HERETICAL ORTHODOXY

Lev Tolstoi was not only one of the world's most famous writers, he was also a deeply concerned thinker and a hugely influential critic of the Church whose impact was felt long after his death. For an entire generation, Tolstoi set the agenda for ethical and religious thought, in Russia and beyond. Most of Tolstoi's main ideas drew on his Christian heritage – selected and creatively combined. While he claimed that his life's work consisted of rediscovering the pure doctrine of Christ as it had been before the Church perverted it, in fact he radically reinterpreted the Christian faith he had encountered in his own life, Russian Orthodoxy. This book offers a new and comprehensive account of Tolstoi's relationship with the Orthodox Church and its teachings, and shows how the Russian Church reacted to the "Tolstoi phenomenon" and attempted to counteract the influence of this new "heretic" – with scant success.

PÅL KOLSTØ is Professor of Russian Studies at the University of Oslo. His previous publications include, as author or editor, ten academic books in English, and numerous journal articles.

IDEAS IN CONTEXT

Edited by DAVID ARMITAGE, RICHARD BOURKE and JENNIFER PITTS

The books in this series will discuss the emergence of intellectual traditions and of related new disciplines. The procedures, aims and vocabularies that were generated will be set in the context of the alternatives available within the contemporary frameworks of ideas and institutions. Through detailed studies of the evolution of such traditions, and their modification by different audiences, it is hoped that a new picture will form of the development of ideas in their concrete contexts. By this means, artificial distinctions between the history of philosophy, of the various sciences, of society and politics, and of literature may be seen to dissolve.

A full list of titles in the series can be found at: www.cambridge.org/IdeasContext

HERETICAL ORTHODOXY

Lev Tolstoi and the Russian Orthodox Church

PÅL KOLSTØ

University of Oslo

Shaftesbury Road, Cambridge CB2 8EA, United Kingdom

One Liberty Plaza, 20th Floor, New York, NY 10006, USA

477 Williamstown Road, Port Melbourne, VIC 3207, Australia

314–321, 3rd Floor, Plot 3, Splendor Forum, Jasola District Centre, New Delhi – 110025, India

103 Penang Road, #05–06/07, Visioncrest Commercial, Singapore 238467

Cambridge University Press is part of Cambridge University Press & Assessment,
a department of the University of Cambridge.

We share the University's mission to contribute to society through the pursuit of
education, learning and research at the highest international levels of excellence.

www.cambridge.org
Information on this title: www.cambridge.org/9781009260411

DOI: 10.1017/9781009260374

First published 2022
First paperback edition 2024

A catalogue record for this publication is available from the British Library

Library of Congress Cataloging-in-Publication data
NAMES: Kolstø, Pål, author.
TITLE: Heretical Orthodoxy : Lev Tolstoi and the Russian Orthodox Church / Pål Kolstø,
University of Oslo.
DESCRIPTION: Cambridge ; New York : Cambridge University Press, 2022. | Series: Ideas in context |
Includes bibliographical references and index.
IDENTIFIERS: LCCN 2022013567 (print) | LCCN 2022013568 (ebook) | ISBN 9781009260404
(hardback) | ISBN 9781009260411 (paperback) | ISBN 9781009260374 (epub)
SUBJECTS: LCSH: Tolstoy, Leo, graf, 1828-1910–Religion. | Russkai͡a pravoslavnai͡a t͡serkov′.
CLASSIFICATION: LCC PG3415.R4 K585 2022 (print) | LCC PG3415.R4 (ebook) | DDC 891.73/
3–dc23/eng/20220607
LC record available at https://lccn.loc.gov/2022013567
LC ebook record available at https://lccn.loc.gov/2022013568

ISBN 978-1-009-26040-4 Hardback
ISBN 978-1-009-26041-1 Paperback

Contents

Preface

This book has made a long journey indeed. It is based on my doctoral project on Lev Tolstoi's relationship to the Orthodox Church, which I began in the early 1980s, and defended a decade later, in 1995.[1] In the meantime, of course, the Soviet Union had collapsed, and Russian politics had become an exciting field of study. So, for two decades I became engrossed in researching more contemporary issues than Tolstoianism and Orthodoxy. Moreover, my thesis had been written in Norwegian, and, having taken up a position as a professor of Russian and East European area studies at the University of Oslo in 1990, I had no time to have it abridged and translated into English. What I did do was to pick out some of the juicier parts, reworking them into articles that were published in various journals.[2]

And then in 2019, the time had come to revisit that thesis and produce a book-length, updated, and thoroughly revised version – which you are now reading. In the meantime, studies of Tolstoi's thinking and Russian Orthodoxy had moved on, but not much had been published on the specific topic of the nexus between the two. The most important new additions of relevance here were two massive volumes by the Russian Orthodox theologian and historian Georgii Orekhanov, who followed an approach very different from mine. His mission was to defend the Church against Tolstoi's attacks and justify its own counterattacks on him. By contrast, my work is not an exercise in apologetics: It lies within the realm of the history of ideas. In describing Tolstoianism as "heretical Orthodoxy"

1 The doctoral committee consisted of Erik Egeberg, Per-Arne Bodin and the late Geir Kjetsaa. I am most grateful for their constructive feedback.

2 "Leo Tolstoy, A Church Critic Influenced by Orthodox Thought," in Geoffrey A. Hosking, ed., *Church, Nation and State in Russia and Ukraine* (Macmillan, 1991, pp. 148–66); "A Mass for a Heretic? The Controversy over Leo Tolstoi's Burial," in *Slavic Review*, 2000, 60, issue 1, pp. 75–95; "The Demonized Double: The Image of Lev Tolstoi in Russian Orthodox Polemics," in *Slavic Review*, 2006, 65, issue 2, pp. 304–32; "The Elder at Iasnaia Poliana: Lev Tolstoi and the Orthodox Starets Tradition," in *Kritika: Explorations in Russian and Eurasian History*, 2008, 9, issue 3, pp. 533–54; "'For Here We Do Not Have an Enduring City': Tolstoy and the Strannik Tradition in Russian Culture," in *Russian Review*, 2010, 69, issue 1, pp. 119–34; "Fame, Sainthood and Iurodstvo: Patterns of Self-Presentation in Tolstoi's Life Practice," coauthored with Ulrich Schmid, in *Slavic and East European Journal*, 2013, 57, issue 4, pp. 525–43; and "Orthodoxie," in Martin George, Jens Herlth, Christian Münch and Ulrich Schmid, eds. (Vandenhoeck & Ruprecht, 2014, pp. 528–40).

in the title of the book, I have intended this not as a theological verdict but as an attempt to convey, in one paradoxical expression, the complexities of Tolstoi's relationship with the Orthodox Church as both continuity and breach.

I have found that some of the ideas that Tolstoi propounded in explicit opposition to the teachings of the Church were in fact remarkably similar to currents within Orthodox thinking and spirituality of his time – in several cases, there had been direct borrowing. Sometimes this affinity was expressed openly, as when Tolstoi wrote that in the Church he had found not only "lies," but also "truths," and also when he lavished praise on specific varieties of spirituality found within the Orthodox tradition, such as "elders," "holy wanderers" and "holy fools." In other cases, less-evident connections between Tolstoianism and the teachings of the Orthodox Church can be traced in certain thought structures that Tolstoi took out of their original context and adapted for his own purposes. We can see this, for instance, in his understanding of God as ineffable and unfathomable, which clearly drew inspiration from "negative" or "apophatic" theology in Eastern Orthodoxy. What I have found so fascinating in studying Tolstoi's ideas against the background of Orthodox thought is how affirmation and rejection go hand in hand.

In the concluding part of this book I examine the relationship between Tolstoi and Orthodoxy from the other end, so to speak: how it was viewed by the leadership and common believers in the Russian Church. Here, we find much of the same duality as in Tolstoi's attitude to Orthodoxy: Whereas the Church regarded him an enemy of the first order – not surprisingly, considering his sharp pen and the harsh language he used in condemning much of what they stood for – there were also some Orthodox authors who recognized and noted the strong residuals of Orthodox theology and spirituality in his thinking. Some of the most influential theologians in the Russian Church around the turn of the nineteens and twentieth centuries – such as Bishop (later Metropolitan) Antonii Khrapovitskii and the philosopher and theologian Sergei Bulgakov – even maintained that, although Tolstoi was not an Orthodox believer, he had a wholesome influence on Russian society. At a time when the Russian intelligentsia were rapidly being de-Christianized and secularized, Tolstoi was one of the few who professed a religious faith and combated materialism, they argued.

More remarkably, even irate Russian apologists who denounced Tolstoi as a servant of Satan and a precursor of the Antichrist sometimes used language that revealed strong connecting lines between their own thinking and his: They attacked him for being a plagiarist who had "stolen the pearl of the Gospel"; he was "a peddler of contraband." As one Orthodox priest expressed it, "his entire beauty Tolstoi has stolen from us, from the Christian Church!." This close affinity between Tolstoianism and the teaching of the official Russian Church made it much more difficult – but also more urgent – for the defenders of the Orthodox faith to combat his message than was the case with, for instance, the atheism of the radical revolutionaries. And so, countless Orthodox writers – laypersons as well as theologians – churned out hundreds of books, pamphlets and articles, seeking to stem his pernicious influence. In 1905, the central church authorities, the Holy Synod, even issued a special Circular Letter against him, a document which normally is referred to as his "excommunication." This is by far the most famous episode in the saga of the relations between Tolstoi and the Russian Orthodox, and the massively negative reaction against this move in Russian society egregiously demonstrated the difficulties the church experienced in communicating its warnings against the new "heretic."

Caroline Serck-Hanssen has kindly read the manuscript and helped me correct some infelicities. All errors and inaccuracies that remain I take the blame for myself.

CHAPTER 1

Introduction

Throughout his long life, Lev Nikolaevich Tolstoi (1828–1910) grappled with the major questions of human existence. Who are we? What is the purpose of life? Where are we going? (Paperno 2014) Almost all his major fictional characters are concerned with these questions and give different answers to them (Orwin 1993). In the autobiographical trilogy *Childhood, Boyhood* and *Youth*, the protagonist "tries out" various philosophical beliefs, seeking to find what can give meaning to human life. These are also the aspects that elevate *War and Peace* from being a purely historical epic to becoming an existential drama.

Around 1879–80, Tolstoi experienced a deep personal crisis. Emerging from it, he believed that he had finally found answers to the questions that he had wrestled with. From there on he appeared primarily as a religious preacher and anarchist socialist (Christoyannopoulos 2016), but without renouncing fiction as a medium. Several of his most important works originate from this period – *The Death of Ivan Ilich, Resurrection, The Kreutzer Sonata* and *Father Sergius*. Also in these novels and short stories, the characters are searching for the meaning of life – and many of them end up finding it in one form or another.

As a philosophical system, "Tolstoianism" may not be particularly significant, but its major role in the cultural history of Europe – indeed, the world – means that it holds great interest also for posterity. Around the turn of the nineteenth century, dozens of Tolstoian communities sprang up in Russia and abroad attempting to put the ideas of their great inspirer into practice (Popovskii 1983; Alston 2014), but his influence was not limited to the groups of professed Tolstoians. At the time, no thinker – with the possible exception of Friedrich Nietzsche – was as influential as Tolstoi. For some twenty-five years – from 1885 to 1910 – it was hardly possible to discuss religious or social issues without taking his views into account, if for no other reason than to condemn them. A few quotations may illustrate the dominant position held by Tolstoi:

> No author has ever put his imprint as strongly on the consciousness of his contemporaries . . . as has Count L.N. Tolstoi (Kuliukin 1902, 818).

> No one has been so much discussed, no one has been so much criticized, no one has had as many worshipers as the late L.N. Tolstoi. No other name has so often shone from the pages of newspapers and magazines, nothing has been so popular in Russia and abroad as the name of Lev Tolstoi (A. Nikol'skii 1911, issue 5, 372).

> L. Tolstoi stands at the centre of criticism and public attention. His moral and social ideas are being discussed everywhere. In the salons, in the learned societies, in the literary circles, among the youth, in the popular press as well as in serious journals, theological as well as secular. Small brochures and thick books, casual remarks and serious scholarly papers, church sermons and public lectures – all of this makes up an impressive library. (Preobrazhenskii 1898, 1)

Famous is also A.S. Suvorin's dictum in a diary entry from 1901:

> We have two Tsars: Nicholas II and Lev Tolstoi. Which of them is stronger? Nicholas II cannot touch Tolstoi, cannot overthrow his throne, while Tolstoi indisputably rocks the throne of Nicholas and his dynasty. (Suvorin [1923] 1992, 316)

These quotes may sound like the effusions of overexcited followers, but all four were in fact written by persons who had no sympathy with Tolstoi's ideas. If they exaggerated Tolstoi's significance somewhat, this only bears witness to how he was perceived in his time – a pertinent fact in itself. "Tolstoianism" deserves considerable attention, greater than what it has received so far in scholarship.

Secondly, anyone wishing to deal with Tolstoi from a literary perspective cannot ignore Tolstoianism. Throughout his towering opus, there is an intimate connection between the thinker and the novelist; it would hardly be doing justice to the great writer if one admired only his stylistic skills, without taking seriously the messages he sought to convey (Orwin 1993). Also, for understanding Tolstoi's early literary works, his later preaching may prove fruitful. Tolstoi's later authorship can be said to have been latent in his early writings, achieving fruition in his mature thinking. These two periods relate to each other as questions and answers: His "conversion" is not so much a rupture as a breakthrough.

With this book, I hope to contribute to our understanding of why Tolstoi thought and taught as he did, by tracing the historical sources of some of his ideas. Tolstoi read extensively, and in his works he referred to a wide range of thinkers and faith systems. Many of these he cited with appreciation, some even with undisguised enthusiasm (e.g., Haase 1928, passim). However, such fascination should not always be taken as confirmation that this or that author or thought system exercised a strong influence on Tolstoi. Often, it indicates texts that Tolstoi saw as confirming his own views, or simply a fleeting interest that did not leave noticeable traces on his thinking.

Many monographs have been written about Tolstoi's relation to other thinkers and cultures.[1] One aspect, however, remains understudied: His relationship with the Orthodox faith. On the one hand, this is surprising: Tolstoi learned about religion from the Russian peasantry, who generally saw religion as synonymous with Orthodoxy. On the other hand, one can understand why this aspect has been largely overlooked for so long: On February 24, 1901, Tolstoi was solemnly excommunicated from the Russian Orthodox Church. In cathedral churches throughout the country, a circular letter from the Holy Synod was read that condemned his "anti-religious and anti-Christian doctrine." Two months later, Tolstoi issued a rebuttal confirming that he had indeed "renounced the church that is calling itself Orthodox." Here he held that the church doctrine was "theoretically a false and harmful lie, and practically a collection of the crudest superstition and witchcraft" (Tolstoi PSS 34, 247). This exchange is by far the single most famous episode in the relationship between Tolstoi and the Orthodox Church, establishing the relationship between them as mutually antagonistic.

Indeed, Lev Tolstoi developed his religious ideas in conscious opposition to the Orthodox faith in which he had been brought up. This opposition was strong and real – but he also clearly took over and implicitly accepted certain aspects of Orthodox theology and spirituality. In *A Confession* (1884), Tolstoi's first religious tract after his deep spiritual crisis in the late 1870s, he claimed that Orthodoxy consisted of both truth and falsehood; he saw it as his task to disentangle the two aspects, digging

[1] For instance, Milan Markovitch, *Jean-Jacques Rousseau et Tolstoi* (1928); Robert Quiskamp, *Die Beziehungen L.N. Tolstois zu den Philosophen des deutschen Idealismus* (1930); Franz-Heinrich Philipp, *Tolstoj und der Protestantismus* (1959). Books that address his relationship with non-European cultures include Pavel Biriukov, *Tolstoi and the Orient* (1925), Derk Bodde, *Tolstoy and China* (1950); Claus Fischer, M. *Lev N Tolstoj in Japan* (1969); A. I. Shifman, *Lev Tolstoi i vostok* (1971); Radha Balasubramanian, *The Influence of India on Leo Tolstoy and Tolstoy's Influence on India* (2013); John Burt Foster, *Transnational Tolstoy* (2013); Natalia Velikanova and Robert Whittaker, eds, *Tolstoi i SShA: perepiska* (2004). Books on Tolstoi's relationship with and influence on other thinkers include Alexej Baskakov, *"Ströme von Kraft": Thomas Mann und Tolstoi* (2014); Charlotte Alston, *Tolstoy and His Disciples: The History of a Radical International Movement* (2014); Henry Pickford, *Thinking with Tolstoy and Wittgenstein* (2016).

out the occasional nuggets of wisdom from what he called the "dung of stale Orthodoxy" (Tolstoi PSS 24, 807). Often he drew a distinction between the teachings of the official Church, which he rejected, and the living faith of simple Russian believers, which he admired.

My own starting point for examining the relationship between Tolstoi and Orthodoxy is that any critique of religion must necessarily be a critique of the religious forms and ideas in which one was raised and socialized. Religion *per se* does not exist – only specific, historical religions; likewise, there is no timeless, ahistorical critique of religion. Any church influences its opponents both positively and negatively – by the elements they take over from it (usually without acknowledging this), and since such rebellion is provoked by precisely the features that are characteristic of that particular faith or denomination.

Tolstoi was deeply imbued with Orthodox ways of thinking and incorporated important elements of Orthodox spirituality into his own religious system. In its basic structure, however, his teaching differed significantly from the Orthodox worldview. The elements he selected from Orthodox spirituality underwent a radical change of meaning when applied to his message. Thus, in determining the relationship of Tolstoi to the Orthodox Church we must emphasize both continuity and break at the same time. To say that Tolstoi was influenced by Orthodox spirituality is not the same as saying that he was in any way an Orthodox believer – clearly he was not. Rather, it recognizes that in nineteenth-century Russia the worldview of the Orthodox Church rubbed off even on some of its most vehement detractors.

I make no claims to originality with this line of reasoning. It has long been used in the study of Western critics of religion, including Tolstoi's great contemporary, Friedrich Nietzsche. It is generally accepted that Nietzsche's militant atheism is incomprehensible unless one understands his love–hate relationship with German Protestantism. Nietzsche himself claimed: "the Protestant pastor is the grandfather of the German philosophy" (Nietzsche 1979, III, 1171), and the same line of reasoning has been applied to him by several historians of ideas. Karl Jaspers wrote that Nietzsche is "gripped by Christian motives" and "uses them in his fight against Christianity" (Jaspers [1938] 1977, 58). Alf Ahlberg argued that, when Nietzsche's teachings are compared with Christianity, the similarities are far more significant than the differences (Ahlberg 1923, 111).

Such analysis of the sources of a thinker's worldview goes beyond the traditional pursuit of conceptual "loans." Rather than "loan," we should speak of ideational "heritage." Applying this metaphor to Tolstoi, we can say that, although the Russian Orthodox Church sought to "disinherit" Tolstoi spiritually with its Circular letter of 1901, and Tolstoi may similarly be said to have renounced any inheritance from the Church in which he had grown up, in both cases this turned out to be only partial. It is indeed possible to break out of the intellectual universe in which one was brought up, but certain mental structures will normally remain. Ideational "legacy" lies somewhere between a legal inheritance, which one can renounce completely, and inheritance in the biological sense, which no one can cast off at will.

Iurii Lotman and Boris Uspenskii of the Tartu-Moscow school of cultural semiotics developed a theory of cultural change that may provide a guide for understanding Tolstoi's relationship to Orthodoxy. They argued that not only languages but entire cultures may be analyzed as *systems of signs*. Russia, they noted, had several times undergone abrupt cultural shifts when, in the course of a few decades, the values of one generation were supplanted by their opposites. Superficially, this interpretation may seem a mere repetition of Russian philosopher Nikolai Berdiaev's thesis that Russians are maximalists who are constantly thrown from one extreme to another (Berdiaev [1937] 1955; Berdiaev [1946] 1970). However, the semioticians emphasized not only the rupture, but also the continuity that is preserved over apparently yawning cultural gaps. The signs of the old culture are not automatically discarded: Sometimes they live on in new forms and with new meanings that the semiotician may disentangle.

In *Historia sub specie semiotica* (1974), Boris Uspenskii discussed the cultural rupture under Peter the Great, seeking to understand the semiotic contrast between the "medieval" and "modern" in Russian culture and what happens when they collide. Contemporary reactions to the shocking cultural and social innovations introduced by Peter were emphatically and unanimously negative – nor could they have been otherwise, Uspenskii maintained. Peter acted as a blasphemer and an iconoclast, and for this he was rewarded by his devout Orthodox subjects with the title "Antichrist." However, in his iconoclasm Peter deliberately – perhaps inevitably – employed and inverted the signs and the symbols of the old culture. From one point of view, Uspenskii claims, Peter's behaviour was not a cultural revolution, but appears as "anti-texts or minus-behaviour within the bounds of the same culture .... However paradoxical this might be, Peter's behaviour in large measure did not exceed the bounds of traditional ideas and norms; it entirely confined itself within these limits, but only by means of a negative sign" (Uspenskij [1974] 1988, 112).

In "Binary Models in the Dynamics of Russian Culture," Lotman and Uspenskii returned to this topic. With regard to Peter the Great, they argued that:

> The new culture demonstrated its blasphemous, anti-ecclesiastical nature with emphatic zeal. Thus it is all the more interesting that the growth of the new culture constantly reveals models of an ecclesiastical–mediaeval type. (The latter, in their turn, are merely a manifestation of the enduring models that have organized the entire stretch of Russian cultural history, including, one may suppose, both the pre-Christian and Christian periods). (Lotman and Uspenskij [1977] 1985, 54)

In their view, Peter's cultural revolution was the most egregious example of a more general tendency in Russian history. (Lotman and Uspenskii did not mention the October Revolution, probably because Soviet censorship would not have accepted it.) They saw Russian culture as characterized by a particularly high degree of binary tensions between the old and the new, between true faith and false, between the norm and breach of the norm. Even after such a breach, much of the old lives on, albeit often in unconscious and distorted form. "Change occurs as a radical negation of the preceding state. The new does not arise from a structurally 'unused' reserve, but results from a transformation of the old, a process of turning it inside out" (Lotman and Uspenskij [1977] 1985, 33). This model, which is clearly related to Hegel's concept of *Aufhebung*,[2] allows a search for the old in the new, for continuity in the break.

Lotman and Uspenskii saw this form of cultural-historical development as peculiar to the Eastern Orthodox cultural environment. They pointed out that in the Western Catholic understanding of the metaphysical universe there were three "spaces" or dimensions: Heaven, hell and purgatory. While heaven is entirely holy and hell purely evil, purgatory is ethically and religiously neutral. This tripartite mental universe made possible the emergence of a secular (de-sacralized and de-demonized) culture between the two extremes. Orthodox theology, by contrast, never developed any teachings about purgatory; Lotman and Uspenskii regarded this as one reason why Russian cultural history has, to a greater extent than Western culture, made convulsive leaps from one position to the opposite (Lotman and Uspenskii [1977] 1985, 31–34).

[2] This untranslatable German term may mean "elevation to a higher level" as well as "cancellation," and Hegel consciously played on this duality. In a change from "thesis" to "antithesis," the old both disappears and is retained at a higher level, as a "synthesis."

Many scholars who are deeply influenced by Lotman's and Uspenskii's theories are nevertheless skeptical to their dichotomization between Western and Russian culture (e.g., Gasparov 1985, 26–28). In my view, their theories can be used as an interpretive key not only for one particular culture, but with general application, as they themselves sometimes did. For example, in his study of the daily life of the Decembrists – the Russian guard officers who rebelled against Tsar Nicholas I in 1825 – Lotman maintained that "a norm and its violations are not locked into a static state of contradiction; they are constantly changing places. Rules arise for violating rules, and violations appear that are essential to norms" (Lotman [1977] 1985, 96).

In *The Social Construction of Reality* (1976 [1966]) Peter L. Berger and Thomas Luckmann developed a theory of socialization at the micro-level that is compatible with macro-level cultural semiotics. They provide a ground-breaking theoretical analysis of how and why the prevailing perceptions of reality in a society are adopted and internalized by its members. Even though there are strong conformity pressures in the vast majority of known societies, totally successful socialization is an anthropological impossibility, they conclude. The individual will always stand both inside and outside the community.

> The symmetry between objective and subjective reality cannot be complete. The two realities correspond to each other, but they are not coextensive. No individual internalizes the totality of what is objectified as reality in his society, not even if the society and its world are relatively simple ones. On the other hand, there are always elements of subjective reality that have not originated in socialization. (Berger and Luckmann [1966] 1976, 153–54)

Berger and Luckmann use the term "unsuccessful socialization" for cases when an individual is unable or unwilling to accept the roles, norms, and conventions of a society. Like totally successful socialization, totally unsuccessful socialization is an anthropological impossibility (except in cases of extreme organic pathology). Successful and unsuccessful socializations are gradations along a continuum, not absolute opposites. Some individuals are closer to one pole, some closer to the other. The factors that push an individual toward unsuccessful socialization and into the role of a deviant, rebel or social critic may be socially or biographically conditioned, or nonreducible idiosyncrasies (Berger and Luckmann [1966] 1976, 183–84).

As a scathing critic of the Church and society of nineteenth-century Russia, Tolstoi placed himself near the pole of "unsuccessful socialization." He had a highly developed ability to see through and dissect fundamental aspects of "the social reality" – indeed, that was among his most important qualities as a writer of fiction. The Russian formalist and literary theoretician Viktor Shklovskii highlighted the "technique of alienation" (*priom ostraneniia*) as a major tool in Tolstoi's prose writing. In his novels, Tolstoi often offers purely external descriptions of well-known social conventions, as if he were an alien from Mars unacquainted with the conventional meanings assigned by society. As an example, Shklovskii referred to battle scenes as well as theater scenes in *War and Peace* (Shklovskii [1967] 1971, 14). With such "tricks" or "devices" (*priomy)*, Tolstoi created an effect of surprise and distance. Here we should note that, for Tolstoi, alienation was not just a technique he employed in his fictional writings, but also an essential element in his criticism of religion, culture and society. Through "uncomprehending" descriptions of institutions, symbolic systems and power structures, he "unmasked" them as man-made constructions – as in the communion scene in *Resurrection,* where the Body of Christ (the communion bread) is referred to as "a piece of loaf" and the chalice as "a cup of wine" (Tolstoi PSS 32, 134). By deliberately removing the sacramental act from its familiar context and refusing to recognize the convention, Tolstoi deprived it of any value.[3]

Although he did not use that term, also Iurii Lotman emphasized the important role of the alienation technique in Tolstoi's prose. His prime example was the short story *Kholstomer* from 1886 (Lotman 1988, 219–20). By describing social relations in Russia as seen through the eyes of a horse, Tolstoi denudes the social conventions and social hierarchies of their accepted meanings and role. A horse has not been socialized into accepting that some people are rich and others poor, some powerful and others not, and is "free" to criticize social phenomena from the outside. That is, the horse does not criticize, but simply *describes* these social relations as perceived by one who does not know the conventional social codes – and in the process exposes them as unnatural and unjust.

The theory of alienation makes a valuable contribution to the understanding of Tolstoi's fictional writing and cultural criticism. However, we must bear in mind that Tolstoi was *not* a stranger in the culture and society he wanted to dissect, although he often experienced it as such. On the contrary, he had deep insights into precisely the culture and society of Russia. Perhaps the alienation technique as a deliberate and effective method can be skillfully employed *only* by a person who possesses intimate knowledge of the phenomenon he or she wants to expose. Only such a

[3] For many more examples of Tolstoi's use of defamiliarization as a subversive device, see Christoyannopoulos 2019.

person can give a description of the outside that causes the readers to pause and to start questioning what they had previously taken for granted. But even more important in our context is that as a non-Martian it was as impossible for Tolstoi, as for anyone else, to dissect *all* sides of the "socially constructed reality" he experienced around him. Also the rebel is a child of his time and his culture, and cannot avoid taking parts of it for granted.

It can perhaps be argued that not much of the older Orthodox religious culture was reflected in Russia's cultural debates toward the end of the nineteenth century. Whereas Peter the Great and his associates, as Lotman and Uspenskii noted, had still been deeply influenced by Christian beliefs and concepts, with the next generations came an accelerating secularization of the Russian upper classes. The Russian intelligentsia that grew up in the nineteenth century was deeply immersed in Western philosophy and social theory: The Church and its teachings no longer laid the premises for the social debate. At the theological seminaries there were astute theologians intellectually on a par with the leading thinkers of the secular intelligentsia, but their overt influence in society was limited. Scholars have noted that in nineteenth-century Russia, there was an almost insuperable abyss between the theological colleges and the secular intellectual communities. With the exception of the early Slavophiles, Fedor Dostoevskii, Nikolai Leskov and Vladimir Solov'ev, few thinkers made any attempt to cross it (Florovskii [1937] 1982). Although Tolstoi should not be regarded as a member of "the intelligentsia" as the term was understood in Russia at the time, there is no doubt that he belonged on the secular side of that cultural divide.

Therefore, it might seem somewhat far-fetched to use Orthodoxy and not secular Russian culture as a framework for understanding his thinking. And yet, despite the high wall of separation between the Orthodox Church and secular Russian culture, the fact remains that important members of the intelligentsia such as Vissarion Belinskii and Mikhail Bakunin experienced intense religious periods in their youth. When Bakunin eventually broke with Christianity, he did not end up as an atheist, but as an antitheist. Bakunin still assigned to God a significant role in human life, but now as a force to be combated and defeated (Bakunin [1882] 1970, 17; Weiant 1953, 120). Intelligentsia ringleaders such as Nikolai Chernyshevskii and Nikolai Dobroliubov were both runaway seminarians and sons of priests, and Nikolai Berdiaev argued that Russian atheism was in fact a religious phenomenon: The nihilism of the intelligentsia was "the negation of Russian apocalypticism" (Berdiaev 1955, 38). Berdiaev also pointed out that strong elements of Orthodox asceticism can be found in Chernyshevskii's main work, *What must be done?* One of the characters in this highly influential novel slept on a bed of nails in order to prepare himself for the self-sacrificing revolutionary struggle (Berdiaev [1937] 1955, 43). "The paradox is that the intelligentsia not only uncompromisingly rejected the church and religion, but unknowingly imitated the theological thinking and the essential features and functions of the Orthodox Church," Alex Fryszman writes (Fryszman 1993, 58). Fryszman's general characterization of the Russian intelligentsia, I will argue, is particularly apt with regard to Tolstoi.

***

In most cases, any theory about an intellectual substrate of Orthodoxy in the thinking of the Russian intelligentsia can be substantiated only by a structural analysis of similarities and parallels in their thinking. This limitation does not apply to Tolstoi, however. Unlike most other non-Orthodox Russian thinkers, he not only wrote an entire library of religious books and articles, but also discussed Orthodox theology in a detailed manner in these writings. That means that we can go beyond a purely structural analysis and engage directly in theological and historical comparisons.

The claim that Tolstoianism contains a strong layer of Orthodoxy has emerged from time to time in the literature, but mostly as casual remarks in passing. For instance, in 1928 Nikolai Berdiaev wrote: "L. Tolstoi is a Russian to the marrow and could arise only on Russian Orthodox soil, even though he made changes to Orthodoxy" (Berdiaev 1928, 77). In *The Russian Idea* from 1946, Berdiaev returned to this idea in a less bombastic way: "For Tolstoi, the Orthodox basis is far stronger than one would normally think" (Berdiaev [1946] 1971, 184). However, Berdiaev did not elaborate on this, and forty years were to pass before another researcher picked up the cudgel. In 1986, Richard Gustafson published *Leo Tolstoy: Resident and Stranger*, a major attempt to understand Tolstoi's ideas with Orthodox theology as the crucial interpretive key. Although Gustafson did not refer to Berdiaev, his main thesis was precisely that a close relationship existed between Tolstoi's worldview and Orthodox theology. He concluded: "Tolstoi may not be an Orthodox thinker, but certainly he is an Eastern Christian artist and theologian within the culture of Russian Orthodoxy" (Gustafson 1986, 457).

The German theologian Martin George concurs, but believes that Gustafson's characterization is too weak. According to George, Tolstoi was "A Russian Orthodox Christian and remained so throughout all turns and twists with explainable consistency" (George 2015, 242). At the same time, George believes that there are good reasons to regard Tolstoi as a heretic, as so many of Tolstoi's Russian Orthodox contemporaries did. A heretic, he explains, is a person who one-sidedly picks out only certain parts of the Christian creed while they discard others (George 2015, 243). With these definitions, George's understanding of Tolstoianism comes close to the deliberately paradoxical title of this book: "heretical Orthodoxy." There is, however, a vital difference in how we use the concept of heresy in relation to Tolstoi. For George, this represents a theological assessment while I use it as a purely descriptive and historical term as an attempt to express, without any normative implications, the duality in how Tolstoi's contemporaries characterized him.

With regard to Gustafson, I believe that his most important insight is expressed already in the title of his book: In the Russian religious tradition Tolstoi was at the same time both a "resident" and a "stranger." It is in this duality that we must look for explanations of Tolstoi's distinct character as an author and thinker (Gustafson 1986, 13). On the other hand, while Gustafson and I end up with very similar conclusions, we reach this endpoint via rather different routes. We diverge in our choice of empirical material to examine, and in our methodological approach. Because our two books are so related and yet so different, it seems relevant to present my own approach through a comparison with that of Gustafson.

Gustafson based his analysis on a "close reading" of Tolstoi's fictional works and diaries and then compared the views expressed in Tolstoi's writings with Orthodox theology. In order to find appropriate sources of this theology, Gustafson went to two extremes: To ancient church texts, and to works written in the twentieth century by some Orthodox and some Western scholars. The Orthodox theologians of the intervening period, including Tolstoi's own century, are consistently overlooked. This, Gustafson explained, was because, in his view, "what passed as theology were but slightly dressed-up versions of Western systems of thought, Catholic and Protestant" (Gustafson 1986, xi). However, Gustafson made no attempt to explain how Tolstoi was able to penetrate beyond these Western-inspired thought systems and find the true Orthodox belief behind them. Implicit in Gustafson's ahistorical approach is the claim that Orthodox thinking and spirituality have not undergone any significant changes over the centuries. He focuses on demonstrating dogmatic coincidences between Tolstoi's thinking and Orthodox theology. This is what I will call "the correspondence method."

Beyond doubt, this method is indispensable in any analysis of this kind. If there is no intellectual affinity, all attempts to prove a genetic relationship must fail. However, such correspondence will have significance only if the common elements found in both Tolstoi's writings and Orthodoxy are distinctive features and not just general ideas. One example: It does not take us very far when Gustafson claims that "Tolstoy's God of Life and Love is an Eastern Christian God. The concept of God as an abstract idea of absolute being has been replaced by a God who dwells in the world of change even as He transcends it" (Gustafson 1986, 108). This is no doubt true, but the view that God is at the same time *in* creation and above it, both immanent and transcendent, lies at the heart of both Western and Eastern mainstream theology. As we shall see, Tolstoi shared this view – but it is methodologically very difficult to claim that this is a specifically Orthodox heirloom.

In this book, I employ two approaches to draw out the connections between Orthodox thought patterns and Tolstoi's thinking, in addition to the correspondence method.

1) Historical-genetic analysis: Through which channels did the Orthodox impulses pass before reaching Tolstoi? And how did he relate explicitly to them? This requires deeper study of Tolstoi's biography and reading. Unlike Gustafson, I focus on the Orthodox literature that Tolstoi read or with a high degree of certainty he can be assumed to have read. Presentations of Orthodox theology from more recent times will be used more sparingly in the analysis.
2) Reception analysis: If Tolstoi really adopted important ideas from Orthodox theology and piety, was this recognized in his lifetime? Those who are closest to detecting such coincidences were the Orthodox themselves, but also other sources will be investigated. Immensely rich and largely untapped sources are available here. Tolstoi's writings sparked a flood of reviews, comments, polemics and scholarly literature, and many Russian Orthodox believers were keen participants in debates about Tolstoi's ideas.

The reception analysis in this book falls into two parts. Some of it is integrated into the thematic analysis (Chapters 2–9) of how certain elements of Orthodox theology and spirituality were integrated in more or less transformed ways into Tolstoi's thinking. Here I draw on sources by Orthodox as well as non-Orthodox commentators. Then, the final part of the book (Chapters 10–13) is devoted exclusively to Orthodox reactions to Tolstoi. Here I emphasize the breadth and diversity of these reactions – official and unofficial, polemical and academic, positive and critical. To my knowledge, these chapters represent the first attempt at offering a comprehensive account.[4]

Russian believers plunged into the debate about Tolstoianism with full weight, but their voices were barely heard outside their own circles. It may seem as if the label "Orthodox" functioned as a kind of disqualification: As the relationship between Tolstoi and the Church was so tense, it was assumed that the Orthodox pamphlets about him could contain nothing but biased slander. In many cases, this was no doubt correct – but Tolstoi's Orthodox critics, with their spiritual worldview, were often in fact more congenial with him than many of his "worldly" critics of the time. On some points, the Orthodox were clearly better able to enter into Tolstoi's worldview, and to shed light on aspects that were overlooked by others. For instance, the Russian philosophy professor A.A. Kozlov, who in 1888 published a recognized monograph, *Count L.N. Tolstoi's religion*, admitted that he was not competent to comment on the veracity of Tolstoi's interpretation of the Bible, and left it to Church historians and theologians to address this issue (Kozlov 1895, 7). Several Orthodox theologians avidly picked up this challenge.

In presenting Orthodox reactions, I examine which insights they can contribute with about Tolstoi's thinking and how they placed themselves in relation to him, explicitly or implicitly. In offering their own standpoints, they also sometimes unwittingly revealed a closer spiritual relationship to him than they were prepared to acknowledge themselves. To the extent that this is the case, it reinforces my theory that there existed a certain set of common beliefs or "self-evident assumptions" (Nygren 1940, 67–70) that Tolstoi shared with (some or most of) his Russian Orthodox opponents of the time. Partly, this is shown by the aspects of Tolstoi's thinking the Orthodox failed to criticize, and partly through the formulation of their arguments in their rebuttals of Tolstoi's criticisms of Orthodoxy.

4 There have been special studies of how Tolstoi's writings were received by other critics in his homeland (Oberländer 1965; Sorokin 1979). Sorokin organized his study according to the writers' ideological position, but there is no chapter for Orthodox critics. Peter Ulf Møller included ecclesiastical writers on a par with other critics in his *Postlude to The Kreutzer Sonata: Tolstoj and the Debate on Sexual Morality in Russian Literature in the 1890s* ([1983] 1988), but that book deals with the debate about a single novella only.

The Orthodox literature on Tolstoi is vast, and not all of it merits our attention here. When selecting texts for this study, I have used several criteria. The official (and unofficial) responses of the national church leaders have a self-evident place, since they were prominent in defining the framework for the Orthodox polemics against Tolstoi (although surprisingly many Orthodox authors, as we shall see, ventured outside this framework). Further, some theologians are represented by virtue of their academic weight; others are included because they had a significant impact upon subsequent history. To bring out the range of Orthodox reactions, I have included many of the most sympathetic and laudatory as well as the most devastatingly critical opinions and abusive characterizations. Some Orthodox writers were willing to go along with Tolstoi's views to a surprising extent, whereas others rejected them out of hand even on those points where it took a trained eye to be able to detect how his teaching deviated from Church doctrine.

The reception analysis provides insights into the general intellectual history of the Russian Orthodox Church around 1900, and its capacity and willingness to confront the spiritual challenges of the time. The struggle against Tolstoianism was not a peripheral matter for Russian Orthodoxy, but something that the Church itself recognized as one of the most taxing tasks on the cultural front. The "Tolstoi affair" figured high on the agenda of the Church throughout the final fifteen to twenty years of Tolstoi's life and was a source of tremendous concern in ecclesiastical circles also before and after that time.

The Circular letter against Tolstoi in 1901 was a momentous act in the history of the Russian Orthodox Church. Although much has been written about this event, historians' perceptions of it have been rife with misunderstandings. This is due partly to insufficient knowledge of Orthodox canonical law and excommunication practice, and partly to the circumstance that the Church leadership itself, for tactical reasons, was deliberately elusive and unclear regarding its own action. To some extent, it is also a consequence of the fact that, for a long time, important Soviet archives were accessible only to Soviet scholars who gave very tendentious interpretations of it.

I have systematically mapped Orthodox writings on Tolstoi and Tolstoianism up until 1917, which was a natural breakoff point. Some more recent literature is also cited, but I have no pretensions to giving a comprehensive account of how Tolstoi was treated in Orthodox émigré literature. After the fall of Communism in the Soviet Union, several polemical and/or academic articles have been written in Russia about

Tolstoi and the Church, primarily by Orthodox authors. Only one author, however, Georgii Orekhanov, has devoted an entire book-length study to the topic – in fact, he has written no less than two bulky volumes of more than 500 pages each. Orekhanov is a Russian Orthodox priest; while clearly a conscientious and thorough scholar, he writes with a specific objective in mind: To vindicate the actions of the Russian Church and launch a counterattack on Tolstoi's criticisms. The title of Orekhanov's second volume is revealing: *Lev Tolstoi: A prophet without honour: A chronicle of the catastrophe.* Unlike Gustafson, Orekhanov finds in Tolstoi's thinking very little influence from Orthodoxy. In his view, Tolstoi's connection to Orthodoxy is primarily "in the negative," and not a matter of influence (Orekhanov 2010, 133–34). He detects "an impassable border" between Tolstoi's views and the teachings of the Church (Orekhanov 2010, 215). As Orekhanov sees it, the significance of Tolstoi's work is that it reflected the deep crisis of spirituality in nineteenth-century Russia, which was expressed in increasingly lower levels of faith and Church culture in Russian society. In my view, however, Orekhanov's perspective, while not irrelevant, is seriously flawed in its one-sidedness and moralism.[5]

To be sure, "Orthodoxy" is not a rounded, unchangeable and clearly demarcated entity. Although Orthodox believers often proudly maintain that their church has remained true to the teaching of the ancients – more faithfully than other Christian denominations – also Orthodox tradition has inevitably evolved over the ages. When I refer to "Orthodox spirituality," or "Orthodox theology" without further specification, what I have in mind is the dominant expressions of this faith as found in Russia in Tolstoi's times. Also with this delimitation, "Orthodoxy" admittedly remains a variegated phenomenon, school theology as taught at the theological seminaries and academies in many respects differed from religious folkways. As Patrick Michelson and Judith Kornblatt point out,

> There was no single, authentic expression of ecclesiastical, Orthodox thought, much less lay religious thought. Rather, there were highly contested, ever-changing choice fields available for those religious thinkers who innovatively deployed their faith to engage public opinion … . Contestation, diversity, even cacophony were the order of the day in late imperial Russia, especially during the last several decades of the old regime. (Michelson and Kornblatt 2014, 8)

[5] Indicatively, the title of the concluding chapter in his second book is "Can the Church forgive Tolstoi?" (Orekhanov 2016, 576). His answer is no.

This was certainly true also with regard to Orthodox polemics against Tolstoi. Although I am unable to delve deeply into the many facets of Russian Orthodoxy as Tolstoi encountered it, I try to show some of the diversity of beliefs, positions and opinions within the Russian Church at the time, in particular as they were expressed in attitudes toward Tolstoi and his message.

In order to decide who is an Orthodox believer, I have used a *subjective* criterion: All who identify themselves as Orthodox are accepted as such. This means that in the early Church, Origen of Alexandria will be included even though he was officially declared a heretic after his death in AD 253. The same is the case with Vladimir Solov'ev who in the late nineteenth century attempted to act as a bridge-builder between the Eastern and Western Churches, and for that reason was viewed with deep skepticism by many in the Russian Church. Also the odd Old Believers who engaged in the polemics about Tolstoi are included in my discussion as matter of course. In the so-called new religious consciousness in the Russian intelligentsia around the turn of the nineteenth century some, like Nikolai Berdiaev (1874–948), wanted to remain a son of the Church, in spite of many misgivings. Others, like Dmitrii Merezhkovskii (1865–941), engaged in lively debates with Russian theologians, but did not see themselves as Orthodox believers.

CHAPTER 2

Tolstoi as a Practicing Orthodox

Tolstoi considered the Gospels to be the most important source of his worldview, next to the works of Rousseau (Tolstoi PSS 75, 234). Indeed, there was no text he worked so much with as the New Testament. Again and again, he would search back *ad fontes*, to the sources, seeking to rediscover the purity of Jesus' words that he felt had been buried or distorted by the Church over the centuries. Tolstoi had an optimistic belief in the possibility of an unprejudiced reading of the sources of Christian faith and claimed that he was forced to "reveal the meaning of Christ's doctrine as something new" (Tolstoi PSS 23, 346). In the following, I will try to show how his Christian understanding was deeply influenced by the form of faith he had known from childhood and with which he was intimately familiar.

When Tolstoi talks of the Christian Church and its iniquities, it is clearly the Orthodox Church he has in mind, even when he explicitly attributes universal validity to his attacks. This is evident, for example, in *What I Believe* (1884), chapter XI, where criticism is first directed at Metropolitan Filaret's *Catechism* and the *Orthodox Explanatory Prayer Book* but is then expanded to apply to all denominations (Tolstoi PSS 23, 433–37). In *The Gospel in Brief* (1884), Tolstoi "updates" the text by consistently translating "the Pharisees" as "the Orthodox" (*pravoslavnye*). Here he is referring to the bigotry and self-righteousness of the Pharisees – while also drawing Russian Orthodoxy directly into the text as the main opponent of Jesus.

Also, in elaborating his positive alternative to the teachings of the Church, Tolstoi takes the Orthodox faith as he understood it as his starting point, whether in order to negate, correct or further develop it. Shortly after his religious breakthrough, he jotted down in his notebook these sentences that can be understood as a rudimentary method.

> After all, the Christ[ianity] of the popes [*popy*], what is it actually? I began to read the catechism. I will not correct them [based on] how everything was to begin with. But I will start from the end. There exists a ch[urch] of practitioners, and [starting there] I will work backwards to the source. (Tolstoi PSS 48, 328)

This quote consists of hurriedly recorded, compressed thoughts, and it has been necessary to add some interpretive brackets for clarity. Still, it seems evident that Tolstoi regarded his rediscovery of Christianity as a regressive movement: He would begin with the existing forms of Christianity and from there move step-by-step, back toward the foundations.

Tolstoi was thoroughly familiar with Orthodox theology and devotional literature and draws on these. Equally important, however, were the impressions he formed by observing and participating in what he called "the Church of the practitioners." Therefore, I will begin by inquiring what Tolstoi's own church attendance and contact with Orthodox believers meant to him.

Childhood and Adolescence

In his childhood, Tolstoi was a practicing member of the Russian Church. He grew up in a wealthy gentry family characterized by traditional values, Orthodox faith among them. He begins *A Confession* (1879–82), his first religious text after his conversion, with these words: "I was baptized and raised in the Orthodox Christian faith. From my childhood years and through boyhood and adolescence, I was instructed in it" (Tolstoi PSS 23, 1). The aunts who were responsible for the upbringing of the Tolstoi children – Lev's mother died when he was two years old and his father when he was nine – were all God-fearing; some of them were very religious. Lev was regularly taken to church and was taught all the prayers (Tolstoi PSS 23, 510).

Tolstoi believed, however, that this training was not very effective. Indeed, he claimed that when, at the age of eleven, he was presented with the "discovery" that God did not exist, this did not shock him. He therefore drew the conclusion that he never had any "serious" faith in his childhood. However, Tolstoi's first biographer and close friend, Pavel Biriukov, claimed that Tolstoi had been "sincerely religious" in his childhood (Biriukov 1905–23, I, 110).

Tolstoi found it difficult to determine exactly when he stopped believing but thought it must have been "very early," adding that this break with his childhood faith was probably "somewhat more complicated than for most enlightened people at the time" (Tolstoi PSS 23, 489–90). He continued to say his prayers and perform other rituals for a period after his inner faith was gone. In an early draft of *A Confession*, he described the ambivalence of his beliefs in the mid-teens: He was convinced that the catechism, which he was compelled to study, was full of lies, but he nevertheless prayed to God to help him pass his exam in religion (Tolstoi PSS 23, 488). Such ambivalence seems to have persisted until he left the university at the age of eighteen. Even after that time, Tolstoi continued to carry with him "a religious love for the good, a striving for moral perfection" (Tolstoi PSS 23, 490). In his notes to *A Confession*, he discussed whether this might have been a remnant of the Orthodox education he had received. Although he did not exclude this, he did not regard it as likely. In the final version of the book, however, he depicts his religious conversion in adulthood as a return to "faith in God, in the moral perfection, and in the tradition that has conveyed the meaning of life" (Tolstoi PSS 23, 46). "The life force that returned to me was nothing new, but the very oldest, what had attracted me in my earliest periods of life" (Tolstoi PSS 23, 46).

Nihilistic Period?

While *A Confession* begins with a short outline of Tolstoi's relationship to "the Orthodox Christian faith" in his childhood, the first words of *What I Believe* (1884) present a kind of religious status report for the next period of his life, the years 1843–78.

> I have lived in the world for 55 years, and, with the exception of 14 to 15 years as a child, I have lived for 35 years as a nihilist in the true meaning of this word: not as a socialist or a revolutionary, as one usually understands this word, but a nihilist in the sense that I had no faith whatsoever. (Tolstoi PSS 23, 304)

Most researchers had taken this statement at face value (see, for instance, Medzhibovskaya 2009, 232). However, we have seen that Tolstoi to some degree misrepresents his attitude toward religion as a child, apparently in order to achieve the greatest possible contrast between the time before and after his "conversion" in the early 1880s. In his categorical condemnation of his manhood years as totally irreligious, he is even guiltier of oversimplification (Zorin 2020, 109). On closer inspection, the thirty-five years that he here lumps together prove to have encompassed a wide range of attitudes to religion in general, and to the Russian Orthodox Church in particular.

The most important sources for understanding Tolstoi's religion, or lack of religiosity, during this period are his diaries and letters. Tolstoi began keeping a diary in 1847 while still living in Kazan, where he was studying at the University, and continued throughout most of his life (Eikhenbaum 1987, 37–39). Only for thirteen years, 1865–78, did he leave the diary untouched in the drawer.

Although Tolstoi may well have considered the possibility that his diaries would be read by other people, the entries are very frank and candid. Day after day, he takes himself to task, lashing out against his weaknesses and vices – cowardice, laziness, vanity, carnal lust, gambling. He sets up strict rules of life for himself, which he time and again recognizes that he is unable to follow. Pretense and whitewashing seem alien to him. Also with regard to religion, Tolstoi lets us follow his innermost thoughts.

For a long time, he appears little preoccupied with religion. Admittedly, already on the second page of the diary he rebukes Empress Catherine the Great for having elevated "glory" (*slava*) to a virtue in her *Instruction* (*Nakaz*) to the legislative commission she had established. "According to the precepts of the Christian Faith, honor is rather something to be blamed" (Tolstoi PSS 46, 5). However, this does not seem to be a personal matter for him. He merely observes, with detached astonishment, the distortions to which it is possible to expose Christianity.

Tolstoi traveled to the Caucasus in 1851, where his brother Nikolai was serving as an officer. In this masculine community where drinking and card games were the usual leisure activities, Tolstoi returned to his childhood practice of praying. The results were remarkable. A fortnight after arriving in the Cossack village where they were stationed, he noted in the diary,

> Last night I hardly slept, and when I had written in the diary, I began to pray to God. It is impossible to reproduce the sweet feeling I experienced during the prayer. I read the prayers I usually say – [Our] Father, To the Mother of God, and Trinity and 'the Gates of Mercy'. I invoked my guardian angel and remained in prayer. If you define prayer as a request for something or as thanksgiving, then I did not pray. I wanted something lofty and good, something I cannot explain even though I clearly recognized what I want: I want to be united with the All-embracing Being. I asked It to forgive my transgressions – no, I did not pray about that, for I felt that when It had given me such a blissful moment, It had forgiven me. (Tolstoi PSS 46, 61–62)

The Swiss scholar Ulrich Schmid quotes this passage and maintains, quite correctly my view, that "already as a young man Tolstoi was definitely religious, and susceptible to mystical experiences" (Schmid 2010, 70). What Tolstoi was describing here was his first, or one of the first, experiences with mystical prayer.

In his short novel *The Cossacks* (1863), he lets the main protagonist Olenin experience moments of mystical rapture, and there can hardly be any doubt that Tolstoi was drawing on his own experience. However, there is a clear difference between the fictional story and the diary. While Olenin experienced this ecstasy in connection with strong impressions outdoors, in the nature, in Tolstoi's own case it was triggered by Orthodox prayers. Even the Trinity, which later would become an object of his most bitter irony, is invoked. The phrase "I read the prayers I usually say" – in the present tense – seems to indicate a relatively uninterrupted, preexisting prayer practice. In any case, this experience is followed by more prayers. Although Tolstoi had experienced wordless, mystical prayer, he continued to take recourse in ritualized Orthodox prayers for help in combating specific sins and weaknesses.

> Prayer: [Our] Father, the Mother of God, remember my loved ones, the living and the deceased. Then: Deliver me, Lord, from vanity, indecision, laziness, lust, sickness, and mental anxiety.
>
> Lord, let me live without sin and suffering and die without despair and fear. With faith, hope, and love, I surrender to Your will.
>
> Mother of God and guardian angel, pray for me to the Lord. (Tolstoi PSS 46, 10)

If God in the first prayer was perceived as "It," an impersonal "All-embracing Being," He here appears as the Lord. One can communicate with Him, also interceding of behalf on others.

Tolstoi's diary from the Caucasus is packed with references to his prayer life. In 1854, he for a while began to write down the days when he had failed to pray, instead of the days he had prayed, which indicates high regularity. His prayers also became increasingly ritualized. In November 1853, Tolstoi decided to drop all self-composed prayers and instead recite only the Lord's Prayer ("Our Father"). "All requests that I can make to God are expressed far more exaltedly and worthily by Himself in the words: 'Thy will be done on earth, as it is in heaven'." In Bucharest, where Tolstoi spent four months with his military unit during the Crimean War, he wrote down the following program for his daily prayers:

> 'Our Father'. Etc. 'For the repose and salvation of [my] parents.' 'I thank you, Lord, for Your mercy and for that and that and that.' (Here you should remember all happiness that has befallen you.) I implore You, inspire in me

> good undertakings and thoughts, and let me succeed with them and find joy in them. Help me to improve in my vices, deliver me from illnesses, suffering, quarrels, debts, and degradation.
>
> Make me strong in what I believe and hope in You, and in the love of others .... (Tolstoi PSS 47, 12)

This private "missal" ends with a thrice-repeated "Lord, have mercy" (*Gospodi pomilui*), the most frequent responsory in any Orthodox service.

At this time, Tolstoi also composed one of his *credos.* Here he explicitly placed himself in the tradition of "the religion of my forebears (*ottsov*)."

> I believe in one almighty and benevolent God, in the immortality of the soul and eternal retribution for our deeds; I want to believe in the religion of my forebears and respect it. (Tolstoi PSS 47, 12)

This quote expresses both intimacy with and distance to the Orthodox faith he grew up with. Although Tolstoi in his own prayer practice made use of the Church's traditional formulae, he seems to have felt that he gave them a divergent meaning.

In his more skeptical moments, Tolstoi asked himself whether prayer was really necessary and useful. He could not give a clear answer but concluded that at least it was not harmful (Tolstoi PSS 46, 130–31). However, his doubt could also become more all-embracing, shaking his very faith in God. After reading Rousseau's "The Creed of a Savoyard priest" ("La Profession de foi du vicaire Savoyard"), Tolstoi admitted that there was no single, weighty proof of God's existence, but also this time he found his footing again: "I cannot comprehend why God must exist by necessity, but I believe in Him and ask [Him] help me understand Him."

For the young Junker in the Caucasus, faith in God was primarily linked to his struggle to live a cleaner, more moral life. Tolstoi complained that sensuality (*sladostrastie*) did not leave him in peace for a moment (Tolstoi PSS 46, 160), but occasionally he prevailed over it. "Yesterday I was tempted by a gorgeous Gypsy girl, but God saved me" (Tolstoi PSS 46, 168). He felt torn between good and evil, between the spirit and the flesh. Immediately after his first and strongest prayer experience, he was horrified by "the narrow, sinful" side of his life:

> I could not comprehend how it could attract me. As from a pure heart, I asked God to take me in His embrace. I didn't feel the flesh, I was pure spirit. But no! The carnal, petty side revenged itself: in less than an hour I could almost literally hear the voice of vanity .... I knew it would destroy my happiness. I fought, but yielded to it. (Tolstoi PSS 46, 62)

Tolstoi rarely shared his inner life with his comrades. If anyone came into the room while he was praying, he would break off in embarrassment (Tolstoi PSS 46, 164). Already in 1853–54, he contemplated publishing religious sermons for the people, but nothing came out of this (Tolstoi PSS 46, 293). With the woman he was wooing at this time, Valeriia Arsen'eva, he did not wish to discuss matters of faith.

> No matter how our future relationships will develop, *we shall never* talk about religion or any matters related to it. You know that I am a believer, but very possibly what I believe differs from yours in many respects. And this question ought never to be discussed, especially not by people who want to love one another. (Tolstoi PSS 60, 128, emphasis in the original, 1856)

It was only when, during a stay in Western Europe in 1857, Tolstoi got in touch with his "Aunt" Aleksandra Andreevna Tolstaia that he found someone with whom he could discuss questions of faith.[1] For a long while she served as his most important confidant, and for several years they conducted an extensive correspondence in which religion was a major topic. Alexandra was deeply religious, and tried in every way to convey to Tolstoi her enthusiasm for Orthodoxy.

In the latter half of the 1850s, two opposite but apparently not contradictory tendencies were noticeable in Tolstoi's religious life. On the one hand, he continued with his Orthodox practices of prayer and church attendance; on the other hand, it seems as if it was precisely through this religious practice that his religious doubts found further nourishment. It is striking how often Tolstoi in his diary and letters touched upon religious topics in the months of March and April, that is, in connection with the Great Lent and the following Orthodox Easter. At that time of the year, Russian Orthodox believers were expected to intensify their religious life. Fasting included not only abstinence from certain types of food and sexual intercourse but also more frequent church attendance and preferably also contemplation over the Gospel. In those days it was common practice not to go to Communion more than once a year, normally during Lent, and one had to prepare for the Sacrament through fasting, prayer and confession (Shevzov 2004, 76–77). In these periods, Tolstoi tried to follow the ordinances of the Russian Church but often came up against an inner barrier that served to distance him from the Church again.

[1] Aleksandra Andreevna was Tolstoi's first cousin once removed, but addressed her as "aunt."

On March 4, 1855, Tolstoi noted that he had been to Communion, and immediately went on to outline "a great, grandiose thought" that had struck him the day before, during a conversation about faith:

> To establish a new religion consistent with the evolution of humanity – the religion of Christ, but purified of faith and mystery, a practical religion that does not promise bliss in the future, but gives bliss here on earth .... This is the basis for a thought I hope I can be absorbed by. (Tolstoi PSS 47, 37–38)

This is one of the earliest clear expressions of Tolstoi's desire to become a religious preacher, and clearly points forward to his later period. However, the connection is ambiguous. Although many staple Tolstoian elements are included in this program in rudimentary form, we also find distinct differences: After 1880, Tolstoi certainly did not attempt to purge religion of faith; on the contrary, he regarded the attitude of faith as of the very essence of any true religion. The quotation ought to be understood in terms of its immediate context. At the time when Tolstoi jotted down these thoughts, he was also working on a proposal for a reorganization of the Russian Army. This was one of his many reform projects; among other things he also had plans ready for how to abolish serfdom. His idea of establishing a new religion can therefore be seen as an expression of a strong reform urge aimed at finding a cause important enough to make it worth his effort.

In 1857, Tolstoi spent the spring months in Western Europe. In Paris, he was haunted by the radical questions of existence that were to return to him over the next decades: "Last night I was suddenly plagued by doubts about *everything*. Even if that doesn't bother me now, it still sits in me. What is it all for? And what am I?" (Tolstoi PSS 47, 118). These questions constituted the very mainspring of his religious quest (Paperno 2014). Three weeks later, Tolstoi decided to buy a copy of the New Testament, pledging to read it every morning and evening (Tolstoi PSS 47, 204). Shortly afterward, he left Paris, having witnessed a guillotine execution that once again evoked a deep sense of meaninglessness (Shishkin 2018, 2–3).

For Tolstoi the best argument for believing was death. Through his own ponderings, he was not able to solve the problem of death: It led him ever deeper into chaos. "Therefore, it is better to assume the old, centuries-old, soothing and childish-simple [faith]. This conclusion is not something I have reached by thinking, but something I feel. Lord Jesus Christ, have mercy on me" (Tolstoi PSS 47, 207).

The next year, 1858, Tolstoi's religious brooding was reactivated in connection with the Easter celebrations. He attended services in the

Kremlin (Tolstoi PSS 48, 10), but could not partake of the Eucharist, because he had not fasted (Tolstoi PSS 60, 256). Tolstoi then noted in his diary: "Christ did not prescribe, but opened up the moral law, the one which always will be the yardstick of good and bad (*durnoe*)" (Tolstoi PSS 48, 11–12). Five days later, he wrote in his notebook: "The Holy Spirit in the Gospel is the unconscious force that lives in all human beings and works in the individual, against his inclinations, but in accordance with the common good and truth (*pravda*)" (Tolstoi PSS 48, 74). The third person of the Trinity is here given a psychologizing interpretation, and seems to be identified with one's conscience.

Three weeks later, Tolstoi recorded his impressions from a moment of prayer:

> I prayed to God in [my] room, before a Greek icon of the Mother of God. The icon lamp was burning. I went out on the balcony; it was a dark, starry night. Stars ... dim stars, groups of bright stars, darkness, the contours of lifeless trees. Here He is (*Vot on*). Fall down before Him and be still! Everything [else] is hollow ... (Tolstoi PSS 48, 76)

These words need not be seen as expressions of heterodox beliefs. Also many Russians intent on following the teaching of their Church should be able to feel the presence of the Creator in the splendor of creation.

The next year, 1859, Tolstoi promised Aunt Aleksandra to fast prior to Easter so that he would not need to be ashamed of himself (Tolstoi PSS 60, 284). However, he was unable to follow-up on this, and in a new letter tried to explain what went wrong.

> I can eat Lenten food, if necessary throughout my entire life, I can pray by myself in my room, if necessary all day long. I can read the Gospels and for a while think that all this is very important; but to go to church and stand there and listen to incomprehensible prayers that I do not understand, look at the priest and at all the different people around me, that is *definitely impossible* for me. (Tolstoi PSS 60, 287, emphasis in the original)

The ascetic aspect of the fasting was no problem for him, quite the contrary. Tolstoi also enjoyed the prayers – in his private devotions. To be part of a larger community of believers, which would later become so important to him, left him cold at this stage.

In her reply, Aleksandra accused Tolstoi of pride, negligence and a lack of understanding of the holy sacraments (A. A. Tolstaia 1911, 127). That provoked him to present his *profession de foi* along with a summary statement of his religious development: In childhood, he had believed "fervently, sentimentally, and unthinkingly," but when religion ran up against the realities of life, he had abandoned the faith, he explained. For ten years he had lived comfortably without any faith. In the Caucasus, on the other hand, he found himself entrapped by an exaltation that he had hardly believed any human being could experience. This, Tolstoi now explained, was because he at that time had been lonely and unhappy, even if he would still characterize it as a good time. "Never, neither earlier nor later, have I experienced such loftiness of thought, never been so able to get a glimpse into 'the life beyond' (*tuda*)." Later, although that experience itself passed, Tolstoi had retained the convictions he had acquired at that time: Belief in immortality and love and in the necessity of living for one's neighbor in order to be eternally blessed.

> I was surprised at the similarity of these discoveries with the Christian religion, so instead of exploring them on my own, I began to look for them in the Gospel, but I found little. I found in them neither God nor the Redeemer nor *sacraments,* nothing . . . . I can say that I have rarely met among people such a passionate longing for the truth as what I experienced at that time. So I held on to my religion, and it made it good to live. (Tolstoi PSS 60, 293–94, emphasis in the original)

However, having read through what he had written, Tolstoi began to wonder if he had not exaggerated somewhat when he had characterized himself as "religious."

> The thing is that I love and respect religion and believe that without it man can be neither virtuous nor happy, and more than anything else in the world I want to acquire it . . . . In brief moments it is as if I believe – but I have no religion and I do not believe. (Tolstoi PSS 60, 294)

It must be on the basis of such recollections that Tolstoi later concluded that his middle years had been "nihilistic." However, this letter to Aleksandra Tolstaia can in no way be taken as proof of indifference: On the contrary, it testifies to a void that had to be filled. Precisely by its absence, faith was a compelling presence for Tolstoi, in the shape of a want.

We can conclude that Tolstoi also as a restless young man grappled intensely with spiritual questions. At times, he lived a passionately religious life, and the framework for this life was provided by the Orthodox faith which he still practiced in part. It was precisely in clashes with "the faith of his forebears" that he was provoked to formulate his own answers. We can detect this pattern even after he had declared himself to be nonreligious. When his oldest brother, Nikolai, died in October 1860, Tolstoi's mind wandered during the funeral. While his brother was being laid to rest with an Orthodox ritual, Tolstoi got the idea of writing a "materialistic gospel," about the life of Christ as a materialist (Tolstoi PSS 48, 30). He never followed up on this. In the end, he did indeed compose his own Gospel, but then the message was fiercely anti-materialistic.

The final aspect of his Orthodox faith that Tolstoi abandoned was prayer. In February 1860, he made a frontal attack against that as well.

> Mechanically, I came to think about my prayer. Whom should I pray to? What actually is God, if it is possible to imagine Him so clearly that it is possible to ask Him about anything, to communicate with Him. If I imagine Him in such a way, He loses all greatness. The God whom is possible to ask for something, and to serve, is an expression of the weakness of the mind. What makes Him God is precisely that I am unable to form any idea about His being. No, He is not a being. He is law and force. (Tolstoi PSS 48, 23)

When prayer slips, the personal concept of God also fades away. But still respect for this God was so great that Tolstoi continued to write His name and pronoun with a capital letter. And in his daily business at the village school at Iasnaia Poliana, which he organized for the peasant children, Tolstoi worked as a religious educator. Instruction was organized in accordance with the Church calendar: Stories about the Apostle Peter were told on St. Peter's Day, and so on. When a *muzhik* died in the village, the pupils were taught about the last rites. In this way, all the sacraments, the liturgy, and feast days were reviewed. A priest visited the school twice a week, but Tolstoi told Aleksandra Tolstaia that he himself had to instruct the priest in how to teach religion to children (Tolstoi PSS 60, 405).

Tolstoi continued to turn to God for help and guidance at critical junctures in life. In September 1862, when he for several days was torn between his affection for Sof'ia Behrs and his fear of proposing, he once again sought refuge in Him. Five times in as many days he invoked the name of the Lord. "No one can help me but God" (Tolstoi PSS 48, 44). The marriage was indeed concluded, and gave Tolstoi several years of "frightening happiness." Stormy, deep love was mixed with jealousy and tiffs. After such quarrels, the couple arranged to pray together (Tolstoi PSS 48, 52). Like so many others in Tolstoi's closest surroundings, his wife was a professing and practicing Orthodox Christian.

As long as Tolstoi was engrossed in his work on *War and Peace*, that project crowded out all other interests. In 1870, however, he once again committed to paper some "thoughts on religion." Now he entered into polemics with himself about which attitude one ought to take toward Christianity. On the one hand, he characterized the Church's answer to metaphysical questions as "soft-boiled hallelujah" (Tolstoi PSS 48, 129); on the other hand, he recognized that it would be useless to try to comprehend Christianity through the faculty of reason: If you try, the only thing you will capture is reason, while to religion with its irrational contradictions slips away (Tolstoi PSS 48, 122). These were thoughts he came to build upon seven years later, when he threw all logical objections overboard, and for a period stood forth as a professing and practicing Orthodox Christian.

Tolstoi's religious crisis probably started in the fall of 1875 or in 1876. Relatively little is known about this phase of his spiritual development. However, his correspondence with Aleksandra Tolstaia offers some insights. In April 1876, Tolstoi wrote that he no longer believed in anything of what religion taught, but at the same time he hated and despised disbelief. He could not see how it was possible to live without religion, and much less how to die without it. Gradually, he formulated his own articles of faith; even though they in his opinion were strong, he regarded them as imprecise and not very comforting. They could give correct answers when his reason asked questions, but offered no support when the heart suffered.

> I, with the requirements of my reason and the answers given by the Christian religion, am like two hands. They want to fold into each other, but the fingers get in the way. The more I struggle, the worse it gets. But at the same time I fully know that it is possible to do this, because these hands are made for each other. (Tolstoi PSS 62, 266–67)

One year later, that handshake had been achieved.

External Adaptation and Internal Maladaptation

Tolstoi's conversion in 1878 came as a surprise to most of the people around him (Orekhanov 2016, 132). It was, however, clearly prepared by a long process of inner struggle and turmoil. The main impetus behind Tolstoi's return to the Orthodox faith of his childhood was the life crisis he experienced in the preceding years. Life as he had known it had become meaningless to him, and now he found a new meaning in faith. However, this explains only his return to a religious worldview as such, and not why the choice fell on Orthodoxy. During his crisis he studied various religions, not only Christianity (Tolstoi PSS 23, 37); and among the Christian confessions official Russian Orthodoxy was not the only possibility. He took an interest in the Irish Evangelist preacher, the 3rd Baron Radstock, who had come to St. Petersburg in 1874. Tolstoi had several conversations with Radstock's Russian disciple A. P. Bobrinskii, and was attracted by the man's "sincere and warm faith" (Tolstoi PSS 62, 261). Still, Tolstoi decided to resume his practice of the Orthodox faith, as a deliberate choice among several religious options.

Throughout his crisis, Tolstoi had stayed in regular correspondence with Aleksandra Tolstaia. However, he later expressly stated that her influence had not been decisive (S. Tolstaia 1978, I, 503). Even though he regarded Aleksandra's faith as deep and sincere, he distrusted it, because it so readily could be combined with an aristocratic lifestyle at court.

What did Tolstoi seek in Orthodoxy that other religions could not give him? More than anything else, it was a sense of *community with the people.* The Church represented connection – diachronically with tradition, and synchronically with the people, the believing masses (Tolstoi PSS 23, 50). "The Church served as a link to the people whom he loved," wrote his daughter Tat'iana (Sukhotina-Tolstaia [1932] 1981, 371). Tradition and the people held the accumulated wisdom of mankind, with insights into the mysteries of life.

> After all the despair and disbelief, I acknowledged as true the meaning which the Christian, toiling people gives life. In the name of this meaning, I submitted to the beliefs (*verovaniia*) that this people professes, that is, to the Orthodox Church. (Tolstoi PSS 23, 307)

Since the people's wisdom was intuitive rather than articulated, it could be communicated only through practice, by taking part in the Christian community of the Church.

In making the worldview and the way of life of the common people a criterion of truth, Tolstoi followed up on an important motif among the Russian intelligentsia: Deep devotion to the people. This attitude found expression among groups as different as the "populists" (*narodniki),* the Slavophiles, and the *pochvenniki.* While the *narodniki* saw a "social truth" in how the simple people lived, to the Slavophiles and so-called *pochvenniki* the people's truth was primarily religious: Their sincere and at the same time practical understanding of Christianity. The most famous *pochvennik* was Fedor Dostoevskii. Like Tolstoi, also he had turned his back on the Orthodox faith in his youth, and returned to it after having been confronted with the meaning-providing faith of the people. These two thinkers had surprisingly similar motivations for becoming Orthodox believers. Both knew the peasantry better than most in the Russian intelligentsia – but still they seemed to idealize it and view it as more homogeneous as regards religion than it actually was.

When Tolstoi had first decided to live as an Orthodox believer, he did not go about it piecemeal or half-heartedly, but gave himself completely over to the ordinances of the Church. He complied strictly with all its prescriptions and fasting days. He recited his prayers every morning, and attended all church services, preferring to go on foot rather than in a carriage. Further, he adhered to the strictest variant of the fasting prescriptions, which banned also fish on fast days (Sukhotina-Tolstaia [1932] 1981, 371).

Tolstoi now talked so much about God that it became a bit too much even for his sincerely devout wife. The village priest often visited Iasnaia Poliana and had conversations with the count that lasted deep into the night (N. Gusev 1970, 442). Tolstoi was deeply engaged in the religious upbringing of his children and made sure that they went to confession and did not skip fasting.

To his bishop, Tolstoi expressed his desire to sell everything he owned and give it to the poor, as Jesus in the Gospel had encouraged the rich young man to do. After some consideration, the bishop discouraged this because Tolstoi's property belonged not only to him but also to his family. On the same occasion, Tolstoi asked to be consecrated as deacon and to be allowed to hold sermons in the church. These wishes were not granted. This conversation took place in December 1879, just a few months before Tolstoi began writing *A Confession*. The priest, A. Ivanov, who related this conversation, emphasized that he understood Tolstoi's requests as being sincere (A. Ivanov 1901a, 259–61). To Ivanov, Tolstoi had proposed that the two of them should publish Christian, ascetic texts in popular editions, but nothing came out of this publishing project. Later, however, Tolstoi did realize these plans on his own, with an entire series of such writings issued by his publisher *Posrednik* ("The intermediator").

The diaries of Tolstoi's wife Sof'ia Andreevna provide insights into how Tolstoi's behavior at this time was perceived by the people around him. She had the impression that he not only adapted to the life of the Church, but devoted himself completely to it, finding great joy in his religious practice. In March 1877, Sof'ia Andreevna remarked that her husband was, in her own words, "happy" in his religion. In August of that same year, she noted that "the religious spirit is becoming increasingly stronger in him." Tolstoi's temperament also changed. While he had always been modest and undemanding, he now became even more humble and patient. His constant struggle for moral perfection had finally been crowned with full victory, his wife believed (S. Tolstaia 1978, I, 503–05).

Also in Tolstoi's letters and notes from this period we can find expressions of serene calm. On January 27, 1878, he wrote to his friend Nikolai Strakhov about his "tranquility and freedom of the soul" (Tolstoi PSS 62, 382). Some words jotted down in 1879 were clearly inspired by St. Augustine's *Confessions* and the Book of Psalms:

> What am I doing here, thrown into this world? Whom can I contact? From whom should I seek answers? From the people? They know nothing. They laugh, and do not want to know. They say: It's a trifle . . . . But I called your name, my Lord, and my suffering ceased. My despair passed . . . . Your path is clear and simple. Your yoke is easy and your burden is light.

However, Tolstoi's protestations of peace of mind were more a programmatic statement than an expression of real experience. Some lines further down in the diary he added, "even though I know that your yoke is easy and your burden is light, it feels heavy" (Tolstoi PSS 48, 351).

Also some other notebook entries from this time indicate that his adaptation to life in the Church was harder than he often made it appear. In 1878, he attempted an explanation of his beliefs arranged in five points:

1. Reason is merely a tool for the early life and cannot provide knowledge of the real issues of life.
2. The fundamental questions include: Why do I live? Why do I experience in myself a division between good and evil? How should I live? What is death? The most general expression of these questions is: "How can I be saved?"
3. Religion is the only thing that is able to give answers to these questions. Because reason is powerless when confronted with them, and will not even acknowledge their legitimacy, we cannot demand of religion that its answers should satisfy the requirements of reason.
4. The different religions each provide their own answers, and these answers are expressed in regulations concerning certain ritual actions – human sacrifice, pilgrimage to Mecca, veneration of relics. These regulations differ wildly, and it is impossible to derive any objective truth from them. The issue of religion, however, is not external truth, but salvation. Common to all believers is that they seek salvation, and find it in self-denial.
5. I say: "I, as a Christian, have thrown aside all the contradictions of icons, relics, and miracles, and allow myself to be satisfied with the Christian means of salvation because I do not know any higher principle than the principle of self-denial and love" (Tolstoi PSS 48, 187–89).

Tolstoi's main reason for accepting the ritual side of Orthodox piety, then, proves to be self-denial. What he is referring to here is not asceticism in the traditional sense, but his willingness to renounce all rational objections, "throw aside all contradictions." The sacrifice required of Tolstoi as an Orthodox believer was nothing less than renunciation of his reason. As a defense for an Orthodox faith, however, this line of reasoning was surely ambiguous at best.

Causes Behind the Break

Tolstoi's overt break with the prescriptions of the Church came in December 1879. As Andrei Zorin (Zorin 2020, 112) remarks, the decision outwardly seemed quick and decisive, but was the result of tortuous inner reflection: On a Wednesday, he suddenly asked to be served by the same lamb chops that the non-Orthodox members of the household ate, despite Wednesday being a day of fasting in the Orthodox Church. After that, he stopped fasting altogether (I. Tolstoi [1913] 1969, 171–72; Biriukov 1905–23, II, 329–30). There is a certain irony in the fact that Tolstoi's "Orthodox period" should end like this, since vegetarianism would later become a part of the Tolstoian form of asceticism. Tolstoi came to perceive vegetarianism and fasting as related phenomena; they were both forms of self-denial. He could also claim that "fasting is an indispensable condition for a good life as it is also the first precondition for a life of abstinence" (Tolstoi PSS 29, 74). And indeed, it was no Epicurean desire to enjoy the pleasures of the table that drove Tolstoi away from the Church. The causes lay elsewhere.

Tolstoi felt more and more strongly that he had to perform the standard Orthodox ritual with "mental reservations." His desire to go all the way with this worship had been hollowed out from within, becoming "piecemeal and divided" – precisely what Tolstoi, with his contempt for hypocrisy, could not tolerate. In *A Confession*, he explained how he found it increasingly difficult to hold back the inquisitive questions of reason, questions that were directed at the most fundamental dogmas. In particular, he found the Eucharist problematical because it forced him to take part in a ritual that expressed the thought of Jesus' vicarious sacrificial death. In addition to rationalist objections of this type, Tolstoi also mentioned problems of another kind: Prayers for the armed forces and for victory over the enemy were a stumbling block not for his reason, but for his moral sense (Tolstoi PSS 23, 50). The same was true of the fragmentation of Christianity into various denominations. These divisions engendered persecution and intolerance, and "the cruelest thing a man can say to another is that you live in falsehood and I live in the truth" (Tolstoi PSS 23, 53).

The frequent prayers for the Tsar and his family also bothered Tolstoi. In *A Confession*, he wrote that he tried to comfort himself by saying that these people were more susceptible to temptation than others and therefore in greater need of intercession. Here, however, there is reason to believe that Tolstoy's memory failed him, and that precisely these prayers were an important reason why he found he could not remain within the Church. In a diary entry as early as May 22, 1878, he wrote: "On Sunday, I went to church. Everything in the service I can give a satisfactory explanation for, but 'Many Years' [for the Tsar. P. K.], and [prayer for] victory over the enemy are blasphemy" (Tolstoi PSS 48, 70). "This was the beginning of the break," maintained Tolstoi's biographer, Henri Troyat (Troyat 1980, 542).

In *What I Believe*, Tolstoi wrote that he was repelled by many things about the Church: The outlandish dogmas; the acceptance of persecutions, the death penalty and war; and the mutual recriminations of the various different confessions.

> But what really undermined my trust in [the Church] was the indifference it showed to what I perceived as the essentials of Christ's teachings, and conversely, the zeal it showed toward what I perceived as immaterial. (Tolstoi PSS 23, 307)

The most important, Tolstoi explained, were the moral commandments given in the Sermon on the Mount. Again, the decisive factor behind the break was what Tolstoi perceived as the moral shortcomings of the Church. True, he admitted that between his own view and that of the Church there was no radical break, only a difference of emphasis. "I could not accuse the Church of denying the essentials, but it recognized them in such a way that it could not satisfy me. The Church did not give me what I expected from it" (ibid.).

Tolstoi's first impulses to confront the Russian Orthodox Church may well have been spurred more by his sense of ethics than by his rationalism. In January 1878, he wrote to Nikolai Strakhov about his Orthodox faith.[2] At this point, the distinction between the knowledge of the heart and the knowledge of reason still held validity for him, and he could therefore

[2] Tolstoy conducted an extensive correspondence on questions of faith with the literary critic Nikolai Strakhov who struggled with many of the same religious questions as he did himself. See Paperno 2010.

claim that for him the doctrines of the Church did not contain anything meaningless. Indeed, he was not even able to see how the criterion of "meaning" could be used as a test of the truth in this matter. If the Church demanded that he once a year should drink wine that they call the blood of Christ and eat cabbage rather than meat on certain days, he would do so even if he did not understand why. It was a different matter when the Church wanted him to pray for the death of as many Turks as possible. "Without asking my mind, I can say from my heart's unclear but nevertheless unambiguous voice that this is wrong" (Tolstoi PSS 62, 381).

Tolstoi's Orthodox period coincided with Russia's war against Turkey in 1877–78. Prior to and during this war, there were strong Panslavist currents in Russia (Kohn 1953). In the propaganda, the war was portrayed as a sacred war of liberation: The Orthodox Southern Slavs were to be freed from the yoke of the infidel Turk. Patriotic and religious motives were so closely intertwined that it was difficult to see where the one ended and the other began.

Tolstoy reacted vehemently against this rhetoric of war-mongering, and also against the fact that the Russian Church was an integral part of the Tsarist state. Looking more deeply into the matter, he found more and more blasphemous effects of the close State–Church relationship, which after the establishment of the The Most Holy Governing Synod under Peter the Great had been organized in a way clearly in contravention of Orthodox canonical law.

In *What I Believe*, Tolstoi quoted a section from Metropolitan Filaret of Moscow's *Catechism*. This was the most commonly used catechism at the time; by 1880, it had been issued in no less than 64 printings. In his commentary on the fourth Commandment, Filaret extended the injunction to love one's father and mother to include reverence for the Tsar, the Fatherland, spiritual pastors and all those in positions of authority in various contexts, such as teachers, judges, officers and the "lords" (*gospoda*) (Filaret [Drozdov] [1880] 1976, 95–96). The latter should be revered by those who "serve them and are owned by them." In particular this last command Tolstoi found more than astonishing: Here the Church was giving its full blessing to the institution of serfdom – twenty years after it had been abolished (Tolstoi PSS 23, 435).

On October 30, 1879, Tolstoi wrote in his notebook:

1) Faith, as long as it remains faith, can in its essence not be subjected to power. Only a bird that can fly is alive.
2) Faith rejects power and authorities (*pravitel'stvo*) – wars, death penalty, robbery, theft, everything that is the essence of government.

> Therefore, the authorities will always want to rape religion . . . . Christianity was raped under Constantine. (Tolstoi PSS 48, 196)

The great Fall of Christianity took place during the Constantinian Revolution in the fourth century, when the Church changed from being a victim of persecution to becoming powerful itself. One of the first pamphlets Tolstoi wrote after his break with the Church was *The Church and the State.* Here, he located the sources of the perversion of true Christianity in the rule of Constantine the Great. "Christianity's consecration of the power of the state is a blasphemy, and the undoing of Christianity itself." True faith is possible everywhere, except where it is connected with the state. The term "a Christian state" is as much a *contradictio in adjecto* as "warm ice" (Tolstoi PSS 23, 479). This concept had led the French to regard Napoleon as being sent them by God, and the Russians were if possible in an even worse position, Tolstoi wrote. They had had to regard a harlot who assassinated her spouse [= Catherine the Great] as if she were God-given. The same they had to believe about The Synod and its chief procurators (*komandiry chinovniki*) (Tolstoi PSS 23, 480). In 1900, Tolstoi read through *Church and State* once more, and commented in his diary: "It says it all" (Tolstoi PSS 51, 116).

At the end of the nineteenth century, there was deep dissatisfaction among a large proportion of the clergy and laity regarding the close relations between State and Church. Due to censorship this dissatisfaction could not be directly expressed at the time, but in the years after the 1905 Revolution, when censorship was lifted, a major debate commenced about the function of the Church vis-à-vis the State and its position in Russian society. It was decided to establish a commission to prepare the convening of a national Church council and to commission proposals for reforms, from all the bishops in the country. It emerged that only two bishops supported the retention of the Holy Synod; the remaining sixty were in favor of abandoning it. This found solid support among the laity and members of the lower clergy (Zernov 1963, 67–72; Pospielovsky 1984, 19–24; see also *Gruppa stolichnykh sviashchennikov* 1905).

Tolstoy was thus not alone in his criticism of the Church's close affiliation with the State; many believers apparently sympathized with this part of his censure. In 1916, the priest Stefan Ostroumov wrote an article in the liberal Orthodox journal *Otdykh khristianina* in which he attempted to tease out the positive elements in Tolstoi's preaching. Ostroumov claimed that the root cause of Tolstoi's critical attitude toward the Church was not the Orthodox doctrine, but was to be found in the attitude of the Church to other religious denominations and not least in its relationship with the State. "Tolstoi rightly felt that state and church are incompatible entities, like power and freedom" (S. Ostroumov 1916, 3, 186).

In 1987, the British scholar Charles Lock noted that "Tolstoy's opposition to the church as hierarchically ordered, itself always subservient to the needs of the state, was part of that broad movement of rebellion and ultimately revolution out of which, and along with much else, modern Orthodox theology was born." Up against Richard Gustafson's harmonizing interpretation of the relationship between Tolstoi and Orthodoxy, Lock made a deliberately paradoxical claim: "... Tolstoy is most Orthodox, and prophetically so, in his attacks on the established Orthodox Church" (Lock 1987, 180).

Tolstoi's Orthodox period foundered on a paradoxical "discovery": He had joined the Church in order to be united with the people, but instead of a Church of the people, what he encountered was the Tsarist Church, with which he would have nothing to do. This attitude was typical among the Russian intelligentsia, who saw all power as evil, and the absolute power of the Tsar as absolutely evil. They therefore rejected everything and everyone who supported this power, including the Russian Orthodox Church. For Tolstoi, the struggle against the Church was unusually bitter and painful because, unlike most other intellectuals in Russia at the time, he was unwilling to abandon his religious worldview. He never gave up the idea that what gave meaning to the life of the peasantry (the *muzhiks)* was their true religious practice, also when they professed Orthodoxy. Tolstoi thus ended up in the same situation as many *narodniki*: He had to instruct the common people about the deep truths that they possessed.

Lies and Truth

Tolstoi's relation to Orthodox faith as he knew it was never unproblematic – neither before nor after his break with the Church. As long as he remained a practicing Orthodox, he was not able to embrace it wholeheartedly; later, he could not fully liberate himself from it. Orthodoxy contained a duality, he maintained: It was "truth interwoven with lies with the finest threads" (Tolstoi PSS 23, 53). In the years 1879–80, he tried in various ways to find a criterion for separating the lies from the truth. In *A Confession* he indicated that this distinction coincided with the contrast between the unreflecting, intuitive beliefs of the common people and the dogmatics of the theologians.

> When I approached the [common] people and heard their opinions about life and faith, I understood the truth more and more . . . . But as soon as I came together with learned believers or took their books in my hands, some doubt immediately arose in me. I was gripped by dissatisfaction and an urge to protest, and felt that the more I studied their talks, the further removed did I become from the truth. (Tolstoi PSS 23, 52)

But Tolstoi soon realized that this contrast did not explain everything. Already in *A Confession* he noted: "[E]ven though I saw that among the people there was less of that mendacious admixture that repelled me among the representatives of the Church, I saw that also in the faith of the people, lies were mixed in" (Tolstoi PSS 23, 56). In an early draft he went as far as to claim that in the faith of the common people there was "even more nonsense" than among believers from his own social stratum (Tolstoi PSS 23, 502).

In his pamphlet *To the Clergy* (1902), Tolstoi introduced a distinction between enlightened and uninformed, un-Christian theology: If one reads what the bishops and the professors of theology write in their journals, one might think that what the Russian clergy preached was a Christian faith, albeit an obsolete one. In this faith, "the gospel truths, after all, have a certain place and are imparted to the people." The activities and teaching of the village priests, on the other hand, he condemned as sheer idolatry (Tolstoi PSS 34, 36; see also Tolstoi 28, 57). In *A Confession*, the primitive, popular belief of the people was presented as positive, while the learned theology provoked only indignation and contempt in Tolstoi. In *To the Clergy*, he turned the relationship between these two forms of Orthodoxy on its head.

Another avenue for finding the pure, unsullied truth of Christianity was to search backward to the sources. This was the program behind Tolstoi's comprehensive Bible studies and Gospel translations. But also this failed to give him a satisfactory explanation. In an unpublished, nameless work written at about the same time as *A Confession*, Tolstoi claimed that the Gospels contained a terrible mixture of "the sublime and understandable on the one hand and the most confused and meaningless teachings on the other" (N. Gusev 1963, 595). In one of his most critical moments Tolstoi claimed that "there are no more godless books than the Revelation and the Acts of the Apostles" (Tolstoi PSS 48, 325). When Tolstoi embarked on his Bible study, he felt as if he had been given a sack of smelly mud. Only through thorough and painstaking work did he discover that in this muck precious gems were hidden (Tolstoi PSS 24, 807).

Thus, while the New Testament could not be embraced in its entirety, the teachings of the Church could not be totally rejected either: "[B]oth the lie and the truth have been passed down to us by the so-called Church" (Tolstoi PSS 23, 56). Those who throughout the centuries had taken care of the pearls together with the muck, not knowing what they were doing, deserve our love and esteem. In one draft variant of *A Confession*, Tolstoi expressed this as follows:

> But what is this priestly [*pastyrskoe*] teaching? What in it is lie and what is true? It has to be truth in it, for it is this priestly teaching which has brought all the Christian truths to us and has taught the people about them. (Tolstoi PSS 23, 508)

A third possibility should also be examined: The lie might be linked first and foremost to the external cult, while the truth of the Church was to be found in its inner core of faith. But also this distinction Tolstoi found problematic. Concerning his depictions of Orthodox services, most scholars have focused on the condemnation of what had been repugnant to him. However, there were also elements in the ritual that attracted him.

> The divine services *(sluzhby)*, the confession and the morning and evening prayers (*pravila*) – all of this was understandable, and aroused in me the happy feeling that the meaning of life was about to be revealed. The Eucharist itself I could explain as an act of remembering Christ, as signifying the cleansing of sins and a complete acceptance of the teachings of Christ … . I felt joy at self-abasement, humbling myself toward my father confessor, a simple and shy priest. Here I could twist out the turmoil in my soul and repent of my vices. Gladly I also in my thoughts joined with the intentions of the Church Fathers who composed the prayers. (Tolstoi PSS 23, 51)

The ritual acts, which Tolstoi here noted as positive and noble, are central elements of standard Orthodox practice. Confession attracted him as spiritual therapy and a concrete opportunity to practice self-degradation. He said the Prayers of the Hours *(ezhechasnye molitvy)* with joy. They were recited morning and evening by the monks in the monasteries and by ordinary believers standing before the icons in the "red" or "beautiful" corner[3] of the house or peasant hut. For the most part, these prayers were identical to those read in church (Ware 1978, 310–11). In his later period, Tolstoi also practiced this in some form. His secretary Nikolai Gusev confirms that Tolstoi recited a ritualized prayer every morning (N. Gusev 1973, 79); and in 1901 Tolstoi noted in his diary three "hourly prayers." In 1907, he wrote to Ivan Tregubov, a Tolstoian and former

[3] "Krasnyi" originally meant "beautiful" but later acquired the more typical meaning of "red."

Orthodox theology student, that he prayed every morning and often made the sign of the cross.

> Especially when I sit down to work, I perform this gesture to induce or strengthen in me the emotional religious mood (*umilenie*) which it has been associated with since my childhood. (Tolstoi PSS 77, 88)

Such a religious "atavism" as this "gesture" would hardly have arisen if Tolstoi had had his background in a Protestant denomination.

The idea that there is the duality in Orthodoxy was not a chance thought or passing idea in Tolstoi's thinking. On the contrary, it stands as the main theme of the last three chapters of *A Confession*, the chord on which that important work ends. He expressed similar ideas in a letter to "aunt" Aleksandra Tolstaia, written at about the same time as *A Confession*: He would much prefer his children to adhere to the faith of the Church than to reject all religious beliefs whatsoever (Tolstoi PSS 63, 6). Only two years later, however, he wrote to aunt Tolstaia that the Orthodox, in his opinion, "belong to their father, the devil" (cf. John 8, 44). "In relation to your religion, Orthodoxy, I am not a lost sheep or a deviant, but one who shall expose it" (Tolstoi PSS 63, 92). The tone in the letter was so acerbic that in the end he decided not to send it (Medzhibovskaya 2009 226).

Researchers have largely ignored the affection/hate attitude that characterized Tolstoi's relation to Orthodoxy in *A Confession* – perhaps because Tolstoi himself moderated it rather quickly. As he sharpened the polemical tone in the next works, there seemed little reason to point out the valuable aspects of the Russian Church. He soon condemned Orthodoxy as "a parasite on true Christianity" (Tolstoi PSS 50, 103) and "one of the most superstitious and harmful heresies that exist" (Tolstoi PSS 50, 87). In *On Violence and Love* (1908), Tolstoi warned the reader against seeing the Christianity of the Church as merely an incomplete or one-sided form of Christianity. No, like a criminal caught red-handed it must either fall apart or commit new crimes. Already in *What I Believe* (1884), he described the teachings of the Church as "the darkness Christ fought against and commanded His disciples to fight against" (Tolstoi PSS 23, 437). But also in this work, Tolstoi admitted that "the teachings of the Church, with dogmas, cathedrals, and hierarchies, are undoubtedly connected with the teachings of Christ" (Tolstoi PSS 23, 448). Historically, he now held, the Church had played an important role: Like a womb, it had provided nourishment while humanity remained at the spiritual fetus stage (Tolstoi PSS 23, 448).

One of the works in which Tolstoi presented the sharpest and most detailed criticism of the Church is *The Kingdom of God is within You*

(1890). Here he claimed that the Church and true Christianity have nothing in common but the name: They represent two diametrically opposed and antagonistic principles. In the Church, all the emphasis is allegedly placed on the outer trappings – icons, prayers, relics and incense. The importance of charitable acts has virtually disappeared, and Christianity has decayed into moral idolatry. However, in this work Tolstoi also posited that the misunderstandings presented by the Church were a historical necessity: If, from the beginning, Christianity had been preached in its pure, untainted form, it would have remained a religion for the enlightened and most insightful of the elite. The masses would simply not have understood it. "But when it was presented in a distorted form, the people who accepted it, slowly but surely, came under its influence" (Tolstoi PSS 28, 147).

In 1895, Tolstoi read a theological thesis on Orthodox soteriology, written by Bishop (later Patriarch) Sergii Stragorodskii (1861–944). It presented the Christian teaching on salvation from the "morally subjective side" (Florovskii 1982, 438), and Tolstoi thought the book was "good" (Tolstoi PSS 53, 50). His reading prompted him to try once more to clarify his relationship to the Russian Church. Tolstoi now stated that those who adhere to Orthodox doctrine undoubtedly become better people, similar to how Evangelical Christians and others are exposed to favorable influences in their respective denominations. This stood in clear contrast to Tolstoi's former claims that the dogmas of the Church are harmful – or at best have no effect whatsoever on the believers' way of life.

But, Tolstoi asked himself, if this is the case, why did he feel such a deep disgust for the teachings of the Orthodox Church? It was because mankind had now managed to grasp the truth in a higher form, as Christ himself had taught it. In relation to the teaching of Jesus, Orthodoxy was indeed "a lie," but "if we had only ignorance and Orthodoxy, then Orthodoxy would no doubt be *a good thing*" (Tolstoi PSS 53, 50, emphasis in the original). Rightly understood, then, the lie of the Church was an outmoded truth.

In 1906, Tolstoi reread Kant's treatise on the philosophy of religion, *Die Religion innerhalb der Grenzen der bloßen Vernunft*. In his diary, he commented on the book and criticized Kant's distinction between statutory (ritualistic) and moral religion.

> Kant is wrong when he claims that the performance of rituals and beliefs in a historical tradition is fetishism, and that this is diametrically opposed to a reason-based belief in the moral law. The belief in a historical tradition and in the necessity of rituals also means faith in a law, even though the moral law here is misunderstood. (Tolstoi PSS 55, 186)

Tolstoi did not want to abolish the distinction between ritualistic and moral religion. He emphasized that all believers, after all, share the same attitude of faith. In the sea of unbelief in the Russia of his times, all believers were sitting in the same boat. Tolstoi could feel a spiritual affinity with some Orthodox believers, in the sense of meeting a "related soul that lives by the same spiritual principle that is in us all" (Tolstoi PSS 81, 184–85). When Tolstoi's secretary Nikolai Gusev in 1903 told that his mother was a sincere Orthodox believer, Tolstoi replied that he esteemed such people (N. Gusev 1973, 44). Three years later, Tolstoi wrote a draft of a story about an Orthodox priest, Father Vasilii. This priest is an entirely positive figure, an example of self-sacrifice and self-forgetfulness. Father Vasilii has the same first and last name as the priest who had baptized Tolstoi, which indicates that he may have served as a model (Tolstoi PSS 36, 594).

In 1906, Sof'ia Andreevna became ill, and requested a priest. Tolstoi gave his consent, noting in his diary:

> I not only accepted this, but gladly contributed [to the priest coming. P. K.]. There are people for whom an abstract, purely spiritual relationship with the source of life is inaccessible. They need a rougher (*grubaia*) form. But also this form is spiritual. And it is good that it exists, even though it is rough. (Tolstoi PSS 55, 243)

The idea of a duality in Orthodoxy lies as an unspoken premise between the lines of much of what Tolstoi wrote and said. Sometimes it was also expressed more explicitly. On January 4, 1908, he had a conversation with Dmitrii Troitskii, an Orthodox priest. Without beating about the bush, Tolstoi referred to the teachings of the Church as "dung" that contaminated the spiritual. On the same occasion, however, he also claimed that

> Yes, you have the truth. If you didn't, you would have succumbed long ago. But together with the truth you also have much lies. A satanic pride has made you believe that you know the truth. (N. Gusev 1973, 77)

Here, Tolstoi expresses the same understanding of the relationship between truth and lies in Orthodoxy as in *A Confession*: The truth of the Church is not just a stage that was later overcome, a thing of the past: It lives on, in fragments, in the present. This view can be found even in his most viciously anti-Orthodox work, *An Examination of Dogmatic Theology*, to which I will now turn.

CHAPTER 3

Tolstoi's Examination of Dogmatic Theology

Why the Book Was Written

During the fall of 1879, Tolstoi felt increasingly uneasy in his Orthodox faith. He had conversations with Nikolai Strakhov and with Dmitrii Khomiakov, the son of Aleksei Khomiakov, and discussed with them his views on faith and the Church (Tolstoi PSS 62, 499). Strakhov counseled him to seek out Orthodox experts on dogmatics, to get the doctrines of the Church presented from the most authoritative sources. Tolstoi followed this advice, and when he went to Moscow in September that year, he had talks with two prominent representatives of the Russian Church. Aleksei (Lavrov-Platonov 1825–90) was the bishop of Mozhaisk and had previously been the principal of the Moscow Theological Academy. Tolstoi's other interlocutor was an even more erudite figure: Makarii (Bulgakov 1816–82) was Metropolitan of Moscow and author of thirteen volumes on the history of the Russian Church. He had also written the two-volume compendium *Orthodox Dogmatic Theology*, which was required reading at all theological colleges in the country. From Moscow, Tolstoi went on to the Trinity-Sergiev Monastery in Sergiev Posad, where Russia's major theological school, the Moscow Theological Academy, was housed. Here he met with several theologians, including the monastery's abbot, Leonid (Kavelin, 1822–96).

There is no record of these conversations, but in a letter to Strakhov on October 4, 1879, Tolstoi wrote that he had not managed to get what he had hoped for. The theologians were "fine and wise people, but I became only more strengthened in my conviction. I am troubled, thrown back and forth, fighting in the spirit and suffer, but I thank God for this condition" (Tolstoi PSS 62, 499).

Apparently, Tolstoi had not yet completely abandoned his belief in the usefulness of seeking out theological expertise. On December 10 the same year, he approached Bishop Nikandr (Pokrovskii 1816–93) in his home town of Tula. To Nikandr, he complained that the Christian denominations too often argued over immaterial matters rather than agreeing on the essentials of faith. The bishop did his best to respond, but ended up referring Tolstoi to the priest A. Ivanov. He was the editor of the diocese magazine, *Tul'skie eparkhial'nye vedomosti*, and was known as a very learned man. He, in turn, recommended Tolstoi to read standard representations of the Orthodox doctrine, and mentioned, *inter alia*, the works of Makarii (Bulgakov) (A. Ivanov 1901a, 264). Referred back to his first interlocutor, Tolstoi had now come full circle.

Although his talks with Makarii had failed to lead to any clarification, only six weeks later Tolstoi embarked on a thorough study not only of Metropolitan Makarii's books, but of all available textbooks in Orthodox systematic theology. The result of all this reading was his *Examination of the Dogmatic Theology* (hereafter: *Examination*), which he worked on throughout the last months of 1879 and the first quarter of 1880. With its 236 pages, it is one of Tolstoi's most voluminous religious treatises and the only one entirely focused on confrontation with Orthodox theology.

In the introduction, Tolstoi explained that when he commenced his investigations, he was still an Orthodox believer. However, he had felt the need for a better understanding of this faith, as its teachings increasingly seemed to conflict with his own immediate perceptions of God and His law. As Tolstoi presented it, it was not academic, scholarly interest that had driven him, but a deep, personal need to gain a firmer grounding. This he still hoped to find in the Church.

In a letter to Strakhov on February 29, 1880, Tolstoi expressed his surprise at the results of his study of Orthodox dogmatics. "If anyone had told me what I would find there, I would not have believed him" (Tolstoi PSS 63, 13). And Tolstoi's conclusions are indeed remarkable: "I finally realized that this whole doctrine of faith, which I once supposed expressed the people's beliefs, is not just lies, but are the fraud of nonbelievers, accumulated over the centuries" (Tolstoi PSS 23, 63). That, he held, also explained why this doctrine tended to produce atheists when it was taught at theological seminaries: It was simply a compendium of nonbelief. Tolstoi denied any value whatsoever to dogmatics, which he described as consisting of "sheer imagination," "blasphemous fever fantasies," "deliberate lies," "pitiful and crooked distortions," etc. Almost overwhelmed by disgust, Tolstoi had repeatedly felt tempted to interrupt his work on this "blasphemous" literature (Tolstoi PSS 23, 80 & passim).

In view of this aggressive language, many readers have doubted Tolstoi's claim that he began his study of dogmatics with an open mind. The

French Tolstoi scholar Nicolas Weisbein believed that Tolstoi went to his theological studies in order to find additional arguments in support of his already negative attitude toward the Christian faith (Weisbein 1960, 149). Henri Troyat used even harsher terms, claiming that Tolstoi wanted to get revenge for the two years of his life he had wasted as a practicing Orthodox (Troyat 1980, 544). Georgii Orekhanov (2010, 197) has expressed a similar view.

However, the invective in *Examination* is interspersed with desperate cries for help. On several occasions, Tolstoi apostrophizes the Orthodox theologians: "I seek the saving faith . . . . Therefore, teach me the truths that God has revealed" (Tolstoi PSS 23, 65). "Show me why my objections are groundless, and soften my callous heart" (Tolstoi PSS 23, 67). Such outbreaks might perhaps be simply rhetorical devices, but can also be taken as expressing a genuine desire for spiritual guidance. If the latter interpretation is correct, the abuses in the book can be understood as Tolstoi's expressing deep disappointment over his unfulfilled expectations.

It seems likely that, at the beginning of his theological studies, Tolstoi was highly ambivalent toward the Orthodox faith. For him it was a system of thought that contained valuable but also highly reprehensible elements. This, as we have seen, was the conclusion he had reached in *Confession*, the work he concluded just before embarking on his examination of Orthodox dogmatics. The two books are closed linked. *Examination* is a necessary follow-up to *Confession;* strictly speaking, they are two parts of the same work. The original version of *Confession* from 1879 ends with the following words:

> I do not doubt that there is truth in the Orthodox teachings, and equally indubitably there are lies in it. I have to find the truth and the lie and separate them from each other. And this I have started with. What I have found of false and what I have found of truth in this doctrine, and which conclusions I have reached, will make up the next parts of this work. If it is worth it and if someone needs it, it will probably be printed somewhere sometime. (Tolstoi PSS 23, 57)

The "next parts" are precisely *Examination*. Nikolai Gusev, who had access to Tolstoi's unpublished manuscripts, explains that in the original draft, the first lines of *Examination* follow immediately after the paragraph quoted above (N. Gusev 1963, 618). In the first printed version, *A Confession* bore a subtitle: "Introduction to an unpublished work."[1] That is why I regard the closing words of *A Confession* as Tolstoi's

[1] Few researchers have commented upon this connection and others have misunderstood it. Inessa Medzhibovskaya (2009, 232) erroneously believes that *A Confession* was given this subtitle because Tolstoi intended it to be an introduction to "the long narrative of confessed wrongdoings and sin."

programmatic statement for his analysis in *Examination*, and will look for places in the text where Tolstoi implicitly or explicitly uncovered elements of truth in the Orthodox dogmatics he encountered.

A Neglected Work

Although Tolstoi probably started to write *Examination* as part of a personal self-therapy, it is clear that he also wanted to reach a wider audience with his message. In the text he repeatedly addressed his future readers, and, as noted, he hoped that the book would be published. That did indeed happen, but only eleven years later. The first edition was issued by a Swiss publisher in 1891, who changed the title to *Criticism of Dogmatic Theology* – apparently to give the book a Kantian touch. This title was retained by all later publishers until the editors of the *Jubilee Edition* of Tolstoi's collected works restored the title used by Tolstoi himself.

Examination was issued only once in Russia in Tolstoi's lifetime, in 1908 – and with a conspicuous lack of impact. Compared to the fury triggered by Tolstoi's other religious treatises, the silence around *Examination* was deafening – particularly striking because it stood in stark contrast to the high temperature of the work itself. In no other writing did Tolstoi's polemical indignation reach such heights. And yet, *Examination* is by far Tolstoi's most neglected work. Compared with the avalanche of polemical writing unleashed by Tolstoi's other religious texts, the Church's counterattack against *Examination* was weak indeed. Why?

Tolstoy's secretary Nikolai Gusev claimed that, in Church circles, *Examination* "did not receive a single response," claiming that this was because Tolstoi's attack on the Church was shattering and irrefutable (N. Gusev 1963, 625). However, there are several other, far more obvious reasons.[2] There seems to have been a widespread perception that Tolstoi's accusations were so grotesque as to be self-defeating. Secondly, many Russian Christians seem to have regarded academic Orthodox theology

[2] Gusev's assertion, as it stands, is not correct. In April 1897, the journal *Pravoslavnyi sobesednik* printed a balanced and insightful article on *Examination* written by Antonii Khrapovitskii, one of the foremost Russian theologians of the time. Also, theology professor A. F. Gusev devoted considerable space to this work in his doctoral dissertation *The Essence of L.N. Tolstoi's Religious-Moral Teaching* in 1902. In several earlier works on Tolstoi, Gusev had attacked virtually all the writer's other religious books; the reason why he had previously omitted *Examination* was that he did not want to attack a book that existed only in illegal, hectograph-duplicated versions (A. Gusev 1886, 1, 136–37; 1902, 79–81).

as a rather inadequate expression of their faith. Even if Tolstoi might have managed to tear into shreds what was taught at the theological seminaries, that did not really concern them (see, for instance, Antonii [Khrapovitskii] 1967c, 176; Novoselov 1905, 116).

Finally, if *Examination* had been published earlier, it might have ruffled some feathers in ecclesiastical circles. When it circulated only as an early *samizdat*, and there were rumors of its existence, Bishop Feofan Zatvornik (Govorov, "the Recluse"), for one, repeatedly tried to obtain a manuscript copy in order to compose a reply (Feofan Govorov 1898–1901, II, 134; V, 78; VII, 188). However, when he finally did get hold of the book, he decided not to respond, concluding that "of all Tolstoi's texts this is the most insignificant" (quoted in Orekhanov 2016, 523).

However, the main reason why Church figures received *Examination* with such equanimity was probably that it aroused even less interest among the secular public than in ecclesiastical circles. When *Examination* was published abroad in 1891, the reading Russian public had already been exposed to both *A Confession* and *What I Believe*, and interest focused on these books, which presented Tolstoi's new teachings in a clearer, more concise and direct manner. With even the enemies of the Church not finding it worthwhile to consider this work, believers saw no reason to spill ink on it either. The secular intelligentsia, for its part, apparently regarded the book as a part of an internal quarrel between Tolstoi and the Church on rather abstruse and uninteresting topics. *Examination* was also large and unwieldy, and very few felt tempted to plough through hundreds of pages when, already in the introduction, Tolstoi announced that he had found the books and dissertations he had consulted devoid of reason and meaning.

But if we can explain why Tolstoi's contemporaries failed to devote much attention to *Examination*, it is harder to explain why modern researchers, with a few honorable exceptions, have overlooked this work. In most modern studies of Tolstoi's thinking, the work is mentioned only *en passant*, if at all (e.g., Spence 1967; Greenwood 1975). Even Richard Gustafson, explicitly seeking to understand Tolstoi's ideas against the background of Orthodoxy, refers to *Examination* only once, in a footnote (Gustafson 1986, 173).

Noting that *Examination* is perhaps Tolstoi's least read work, E. J. Simmons suggests that it is high time to rehabilitate it, since "it is an unusually fervent and compellingly logic attack on revealed religion and especially on the Russian Orthodox Church" (Simmons 1969, 99). However, Simmons does not analyze the book himself. In his Tolstoi biography, there is only one reference to it, in a footnote. Of Tolstoi's biographers, only Nicolas Weisbein, A. N. Wilson and Daniel Rancour-Laferriere declare that they have actually read it. Rancour-Laferriere admits how he had to struggle to get through it: "Tolstoi's tract is too bitterly sarcastic to be understood as serious theology in its own right . . . . Even for an atheist former Christian like myself the work is off-putting" (Rancour-Laferriere 2007, 79).

Regardless of its literary qualities or lack thereof, *Examination* is important for understanding Tolstoi's religiosity. It contains various statements in which Tolstoi makes clear what he himself believes, and we can also, to some extent, reason antithetically from the doctrines he rejects, to get his own positive view. However, it is perhaps less interesting to ask *what* Tolstoi rejected in Orthodox theology than to look for the reasons *why* he rejected it. The criteria underlying Tolstoi's criticism can say much about how he related to Orthodox modes of thinking.

The Examined Books

Tolstoi did a thorough job in his study of Orthodox dogmatics. In the introduction to *Examination*, he writes that he read

> . . .all our catechisms – Filaret's, Platon's and others. I read the *Epistle* of the Eastern Patriarchs, then Peter Mogila's *Orthodox Creed* and John of Damascus' account of Orthodox faith. Finally, as a summary of all this, I read *Introduction to Theology* by Makarii and *Orthodox Dogmatic Theology* of the same Makarii. (Tolstoi PSS 23, 61)[3]

Tolstoi had long been unable to decide which of these books he ought to use as basis for his investigation. He eventually settled on Makarii's *Orthodox Dogmatic Theology*, because, as he explained, it was the newest and fullest (more than 1200 pages). Makarii also cited extensively all the other above-mentioned works, so that a refutation of his book would at the

[3] Filaret's (Drozdov, 1782-1867) book *Extended Christian catechism for the Orthodox Church* was published numerous times between 1827 and 1909. According to George Maloney, many Orthodox regarded it as one of the symbolic books of the church (Maloney 1976, 52). It replaced all earlier Russian catechisms and remained in use at least until the 1970s (Haupmann 1971, 66). Metropolitan Platon's (Levshin 1737-1812) *Orthodox theology in brief* from 1775 was the first attempt to "create a theological system written in Russian" (Florovskii 1982, 111) since Platon's predecessor as Metropolitan of Kyiv, Peter Mogila (Mohyla), had written his *Confessio fidei* (1640) in Latin. In the seventeenth century, the theological environment in Kyiv was strongly influenced by Western theological traditions, since most of Ukraine at the time was part of the Polish Commonwealth. *Confessio fidei* was nevertheless accepted at the church council in Jassy (Iaşi) in 1642 as a correct presentation of the Orthodox faith.

same time serve as a repudiation of the entire Orthodox theological tradition, Tolstoi argued. An underlying premise for this reasoning is that Makarii correctly reproduced the thoughts of his predecessors, which Tolstoi believed to be the case: All of those books "contain one and the same thing, the difference lies only in the degree of completeness in the account" (Tolstoi PSS 23, 61). However, Tolstoi does point out a few differences between Makarii and the other theologians, and then consistently in favor of the older works.

Nicolas Weisbein believes Tolstoi made a poor choice of objects to investigate. He claims that Makarii's works were poorly composed, without classification, chronology or method (Weisbein 1960, 176). Historian of Orthodox theology Georgii Florovskii expressed the same view, and held that *Orthodox Dogmatic Theology* is "bureaucratic," "lifeless" and "without conviction . . . . It is only answers to questions that have not been asked" (Florovskii 1982, 222). Florovskii can also underpin his harsh judgment with statements made by Tolstoi's contemporaries. Lay theologian Aleksei Khomiakov, for instance, called Makarii's *Introduction to Theology* "enchantingly foolish," and thought it would be a pity if a foreigner should take these scribblings as an expression of Russian Orthodox theology (Khomiakov 1900–14, VIII, 189). Metropolitan Filaret (Gumilevskii) dismissed Makarii's book as "an insane hodgepodge," "without logical order or power in the proofs."[4]

Weisbein believes that if Tolstoi had chosen Thomas Aquinas' *Summa Theologica* instead of Makarii's work as basis for his investigation, he would have emerged with a more positive view on Christian theology (Weisbein 1960, 177). Besides the counterfactual character of Weisbein's hypothesis, which necessarily makes it rather irrelevant, it reveals a poor understanding of Tolstoi's situation. It was the Orthodox Church to which he had belonged and which he needed to explore. Makarii's work had been recommended to him by several Orthodox believers. Indeed, Makarii was read not only in his own time but remains a theological authority in the Russian Church also today. According to Orekhanov (2016, 138), Makarii's lectures in dogmatic theology have been in continuous use as a handbook for students at Russian theological schools "right up to our own days." At the same time, he maintains that metropolitan Makarii's *Dogmatics* is indeed "characterized by scholasticism, and Tolstoi with his

[4] That was exactly the same conclusion that Tolstoi reached: He characterized *Orthodox Dogmatic Theology* as self-contradictory and "without internal connection between the parts" (Tolstoi PSS 23, 61).

very delicate, one might even say hypersensitive, artistic flair . . . could not fail to note precisely this weak side of metropolitan Makarii's book" (Orekhanov 2016, 144, 148). With such an inauspicious starting point, it is all the more remarkable that Tolstoi managed to find some points in Makarii's books that he could relate to.

Tolstoi's Assessment Criteria

Nicolas Weisbein is one of very few modern scholars who have tried to penetrate the *Examination of Dogmatic Theology*. He gives a thorough account of its content, and concludes that it is permeated by rationalist criticism of theology. According to Weisbein, Tolstoi had stood St. Anselm's maxim on its head: Instead of *credo ut intelligam* – I believe in order to understand – his motto was *intelligo ut credam* (Weisbein 1960, 155). This impression of Tolstoi as anti-Anselm has stuck and been repeated by other commentators (Simmons 1969, 99). Indeed, parts of *Examination* can be given such an interpretation – like the claim "one cannot believe that which one does not understand" (Tolstoi PSS 23, 106). However, many passages go in other directions, and should warn us against reading this statement too bombastically.

Although reason is not the main truth criterion in *Examination*, it undoubtedly occupies a prominent place. Tolstoi claims that the commitment to reason is based on the linguistic medium itself:

> Help my weak understanding, but do not forget that whatever you say, you address it to the mind. When you convey the truths of God, you must express yourself in words, and words, after all, can only be perceived by the mind. (Tolstoi PSS 23, 67)

Several of the most basic Orthodox beliefs, according to Tolstoi, appear devoid of meaning. This applies, for example, to the dogma of the Trinity:

> Let us assume that some claimed that God lives on Olympia, that he is made of gold, that there is no god, that there are fourteen gods, that God has children or a son. All of these are strange, barbaric claims, but each of them at least corresponds to a concept. But that God is one and yet three, that cannot be connected with any concept. (Tolstoi PSS 23,120)

Secondly, Tolstoi at times claims that Orthodox theology is self-contradictory. It teaches both that man cannot achieve anything without the help of divine grace, and that grace does not abolish human free will. When Makarii adds that this is beyond human understanding, Tolstoi suspects that this is an attempt to escape the rules of logic (Tolstoi PSS 23, 237).

A third way Makarii sins against reason is in his use of circular arguments. First, he declares that Scripture and tradition are true because they are preached by the Church; then he claims that the Church is true because it recognizes Scripture and tradition (Tolstoi PSS 23, 64–65).

An important reason why the rationality criterion is so effective against Makarii is that the bishop goes a long way toward recognizing the competence of reason in theology. He holds that most dogmas can be deduced from both Scripture and reason independently, and he tries to prove both the existence of God and His most important qualities by means of purely deductive arguments. Makarii even claims that the doctrine of the dual nature of Christ – as fully human and fully divine – is in accordance with common sense (Tolstoi PSS 23, 178–79).

According to the modern Russian theologian Georgii Orekhanov (Orekhanov 2016, 153), the main motif of Tolstoi's criticism of Orthodox dogmatics was the relationship between the faith of the Church and contemporary scientific knowledge. This is not what I find. In my view, most important for Tolstoi was the requirement that the doctrine of faith must be relevant to the everyday lives of human beings.

> Even if I should come to see that what the theology tells me about [providence and redemption] is sensible, clear, and proven, it would not interest me . . . . What is particularly important and dear to me is to get guidance on how to behave. (Tolstoi PSS 23, 159)

The crucial point for Tolstoi is therefore the moral content and applicability of the dogmas. The most valuable thing belief can give people, as Tolstoi sees it, is ethical guidance – and he finds it difficult to see what moral consequences can be drawn from, for instance, the doctrine of the Trinity. Makarii ends every main section of his book with a point where he derives a "moral application of the dogma," but the connection between the dogma and the practical implications Makarii draws from it are often so arbitrary that the method undermines rather than supports the ethics, as Tolstoi is quick to point out (Tolstoi PSS 23, 67).

Finally, Tolstoi accuses Makarii of subterfuge in his exegesis. On the whole, the theologian has a rather cavalier attitude toward Biblical texts, paraphrasing them as he sees fit. A gross example of this Tolstoi sees in the account of the Fall in Genesis, where Makarii replaces the "serpent" with "the devil" (Tolstoi PSS 23, 139). This part of Tolstoi's criticism, however, backfires on himself. His own paraphrasing the Bible is, to put it mildly, not always very precise. In his version, for instance, the story of the Fall can be rendered as follows:

> God made man, but wanted to make him like the beasts, who do not know the difference between good and evil. Therefore, he refused to let him eat of the tree of knowledge about good and evil. And to scare him, God fooled him into thinking that he would die if he did. But man exposed the deception of God through wisdom (the serpent) . . . .
>
> One can like it or not like it, but it is how this story is written in the Bible. (Tolstoi PSS 23, 139)

With this imaginative narration of Genesis 1–3, Tolstoi can hardly be said to be living up to his own demands for exegetical accuracy.

The parts of Tolstoi's criticism of classical Orthodox theology that I have analyzed so far have been purely destructive. They seem to indicate that Tolstoi did not find anything valuable in the dogmatic treatises he read. Occasionally, however, he did not reject outright what Makarii had written, but was dissatisfied with the way the Bishop expressed it. Makarii, like other Orthodox theologians, he held, treated a subject in the wrong order or put too much or too little emphasis on certain details. At the same time, they insisted that their way of presenting it was the only one to salvation. "But as soon as they begin to claim that the very formula in which they express their thought is the only truth, then I can no longer accept what they say" (Tolstoi PSS 23, 175). On the other hand, there is little point in criticizing a writer for formal errors if one believes that what he is saying is utter rubbish. Such "internal" criticism presupposes a certain degree of factual agreement.

Even Orthodox dogmatics, it emerges, contains not only lies but also some fragments of truth. A few times, Tolstoi explicitly describes certain dogmas as being "not untrue but coarse and incomplete" (Tolstoi PSS 23, 175). Such partial agreement can be found not only concerning isolated, peripheral points, but also on basic matters such as the understanding of salvation, the nature of man, and the essence of God. Moreover, there is much to indicate that this is not just a matter of converging beliefs, but of direct influence.

Doctrine on Salvation

Tolstoi rejected the doctrine of the objective foundation of atonement through Jesus' vicarious sacrificial death. Since this doctrine is of fundamental importance to any Christian denomination, this is one of the points where Tolstoi most clearly departed from the common Christian creed. However, Christian soteriology contains not only a doctrine of the objective basis for salvation, but also theories of how salvation is subjectively communicated to human beings. Grace has not only a sender but also a recipient. With regard to the "human" side of salvation, there has historically been considerable disagreement among the Christian churches. It was not least on this point that Luther had criticized medieval Roman Catholic theology. He believed that man was credited with too much self-effort in the salvation process, and presented the idea of salvation by faith alone, without deeds: *Sola fide*. Confronted by God's offer of mercy, man stands empty-handed. The only thing he can give in return is faith – and even that is a gift of God.

The Orthodox Churches have never accepted this view. Drawing on an understanding of salvation as *synergeia* between the efforts of God and man, they teach that both faith and deeds are necessary. This is a central point in most of the theological textbooks that Tolstoi consulted: It is often the postulate with which the presentation of dogma begins (*Poslanie,* not dated, 9; Filaret Drozdov [1880] 1976, 3; Petr 1841, 1). In their epistle from 1723, the Eastern patriarchs went so far as to declare anathema all those who proclaim salvation without works, deeming them worse than the unbelievers (*Poslanie,* not dated, 11).

Tolstoi's vehement attack on Christian atonement must be understood first and foremost from a moral point of view: He wants to make room for the independent, responsible actions of human beings. The struggle between good and evil, in his view, takes place within each individual – but the doctrine of the objective basis of reconciliation makes this struggle an entirely external event located in the past, in which man does not participate. "Adam has once and for all committed evil on my behalf, and once and for all, Christ has corrected it" (Tolstoi PSS 23, 376). Man is reduced from actor to spectator. When people can come again and again, asking forgiveness for their sins, they do not have to bear the full consequences of their actions, he maintained.

> If man can be saved through redemption, sacraments, and prayer, he does not need to do good works. The Sermon on the Mount, or the Creed – it is impossible to believe in both at the same time. (Tolstoi PSS 28, 60)

Theology of Man

Protestant anthropology often takes as its starting point the dual distance between God and man: What is created is different from the Creator, and after the fall of Man, mankind has been removed even further from its origin. Sin has become an inseparable part of human nature as Original sin. Sin is not just something we have, but something we are.

By contrast, classical Orthodox theology strongly emphasizes the similarity between God and humans. Psalm 82, 6 is frequently mentioned: "I have said, Ye are gods; and all of you are children of the most High . . . ."[5] Even more important is Genesis 1:26: "Then God said, Let us make man in our image, after our likeness." Here, Godlike-ness is linked to the act of creation. It has been laid down in human nature from the very beginning, and even though the "image" was soiled by the Fall, it has not been crushed. This text has a "fundamental and essential meaning" for Orthodox theology, according to Sergei Bulgakov (S. Bulgakov 1937, 221).

Most Protestant theologians make little use of Genesis 1:26. For Luther and Calvin, *Imago Dei* was an expression of man's original state of justice (*justitia originalis*) that was lost with the Fall (see, e.g., Hägglund 1975, 207). By contrast, for Orthodox theologians, Genesis 1:26 is a cornerstone, and Tolstoi would have encountered references to this scriptural passage in most of the theological treatises he read. It is of great importance to Orthodox theologians that this verse uses two different expressions for man's Godlikeness, in Hebrew: *Selem* and *demut*, Septuagint: *Eikon* and *homoiosis*, Latin: *Imago* and *similitudo*, Russian: *Obraz* and *podobie*.

Although Genesis uses two parallel words, these do not in Hebrew express a double meaning but are to be understood as reinforcing synonyms (Thunberg 1985, 297). This becomes evident when we compare with verse twenty-seven where the same reinforcing effect is obtained by using one word, *selem*, twice. However, in the standard Orthodox understanding, each of these two words expresses one particular aspect of man's divinity. The specific details of this doctrine vary somewhat from theologian to theologian, but there is relatively broad consensus that image or *obraz* refers to the formal aspect – generally: Reason – and likeness or similitude (*podobie*) to the real aspect – virtue or holiness. Lars Thunberg notes a tension between the "ontological" character of the image and the "morality" of similitude (Thunberg 1985, 293). In Orthodox systematic theology, both in Tolstoi's time and later, the image anthropology is one of the most important preconditions for the doctrine of *theosis*, the deification of man: When a human being is made divine, he or she does not, strictly

[5] See also Acts 17, 28: "For we are also his (= God's) offspring."

speaking, acquire a new nature; instead, our innate, latent divinity is purified and realized (see, for instance, Vyscheslavzev 1937, 316).

Metropolitan Makarii summarizes the Orthodox *obraz–podobie* model as follows:

> To be God's *obraz* is characteristic of us in the way we are originally created, but to become God's *podobie* depends on our will. It exists in us only as an opportunity; while we actually acquire it through our behaviour. (Makarii [Bulgakov] 1895, I, 457)

Tolstoi occasionally employed *obraz–podobie* thinking in his writings. For example, in his diary for 1894 he expressed the idea that reason is "given by God and is like Him (*podobnyi*)" (Tolstoi PSS 52, 155–56). In 1900, he claimed that it would be insane hubris and a sin to claim that we are like Jupiter or the militant Lord of Sabaoth. On the other hand, to be like the God we know through love and reason is a necessary condition for achieving peace and joy. "In order to be God *podobnyi*, it is enough to love" (Tolstoi PSS 54, 39). In *The Way of Life*, Tolstoi similarly taught that to live "godly" (*po-bozhii*) is to be like God (*podobnyi*). More important than these individual quotes, however, is the fact that Tolstoi's general scheme of salvation shows clear structural conformity to the teaching of Orthodox school theology on this point. Tolstoi strongly emphasized the divine nature of man. He perceived the relationship between God and man as a whole–part relationship, and this should not be understood statically, as a mathematical fraction. Tolstoi's conception of salvation was distinctly dynamic. Therefore, when he claimed that we are "part" of God, that should be taken as an invitation to participate in God (*partisipere, u-chast-vovat'*, Gustafson 1986, 335). Tolstoi always understood the divine nature of man under two parallel viewpoints: As an "already now," and as a "not yet." Man *is* divine, insofar as he realizes it, but he must also earn his divinity through his way of living. "Christianity says: Live in accordance with your nature (and by that is meant: Your divine nature)" (Tolstoi PSS 28, 85).

In a diary entry from 1908, Tolstoi discussed the relationship between man's call to make himself "perfect" (*sovershenstvovat'*) and his divinity:

> If the meaning of life is *sovershenstvovanie*, it is clear that this cannot mean to make the soul perfect (it is divine, and therefore already perfect). It must therefore be to annihilate what prevents the perfection from emerging – one's sins. (Tolstoi PSS 56, 91)

Richard Gustafson holds unreservedly that Tolstoi's model of salvation is the Eastern Christian doctrine of deification (Gustafson 1986, 457). I believe this conclusion can be defended if we by "model" mean that

Tolstoi took this as the inspirational starting point for his own creative adaptation of this idea, and not as a template that he copied slavishly.

Also on another level we find coincidence between Tolstoi's and the Eastern Churches' understanding of human nature: In their view on the relationship between soul and body. Richard Gustafson claims that "in Eastern Christian anthropology, there is little of the tendency towards a simple dualism between body and soul or mind that is so characteristic of Western modes of thinking even before Descartes" (Gustafson 1986, 267). Instead, he maintains, the Eastern Churches operate with a three-part image of human nature in accordance with 1 Thessalonians 5: 23 – spirit, soul and body. He sees a clear parallel with Tolstoi's view, ascribing a similar trichotomic anthropology also to him. Gustafson refers to Tolstoi's idea that man has two consciousnesses: A lower, animal consciousness and a higher "I." The latter, Gustafson believes, fulfills the same role as man's "spirit" in Christian anthropology.[6]

However, *if* Tolstoi had adhered to a trichotomic anthropology, that would set him apart from the dominant trend in Eastern Church theology. Admittedly, the three-part formula had many supporters in the early Greek Church; also more recent Orthodox theologians have advocated this model (e.g., Ware [1979] 1981, 60–61). Other modern theologians, such as Vasilii Zen'kovskii and Vladimir Lossky, vacillate between dichotomy and trichotomy (Zen'kovskii 1951, 21; V. Lossky [1957] 1973, 127). In the Middle Ages and until the end of the nineteenth century, however, Orthodox anthropology was clearly and unambiguously dichotomist. In our context, it is particularly important to recognize that the Orthodox sources Tolstoi read adhered strictly to this view (Filaret Drozdov [1880] 1978, 31; Platon Levshin [1775] 1969, 45–48). Makarii devoted a whole section of his *Orthodox Dogmatic Theology* to "the composition of the human being." Here, he explicitly polemized against the idea that man consists of three parts. In the Bible, man is sometimes attributed body and soul, at other times body and spirit. "This means that soul and spirit are only two different names for the same component," the bishop claimed (Makarii [Bulgakov] 1895, I, 444). Makarii admitted that the New Testament contains a few statements where the spirit is clearly separated from the soul, but these must be interpreted in light of the

6 Somewhat confusingly, Gustafson also claims that "Tolstoy's doctrine of person as a divine core covered by the crust of animality finds its source in Eastern Christian anthropological thought" (Gustafson 1986, 176).

dichotomic statements of the Bible, since the word of God cannot contradict itself.

> In each of us there are not one, but two people, an inner and an outer, a spiritual and a carnal. We shall therefore follow the precept 'That ye put off . . . the old man, which is corrupt according to the deceitful lusts; And be renewed in the spirit of your mind; And that ye put on the new man, which after God is created in righteousness and true holiness'. (Makarii [Bulgakov] 1895, I, 91, quoting Eph. 4, 22–24)

This quote it is strikingly similar to Tolstoi's view as he formulated it in *What I Believe*: "The battle between what draws us towards the animal life and what draws us toward the reasonable life, . . . is embodied in every person's soul and constitutes the essence of the individual's life" (Tolstoi PSS 23, 376).

An essential characteristic of human existence, according to Tolstoi, is that we live at the intersection between two worlds – the spiritual and the material. As seen from the outside, man is an animal, subject to the laws of nature, but this is literally speaking a "superficial" description. Man has also an inside, which is divine:

> The animal and purely animal existence in man is not the human life. Neither is life according to the will of God the human life. The human life is composed of the animal and the divine life. (Tolstoi PSS 28, 79)

Normatively, according to Tolstoi, human life consists in a movement toward the divine life: "The more this composite life approaches the divine, the more life" (same place). Or expressed figuratively: "[the Christian teaching] says that man is neither a wild animal nor an angel, but it is an angel which is being born from a wild animal, a spiritual entity born out of an animal entity. This is what our entire existence in this world consists of" (Tolstoi PSS 39, 123). The similarities between the anthropology of Tolstoi and the Eastern Churches, then, must be based on shared dualistic beliefs, not trichotomic ones.

God's Incomprehensibility

Makarii is a distinctly theocentric thinker: Whatever subject he examines, he starts from God, and the first 350 pages of his dogmatics are exclusively devoted to God "an sich" (*v samom sebe*). He begins by discussing which possibilities we humans have to know anything about God at all, and declares that God is unfathomable. This is explained in various ways. God is unlimited, while the human spirit is limited – and the infinite would no longer be infinite if it could be fully understood by a finite being. In addition, the human spirit is united with the body, which, like a fog, lies between us and God. Finally, human knowledge is obscured by sin (Makarii [Bulgakov] 1895, I, 69).

With this introduction, it might seem that Makarii's attempt to develop a positive theology about God would have stranded before it could get off the ground: After all, there is not very much one can say about a completely incomprehensible God. However, for Makarii, God's incomprehensibility is not absolute: God has revealed Himself to mankind, through His creation and by supernatural revelations. "The first dogma that [the Orthodox Church] will impress on us is the following: God is incomprehensible to human reason, humans can only have partial knowledge of Him" (Makarii [Bulgakov], 1895, I, 66). To this, Tolstoi retorts: "If the author [Makarii] had understood incomprehensibility as incomprehensibility, he would not have tried to prove that we can comprehend God partially but would have acknowledged straightaway that we cannot comprehend Him" (Tolstoi PSS 23, 70).

For Makarii, the little word "partial" functions as a launching pad to the substantial part of his dogmatics. Having first expressed the minor caveat that the Orthodox Church "does not intend to define God, whom it recognizes as incomprehensible and therefore strictly speaking indefinable," Makarii goes on to list some of the most important qualities we can attribute to God: He is infinite, autarchic, autonomous, omnipresent, eternal, immutable, omnipotent, all-knowing, all-powerful, perfect freedom, perfect holiness, goodness, truthfulness, faithfulness and righteousness (Makarii [Bulgakov] 1985, 94–150). Tolstoi's standard objection to each of these is that Makarii's definitions are illegitimate because they fail to take the incomprehensibility of God seriously (Tolstoi PSS 23, 72; 73, 85, 92, 97, 99).

The idea of God's incomprehensibility is a central and fundamental idea in all varieties of the Orthodox doctrine of faith, ancient and modern. It goes back to the Old Testament prohibition against making graven images or likenesses of God. Even Moses, who encountered Him in a fiery bush of thorns, was not permitted to see His face, but could only see Him "from behind" as He passed by (Ex. 33, 23). In the New Testament, this strict Jewish transcendentalism was modified by the fact that God Himself as the incarnate Jesus Christ dwelled among men, but here too the Father is perceived as strictly inaccessible and unimaginable: He "hath immortality, dwelling in the light which no man can approach unto; whom no man hath seen, nor can see" (1 Tim. 6:16).

The idea that there are immense depths in God that evade revelation is found in all Christian denominations. To respect God's greatness, Calvin, like Makarii, taught that "what is finite cannot grasp the infinite" *(finitum non capax infiniti)*. Luther spoke of "the hidden God," "*Deus absconditus*," and warned his followers against trying to penetrate the obscure sides of God. To search behind the revelation to elicit from God His secrets is *lèse-majesté*. In the Eastern Churches, on the other hand, this is a mystery to dwell upon, and an entire theological tradition has developed around the concept of incomprehensibility: Apophatic or negative theology. This theology has been associated in particular with *Corpus Areopagiticum*, a collection of writings attributed to the Greek Councillor Dionysius (who, according to Acts 17: 34, was converted by Saint Paul at the Areopagos), but it probably originated from a sixth-century Syrian monastic environment.

One of the Areopagitic writings, *About Mystical Theology*, distinguishes between two fundamentally different ways of approaching knowledge about God – the cataphatic and the apophatic. According to the cataphatic method, men attempt to determine the being of God by attributing to Him qualities such as good, omnipotent, omniscient, etc. The reason why such positive descriptions of God are possible is that He has revealed Himself to mankind in successive theophanies, of which the Incarnation of Christ is the highest.

A higher form of theology is the apophatic. That it is "higher" does not mean that it gives more precise knowledge of God – indeed, it does not offer any precise, positive knowledge whatsoever. The apophatic theologian approaches God through negatives, expressing only what God is *not*. Like the sculptor who chips away everything superfluous from a block of stone in order to bring out the subject's characteristic features in a statue, the apophatic mystic removes all definitions and ideas about God that have accumulated around Him. However, also the analogy with the sculptor does not hold: Because God is so infinitely more difficult to "portray," the negative theologian must act far more radically than the artist.

This method is regarded as genuinely biblical. In the Areopagitic text *On the heavenly hierarchy*, it is claimed that

> Occasionally, the Holy Scriptures praise God by describing which features are completely different from His. Thus, he is called invisible, unlimited, and unsearchable (1 Tim 6, 16; Psalms 144, 3[7]; Rom. 2:33). This other way

[7] Western numbering: Psalms 145, 3.

> is, in my opinion, even more appropriate to use about God [than the cataphatic way]. For although we do not know God's infinite, incomprehensible, immeasurable, and limitless being, we can, on the basis of the esoteric Holy tradition, conclude that God has nothing in common with anything that exists. (Dionysius, Pseudo- 1974, 9–10)

The apophatic path starts "from below," from the material, by reminding us that God does not have body, form or shape. Accordingly, He is not subject to human change or passions. But God is not soul or intellect either. He is neither big nor small, neither time nor eternity, neither truth nor falsehood. Pseudo-Dionysius explains that all affirmative statements employ distinctions or contrasts; they assume that there is something to be compared *with*. God, however, transcends all distinctions. Even the predicate "being" is too narrow to be used about Him (Dionysius, Pseudo- 1968, 186–87).

If all affirmative statements turn out to be insufficient, then the negative ones also come to grief. God is not light – but He is also not not-light. To God, not just words, but even thought must be silent. He appears not only as the Invisible, but as the Unimaginable. For pseudo-Dionysius, God's incomprehensibility is rooted in God himself and not merely the result of man's limited capacity of understanding, in the way Makarii presented it (Lossky [1957] 1973, 31).

Cataphasis and apophasis are opposite but not mutually exclusive methods. The former is made possible by God's immanence, whereas the latter guards His transcendence. Cataphasis ends up by conferring on God a plurality of epithets, a "polionymity." The apophatic method leads to the contrary claim about God's absolute "anonymity," but these are two expressions of the same matter. They are both helpless attempts at grasping what is incomprehensible.

The negations lead into "the darkness of ignorance," but that does not mean that they end up in emptiness, an absence. On the contrary, they lead the believer toward a Presence, a meeting with the living God. Apophasis is not abstract speculation, but a form of cleansing whereby the believer is emptied of all concepts, to be filled by Him. The goal is not *knowledge* of God, but *union with Him*.

It is probable that the Areopagitic writings were composed in a heterodox, monophysitic environment. However, they were nevertheless accepted by the Orthodox Churches, primarily because they were strongly advocated by Maximus Confessor. He was a leading theologian in the seventh century, and his orthodoxy was not questioned.

Later, apophasis was taken up and elaborated by other theologians. An important contribution to the development of Orthodox doctrine was provided by the Athos monk Gregory Palamas in the fourteenth century. The task he set himself was, on the one hand, to determine the relationship between the incomprehensibility of God and the doctrine of man's divine nature. Between these two core points in Palamite theology there was an obvious tension: If the Christian can become "like God" already here on earth, how can one simultaneously claim that God is radically different from, or indeed incomprehensible, to us? Although man is created in God's image, He surpasses, according to Orthodox theology, any image we can form about Him. To deal with this tension, Gregory developed a distinction between God's "being" (*ousia*) and his "energies" or manifestations. What the mystic sees in contemplation is only the latter: God Himself is essentially inaccessible (Meyendorff 1974, 122–24).

The Areopagitic writings made an impact also on Western theology. Their influence can be traced as an undercurrent in the Middle Ages in the platonic-mystical tradition from Johannes Scotus Erigena (who translated them into Latin), to Nicolaus Cusanus. In recent times, however, the influence of the areopagitic writings has waned in the West, whereas the Eastern Church has returned to them. One theologian who has contributed notably to renewed interest in apophaticism is Vladimir Lossky, who sees apophasis as "truly characteristic of the whole tradition of the Eastern Church" (V. Lossky [1957] 1973, 42; V. Lossky [1963] 1983).

***

Incomprehensibility is a central element in Tolstoi's understanding of God. In his diaries, he constantly returned to this theme. In 1904, he described God as analogous to the mathematical sign "x": He is the unknown entity, but without Him we would not be able to set up the equation of life, much less solve it (Tolstoi PSS 55, 98). That same year, Tolstoi described God as

> . . .eternal *Deus absconditus*, incomprehensible. . . . He is unknown to me, but I know that my destination is in him, and also that my participation in him constitutes the unshakable foundation of my life. (Tolstoi PSS 55, 51)

Tolstoy returned to the concept of *Deus absconditus* in his diary in 1906, where God is also referred to as "the incomprehensible, mysterious principle (*nachalo*)" (Tolstoi PSS 55, 226).

Polemicizing against dogmatic Christian theology, Tolstoi wrote in his diary on September 27, 1894:

> The more seriously and sincerely I think about myself, about life and its origin, the less need I have for a concept of God, the more devastating it becomes. The closer I get to God, the less I see Him. Not because He does not exist, but because it becomes more frightening to talk about Him, and even more so to define Him, mention Him. (Tolstoi PSS 52, 144)

Here, God's existence and the concept of Him (the attempt to seize Him) are seen as opposites. The more one strives toward the latter, the less will one experience the former.

Tolstoi is on guard against any attempt to become "buddies" with God. In 1910, he warned against the danger of familiarity (*panibratstvo*) in the relationship to God. "It is better to leave God completely in peace and perceive Him as something fully inaccessible to us" (Tolstoi PSS 58, 114–15).

In the short pamphlet *Thoughts on God*, Tolstoi provided an important description of his understanding of the apophatic way:

> My life consists in approaching Him, but this movement in no way increases my knowledge about Him . . . . Any attempt to form an imagination of Him (e.g., that He is Creator or merciful), removes me from Him. (Tolstoi 1912/13, XV, 59)

Tolstoi had the same experience as that underlying the apophaticism of the Areopagite. Importantly, this was not just a matter of a common psychological experience, but an insight communicated to him through Church tradition. Tolstoi had direct knowledge about the negative theology of the Eastern Church, and accused Metropolitan Makarii of having "distorted the deep and sincere speech of the apostles and Church fathers who prove that God is incomprehensible" (Tolstoi PSS 23, 71). Drawing on this tradition, he could attack Makarii for not being *sufficiently Orthodox*.

Oddly enough, this clear reference has hardly been noted in Tolstoi scholarship. Richard Gustafson is the first to employ apophaticism as an explanatory model for elucidating Tolstoi's concept of God (Gustafson 1986, 92–95). However, as he was obviously only superficially familiar with *Examination*, he did not see any causal relationship and did not progress beyond detecting the structural parallels.[8] With the exception of

[8] In *The Image of Christ in Russian literature: Dostoyevsky, Tolstoi, Bulgakov, Pasternak*, John Givens maintains that in *Resurrection*, Tolstoi presents an apophatic picture of Christ since "readers discover who Christ is in the novel by understanding what Christ is *not*. Christ is not to be found in the Jesus preached by the evangelical English missionaries . . . . Christ is not to be found in the lives of the privilege classes or the unwashed masses . . . . Finally, Christ is not to be found in the crucifixes, icons, and paintings in the courtrooms, prisons and churches" (Givens 2018, 118). Givens' usage of apophaticism as a literary method, however, is far removed from the negative theology taught by the

my own articles (Kolstø 1991, 153–56; Kolstø 2014, 533), only Martin George (2015, 236–40) has pointed out the significance of this paragraph. George concludes that apophaticism is an essential element in Tolstoi's thinking about God.[9]

In *Der Gottesbegriff bei Tolstoi,* Robert Quiskamp (1937) mentions that Tolstoi in *Examination* explicitly invoked the Church Fathers in support of his view, without drawing any consequences from this. He consistently used German theological and philosophical tradition as frame of reference for his analysis of Tolstoi's concept of God, assuming that in his theology Tolstoi was a convinced student of Immanuel Kant. In *Kritik der reinen Vernunft* Kant had argued that our intellectual categories are structured in such a way that we humans are prevented from acquiring rational knowledge of God, something Thomas Aquinas had claimed was possible (Quiskamp 1937, 58–60). The existence of God was for Kant "incomprehensible" in the sense that all knowledge about Him being inaccessible to "pure" reason.

Quiskamp points out that Tolstoi had read *Kritik der reinen Vernunft* already in 1869, and was very excited. (*Kritik der praktischen Vernunft*, however, he did not read until in 1887.) In some of his formulations, Tolstoi indeed sought to express his apophaticism in Kantian language (e.g., PSS 23, 71). If Tolstoi's understanding of the incomprehensibility of God could be fully explained by his reading of Kant, his references to the Church Fathers would be less important. However, the Church Fathers and the German idealist perceive the incomprehensibility of God very differently: While Kant rejected the possibility of knowing anything about the *existence* of God, Orthodox theologians took His existence for granted, denying only the possibility of expressing anything about His *essence*. Tolstoi's thinking here was in line with the Eastern Church, and in opposition to German idealism:

> If we speak about the origin of all things, about God, then it is clear that we recognize, comprehend, His existence. But if we talk about the very essence (*sushchestvo*) of God, it is obvious that we cannot comprehend Him. (Tolstoi PSS 23, 69)

Eastern theologians. Jesus is not and cannot be *deus absconditus*, since he is the incarnated, revealed God. Christology therefore belongs to and must be treated under cataphatic theology.

[9] In a short but instructive article, George concludes (George 2014, 369) that "in several respects Tolstoi turns out to be a representative of the apophatic teaching on God in the Eastern Church, not too different from the most conspicuous representative of this tradition, Pseudo-Dionysios'. However, George also concludes that on many pivotal questions Tolstoi's teaching on God, as seen not only from an Orthodox but also from a Western – Evangelical or Roman Catholic – theological viewpoint must be regarded as heterodox, indeed as not Christian" (George 2014, 369).

Here, Tolstoi does not at all question that God "is"; the incomprehensibility applies only to the "how." He claims that Makarii's infelicitous idea of "partial" recognition of God is due to the bishop's failure to keep these two issues separate.[10]

Tolstoi may have encountered Orthodox apophaticism in various places. John of Damascus summed up the ancient tradition in a classic formulation in *De fide orthodoxa – On the Orthodox Faith* – one of the Orthodox theological treatises that Tolstoi read while working on *Examination*:

> Consequently, the Godhead is infinite and immeasurable, and all we can understand about Him is His limitlessness and incomprehensibility. All we can express affirmatively about God does not show His nature, but only what can be related to His nature. If you ever talk about goodness, justice, wisdom or the like, you do not describe God's nature, but only what can be related to His nature. (John [Damascenus] 1970, 172)

One of the most important renewers of Russian Orthodox theology in Tolstoi's time was the learned bishop and mystic Feofan Zatvornik (the Recluse). In his *Letters on the Christian Life* from 1860, Feofan wrote:

> God is infinitely incomprehensible as regards His being, His perfection and deeds. Marvel! ... He is not one of the things we know from the created world: neither power nor light, neither life nor mind, word or thought, anything whatsoever that we can imagine with our mind. And then, when our gaze has seen all these negatives, we are led instantly into a kind of divine darkness. (Feofan [Govorov] [1860] 1880, 337–38)

We know that Tolstoi was interested in the writings of Feofan, but cannot say anything specific about when this interest was awakened. His own copy of *Letters on the Christian Life* is from 1891.

Orthodox apophaticism is also reflected in the liturgical books of the Orthodox Churches. In the Service Manual (*Sluzhebnik*), God is addressed as "inexpressible, unimaginable, invisible, incomprehensible" (edition 1817, sheet 81). In the Book of Rituals (*Trebnik,* or "Book of Needs"), He is worshiped as "eternal[11] Tsar, invisible, inexplorable, incomprehensible and inexpressible" (edition 1836, sheet 234). If Tolstoi was not already familiar with these prayers, he certainly encountered them in

[10] In 1981, Gary Jahn examined Tolstoy's intellectual relationship with Kant and concluded that they both believed in "one true 'rational religion' consisting solely of moral precepts" (Jahn 1981, 65). The points of overlap in their thinking that Jahn identified, however, consisted mostly of general ideas prevalent in liberal theology in eighteenth and nineteenth centuries.

[11] "Eternal": *beznachal'nyi,* literally "without beginning."

Makarii's book, as the bishop referred to both of them (Makarii [Bulgakov] 1895, I, 67).

Makarii's *Orthodox Dogmatic Theology* is the most important link between Tolstoi and the thinking of the Church Fathers. In this work, the bishop refers to a large number of theologians who professed apophatic views – Gregory of Nyssa, Basil the Great, Efrem the Syrian, John Chrysostom, Simeon the New Theologian and others (see Makarii [Bulgakov] 1895, I, 69–70). In most cases, Makarii also provides accurate references to accessible Russian translations that Tolstoi could check. Thus, Makarii was the central supplier of the arsenal of arguments Tolstoi used against him.

The Attributes of God

Although apophasis is an essential element in standard Orthodox theology, it would be misleading to emphasize it at the expense of cataphasis. As Orthodox theologians see it, it is not negative theology alone, but the duality of negative and positive theology that constitutes the genuinely Orthodox approach.

For Tolstoi, his understanding of God's incomprehensibility did not lead him into agnosticism. He made clear, affirmative statements about God; also in this part of the theological landscape he oriented himself by means of an Orthodox map at times. In the following, I examine what he had to say about some of the most important attributes of God – His unity and personality, love and will – as they were developed in Orthodox Church theology and by Tolstoi.

Unity. The idea of God's unity is reintroduced in the Orthodox theological books that Tolstoi read as the first and most fundamental postulate of cataphatic deduction. But the use of the mathematical concept of "one," bishop Makarii explains, like all cataphatic provisions, is based on analogy, and therefore has only limited validity.

> When we say that the Eastern Churches believe in one God, Father, Almighty (*vsederzhitel'*), and one Lord, we must understand that He is called 'one' not in the sense of the number 1, but that He is complete (*vsetselo*). (Makarii [Bulgakov] 1895, I, 77, quoting Rufinus)

Tolstoi heaped scorn on this claim: This is like saying that the leaf is green, but not in color. "The words 'one' and 'only' are words that express numbers, and therefore cannot be applied to the God we believe in" (Tolstoi PSS 23, 79). But also for Tolstoi, the idea of unity proved central to his understanding of God. In *Thoughts on God* he claimed: "About God we can only say what Moses and Muhammad said, that he is one" (L. Tolstoi 1912–13, XV, 68, originally a diary entry from 1896, PSS 53, 119). Although Tolstoi here refers to Moses and Muhammad, it is more natural to see Eastern Christian theology, and not Jewish and Islamic monotheism, as the source of inspiration for his concept of unity. (Tolstoi's knowledge of both Islam and Judaism was rather fragmentary. See, e.g., Koblov 1904; but see also Schmid 2014 for a slightly different view). Moreover, in clarifying the idea of the unity of God, Tolstoi repeats Makarii almost literally: "About God one cannot even say he is one in the sense of the number 1, but only in the sense that he is one-centred (*odnotsentren*)' (same place)." That statement was made sixteen years after Tolstoi wrote *Examination*. The purpose of juxtaposing them here is not primarily to catch Tolstoi in contradictions, but to show that he must have received stronger impulses from Orthodox thinking than he realized himself.

The most detailed discussion of God's unity in Tolstoi's writings can be found in the diary note from 1896 from which I have already quoted several times. It is one of the best summaries of Tolstoi's understanding of God in general:

> [God is] the highest, spiritual being who lives in everything. He is one in the sense that He is a being you can turn to, if not pray to. There exists a relationship between me with my limited individuality, and the incomprehensible but existing God. The most important reason why God is incomprehensible for us is precisely that we know Him as a unified being. We cannot perceive Him differently. A being that fills everything must be unified. If God is not one, then He falls apart, and He is no longer. (Tolstoi PSS 53, 118–19)

Personality. The God of Christians is a personal God who thinks, speaks and – not least – acts. Tolstoi, on the other hand, insisted that God is not a person.

> With prayer we turn to a personal God, not because God is personal (I even know for certain that He is not personal …), but because 'I' is a personal being. (L. Tolstoi 1912–13, XV, 68)

Not least due to such statements, many readers have concluded that there is an insurmountable chasm between Tolstoianism and the Christian concept of God.[12]

[12] Vladimir M. Paperni (Paperni 2019, 84) emphasizes this aspect of Tolstoi's concept of God, and sees it as an expression of mystical religious metaphysics. At the same time, this did not in his view make Tolstoi a mystic in any meaningful sense of the word; instead, he describes Tolstoi's position as "countermysticism."

Hugh McLean quotes an excerpt from Tolstoi's diaries from 1900 in which he engages in a dialogue with himself:

"That God who is in me hears me, of that there can be no doubt.

Then you are praying to yourself?

Yes, only not to my lower self, not to my whole self but to that part of me that is divine, eternal, loving. And it hears me and answers. I thank Thee and love Thee, O Lord, who dwellest in me" (Tolstoi PSS, 53, 15). In McLean's interpretation, Tolstoi here suggests that "'in praying to God one is in fact simply addressing what is holy within oneself" (McLean 2010, 157). In my view, this would have been reasonable reading were it not for the two last sentences. They seem to indicate that Tolstoi's God is closer to the immanent Godhead of many Christian mystics.

Tolstoi's alleged rejection of God's personality may well be based on a semantic misunderstanding. In Russian the word "person" must be expressed with the noun "*lichnost*," which also means "individual." To claim that God is an "individual" is not a Christian idea; many might even regard it as a meaningless statement. When Tolstoi argued against God's "*lichnost*," he usually claimed that "*lichnost*" represents a limitation and God is unlimited. (L. Tolstoi 1912/13, XV, 64). And indeed, individuality undoubtedly does represent a limitation – but personality cannot in the same way be said to do so. Tolstoi's line of reasoning here may indicate that it is God's "individuality" rather than His personality he seeks to refute. In *Der Gottesbegriff bei Tolstoi*, Quiskamp writes:

> Tolstoi constantly repeated that he did not want to believe in the personality (*Persönlichkeit*) of God. Here, however, one must be aware that his concept of personality is always associated with bodily individuality. (Quiskamp 1937, 118)

Quiskamp therefore concludes that "for [Tolstoi] God is *no person, but unquestionably for him he is a personality*" (Quiskamp 1937, 141, emphasis in the original).

When Tolstoi rejected the idea of God as "*lichnost*," it is not least because he feared that it would unleash anthropomorphism in theology:

> The human being in the world is unthinkable other than as a *lichnost'*. But how can one say about God that he is a *lichnost'*, that he is *lichnyi*? This is the root cause of anthropomorphism. (Tolstoi PSS 53, 118)

Elsewhere Tolstoi admitted that we cannot avoid being anthropomorphists (Tolstoi PSS 55, 169). We cannot operate without certain positive characterizations of God. Expressed in the terms of Eastern Church theology: Apophatic theology must be supplemented with cataphasis. This is the same duality within which also Tolstoi's thoughts about God revolved.

God's love and will. The Christian idea that God is a "person" is primarily a way of expressing that He is in possession of reason and will and is genuinely interested in the well-being of His creatures. God embraces every human being in His care and love. For Tolstoi, too, the idea of God's love was fundamental. It is true that in his apophatic zeal he occasionally rejected the idea that God is reason and love: These two qualities are solely characteristics of human beings (Tolstoi PSS 54, 33). Even so, Tolstoi very often made the words of John the Apostle his own: "God is love." In addition to this substantive identification, he also used the verbal construction "God loves." Sometimes this thought was expressed in a way that indicated a personal concept of God: God loves "tête à tête" with the individual believer (Tolstoi PSS 56, 151; PSS 57, 58).

Also another cataphatic description of God, in addition to God being love, appears frequently in Tolstoi's writings: That God has *will.* This is not an undifferentiated will à la Schopenhauer, but an individualized will for each human person. Tolstoi often declared that the meaning of human life is to recognize and perform the will of God. Occasionally, he combined this thought with distinctly apophatic formulations: "Surrender yourself completely to God – *Deus absconditus*, this incomprehensible, mysterious source (*nachalo*). Put your life into the execution of His will, and everything will be easy" (Tolstoi 55, 226).

In an often-quoted letter to V. K. Zavolokin in 1900 Tolstoi wrote:

> *Man did not come into the world by his own will, but by the will of the one who has sent Him to the world. Therefore, he should not live according to his own will, but according to His will, who has sent him.* (Tolstoi PSS 72, 527, emphasis in the original)

These words were reproduced in 1952 by the Russian writer in exile Vladislav Maevskii, who commented on them as follows:

> These and similar lines in Tolstoy's works, and not least his entire ethical construction, leave no doubt whatsoever that his God, *according to His being, is transcendental and provided with personal will and personal reason. It is the God of the Church.* (Maevskii 1952, 76, emphasis in the original)

This writer went so far as to abolish any contradiction between Tolstoi's concept of God, and that of the Church.

In 1900, the brochure *Thoughts on God*, which Vladimir Chertkov compiled of excerpts from Tolstoi's diaries and letters, included many of the quotes presented in this chapter. Some Orthodox writers perceived the concept of God which Tolstoi presented in this booklet as utterly un-Christian (e.g., P. I. 1912, 1344); others concluded that a new and softer

Tolstoi had emerged. Having read *Thoughts on God*, the Orthodox priest Sergei Strakhov claimed that Tolstoi's worldview was now turning from pantheism to theism – but might easily shift back again (S. Strakhov 1903, 2, 183). The priest-monk Mikhail – later Old believer Bishop – believed that "theism leads to the Church, even when expressed in such an unclear form as in L. N. Tolstoi's brochure *Thoughts on God*" (Mikhail [Semenov] 1902, 359).

In Tolstoi's published texts, his thoughts on God often acquired a polemical sting aimed at Orthodoxy and the Christian concept of God. In the diaries, however, he was primarily concerned with clarifying his own, personal relationship with God: Maintaining a strict demarcation line against Orthodoxy was a less pressing concern. In one instance, Tolstoi argued that "God is not a concept, but a being, what the Orthodox call 'the living God' as opposed to a pantheistic God" (Tolstoi PSS 53, 118). Here, he explicitly drew a positive comparison between his own understanding of God and that of the Orthodox. This statement might be expected to interest many Orthodox believers, but comments on it have been surprisingly few. That may be because most Orthodox had already made up their mind that Tolstoi was a pantheist, and they did not know how to relate to his explicit anti-pantheism. Such confusion seems to underlie the reaction of the theologian Nikolai Makkaveiskii. He first asserted that Tolstoi was a pantheist, but then reproduced the quote that God is what the Orthodox call "living God," and then asked: "How, then, should we understand Tolstoi's religious worldview? It is vague, nebulous, confused, inconsistent and difficult to understand" (Makkaveiskii 1902, 23).

Makkaveiskii's reaction was in many ways understandable. Tolstoi's teachings about God did indeed at times give the impression of being "confused" and "inconsistent." Although I believe that attempts to define Tolstoi as one-sidedly pantheist are faulty, the pantheistic elements should not be swept under the carpet. The "pro-Orthodox" statements evident in his writings should not be accorded precedence over the clearly anti-Orthodox. Both trends belong to the overall picture: Both Tolstoi's closeness and his distance to historical Orthodoxy must be underlined at the same time.

Tolstoi scholars have been very much in agreement in their characterizations of *Examination of Dogmatic Theology*, it is based on undiluted rationalism. Henri Troyat: "In the name of reason, he rejects all that is beyond his understanding" (Troyat 1980, 549). Ernest Simmons: "He was not disposed to accept anything that would not stand the test of reason"

(Simmons 1969, 99). Lev Shestov: "Reason has done its work: No trace of the Scripture is left" (Shestov 1964, 166). Nikolai Losskii: "In his book *Criticism of Dogmatic Theology,* his abstract rationalism reaches extreme levels and creates an almost comical impression" (Losskii 1928, 239).

Thus, Weisbein's assertion that reason is Tolstoi's only criterion of truth in *Examination* is part of a well-established tradition. There is some evidence to support such an interpretation, yes. However, there is also so much that undermines it that it must be abandoned. As I have shown, *Examination* is one of the works in which Tolstoi was most open to the mysterious, the unfathomable.[13]

In this chapter, I have discussed some points where Tolstoi's teaching coincided with the theological tradition of the Eastern Church. That certainly does not mean that he was a "crypto-Orthodox" or an "Orthodox reformer." He completely rejected not only the doctrine of Trinity, but also such a central theological discipline as Christology, because for him what mattered was not the person of Christ, but His teachings. In addition, he regarded ecclesiology and sacramental theology as regrettable derailments from the true theme of religion – the relationship between God, Man, and Life. Therefore, it seems unlikely that he would have come to a very different assessment of Orthodox theology if he had examined another textbook of Christian dogmatics instead of Makarii's compendium.

Moreover, also on the points where we can note significant coincidence between Tolstoi's thinking and standard Orthodox theology, Tolstoi often combined the elements in ways that yielded a very different result. Take, for instance, their respective understandings of the relationship between God and man. While Orthodoxy is strictly theocentric, and treats man in light of God's creation as a derivative entity, Tolstoi is consistently anthropocentric (Patterson 1990). For him, the existence of man on earth is the starting point, with God entering the picture as the element that can

[13] This is similar to the conclusion that the modern Russian theologian Georgii Orekhanov seems to reach, although his views on the matter are somewhat contradictory. On the one hand, he claims that "Tolstoi shows himself as a rationalist and moralist with the absence of any kind of mystical connection between God and man" (Orekhanov 2010, 210). Six years later, however, Orekhanov argues that Tolstoi's rationalism differs from the rationalism found in the Western world which in the nineteenth century took the form of positivism and scientism. Tolstoi's rationalism, in Orekhanov's view, was paradoxically "irrational" and "not too far removed from Christian mysticism … . In Tolstoi's rationalism there are 'Russian' and even 'Orthodox' elements" (Orekhanov 2016, 201). It is a pity that the potentially rewarding line of enquiry indicated by these scattered remarks was not followed up anywhere in Orekhanov's two massive books on Tolstoy's relationship to the Orthodox Church.

give meaning to human life – a very different way of reasoning from that of Orthodox dogmatics.

Tolstoi reacted not only to the individual dogmas in the Orthodox school theology he read, but also to the genre of dogmatics as such. In his opinion, it was far too concerned with issues not directly related to the immediate interests and needs of human beings. In his diary, he noted in 1880:

> Who has ever benefited from interpretations of sacred tradition? Have they opened anybody's hearts? No .... And where is it written that we shall interpret? Nowhere. Everywhere we are told to be like children. What is hidden from the wise is revealed to the children and to the poor in spirit. (Tolstoi PSS 48, 328)

Tolstoi's ingrained skepticism toward distinctions and definitions was a major reason why his knee-jerk reaction to Orthodox dogmatics was one of protest, also when he was deeply in agreement with the theologians. However, there are other genres in Orthodox literature that are far less intellectualistic than dogmatics, and more closely related to the lives and experiences of believers. This is the case with devotional books, sermons and, not least, the entire ascetic-mystical monastic literature. From the outset, Tolstoi had a far more positive attitude toward these genres. In the following chapters, I examine his use of such sources.

CHAPTER 4

Tolstoi, Orthodoxy and Asceticism

Asceticism occupies a central place in Tolstoi's religious thinking: Even if he rejects the term "asceticism" (*asketizm*) as such, his ideal of virtue is clearly ascetic. As he understands *asketizm*, it denotes "self-inflicted torment," and what Christ demanded was not that we should hurt ourselves, but that we should realize ourselves (Tolstoi PSS 23, 415). If, however, asceticism is understood as "cleansing of all carnal lusts, demands and desires," then Tolstoi's ethics are clearly covered by this definition. He taught, for instance, that "virtue consists in the repression of passions through self-denial . . . . This is the eternal, highest law" (Tolstoi PSS 35, 184). G. W. Spence and Alexandre Christoyannopoulos attach great importance to this aspect of Tolstoi's teaching (Spence 1967; Christoyannopoulos 2020). In his study *Tolstoi the Ascetic*, Spence holds that Tolstoianism must be understood against the background of "primitive Christian thought" (Spence 1967, 83). In this chapter, I examine Tolstoi's relation to some of the ascetic traditions in Orthodox spirituality.

The emergence of ascetic ideals in Christianity is closely linked to the establishment of monasticism. Indeed, Henry Chadwick calls the first monks and nuns "the ascetic movement" (Chadwick 1978, 174). It is no coincidence that this movement received a powerful boost in the fourth century, when Christianity became a state religion in the Roman Empire. The monastics wanted to maintain their uncompromising severity and distance to "the world" at a time when the Church had begun to adapt to it. The first colonies of monks were established in the third century in the Egyptian desert; the movement soon spread to the entire Mediterranean region, with strong monastic groups emerging in Palestine, Syria and Asia Minor. In the Greek Church, the monasteries at Mount Athos on the Khalkidhikí Peninsula in the north-western Aegean were destined to play a very special role. In its heyday, as many as 40,000 monks lived on Mount Athos, and the specifically Orthodox form of contemplative mysticism known as Hesychasm was developed here in the fourteenth century by Gregory Palamas and others.

In all these settings, devotional texts were produced in which experienced monks offered directions for a life of prayer, fasting, self-denial, and Biblical study. These texts were read by later generations of monks, who compared them to their own spiritual experiences and wrote new treatises. Eventually, an entire library of mystical and ascetic literature was created. Some of the most important texts were collected in the eighteenth century by two Athos monks, Nicodemus of the Holy Mountain (1748–1809) and the Archbishop Macarius of Corinth (1731–1805). This collection was published in Venice in 1782 under the title *Philokalia.* Shortly after, the texts were translated into Church Slavonic by abbot Paisii Velichkovskii (1722–94) and his assistants, under the title *Dobrotoliubie.* This became one of the best-known works in Slavonic religious literature (Bolshakoff 1977, 90), and "enjoyed far greater influence in Russia than it did in Greece" (Coates 2014, 157).

Tolstoi had a copy of *Dobrotoliubie* in an 1851 edition, in which he had underlined many passages. We cannot say for sure when he read the book: The first evidence is from 1886.[1] Of course, he may have obtained the book from a second-hand bookstore, or it could have been standing untouched on his bookshelf for thirty-five years before he opened it. The latter seems unlikely, given its central importance in the environment around the monastery of Optina Pustyn with which Tolstoi had a strong interest in (see Chapter 5). If he became aware of the book only in 1886, it would not have been necessary to buy Paisii's old Church Slavonic translation: In 1876, Bishop Feofan Zatvornik (Govorov) had begun on a new Russian translation, with a larger number of texts. Despite these uncertainties as to dates, I regard *Dobrotoliubie* as a likely source of Tolstoi's asceticism theories, which in any case continued to evolve also after 1886. On important points there is a strong overlap between Tolstoi's ideas and the Philocalic tradition in Orthodox monasticism.

Dobrotoliubie is a multifaceted work. The texts in it span almost a thousand years and originate from more than twenty authors in the Church Slavonic translation (forty in the Russian version). Three of them – Antonius the Great, Marcus the Ascetic and Evagrius Ponticus – were among the Egyptian desert fathers. Antonius, who must have lived between 251 and 356, is often considered the "father of monasticism." Although the texts in *Dobrotoliubie* ascribed to Antonius were most

[1] He consulted it also in 1887 and 1898; see *Biblioteka* 1972, Ia, 265–66.

probably not authored by him (Ware 1984, 1339), they gained considerable authority by being linked to his name. We have little information about Marcus the Ascetic except that he probably lived in the late fourth century. It is uncertain whether the writings of *Dobrotoliubie* that carry his name were actually written by him. And thirdly, Evagrius (345–99) introduced the thoughts of the famed third-century theologian Origen to the monastic environment in Egypt, and was a major ideologue of early monasticism. Among other things, he compiled a list of eight core vices that later generations reworked into the seven deadly sins. As a follower of Origen, some of whose teachings had been declared heretical, Evagrius was condemned at the Fifth Ecumenical Council in 553, and many of his writings survived only by being assigned to other authors (Lossky [1963] 1983, 104–06). In any case, the texts in *Dobrotoliubie* that bear his name are probably authentic.

Among later authors represented in *Dobrotoliubie*, Simeon the New Theologian (949–1022) and Gregory of Sinai (1290–1346) are the most significant. Simeon left a number of mystical writings and is considered a precursor to the Hesychast movement. Gregory lived at Mount Athos at the same time as Gregory Palamas and further developed the Palamitic prayer technique. They are both represented in *Dobrotoliubie* with several longer texts. The other contributors to the Church Slavonic edition of *Dobrotolubie* are less well known.

Most of the writings in *Dobrotoliubie* consist of brief exhortations and teachings, often arranged into groups of one hundred. The instructions cover a wide range of subjects, so the thematic range of each writing is often large. Many of the authors are concerned with the contemplative "Jesus prayer" and other forms of prayer technique. However, this topic is not as dominant, as the secondary literature has often presented it as being. E. Kadloubovsky and G. Palmer called their English translation of some of these texts *Writings from the Philokalia on Prayer of the Heart*, which leaves a somewhat misleading impression. In *Dobrotoliubie*, the ascetic teachings are at least as prominent as the mystical ones, if not more so.

It is the ascetic teaching that is the focus of this chapter. Instead of attempting to offer an exhaustive analysis of all aspects of the ascetic message in these texts, I limit myself to a presentation of certain issues that foreshadow Tolstoi's teaching. For the sake of simplicity, all *Dobrotoliubie* authors will be dealt with together. Although there may be significant nuances between their ideas, I find it justifiable to speak of "une spiritualité spécifique de la *Philocalie*," as Kallistos Ware put it (Ware 1984, 1348). Because *Philokalia* is composed of texts from so many different sources, it provides a cross section of Orthodox monastic literature, offering a good entry point to the tradition of Eastern Christian asceticism in general.

The Body

We saw in Chapter 3 that the compendia of Orthodox dogmatics that Tolstoi had read operated with a dualistic anthropology, in which the body was juxtaposed to the soul, alternatively to the spirit. Most of the *Dobrotoliubie* Fathers advocated the same dichotomy, and took it one step further, regarding the body as something harmful that the Christians must fight against or liberate themselves from. For instance, Philotheus of Sinai cites Rom 8, 6–8: "For to be carnally minded is death; but to be spiritually minded is life and peace .... So then they that are in the flesh cannot please God." In these verses, St Paul uses the Greek word *sarks* for "flesh," not *soma* (body), and there is no reason to interpret him as an opponent of the body. However, that is exactly what Philotheus does when commenting on these Scriptural verses in *Dobrotoliubie.* He claims that "it is impossible to fight against powers and authorities when you have a full stomach, when you are tied to the flesh, which is heavy and always lusts against the spirit" (*Dobrotoliubie* 1902, 1/2, 25b[2]). In this quote "the flesh" is "heavy," which shows that it is perceived as something material. Hesychius of Jerusalem (ca 450) presents a similar view: "... If you want to be hostile, then be it towards the body. The flesh is a treacherous friend, and when it is cosseted, it rises against you even more. So, be an enemy of the body and wage war against the belly (*chrevo*)" (Dobrotolubie 1902, 1/2, 22b). In this text, body (*telo*) and flesh (*plot'*) are conflated: Once more we are taught that the stomach is an important accessory to "the flesh."

Pseudo-Antonius claims that it is impossible for the body to be free from evil and adds:

> The sensible (*slovesnaia*) soul who realizes this, throws away the burden of matter, that is, of wickedness. It rises liberated from its weight and acknowledges everyone's God while closely guarding the body and distrusting it as an enemy and an adversary. (*Dobrotoliubie* 1851, 1/1, 6a)

The statement that "matter" is evil borders on the Manichaean heresy. Such extreme ideas are found in *Dobrotoliubie* only in the Pseudo-

[2] In *Dobrotoliubie* only every other page is paginated. I indicate on which side of the leaf the quotation is found by adding "a" (front) or "b" (reverse side).

Antonian texts. However, they may be an implicit premise for some other *Dobrotoliubie* authors as well when they teach that the body is the "enemy" of man.

In Tolstoi's writings, we find much of the same negative view of the body. He never wrote that the body is "evil" or "sinful," but he saw it as something partly harmful, partly illusory. Especially in his diary from the last few years of his life, Tolstoi returned to this idea repeatedly. The enlightened man, he wrote, perceives the physical life as something unreal (*nereal'noi*). "As soon as a person reaches the true life, he throws away the bodily life that has become unnecessary for him" (Tolstoi PSS 54, 198). Since self-denial is the basic law of human life, there is nothing more harmful than to be concerned with physical well-being (Tolstoi PSS 56, 49). Life, Tolstoi explained, can be depicted figuratively as "the uprising of love from the grave of the body" (Tolstoi PSS 56, 74). In 1908, Tolstoi asked God to help him to "despise and forget my physical self" (Tolstoi PSS 56, 148). Writes Rene Fueloep-Miller: "Tolstoy, who had once glorified the body, now preached that the flesh had to be forcibly broken to bring about the liberation and salvation of the soul. He demanded the mortification of the body, and he was no less insistent in this demand than Saint Anthony or the pillar saints in the Lybian desert" (Fueloep-Miller 1960, 101–02).

In his published writings, Tolstoi usually employed a slightly different terminology, replacing the spirit/body opposition with the contrast between the "divine" and the "animal" forms of human existence. The latter term encompasses more than the body itself: It includes the entire empirical side of human life, everything we have in common with the animal world. This form of existence constitutes the "shell" (*obolochka*) that surrounds our spiritual being. It is our task to move our consciousness from our animal "I" to our divine "I" (Tolstoi PSS 26, 342–83).

These same expressions occur in *Dobrotoliubie*. Pseudo-Antonius claims that "through his mind, man is united with the unfathomable and divine force, but with his body he is akin to the beasts" (*Dobrotoliubie* 1851, 1/1, 5a). The soul is divine and immortal in the sense that it is infused by God. It has been united with the body for a pedagogical reason: The soul is to be tested (*iskushenie*) and (if it passes the test) become divine (*ubogotvorenie*) (*Dobrotoliubie* 1851, 1/1, 14a). Gregory of Sinai teaches that we are created indestructible, but since we also have bodies, we are nevertheless subject to corruption. By being disobedient, we "became animals instead of beings with reason, wild animals instead of divine" (Dobrotolubie 1851, 1/1, 88b).

Several contemporaries of Tolstoi drew parallels between the understanding of the body in Tolstoi's writings and the ancient Church. The German Lutheran Church historian Adolf von Harnack considered dualism to be one of the most important characteristics of Eastern monasticism, one of the features that in his view most clearly distinguished it from Western asceticism. Harnack noted Tolstoi's teaching as an example of where the Orthodox dualism could lead when taken to its extreme. Tolstoi was a layman, but he wrote "as a true Greek monk" (Harnack 1903, 43). Also the Russian Marxist Gennadii Plekhanov saw the downgrading of the flesh in favor of the spirit as a distinctive feature of Tolstoi's teaching. Plekhanov argued that "such a disparagement was once characteristic of the Christians, and from that point of view, Tolstoi's teaching has indeed much in common with the Christian doctrine" (Plekhanov 1977, 314–15).

The Passions

In *What is Religion and What is its Essence?* from 1901–02 Tolstoi defined virtue as the suppression of the passions through self-denial (Tolstoi PSS 35, 184). This was a core insight that he had acquired already as a young man. In his diary from 1852, he had written: "I have long been convinced that virtue, even at its highest level, consists in the absence of bad passions" (Tolstoi PSS 46, 93). Also in the Hesychast tradition, the struggle against the passions was a crucial element in their ascetic program. According to Pseudo-Antonius, in order to be truly free, one must prevail over one's own passions. The man who is evil or without moderation cannot be called free even if he is a prince, for he is a slave of his passions (*Dobrotoliubie* 1851, 1/1, 3a).

To rid oneself of the passions, one must first identify them. According to Hesychius, many passions lie hidden in every soul, and are discovered only when something activates them (*Dobrotoliubie* 1902, 1/2, 9a). He regarded vanity, self-indulgence (*slasti*) and love of money as the three most dangerous passions (*Dobrotoliubie* 1902, 1/2, 7b). According to Pseudo-Antonius, we can be slaves of our passions if we so wish, but we also have the possibility to be free and not succumb to them (*Dobrotoliubie* 1851, 1/1, 8a).

Tolstoi agreed that humans both can and must fight the passions with all their might. This is not a sacrifice but in our own self-interest. Tolstoi explained that the passions may indeed bring brief moments of pleasure, but never genuine satisfaction. Our animal nature will always develop more and greater desires as soon as the first ones are satisfied. The person who toils as a slave under his animal nature will therefore feel a constant deficit of pleasure (Tolstoi PSS 26, 425). It is those who follow their lusts and desires who become the true martyrs, not the Christians (Tolstoi PSS 23, 423).

The *Dobrotoliubie* author who most systematically elaborated a teaching of the passions was Gregory of Sinai. He declared that the activity of the passions deprives men of access to grace. A soul that loves the passions and sin will readily become an abode of demons, both in this world and in the next (*Dobrotoliubie* 1851, 1/1, 89a). Gregory therefore does not hesitate to call passionate habits "the torments of hell." They are like stinking worms, snakes, toads and leeches that torture the soul (*Dobrotoliubie* 1851, 1/1, 92a).

Gregory gives several slightly differing explanations as to how the passions arise. In one place he teaches that they are begotten by sinful deeds, and that the passions in turn beget harmful thoughts (*pomysli*). In another place he claims that "*pomysli* are the words of demons and the forerunners of the passions" (*Dobrotoliubie* 1851, 1/1, 94b). The message in both cases is of the close relationship between our thoughts and our emotional life. In his text no 74 we can read:

> When the passions are in action, some *pomysli* are at the forefront while others follow from behind. In front are the daydreams, and after them come the passions. The passions precede the demons, and the demons follow the passions. (*Dobrotoliubie* 1851, 1/1, 95ab)

Perhaps not so many people today will find this explanation very convincing. In July 1898, however, Tolstoi wrote in his diary: "*Pomysli* lead to daydreams, daydreams to passions, and passions to demons (from *Dobrotoliubie*)" (Tolstoi PSS 53, 204). Tolstoi did not state where in *Dobrotolubie* he found this formulation, but it must have been in the above-quoted text by Gregory of Sinai.

In Gregory's view not all passions are evil. He distinguishes between voluntary passions, which arise from some kind of excess, and inevitable ones, which are awakened by their surroundings or by their natural qualities (*svoistva*). In the latter case, they are not shameful (*Dobrotoliubie* 1851, 1/1, 95b). An echo of this idea can be found in Tolstoi's diary from 1907, where he wrote that passions are merely exaggerations of natural and legitimate inclinations (*vlecheniia*) (Tolstoi PSS 56, 43).

Gregory divides the various specific passions into categories. He mentions a total of sixty-eight, noting that the list could easily be extended. So that the novice will not get lost in this jungle of passions, Gregory singles out some as particularly important. Like Evagrius, he argues that there are eight dominant passions: gluttony, greed, vainglory, despair, lust, wrath, pride and sloth. Of these, the first three are primary and the last five are secondary (*Dobrotoliubie* 1851, 1/1, 98b). In his copy of *Dobrotoliubie* Tolstoi underlined them all, and in his own works we can find similar catalogues of vices. In *A Confession*, he wrote about the attitudes and qualities he had been encouraged to cultivate as a young man: Ambition, lust for power, selfishness, carnal lust (*liubostrastie*), pride, anger and revenge (Tolstoi PSS 23, 4). That list includes most of the main vices on Gregory's list. Those that are missing are dealt with elsewhere.[3]

Later in his presentation of the vices, Gregory argues that debauchery and despondency are "particularly cruel and burdensome" passions (*Dobrotoliubie* 1851, 1/1, 102b). In the margin next to these in his copy of Philocalia, Tolstoi wrote "these are the worst" (*Biblioteka* 1972, vol 1a, 265). Another place Gregory singled out gluttony as perhaps even more deleterious. The stomach is called "the Queen of the passions." Gluttony is a clear example of a passion that pulls others after it. Under the influence of the vapors produced when eating too much food, man becomes drowsy and longs to sleep rather than pray. Too much eating not only leads to laziness, but, according to Gregory, also excites carnal desire. "When you over-eat, you open up the door to lechery (*Dobrotoliubie* 1851, 1/1, 125b). Modern readers may find this claim somewhat puzzling, feeling that overindulgence temporarily slakes the sexual urge. Tolstoi, however, was obviously intrigued by this thought. In *The Kreutzer Sonata*, the protagonist Pozdnyshev explains: "[O]ur stimulant superfluous food together with complete physical idleness is nothing but a systematic agitation of [sexual] lusts (*pokhot'*)" (Tolstoi PSS 27, 23). The idea of a close connection between gastronomic and sexual excesses emerged also in *The First Step* and *Circle of Reading* (Tolstoi PSS 29, 73; 41, 148).

Apatheia

The struggle against the passions, according to the Philocalic authors, is crowned with victory when the monk has reached a state of passionlessness

[3] In his catechesis *Christian teaching*, Tolstoi presented his own vice catalogue of six deadly sins that only partly overlaps with Gregory's list: Drunkenness, idleness, immoderate desire, avarice, lust of power, and fornication. Gary Hamburg suggests that despair is omitted since Tolstoi might have regarded it as a "monkish" vice unlikely to affect "genuine Christians" (Hamburg 2010, 153). However, in *Circle of Reading*, Tolstoi devotes considerable attention to despair or despondency (*unynie*) (Tolstoi PSS 41, 445–47). Similarly, Hamburg's attempt to explain the absence of pride in *Christian teaching* is not convincing: "Perhaps as a Russian aristocrat with an imperious character, Tolstoy preferred not to confront his own pride" (Hamburg 2010, 154). But already in *A Confession*, Tolstoi castigated himself for his "vainglory, greed and pride" (Tolstoi PSS 23, 4), and attacks on pride are littered throughout his compilations of devotional texts such as *Circle of Reading*.

or *apatheia* – in Church Slavonic *bezstrastie*. This ideal can be found in the texts of virtually all *Dobrotoliubie* authors. Callistus and Ignatius consider *bezstrastie* a necessary, but not sufficient, condition for achieving genuine prayer (*Dobrotoliubie* 1902, 1/2, 102b). Evagrius Ponticus believes that the nuptial garments in the wedding of the king's son in Matt 22, 1–14 must be understood as the *bezstrastie* of the sensible soul. Thus, he makes passionlessness, as it were, the very entry ticket to Heaven (*Dobrotoliubie* 1851, 1/1, 146b). Gregory the Sinaite expresses himself even more explicitly when he calls *bezstrastie* "the promised land" (*Dobrotoliubie* 185l, 1/1, 93a).

The fullest account of the *apatheia* or *bezstrastie* ideal in *Dobrotoliubie* is given by Simeon the New Theologian. He asks his readers not only to refrain from wealth and gold, but also to drive out of their souls the very *desire* for these things. "Let us hate not just the lusts of the body (*slasti telese*) but also its uncontrolled (*bezslovesnye*) movements" (*Dobrotoliubie* 185l, 1/1, 5 4a). In Simeon's view, a man cannot eradicate the passions within himself, but he can prevail over them. "I call a man passionless when he not only does not follow the dictates of the passions, but the very desire after them is alien to him." Holy people have mortified their limbs and cleansed them of all impurity and passionate desires (text 118).

Some modern Orthodox theologians have downplayed the importance of the *apatheia* ideal in the Eastern Church (e.g., Fedotov 1981, 490). However, other authorities like Kallistos Ware and Vladimir Lossky accept the term as a valid expression of a life of high moral quality (V. Lossky [1963] 1983, 52–54, lo5–8). Ware explains this as a state of "purity of heart": "[I]t signifies advancing from instability to stability, from duplicity to simplicity or singleness of heart" (Ware 1981, 156). There can thus be no doubt that the *apatheia* ideal has retained its role in Orthodox piety and is a central concept in Eastern monastic literature.

Passionlessness was an ideal of fundamental importance for Tolstoi. Also for him the final aim of asceticism is the total cessation of all bodily lusts and desires. The person who manages to place the meaning of life completely in the inner, spiritual dimension will be delivered from pain – as well as from pleasure, as there is no pleasure without pain. These are two opposite states that mutually provoke and are conditioned by each other:

> According to Christian doctrine, life in its true meaning ... is neither joy nor suffering but consists in the birth and growth of man's true, spiritual 'I'. This excludes both joy and pain. (Tolstoi PSS 39, 189)

Ascetics may be affected by physical pain – indeed, they must be prepared for deprivations and sufferings every moment of their lives, but this no longer affects them. They have achieved an "imperturbable spiritual tranquillity" (Tolstoi PSS 42, 167). The true believer wants nothing and fears nothing (Tolstoi PSS 42, 342).

Tolstoi used the word "apathy" (*apatiia*) in the common, negative meaning it has taken on in modern European languages, as dullness or lethargy (e.g., Tolstoi PSS 54, 65). He did not use the Russian equivalent *besstrastie* in his writings either, although he was familiar with it. This term occurs in Tolstoi's diary as early as in 1854, where he claims that "*besstrastie*, that is, an always unchanged, cold-blooded gaze, constitutes the wisdom of the old" (Tolstoi PSS 46, 222). This he wrote during his stay in the Caucasus, at a time when the diary frequently testified to his desperate struggle against the passions. At that time, he perceived *besstrastie* as desirable, but for him an unachievable state of mind.

Instead of using Orthodox ascetic terminology, Tolstoi developed his own when he stood forth as an ascetic religious preacher. He used the word *ravnodushie* – which Russian thesauruses list as a synonym of *apatiia.* Directly translated, *ravnodushie* means "equanimity," and Tolstoi occasionally used it in that sense. However, he frequently employed it as a technical term, to mean the absence of passions, both good and bad. In *Examination of Dogmatic Theology*, for example, he claimed: "Jesus gave us an example of full *ravnodushie*, if not to say contempt, for tsars, taxes, inheritance litigation and the execution of a fallen woman . . . . Nothing of what is not your soul should concern you" (Tolstoi PSS 23, 303). Here Tolstoi is clearly influenced by the Greek *apatheia* ideal.

Here it might be objected that, in addition to indifference or *ravnodushie*, Tolstoi also sets up "contempt" (*prezrenie*) as an ideal. It can be argued that a contemptuous attitude presupposes agitation and a lack of equanimity. But also the idea of a "contemptuous indifference" can be found in Orthodox ascetic texts. For instance, in the sixth-century classic *Ladder of Divine Ascent* (*Lestvitsa)*, John Climacus taught that the individual who wants to free himself from the passions must "abstain from everything, despise everything, laugh at everything, and reject everything" (Climacus 1963, 4).[4]

Tolstoi's peculiar use of the *ravnodushie* concept crops up in many unexpected places. For example, in an article on the 1905 Revolution he wrote that the Russian upper class should go out into the countryside and

[4] However, on other occasions, Tolstoi drew a distinction between *prezrenie* and *ravnodushie*. In 1907, he claimed that he did not despise the Constitutional Democrats, the so-called *Kadety*. Rather, he tried to disregard completely what they said (N. Gusev 1973, 103).

take part in the toil of the people. In that way, they would be able to acquire the peasants' patience and joy of work, *ravnodushie* and contempt for the authorities (Tolstoi PSS 36, 261). To a woman who had an unfaithful husband, Tolstoi wrote that if she had been utterly clean herself, she would have been completely *ravnodushnaia* with regard to how her husband sought satisfaction for his passions (*strasti*) (L. Tolstoi 1901, 111).

At times, Tolstoi himself acquired a state of indifference or passionlessness (Tolstoi PSS 52, 80). In his diary in 1909, he noted:

> Yesterday, for the first time, I experienced a very joyful new feeling: complete surrender to His will, full *ravnodushie* to everything that might happen to me, absence of any desire except this one: to do what He wants. (Tolstoi PSS 57, 81)

We should not take literally Tolstoi's claim that was "the first time" he experienced this feeling. Three years earlier, he had written, "I am experiencing a completely new state of consciousness . . . : *Ravnodushie* to the opinions of men, to the state of the body, even to my own creativity" (Tolstoi PSS 55, 262). When this feeling was experienced as something "new" three years later, it might be because the sensation was different every time. Each individual case was unique.

More important than Tolstoi's terminology, however, is the content of his teaching. It is evident that the ideal of the *ravnodushie* influenced very many different aspects of his moral philosophy. Tolstoi set up a number of practical rules of life: Nonviolence, celibacy, propertylessness, vegetarianism, physical work and abstinence from all kinds of drugs. At first sight, this list might seem somewhat mixed up, and Tolstoi did indeed argue in different ways for the various rules. There is, however, one common feature: The need to suppress the passions in order to achieve peace of mind. This is what links Tolstoi's maxims together into one whole. Below, I demonstrate how his teaching on the passions permeates different sides of his thinking. I will not attempt an exhaustive account of all of these aspects of his teaching – some of which would merit an entire chapter – but focus on the one common factor that joins them: The *ravnodushie*-ideal.

Nonviolence (nonresistance): Nonviolence is usually justified on the grounds that it is wrong to hurt other people: You shall not inflict suffering on your neighbor, even if he has injured you first. For Tolstoi, however, this was only part of the argument. Equally important is how your violence affects *yourself*: Nonviolence is a condition for achieving happiness and spiritual growth. The violence to which you yourself are exposed harms only your body, whereas the violence you afflict on others damages your soul. The opposite of nonviolence here is care for your own body. In Gethsemane, according to Tolstoi, Jesus was tempted to ask God to spare him bodily suffering, but was given the power to choose surrender without exhibiting resistance to the violence of men (Tolstoi PSS 24, 702–06).

In *What I Believe*, Tolstoi juxtaposes the upper classes and the working people in various ways, to bring out the superiority of the life of the uncouth simple peasants. For example, he argues that, whereas the people of the upper classes put up resistance whenever they encounter difficulties, the attitude of the common people is characterized by passive acceptance of the conditions of life. Unlike those in Tolstoi's social circles who fume and become indignant at the deprivations and sufferings fate sends them, the lower classes accept grief unquestioningly. They remain calm, firmly convinced that this is the way it must be (Tolstoi PSS 23, 40). This view is an important aspect of Tolstoi's attitude toward nonresistance. The aim must be to meet natural disasters and human evil as basically the same thing: As *external* calamities.

Abstinence: The connection between Tolstoi's teaching about the passions and his maxim of sobriety is obvious, although he used various arguments in preaching abstention from drugs, alcohol and tobacco. Production of these substances prevents people from using the earth to grow good, healthy food. More important in his view, however, is that these substances create artificial physical needs. Moreover, they blunt our conscience so that we more easily succumb to passionate and violent desires. This is the reason why men so often get drunk before going to a brothel, or to war (Tolstoi PSS 27, 272–73).

Ethics of sexuality: In *The Kreutzer Sonata* and the *Afterword to the Kreutzer Sonata*, Tolstoi makes absolute sexual abstinence an ideal for everyone, within as well as outside marriage. This ideal, too, must be understood in relation to his general teaching on the passions. Tolstoi holds up complete chastity as the ideal because he sees the sexual instinct as being one of the strongest expressions of animal life in us. It is "the strongest, meanest, and most stubborn of the passions" (Tolstoi PSS 27, 30). It provides the highest possible pleasure, but also the greatest pain. The main protagonist in *The Kreutzer Sonata*, Pozdnyshev, explains how cohabitation with his wife had been characterized by a constant pendulum movement between active sexual life and violent bitterness. "At that time we did not understand that this love and this wickedness (*zloba*) against each other was one and the same animal feeling, seen only from opposite ends" (Tolstoi PSS 27, 45). Only a couple living in a purely platonic relationship can therefore have a chance to avoid enmity.

Physical labor: In line with his high regard for the peasant way of life, Tolstoi recommends manual labor as a means of acquiring good health. Only physical labor is genuine, decent work, since only such labor can provide food and other necessities. All those who are engaged in "intellectual work" ultimately exploit the physical labor of others. At the same time, Tolstoi's work ethics can also be regarded as an outgrowth of his ascetic thinking. Some ascetics of earlier centuries had questioned the value of physical work, which they thought distracted man from the spiritual life. Tolstoi's ascetic program, however, includes manual labor as a suitable means of subduing the passions. Those who have exhausted themselves in the fields have neither the time nor the strength to excite their unnatural lusts after the end of their working day. "Work in the fields ... makes everybody equal, and hacks off the wings of luxury and passion" (Tolstoi PSS 25, 467).

Propertylessness: Tolstoi did not only present an ideal of poverty; he went further and maintained that people should renounce all kinds of property ownership. This view can be perceived as an egalitarian program: Real estate is the major source of inequality between people: Therefore, the principle of owning private property is unjust and should be abolished. Such considerations clearly were part of Tolstoi's reasoning. More important, however, was his belief that all property is harmful to the owner himself: The proprietor will inevitably be seized by the passion of self-interest or greed (*korystoliubie*). Property is a means to satisfy the desires of the flesh. One must choose between God and the flesh; one cannot serve two masters at the same time (Tolstoi PSS 24, 823).

According to Tolstoi, the craving for material goods is often triggered by the belief that it is necessary and possible to secure life by external means. This belief he rejected as a delusion. Those who first begin to amass goods will not find any natural limit to their hoarding (Tolstoi 1902, 40–42). Jesus taught that those who try to save their lives shall lose it (Cfr Matt 10, 39). Only those who are not worried about the day of tomorrow can find equanimity of mind.

The *ravnodushie* ideal is an important element also in Tolstoi's socio-economic theories. Tolstoi presented these first in *What Can We Then Do?* (1886), but also the follow-up *The Slavery of our Time* (1900) is relevant. Tolstoi offered a fierce criticism of the capitalist exploitation of the working class, phrased largely in terms of traditional socialist approaches. Tolstoi's peculiar twist to this message appeared when he also criticized materialistic socialism for what he saw as a contradiction: The socialists correctly claim that the superabundance of the bourgeoisie is built on the poverty of the lower classes, but at the same time they also teach that in the future, classless society, everyone will share in the riches and luxuries. The claim that all would then receive according to their needs was in Tolstoi's opinion unsustainable, because "in such a society, the needs are always infinitely greater than the possibilities to satisfy them" (Tolstoi PSS 34, 161). "Needs" readily becomes another name for animal passions, and if one has first begun to yield to the lusts of the body, then there is no limit to the costly, "refined habits" one can develop. Tolstoi was unwilling to take part in the struggle for a fairer distribution of material goods for the simple reason that he did not perceive them as being "good" at all.

Apatheia and *Theosis*

For Tolstoi, deliverance from the tyranny of the passions was a necessary condition, not just for a good life, but for correct thinking as well. In his December 1890 diary, he wrote that only a person who is holy can think accurately and fruitfully. Sinful people are full of desires, aversions, hopes and passions (*pristrastiia*), and their thoughts serve all this. Therefore, in order to understand something fully, what is needed is not to penetrate, ponder and analyze it, but instead to purify (*ochishchat'*) one's heart of desires, passions and mundane hopes – in short, get rid of one's sins and enhance love (Tolstoi PSS 51, 112–13).

Asceticism is seen as a purification of mind and body that enables man to acquire true insight. The same idea was expressed by the Greek monks in their teaching of *catharais* (cleansing) as a prerequisite for *gnosis* – true knowledge. Formulated positively, Hesychius of Jerusalem proclaimed that "the path to reason (*razum*) passes through *bezstrastie* and humility" (*Dobrotoliubie* 1902, 1/2, 8b). Negatively, it was claimed that "the night of passions" is identical to "the darkness of ignorance" (*Dobrotoliubie* 1902, 1/1, 92a). Several scholars have emphasized that Orthodox asceticism becomes meaningful only in this perspective. E. Kadloubovsky and G. H. E. Palmer explain that asceticism "consists primarily of efforts to attain sobriety of mind and its spiritual fruits, whilst the mastery of the body and of the passions are subordinate and proportionate to this aim" (Kadloubovsky & Palmer 1976, 18). Orthodox monastic tradition expresses this through the doctrine of the two parallel paths: *Praxis* and *theoria* – asceticism and contemplation. These paths precondition and affect one another; the monk must always follow both of them simultaneously (V. Lossky [1957] 1973, 202). The end goal of both is deification – *theosis*. *Apatheia*, therefore, is "the beginning of deification" (V. Lossky [1957] 1973, 48).

Several authors in the *Dobrotolubie* compendium refer to *apatheia* as a divine state. Callistus and Ignatius claim that "*bezstrastie* is the resurrection of the soul before the body, as far as is possible for man. It is to put on God's image and likeness (*obraz i podobie*)" (*Dobrotoliubie* 1902, 1/2, 12a). Theoleptus of Philadelphia explains that whenever God causes man to be dead toward the passions and sin, He makes him a participant (*prichastnik*) in divine life (*Dobrotolubie* 1902, 1/2, 47a). Pseudo-Antonius claims that God is passionless and immutable: He cannot rejoice or be angry, for joy and anger are passions. As it is the task of man to become as similar to God as possible, we too should strive to free ourselves from the passions (*Dobrotolubie* 1851, 1/1, 16ab). All these authors see the passions as chains that keep us bound to the "world." Only when these moorings are cut can the soul ascend to God. By suppressing the flesh, we can realize our inherent possibilities and fulfill our destiny: To become like God.

For Tolstoi, the ideal of passionlessness was closely linked to his teaching about the divine nature of man. In his diary for 1909 he wrote: "Self-abnegation is to acknowledge one's divinity and eternity" (Tolstoi PSS 57, 62). Also in his published texts from the final decade of his life we find this view. In *What is Religion and What is its Essence?* (1901–02) he taught that by suppressing the passions we can increase the divine principle within us (Tolstoi PSS 35, 190). This idea was developed more extensively in *Circle of Reading*:

> As soon as you feel the desires of passion stirring in you, then evoke the awareness of your divine nature. As soon as you feel that the divine nature is obscured [in you], know that you have become possessed by passions, and must fight them. (Tolstoi PSS 42, 289)

The ascetic struggle against the passions is held to affect consciousness; conversely, concentrating our consciousness on the divine dimension will affect our sensual life. Only those who are passionless can realize their godly nature.

Apatheia and *Agape*

Tolstoi's ideal of *apatheia* has been overlooked, misunderstood and even denied. Richard Gustafson, for example, claims that Tolstoi had no such ideal at all. In his opinion, Tolstoi's aim was "not stoic *apatheia*, if this is understood as passionless detachment from everything else. The goal is to set loose love for all, our self and everything else" (Gustafson 1986, 178). If

Gustafson wanted to say that Tolstoi advocated a *Christian* ideal of *apatheia* rather than a stoic one, that is in my view a defensible position. In the context, however, it seems more likely that, in Gustafson's opinion, *apatheia* can be imagined only within a stoic context. As I hope to have made clear, that is not the case.

At the same time, there can be no doubt that "to set loose love for all" is indeed a central aim for Tolstoi, as Gustafson claims – but, for Tolstoi, this is not opposed to "passionless detachment," rather, it is conditioned by it. This view is clearly expressed in several of Tolstoi's works. In *The Law of Violence and the Law of Love* (1908), he explains that people can strengthen their love by exterminating (*unichtozhenie*) the mistakes, sins and base passions that prevent it from appearing (Tolstoi PSS 37, 211). Here, the passions and love are presented as opposites. The less is left of the passions in a human being, the more there is room for love. This idea is expressed even more clearly in *The Kreutzer Sonata.* Here, the dual struggle *against* the passions and *for* love is elevated to the level of world history. In a magnificent vision Pozdnyshev sees the universal Kingdom of Peace at the end of times:

> If the goal of mankind is, as it is written in the books of the prophets, that all human beings shall be united in love, that they shall hammer their spears into scythes, etc., what is it that prevents us from attaining this goal? It is the passions . . . . If the passions were destroyed, then the prophecy would be fulfilled. (Tolstoi PSS 27, 30)

Tolstoi did not perceive love as a passion or feeling as we generally do today. Instead, it is primarily a form of *action*, an activity. That made it possible to maintain the ideals of passionlessness and love at the same time, although living up to this double ideal is often difficult in practice. In the last year of his life, Tolstoi lamented in his diary that he could not manage to be *ravnodushnyi* in the sense of having "love to those who are not kind" (Tolstoi PSS 58, 131). This entry makes it clear that Tolstoi expects a genuinely passionless person to show love toward his fellow human beings – including those who do not deserve his love.

Also in the Christian monastic tradition, asceticism and love are inextricably interlinked. "Only a harmonious union between them can lead man to Christ and make him worthy of the eternal life," one ascetic author writes (Iastremskii 1913, 37). In *Dobrotoliubie* we find several testimonies about this attitude. Abba Philemon describes a spiritual chain reaction:

> Silence begets asceticism, asceticism – crying, crying – fear, fear – humility, humility – reflection, reflection – love, and love makes the soul healthy (*bezboleznennyi*) and passionless. (*Dobrotoliubie* 1902, IV, 144a)

Here, *apatheia* is presented as the end product, with agape as the immediate mechanism of release.

As we have seen, the fusion of asceticism and the ethics of love that Tolstoi advocated has clear models in Orthodox monastic literature. The Russian Orthodox writer P. Apokrif suggested this, cautiously, when he claimed that "it is almost as if Tolstoi's doctrine of love contains the centuries-old, *ecclesiastic-Christian* teachings about the need to renounce the world of passions, but in a severely degraded form, adapted to his own peculiar religious-philosophical opinions . . ." (Apokrif 1903, 13l, emphasis in the original).

This is not to say that the Christian tradition is the only source of Tolstoi's ascetic ideal. To some degree, the Orthodox *apatheia* ideal draws on Stoicism – a moral philosophy familiar to Tolstoi. In *What I Believe*, he refers to Seneca, Epictetus and Marcus Aurelius. Tolstoi read Epictetus in 1882 and found him "very good" (N. Gusev 1958, 553). Also in Schopenhauer as well as in Buddhism, Tolstoi found kindred ideas (Biriukov 1925; Quiskamp 1939). The reading of Schopenhauer, the Stoics and the Orthodox monastic literature were three major impulses that pulled Tolstoi in the same direction.

Asceticism for Everyone

The earliest monastic movement was basically individualistic and elitist. The first hermits upheld the demand for full self-denial – but only for the individual. The ascetic ideal did not extend to all of society. On the contrary, the hermit left human society behind, sought salvation in seclusion, and urged others to do the same. If he returned to "the world" at times, this was to preach the word of God to others, and give them a chance to turn around, take a new direction (*metanoia*). The monk had a certain responsibility toward his fellow men. Like the enlightened person in Plato's parable, he must reenter the "cave" to preach the divine truth to those who have not yet seen the light. But he had no responsibility for society as such.

Also Tolstoi maintained that the Christian should not try to transform society by political or social activism, but should instead concentrate on his own self-perfection (*samosovershenstvovanie*) (Tolstoi PSS 28, 182, 184; Tolstoi PSS 36, 262). However, he did not recommend the reclusive life of the hermit as the outer framework for asceticism, for two related reasons. Firstly, he could not accept that the ascetic ideals should apply only to a few, select, persons. Tolstoi retained his basic individualistic understanding of ethics, but wanted everyone to join the elite of ascetic individualists. We could say that Tolstoi abolished the distinction between the monk's life and "the world" by universalizing the ascetic demands. Secondly, in Tolstoi's view, the proper place for the ascetic is precisely the world: Only there can the ascetic influence his fellow human beings through his example. Tolstoi's model is therefore an "inner exodus," in contrast to the hermits' exterior withdrawal.

For Tolstoi, then, asceticism is not a lifestyle for a few zealots only, but part of a universal moral program. In fact, his teaching on this point was nothing new. The Orthodox Church does not operate with a double ethical standard, with one set of requirements for lay people and another for the monks. On the contrary, the lofty standards of the monks are to serve as a model for everyone. Those who issued and wrote the preface to the Church Slavonic edition of *Dobrotoliubie* wanted this to be a manual for all Orthodox Christians, laity as well as monks (*mirstii, vkupe i inotsy*) (*Dobrotoliubie* 1851, 1/1, *preface*).

This attitude was adopted and further developed by later Orthodox writers. Patrick Lally Michelson explains that in the strand of Russian spirituality that emanated from the philocalic texts, asceticism was not exclusive to monasticism "but was accessible to and incumbent on all Orthodox Christians, although to varying degrees" (Michelson 2017, 148). Virtually all modern books on asceticism by Orthodox authors emphasize that this program has relevance for all believers, irrespective of their life situation.[5] Therefore, we can see Tolstoi's preaching of "asceticism in the midst of society" as a further development of tendencies already latent in the Orthodox ideal of a godly life.

[5] "When we talk about the monastic life, we are therefore talking about a life with which every Orthodox has a close and intimate relationship," writes the Orthodox monk Sofronii (1953, 6). According to the Finnish Orthodox writer Tito Colliander, "There no place, no society, no external circumstances that are not suitable [for fighting the ascetic struggle]" (Colliander 1985, 26). And: "There is no Christian who is not an ascetic. In rough terms, the entire world, the monastery and all Orthodox believers, each in their own rank, should live as a monk" (Volzhskii 2002, 421). The monastery and the "world" are merely two different settings for the unfolding of the same ascetic endeavour. "Not only those who have withdrawn from the world to save their souls can be ascetics. The same is true of lay people in the most diverse social situations" (*Asketizm i monashestvo*, not dated, 36).

CHAPTER 5

Lev Tolstoi and Orthodox Forms of Spirituality: Elders

In the pamphlet "Thou shall not kill" (1907) Tolstoi wrote:

> From time immemorial, an unofficial, vigorous faith has persisted among the Russian people alongside the official faith. By some strange means it has become deeply rooted among the people, in their sayings, tales and legends, disseminated by way of the holy lives of elders, holy fools, and wanderers (*startsy, iurodivye, stranniki*). (Tolstoi PSS 37, 47–48)

Here Tolstoi singles out for praise three forms of piety developed within the Orthodox Church: *Eldership*, *holy foolishness* and *holy wandering*. This was no slip of the pen or a mere passing attraction: Tolstoi maintained a constant interest in these religious practices. In this and the three following chapters, I discuss Tolstoi's relationship to these forms of spirituality.

Tolstoy's biographer A. N. Wilson sees Tolstoi's attempts to emulate the *elders* and the *holy fools* as reflections of his literary, artistic approach to life:

> There was Lyovochka the village idiot or *yurodivy,* muttering his holy thoughts, mowing (very badly) in the fields or attracting the derision of simpletons or sophisticates alike by his hamfisted attempts to make his own boots. There was the bearded prophet, doling out wise saws and advice to pilgrims with the portentous self-confidence of the *starets*. There was, still refusing to go away, the retired army officer and the landed aristocrat .... (Wilson 1989, 305)

All this was only a matter of trying on various theatrical masks, one after another, Wilson asserts:

> ... all these completely inconsistent roles – squire, *starets, yurodivy,* lecher, saint, husband, historian, private landowner, public dissident, etc. etc., are revealed as cameo roles designed to show off the virtuoso skills of a crude but self-assured actor. This is not to say that Tolstoy was in control, or that he was hypocritically pretending to be any of these figures; merely that the

> instinct in a novelist of trying on masks is so strong that it will continue even after the practice of fiction has been abandoned. (Wilson 1989, 305)[1]

If Wilson is correct, Tolstoi was interested in eldership and holy foolishness only as *forms*, not as genuine expressions of religious piety. Was this mere histrionics, part of an ingenious stage production, as Wilson would have us believe? I think not, and will in the following attempt to show that Tolstoi's attitude toward eldership was highly ambivalent. On the one hand, he held the individual elders whom he had met in very low esteem, but at the same time he highly respected the institution of eldership as a form of piety. Moreover, he emulated this institution in his own practice of spiritual guidance; several contemporary observers identified him as a new and "modern" kind of elder. In my view, eldership to Tolstoi was not a "mask" to hide behind, but a religious and pedagogical practice readily available in the Eastern Orthodox tradition that he remoulded for new purposes.

The Elders and Spiritual Guidance in Traditional Orthodox Theology

An *elder* was usually an experienced monk (and some nuns) endowed with special gifts of spiritual wisdom and who acted as a mentor for other monks/nuns. Such persons often sought out total isolation in the wilderness before returning to human company to share the fruits of their spiritual experiences. The institution of eldership was linked to the prominent place of asceticism in monastic piety. The path of self-denial was considered to be so fraught with difficulties and perils that anyone wishing to pursue it required the support of someone who had gone before.

Between the elder and his disciples a powerful, almost unbreakable, bond of obedience prevailed (Pärt 2010, 147). Although the first Eastern monks had considered obedience as ranking below the other classical monastic virtues of celibacy and poverty (Chadwick 1978, 179), in the Western tradition originating with St Benedict, obedience became the hub around which the whole life of the monastery revolved. In places where eldership gained a following in the East, Orthodox monastic pietism was also distinguished by the prominence accorded to obedience, even though it differed clearly from the Benedictine model. While Roman Catholic

[1] Also Rosamund Bartlett (Bartlett 2010, 333) uses the expression "mask" to describe Tolstoi's attitude toward holy foolishness.

monks take vows regarding the monastic rules and the community (personified in the abbot), the dominant form of Orthodox obedience, both historically and today, is much more a personal relationship between the novice and his personal mentor or advisor.

The term "elder" or *starets* is a translation of the Greek word *geron*, meaning "old man," which in the ancient Greek church designates a special kind of spiritual adviser. The elder was not necessarily the oldest monk in the monastery or most senior in rank: Instead, the title indicates profound respect for that person's spiritual maturity.

An elder might have one or many disciples, and there could be one or several elders in the same monastery. There were no predetermined procedures according to which elders were selected and appointed. The service was purely charismatic, based solely on the belief of the other monks that the elder was in possession of special faculties to guide others. A new elder could be chosen by the novices or nominated by a previous elder as his successor. Ordination to the priesthood was not a requirement: Indeed, the elder institution bypassed the established, hierarchical order in the monastery (Pärt 2010).[2] In *The Brothers Karamazov* Dostoevskii gives a literary account of the tensions that this could engender. While not denying that the authority of the elder could lend itself to misuse, Dostoevskii nonetheless describes the service as "a thousand-year-old instrument for the moral regeneration of mankind from slavery to freedom and to moral perfection" (Dostoevskii 1888, 13, 37).

Novices were not the only persons to seek the spiritual and practical guidance of the elders. Lay people did so, too. It was widely believed that elders possessed prophetic as well as therapeutic skills. Questions put to them might range from how to save one's soul to whom one's daughter should wed. It was usual for the spiritual children of an elder to confess their sins to him. This "confession" was not necessarily of a sacramental nature. Nevertheless, it was frequently confused with the Church's institutionalised sacrament of penance, not least because an elder would often prescribe a form of *epitimiia* – an ecclesiastical sanction or penance (see Smirnov 1905, 19).

Individual, spiritual counseling was not unknown in the West either, as distinct from the sacrament of confession. For instance, Teresa of Avila wrote in her autobiography, "the novice is in need of advice to know with

2 Patrick Lally Michelson maintains that apologists of philokalic asceticism, which the reinvigorated movement of elders was a part of, "were calling into question, perhaps unwittingly, the vertical, centralized structure of the Russian church" (Michelson 2017, 149).

certainty what benefits him the most. To this end an advisor is of the utmost importance, but he must be a man of experience" (Teresa of Avila [before 1567] 1963, 79). In Roman Catholicism, however, this did not result in the same antagonism as in the East because, for one thing, the spiritual mentor was almost always an ordained priest. As one Western scholar explains,

> Spiritual direction in Western Christianity, in particular, has usually connoted a more limited, less personal relationship than the phenomenon of spiritual master and disciple in other spiritual traditions. Spiritual direction in Western Christianity became increasingly the province of ordained clergy. Because of the link to sacramental confession it often tended to have a strong moral emphasis, ……. .
>
> The care of souls in Orthodox Christianity focused on the pursuit of holiness in general rather than the more narrow concern or morality. Above all, the Christian East has always retained a strong sense of the role of the Holy Spirit–the pneumatic element in guidance of souls.. (Corcoran 1985, 445)

A concise presentation of the ideology underlying the Orthodox *institutional elderdom* as understood in Russia in Tolstoi's time is provided by the signature *Pustynnozhitel'* ("Desert hermit") in the journal *Dushepoleznoe Chtenie* (1906). The author of the article feels a need to respond to claims that eldership is a wasteful and useless invention and thus indirectly acknowledges the controversial nature of this form of spirituality. Even among monks he has heard allegations that this institution of spiritual guidance is characterized by its proclivity to inform on people and spread gossip. "Desert hermit" himself holds the opposite view: Eldership represents a necessary precondition for the regeneration of Russian monasticism. Only monasteries that establish the institution will have any chance to experience spiritual growth (Pustynnozhitel′ 1906, 2, 211).

"Desert hermit" wants first of all to show that eldership is deeply rooted in the Scriptures. In several places in the Old Testament, terms for "old" and "eldest" are translated as "elder," especially for expressing respect for old age (Lev 19, 32; Deut 28, 50; Job 5, 10). In cases in which the elder is given a special advisory role, the Scriptural passage is construed as lending support to the office of the eldership (Deut 32, 7, cited by Pustynnozhitel' 1906, 2, 217).

Of particular importance as a justification of eldership is the example of Jesus Himself. "I am the way," He said to His disciples (John 14, 6), and undoubtedly meant by this that he who aspires to perfection must follow Him in all things (Pustynnozhitel' 1906, 2, 212). But, according to the evangelists, the role of Jesus as counselor is so exceptional that no one should attempt to follow it. "Neither be ye called masters: For one is your Master, even Christ" (Matt 23, 10). In the eldership tradition it is therefore not the *teaching* of Jesus that is stressed as an example, but His humility. Jesus is the prototype not of the elder, but of the elder's *disciple*, and shows the necessity of subjecting oneself to the will of another. "For I came down from heaven, not to do mine own will, but the will of him that sent me" (John 6, 38). In Gethsemane, Jesus entreated the Father, "not as I will, but as thou wilt" (Matt. 26, 39), and showed thereby that he was "obedient unto death, even the death of the cross" (Phil. 2, 8) (Pustynnozhitel' 1906, 2, 211; see also Smolitsch 1936, 25–26).

If the elder–disciple relationship is regarded as analogous to that between God the Father and God the Son, the underlying pretensions become considerable. The elder acts with divine authority, and those who will submit themselves to him must bend their own will and entire thinking to the will of the elder. Obedience must be total and all-inclusive, flowing from genuine love of, and faith in, the elder. A disciple must be willing to lay bare his life even in the smallest details. It is impossible to renounce one elder for another. Not even when the orders of the elder cause bewilderment or seem far too strict is criticism of his decisions permissible (Pustynnozhitel' 1906, 6, 203).

"Desert hermit" uses most of his article to provide support for eldership by reference to the writings of the Church Fathers, those quoted in *Dobrotoliubie* in particular. Several of the authors represented in this collection champion the cause of eldership. Here I limit myself to those included in the Old Church Slavic edition, which Tolstoi read. Callistus and Ignatius assert that he who will walk with the Lord without stumbling on the path of silence must choose perfect obedience. He must therefore do his utmost to find a mentor and guide in whom the Spirit resides and who lives as he preaches.

> When you have found such a one, you must cling to him body and soul as a devoted son clings to his father. From then on you must obey all his commands, agree with him in all things, and regard him not simply as a human being, but as if he were Christ Himself. (*Dobrotoliubie* 1902, l, section 2, 58b)

The elder shall be the disciple's prototype (*pervoobraz*) whom the disciple is to emulate as if he were his own mirror image. True, it had occasionally happened that some of the Holy Fathers in past centuries succeeded in attaining divine silence and perfection without such obedience, but this was due to a special God-given faculty that is given to only a very few, Callistus and Ignatius claim (*Dobrotoliubie* 1902, 1, section 2, 61a).

Similarly, Simeon the New Theologian entreats the monk to beseech God with tears to deliver a holy guide for him (*Dobrotoliubie* 1902, 1, section 1, 55a). The reason given is that he who obeys the will of another will not only learn self-denial but will become as if dead to the world (*Dobrotoliubie* 1902, 1 section 1, 56a).

> The devils rejoice when a man gainsays his [spiritual] father, but he who humbles himself before him even unto death awakes the amazement of the angels. For such a man performs God's deeds and emulates God's Son, He who obeyed his Father even unto death, yea, even death on a cross. (*Dobrotoliubie* 1851, section I, 56b)

Here the obedience of the disciple is compared with that of Jesus, and Simeon does not hesitate to draw the logical conclusion: The elder stands in the place of the Lord. "Regard your teacher and guide as you would regard God Himself, then you cannot gainsay him" (*Dobrotoliubie* 1902, 1, section 1, 55a). Such advice appears to indicate that Simeon advocates blind submission to the authority of the elder. However, he also introduces an important distinction between good and bad teachers and emphasizes the importance of being able to distinguish between them. He gives two main criteria to help in making such discernment. Firstly, the elder, by his way of life, must demonstrate that he follows the path of asceticism: He must have suppressed his passions. *Bezstrastie* is therefore an absolute prerequisite of a good elder. The other prerequisite is loyalty to Holy Scripture and tradition. The disciple is encouraged to investigate on his own (*sam*) the Bible and the ascetic writings of the Church Fathers and hold their meaning up "as a mirror" to the precepts instilled by his elder (*Dobrotoliubie* 1851, section 1, 55a). Thus, we see that the disciple's own faculty of judgment is not ruled out after all. Even though the substance of the teachings of the elder must be judged according to objective, external criteria – the Scriptures and tradition – in the end, the disciple himself must determine whether he is able to find consistency. Apparently, however, this critical examination must take place only during the period under which the elder is *being selected.* From the moment a true guide has been found, his word counts as indubitable law.

At times during the history of Orthodoxy, the institution of the elder was partly disregarded or even forgotten. After a lengthy period of decline, it was reactivated by Simeon the New Theologian in the eleventh century. Simeon won few disciples over in his own lifetime, however, and it was not until the 1300s that his thinking was revived and elaborated upon within the Hesychast tradition. This mysticism was developed primarily on Mt Athos, but had offshoots in Russia, with Nil Sorskii as the leading spokesman of the movement. His group of "trans-Volga elders" encountered opposition from powerful sources within the Russian Church and was dissolved in the course of the 1500s (Bolshakoff 1977, 18–38). When Paisii Velichkovskii's disciples reintroduced the eldership institution in the early 1800s, the institution was seen as an innovation, and many monks held critical views.

In Russia, the Optina Pustyn' monastery in the *guberniia* of Kaluga close to the town of Kozelsk occupied a special place in the eldership movement. It had been founded back in the Middle Ages and had survived many periods of decline, but around the year 1700 there were no more than about a dozen monks. Optina did not experience a spiritual blossoming until early in the 1800s under its abbot Moses, who had become acquainted with Paisii's revivalist movement. Under the leadership of Moses, Leonid (Nagolkin) (1768–1841) became attached to the monastery in 1829 as its first elder. Makarii (Ivanov) (1788–1860) succeeded Leonid as elder in 1839. The last of the three great Optina elders was Amvrosii (Grenkov) (1812–91) who became elder on the death of Makarii. Makarii and Amvrosii were ordained priests, in contrast to Leonid, who was not (Bolshakoff 1977, 164–95).

The elders did not live within the monastery itself but dwelled in a *skit* – a smaller separate community – some distance away in the forest. Life in a *skit* is something somewhere between the total isolation of the hermit and the ordered world of the coenobitic monastery. The elder participated in the liturgical community of the monastery only on feast days and other special occasions. Otherwise he said his prayers alone or in the company of a few disciples.

Amvrosii was denied the opportunity to live a life of a recluse devoted to meditation. Most of his working days were devoted to receiving visitors and providing counsel or spiritual guidance. In addition he dictated hundreds of replies to persons who had contacted him in writing. So widespread was his fame that it became difficult to attend to the numbers of people queuing in front of his hut. Many waited for days at a time before gaining entry – some even for weeks. Amvrosii had three assistants who grouped the crowd according to sex and rank. The men were received first, then the women. The evening was set aside for talks with the monastery's own monks. Prominent visitors, however, could expect to be granted an audience without having to wait in line.

As a rule, Amvrosii formulated his advice in concise sentences, often in rhyme. He always said that those who approached him must acknowledge his words as the will of God. If they did not, then his advice would be useless. He warned that people who did not act in accordance with his directions would experience adversity and misfortune (Bolshakoff 1977, 193). Countless were the stories of his prophetic gifts and there were many who said that they had been cured after his intercession on their behalf (Smolitsch 1936, 199–202).

Excerpts from Amvrosii's letters of spiritual guidance, published in several volumes, generally contain fairly conventional Orthodox admonishments. The advice he gave tended to revolve around attending Confession and Communion with greater frequency, the observance of stricter fasts, and, above all, demonstrating greater humility. The term "humility" as used by Amvrosii nearly always had connotations to "obedience." The obligation to subject oneself to authority – be it the Church, or one's parents and guardians – was a recurrent theme ("The egg should not teach the hen to lay") (Amvrosii [Grenkov] 1908, 86 and 125). Among other things, he defended the support lent by the Church to the military power of the State, by saying that all authority would be undermined if the Church were to advocate actions contrary to those pursued by the State (Amvrosii [Grenkov] 1908, 203–05).

* * *

Several Russian men of letters visited Optina Pustyn'. In Makarii's time, the writers Nikolai Gogol and Aleksei Khomiakov, the philosopher Ivan Kireevskii and the historian Mikhail Pogodin all made pilgrimages there. Fedor Dostoevskii visited Amvrosii in 1878 together with his younger friend, the philosopher Vladimir Solov'ev. It is generally assumed that Amvrosii is one of the figures on whom the character of Father Zosima in *The Brothers Karamazov* – which Dostoevskii was working on at the time – is modeled.

Since Optina Pustyn' is located fairly close to Iasnaia Poliana, it is probable that Tolstoi visited the monastery in his adolescence or youth (Orekhanov 2016, 552), but we have no information about that. What we do know is that the year before Dostoevskii's visit, in July 1877, Tolstoi had called on Amvrosii, together with Nikolai Strakhov. This was during Tolstoi's "Orthodox period," and he evidently had high hopes for the meeting. In a letter to Aleksandra Tolstaia dated February 1877, he touched on his reasons for setting out on the journey: Both he and

Strakhov were convinced that it was impossible to live without religion, but nevertheless could not get themselves to believe, he explained. Tolstoi wanted to present his predicament to the monks at Optina (Tolstoi PSS 62, 311).

The evidence is conflicting as to what Tolstoi actually gained from the visit. According to his wife, the wisdom, sophistication and conduct of the monks had pleased him greatly (S. A. Tolstaia 1978, 1, 503). Aleksandra A. Tolstaia claims that Tolstoi returned "utterly persuaded of our Church's holiness and truth" (A. A. Tolstaia 1911, 22). However, Tolstoi's biographers describe the meeting with Amvrosii as a disappointment (Tolstaia 1975, 221–22). According to some sources, Tolstoi had begun to cross-examine the elder on his interpretation of the Gospels, and was not particularly impressed with the answers rendered by Amvrosii. The elder, in turn, was apparently just as unhappy about the visit as Tolstoi – but also on this point opinion is divided.[3] With his friend Pavel Matveev (who was an Orthodox believer) as the source, Nikolai Strakhov wrote to Tolstoi to say that "the fathers [at Optina] are full of your praise and are of the opinion that you have a beautiful soul" (N. Strakhov 1914, 126). Tolstoi replied that it gave him great pleasure to recall the elders (Tolstoi PSS 62, 338).[4]

According to Pavel Matveev, while Tolstoi was at Optina he received news from home that one of his children had become seriously ill. He broke off the trip earlier than originally intended, but paid Amvrosii a farewell visit. The elder gave a performance of his prophetic gifts, declaring that the child's condition was not grave. Tolstoi could therefore safely conclude his fast at the monastery before returning home, he said. If not, he would suffer depression and despondency. Tolstoi chose not to follow this advice, and Matveev sets this event in connection with the thoughts of suicide which, according to *A Confession*, were to plague Tolstoi during these years (P. Matveev 1907, 4, 153–55; see also Tolstoi PSS 23, 12–13).

Whatever the outcome of this first visit to Optina, Tolstoi returned four years later, in June 1881, traveling together with his valet Arbuzov. This

3 According to one report, on taking his departure, Tolstoi had kissed Amvrosii on the cheek. This was an ordinary way of showing respect in Russia in secular contexts, but inappropriate in a relationship between a man of God and a lay believer. Amvrosii firmly believed therefore that Tolstoi had done this to ward off the blessing the elder was about to confer on him. This the elder judged to be an expression of spiritual arrogance; he had been so reduced by his conversation with Tolstoi that he was hardly able to breathe afterwards (V. E. 1902, 128).

4 Pavel Basinskii writes that "the monks detected an elder in him. They understood that not in his writings but in his very way of life Tolstoi was closer to the archetype of Christian ascetic (*podvizhnik*) than many in the official clergy (Basinskii 2019, 500). Basinskii, however, does not reveal which source/s he bases this claim on.

time Tolstoi kept a diary of the trip, where he recorded his impressions. In the queue outside Amvrosii's cell, he probed the reasons why others had come to the elder. Can a *panikhida* be prayed for the departed soul of a husband who has drunk himself to death during a baptism? Another wanted to inquire if he ought to make a pilgrimage to the Holy Land. Others were concerned with questions of a more mundane nature. Will my daughter ever be married? Should I build a house? One person wondered if he ought to start a business or open a tavern. Tolstoi's notes do not reveal whether he himself saw such concerns as trivial or subjects worthy of an elder's attention (Tolstoi PSS 49, 143).

During this visit, Tolstoi spent several hours together with the elders, who were aware of his free-thinking position and attempted to steer him back into the Orthodox fold. The conversation came to revolve largely around the authority of the Church. Amvrosii is credited with saying that the writings of the Church Fathers and the resolutions adopted by the Church Councils are revelations of God in line with the Gospels and the Letters of the New Testament. He also approached the subject of the hierarchic order in heaven: As there is a difference between a general, a colonel, and a lieutenant on earth, so will there be differences in rank in the Kingdom of heaven. Tolstoi found the analogy distasteful, to put it mildly, and suspected that Amvrosii was concerned about his own future ranking in the hereafter (Tolstoi PSS 49, 144).[5]

If opinion is divided on the end result of Tolstoi's first visit to Optina, then consensus is no greater on his impressions after his second visit. According to the signature "V. E." in the Orthodox journal *Dushepoleznoe Chtenie* (1911), Tolstoi is said to have spoken of Amvrosii as being "a totally holy man." "When you speak with such a person, you

[5] Tolstoi claims that he caught Amvrosii out misquoting Matthew 18, 15–17: "Moreover if thy brother shall trespass against thee . . . let him be unto thee as a heathen man and a publican." In these verses the Eastern Church finds its most important endorsement of Church discipline, and Amvrosii often refers to them in his letters of guidance (see, for instance, Amvrosii 1908, 86). Tolstoi relates that Amvrosii left out the words "against thee" (Tolstoi PSS 49, 144). However, a misrepresentation such as this cannot be said to impinge upon the meaning of the text; and it is far from "flagrant," as Henri Troyat has asserted (Troyat 1980, 568). The two words Amvrosii skipped over are not to be found in the oldest handwritten scripts and have also been removed from many recent translations of the Bible. The situation is slightly ironic: In *What I Believe* Tolstoi accused the Orthodox Bible translators of deliberately twisting the words of Jesus when they keep to a newer, fuller textual variant (Tolstoi PSS 23, 348–55). At Optina, however, he attempted almost to make a heretic out of Amvrosii because he recites the shorter and older version. As early as in *Examination of Dogmatic Theology* Tolstoi had branded the treatment by the Orthodox of these verses as unreliable (Tolstoi PSS 23, 261). Neither Tolstoi himself nor any of his biographers appear to have noticed this inconsistency (see, for instance, Biriukov 1905–23, vol II, 389).

sense the presence of God" (V. E. 1911, 23). This statement has subsequently been repeated by several biographers and commentators of Amvrosii (Chetverikov 1912, 271; Smolitsch 1936, 198; Fueloep-Miller 1960, 109–10); in a modern Amvrosii biography, it is even reproduced in epigrammatic form on the jacket (Dunlop 1972). In the oldest biography of Amvrosii (Agapit 1900), however, there is no reference whatsoever to any such utterance: There is good reason to believe that it is a later apocryphal addition. We know that Tolstoi was aware of its existence (*Biblioteka* 1972, Ia, 273–74). and did not disclaim it – but it does not rhyme well with Tolstoi's own notes, and most of his biographers have preferred to ignore it. Biriukov alleges that Tolstoi "returned home with an even poorer view than the first time" (Biriukov 1905–23, II, 388), and Tolstoi's daughter Aleksandra writes that the stay at the monastery "pushed him even further away from Orthodoxy" (A. L. Tolstaia 1975, 242).[6]

Nevertheless, we must conclude that Tolstoi found it impossible to rid himself of thoughts of Amvrosii. In February 1890 we find him in the Optina monastery for the third time, now accompanied by two of his daughters. According to some reports, he is held to have said after the meeting, "I am shaken, shaken" (V. E. 1911, 24; Chetverikov 1912, 271). Judging from Tolstoi's diaries, however, the outcome of the meeting was rather slim. Amvrosii is characterized as "pathetic." "Woe be to them [the monks], for they live off the labour of others," he wrote in his diary during the visit. Therefore, it is surprising to read that he felt that he had learned, during this visit, to show tolerance toward Orthodoxy (Tolstoi PSS 52, 23).

Amvrosii died the year after Tolstoi's last visit, and his successors as the elders of Optina, Anatolii and Iosif, lacked the former's fame and reputation. The stream of pilgrims to the monastery tailed off, nor did Tolstoi visit the elders again.[7] However, Tolstoi was to make a final trip to Optina. In October 1910, when he left his home for good, he lodged at the monastery inn there (see Chapter 6). During this stay he seriously contemplated requesting a meeting with the elders. Twice he started out in the direction of the *skit*, but on both occasions he changed direction and wandered into the forest instead (Makovitskii 1979, IV, 404–06).

6 Aylmer Maude reproduces Tolstoi's positive account of Amvrosii but notes that its trustworthiness may be open to discussion (Maude 1905, II, 75).

7 According to the *Jubilee Edition* of Tolstoi's collected works, volumes 53 and 83, he is said to have traveled to Optina in 1896 (Tolstoi PSS 53, 453; Tolstoi PSS 83, 239). This has been refuted by Nikolai Gusev and is in all likelihood incorrect (N. Gusev 1960, 215).

It is impossible on the basis of such fragmentary evidence to form any firm conclusions regarding Tolstoi's opinion of the activities of the Optina monks. It does seem, however, that neither monastery life in general, nor the teachings of the elders in particular, held much appeal for Tolstoi. Neither does Amvrosii's personality appear to have made a favorable impression. But, given that Tolstoi returned time after time, there must have been *something* he was looking for at Optina Pustyn' that he was unable to find elsewhere.

In many ways it seems as if Tolstoi was just as taken by the "atmosphere" surrounding the elder's *skit* as by the actual discussions on spiritual matters with the elder. In the travelers' dining room and in the queue outside the elder's house, he absorbed impressions. Whereas the people around him had come to experience the elder, Tolstoi came apparently just as much to study *eldership* as a religious-cultural institution; in time, he himself began to act as a heterodox elder.

As we have seen, the service of the elder was linked to the person rather than to the monastic institution as such. As early as in the case of Makarii and Amvrosii, the connection to the monastery was looser than it was for the ordinary monks: The elders lived half a *verst* from the main buildings and were mostly exempt from having to follow the rules of the monastery. Since eldership was an independent, autonomous service, it was possible to detach it even further from its monastic environment and situate it within a new framework outside the Church.

As a preacher Tolstoi did not travel the roads as a popular speaker but received visitors at Iasnaia Poliana, people who came to ask for spiritual guidance and advice. During the final years of Tolstoi's life, his home had become as popular a pilgrimage site as the Optina monastery. Like the monks, Tolstoi was sought out by the common folk as much as by representatives of the intelligentsia. Tolstoi was loath to turn people away without having considered their case, "since he had no right, he felt, to forsake the faithful. He was a lay equivalent of the elder Amvrosii," according to his biographer Henri Troyat (Troyat 1980, 652). Iasnaia Poliana had no inn for pilgrims, but no one was hindered from spending the night there. Everyone found somewhere to lie down for the night, in the main building, in the servants' quarters, or simply in a shed.

Tolstoi's last secretary, Valentin Bulgakov, has given an account of the motivations underlying people's desire to meet Tolstoi. Some came to win his support for some cause or another, such as a peace congress or a new school development. One said that he was a police spy and was hoping to find moral support in his struggle to unmask the revolutionaries. Many asked for money, for instance to finance a dowry, an education, or to escape from the country. One lady's prime ambition was obviously to secure a "relic," to which end she asked for a strand of hair from Tolstoi's head (V. Bulgakov 1957, 167). Others, however, sought spiritual guidance. A consumptive Tolstoian confessed, on a bench in the park, that his illness tormented him (V. Bulgakov 1957, 62–70). It was Bulgakov's job to answer routine enquiries and attend to the least needy among the callers. In many ways he functioned as a counterpart to Amvrosii's *keleinik*, the lay brother who assisted the elder.

Tolstoi received quantities of letters from people wanting to know his opinion on various questions. No fewer than 50,000 such letters have been preserved. Following the publication of *The Kreutzer Sonata,* a great many letters arrived inquiring about his opinion on matters concerned with married life (Møller 1983, 130–41). Advice by letter from elders was no novelty. Amvrosii's correspondence had been voluminous, and Bishop Feofan the Recluse, throughout his time as a hermit, had kept in touch with his flock solely with the aid of the postal services.

Tolstoi replied to most enquiries, irrespective of whether they came from high or low. The majority of his answers have been preserved, and comprise an important background for understanding his work as spiritual advisor. A striking feature is the heterogeneity of his answers. In *The Path of Life* Tolstoi wrote, "Christianity does not set out the same rules of life for everybody" (Tolstoi PSS 45, 125). This was an insight that only to a small degree found expression in his public writings, where general, categorical utterances abound. In his letters of guidance, however, Tolstoi was at pains to individualize his advice as much as possible, commensurate with the petitioner's situation. This was why he often wrote for further details concerning a person's circumstances before offering concrete advice (Tolstoi PSS 75, 55).

A great deal depended on the tone, the atmosphere, of the letter addressed to him. In 1904, within the space of two weeks, Tolstoi received letters from two women who desired to know whether it would be appropriate to take part in (the Russian–Japanese) war as nurses. One of them denounced such Samaritan participation in war, and Tolstoi was in complete agreement with her (Tolstoi PSS 75, 42). The other was less decided; to her, Tolstoi wrote that this was a question she must try to resolve on her own. The essence of the matter concerned the attitude with which she intends to play her part (Tolstoi PSS 75, 35–36). This latter piece of advice is typical of many of Tolstoi's replies. He indicates a few general guidelines, then sends the ball back into the court of the enquirer.

It was important for him to stress the need for personal independence and responsibility. As an elder, Tolstoi had no wish to function as an oracle but rather as a "Socratic midwife."

On the other hand, others received very specific recommendations and diagnoses: "When you complain of fits of cheerlessness, it merely shows that your soul in ordinary circumstances is a strong soul. With all my heart and soul, there is nothing I want more than that you more and more often and more and more powerfully will acknowledge yourself as God's son and live for Him" (Tolstoi PSS 75, 54). In some cases, Tolstoi attached a prediction to his advice:

> I think it would be best for you to return to your father and do try to induce in yourself good sentiments regarding his person. If you are successful in this, it will induce similar sentiments in him towards yourself. (Tolstoi PSS 75, 62)

A recurrent feature in his replies is that Tolstoi recommends the writer to endure his or her circumstances, even when this compels them to lead a life that conflicts with Tolstoi's teachings. A young cadet writes to say that he wants to leave the naval academy and establish himself as an honest farmer. Tolstoi dampens his aspirations: "If it is at all possible [for you] to continue in your present walk of life, then do so" (Tolstoi PSS 75, 68). A priest who wants to leave the service of the Church is requested to think carefully through his intentions. The path he would follow will be a path of self-sacrifice and martyrdom (Tolstoi PSS 75, 76). One Tolstoian wonders if he ought not to yield to his parents' entreaties to arrange a church wedding. He is told that it is extremely difficult to set oneself apart from the conventions of society without simultaneously breaking God's most important commandment: Love of one's neighbor (Tolstoi PSS 75, 4).

People requesting the elucidation of general points in Tolstoianism without mentioning any connection to problems in their personal life are usually referred to his published writings, or asked to exemplify their question (e.g., Tolstoi PSS 75, 50). The prayers of autograph hunters are often answered (Tolstoi PSS 75, 92), whereas people requesting money are generally bluntly reproached:

> You seem to forget that I receive several letters like yours every day, and even though I might be of a mind to do so, I am not in a position to satisfy your wishes . . . . Be so kind not to write to me more often. (Tolstoi PSS 75, 22)

Tolstoi finishes this letter by wishing the addressee "greater peace and humbleness." As did Amvrosii, Tolstoi demanded a certain amount of respect from his supplicants before meeting them halfway. Nonetheless, appeals for money continued to pour in, and in 1907 Tolstoi felt compelled to place an announcement in two of the country's largest papers, making it plain that requests of that nature would not be countenanced (N. Gusev 1973, 54).

It occurred that Tolstoi was approached by people entertaining thoughts of suicide or suffering from serious nervous ailments (see, for instance, Tolstoi PSS 75, 51). On several such occasions he said that he found it taxing to have to bear the distress of so many strangers. After a young seminarian had visited him for help with his masturbation problem, Tolstoi wrote in his diary,

> I was absolutely unable to give him any help at all. I spoke with him and gave him the money I had on my person. This is possibly one of the most difficult situations: A young person has completely exaggerated and fallacious ideas about me .... He comes here expecting total redemption, and nothing happens .... This is a *drawback*[8] of my otherwise enjoyable situation. The essential thing is not to hurry. And I who didn't even pray in his presence, together with him. (Tolstoi PSS 50, 63)

The need to approach all deeds with prayer was something Tolstoi had learned not least from the elders: "Yea, *everything, everything must be performed with prayer*, as also the elders have said. Not merely by a prayer of words, but by thinking of God and His will," he noted in his diary a month later (Tolstoi PSS 50, 79, emphasis in the original). In fact, this was closer to the elders' concept of prayer than Tolstoi admits: The elders made efforts to detach themselves from word-prayers, to cultivate the mystical inner prayer of the heart that prays itself incessantly.

There is considerable evidence that the role of the elder was a role into which Tolstoi was forced first and foremost by his countless adherents and admirers. As so many other elders, he saw his counseling responsibilities as a cross he had no choice but to bear, and he accepted it as a necessary aspect of his work. It troubled him that he seldom managed to live up to the expectations his visitors had of him. In April 1909, Tolstoi wrote in his diary, "As I went out onto the balcony, I was surrounded by supplicants, and I was simply unable to show kindness to all of them" (Tolstoi PSS 57, 51). Two nights before, Tolstoi had seen one of the Optina elders in a dream. (Which of them he was unable to recall.) The elder sent a letter to Tolstoi containing many paragraphs of "beautiful, calm and affectionate elder wisdom." Tolstoi was intrigued by especially one of the thoughts in

[8] Tolstoi used the English word in the original.

the letter: The elder had written that he was no longer able to teach anything or advise anybody to live this way or that. Firstly, he had realized that he was no wiser than others; secondly, that everything people need to know is already revealed in the Scriptures; thirdly, all that transpires in the external world is immaterial (*bezrazlichno*), and has absolutely no effect on people's possibilities of attaining inner, authentic rewards (Tolstoi PSS 57, 50).

This dream can be interpreted in a myriad of ways, of course. I shall simply indicate what I believe might be helpful for shedding light on Tolstoi's relationship to eldership. He was obviously struck by the paradox that one who himself was both an elder and teacher approached him to divulge his problems. The roles had been changed: Instead of Tolstoi coming to visit the elder, it was the elder who came to him. In the dream Tolstoi was acknowledged in some way as the "elders' elder." But this acknowledgment was undermined immediately thereafter. If the elder is unable to counsel others, then neither may Tolstoi. Tolstoi has no choice but to admit the relevance of the elder's arguments against spiritual guidance, simply because they had been culled from his own religious writings. Thus, the dream gives expression to both Tolstoi's self-awareness as a religious teacher and counselor, and to his doubts concerning the value of his work. We find a similar ambivalence in other entries in his diary for the same period. Three months later, Tolstoi wrote that "I cannot help but wonder why God has chosen (*izbral*) a reptile like myself through whom to communicate with mankind" (Tolstoi PSS 57, 93). Even though Tolstoi here describes himself as a reptile (*gadina*), he did not allow this to shake his conviction that he had a divine message to convey.

* * *

For most modern Russians at the turn of the nineteenth and twentieth centuries it was no longer *comme il faut* to visit the monks at Optina. They belonged to a bygone age. Above all they were associated with the official Church, which in turn was identified with the authority of the State. It was here that Tolstoi represented a "modern" alternative. Tolstoi's creed was purged not only of all forms of "superstition" but also of all connections with tsarism. One could travel to Iasnaia Poliana without being suspected of harboring reactionary sympathies and supporting the regime.

Among the people who called on Tolstoi was the well-known *fin-de-siècle* writer Leonid Andreev (1871–1919). In 1911, Andreev published his impressions in the magazine *Solntse Rossii*, giving what was almost a hagiographic account of Tolstoi, and asking: "Where else in this world would it be possible to meet such a good elder?" (Andreev 1911). Others, however, were extremely critical of their reception at Iasnaia Poliana. In 1909, a letter was published in the newspaper *Slovo* from an anonymous worker who described his unsuccessful meeting with Tolstoi: "I had hoped that he would be able to read, to define, the spiritual condition I was in, that he would understand and help me, etc. Good God! How I was suffering at the time. But the great thinker did nothing for me." The worker had shown Tolstoi a few small articles he had penned but was advised to burn them as soon as possible – they were that hopeless. Finally, Tolstoi had asked if he did not feel inclined to go by the kitchen to get some food, thus letting him understand that the audience was at an end (Chepurin 1909, 115). Episodes such as this were exploited by Orthodox anti-Tolstoian writers who claimed that Tolstoi's interest in his visitors was limited to the materials they could furnish for his writings (ibid.).

Among the first people to draw a parallel between Tolstoi's work as proselytizer and eldership was Nikolai Mikhailovskii (1842–1904), one of the leaders of the Narodnik movement. Mikhailovskii surmised that Tolstoi, like Gogol' and Dostoevskii before him, had a penchant for telling others what to think. Prior to 1880 there had been a certain balance in Tolstoi's teachings: While preaching fatalism and obscurantism with his "left hand," his "right hand" was engaged in public debate. After his religious conversion, however, the right hand had withered completely away: The great Russian man of letters had become left-handed.

> He despises, quite simply, life, with all its complicated forms. He has dug for himself "a monk's cell under a fir tree" and allows everybody to come and pray. From his cell he peers out with derision on the whole of the created world: thrall or freeman, barge-pullers or independent noblemen – everything is insignificant! Everything is inconsequential, nothing means anything, if only one listens to the elder in his cell under the fir tree. (Mikhailovskii 1886, 216)

Most of the people who identified Tolstoi with the role of elder did not do so with the intention of making a fool of him, but to pay homage. Not least after his death, "elder" became a frequently used epithet about him (see, for instance, Meilakh 1979 [1960], 29, 34, 37; Petrov 1978, 98). At this stage, the term "elder" was evidently perceived as a mark of respect that could be used to describe Tolstoi without having to convert to his creed. Soon after his death, a commemorative volume was published, including obituaries and other items on Tolstoi. Culled exclusively from the liberal and free-thinking press, they contained various crude attacks on the Church for its treatment of Tolstoi. The style was generally pretentious, the metaphors often hyperbolic. With the demise of Tolstoi, the world had become "fatherless" (*osirotel*); in other words, Tolstoi had been the "father" of mankind. Another term frequently used to describe him was "*elder*," often augmented by the prefix "the great." Nikolai Asheshov, in particular, invokes this term of honor repeatedly as if it were a litany and capitalizes the first letters of both components (*Pamiati* 1911, 33–35).

The Orthodox Bishop Nikon of Vologda protested that the enemies of the Church had stolen the name "elder" from the holy language of the Church to apply it to an apostate (*bogootstupnik*). In the opinion of Nikon, the term should be reserved solely for ascetics (*podvizhniki*) (Nikon 1910, 896). But it was far from only the enemies of the Church who applied the designation of "elder" to Tolstoi. It appears in the writings of Christian authors, too (for instance, Gladkov 1914, 54; D. Skvortsov 1911, 8; I. Grigor'ev 1912, 164). This supports the theory that the institution of eldership was perceived as a transplantable external form not indissolubly bound to a given spiritual content.

The opinion one had of Tolstoi could be expressed, moreover, by placing selected epithets in front of this title. To the reactionary Orthodox writer I. Aivazov, Tolstoi was a godless (*nechestivyi*) elder (Aivazov 1908, 1624), whereas the liberal ecclesiastical author N. Smolenskii employed the distinction "Honourable (*Mastityi*) elder" with an upper-case "H." The priest Dmitrii Kazanskii viewed Tolstoi as a "thinker-elder," in contrast to an "elder of the faith" (Kazanskii 1910, 1616). In fact, the elder designation has continued to be appended to Tolstoi's name by Orthodox apologists (for instance, Orekhanov 2016, 267). In 1939, the Archimandrite Ioann (Shakhovskoi) called Tolstoi an "elder" in the same breath that he asserted that the philosopher of Iasnaia Poliana was under the influence of the powers of darkness (Ioann [Shakhovskoi] 1939, 9, 14). In Vladislav Maevskii's *Lev Tolstoi's Tragic Search for God* (1952), Tolstoi is mentioned about a dozen times as an elder, without any apparent irony intended (Maevskii 1952, passim; see also Kontsevich 1960, 29).

Several Soviet scholars applied the appellation of elder to Tolstoi (for instance, Bonch-Bruevich 1929, 60); Meilakh [1960] 1979, 261, 274). However, in such cases, its significance had become considerably diluted. No longer did it refer to an authoritative spiritual counselor, but a pious, elderly man, with the stress on "elderly" ... thereby returning to its etymological starting point. This can also explain why "elder" came to be used with increasing frequency about Tolstoi as he grew older. The age aspect often resonates in the writings of ecclesiastical authors as well (e.g., A. Ivanov 1901a, 257–72; Rozhdestvin 1902, 14).

Tolstoi drew on the elder tradition in several of his novels. In *The Three Elders,* the title refers primarily to holiness and great age rather than anything to do with spiritual guidance. On their deserted island in the White Sea, the elders have no disciples – and would probably have been incapable of teaching them anything had they had any. On the contrary, they themselves become students of a bishop passing through on a ship who tries, unsuccessfully, to get them to learn The Lord's Prayer by heart. On the ultimate page, however, the tables are turned: As the elders, walking on the water, approach the bishop to ask him to repeat the words of the prayer once more since they had forgotten them again, he realizes that spiritual authority has little to do with book-learning. "'It is not I who should teach you. Pray for us sinners!' At which the bishop prostrated himself at the feet of the elders" (Tolstoi PSS 25, 105). After all, then, the three old men did qualify to be called elders, also in the technical sense.

It does not appear that Tolstoi ever styled himself "elder."[9] Tolstoi, however, was well aware that others classified him as an elder. For instance, he read the graffiti left by the visitors to Iasnaia Poliana in the gazebo in the grounds. Among the panegyric utterances there was a homage to "the great, famous elder." Two others left the signature "pilgrim." Tolstoi said that he found the inscriptions "uninteresting" (V. Bulgakov 1957, 397–99).

There were not only similarities between Optina Pustyn' and Iasnaia Poliana, there were obvious differences too, of course. Several of the attributes generally associated with an elder were not found in Tolstoi. The supernatural abilities of prophesy and healing were absent, as was the subjecting to spiritual authority. Tolstoi emerged as more of a "democratic" version of the invariant, with greater stress on dialogue than on commandments. We could say that Tolstoi took the form of the tradition, but employed it in a new context. To draw a perhaps daring parallel: In His teachings, Jesus continued the late Rabbinic tradition while also

[9] In 1913, the Orthodox priest Dmitrii Troitskii did print some letters Tolstoi had written to him in which the expression occurs: Tolstoi speaks of himself as "an eighty-two-year-old *starets* (D. Troitskii 1913, 41). In the *Jubilee Edition,* however, the same letter is published in a different version: *Starik* (old man) is here substituted for *starets* (Tolstoi PSS 82, 186). This difference is of little significance, however; in both cases it is quite obvious that Tolstoi's intention was to refer to his great age.

transcending it by His unprecedented and consummate interpretation of the authorities ("but I say unto you"). In like manner, Tolstoi embarked upon the Orthodox elder tradition but broke with it by giving it a new content. The same duality characterized his relationship to holy wanderers, to which we turn in Chapter 6.

CHAPTER 6

Tolstoi and the Wanderer Tradition in Russian Culture

The Russian word *strannichestvo* can be translated as "pilgrimage" – a concept familiar within the Roman Catholic Church as well. In the Russian concept of a *strannik* or wanderer, however, the focus is not primarily on reaching a sacred site in order to worship, but on the journey, on being underway. Wandering, movement, becomes a goal in its own right. In fact, Russian has a separate term to denote a conventional pilgrimage: *Palomnichestvo*. But *strannichestvo* and *palomnichestvo* cannot be kept strictly apart. Using an analogy from linguistics, we might say that they express the imperfective and perfect "aspect" of the same action: They relate to each other as a process to result, as "seek" to "find."[1]

Eastern Christian theologians find the *strannichestvo* motif in the Old as well as in the New Testament. The story of the Jewish people's forty-year wandering in the Sinai desert is perceived as an image of the Church, which is constantly on the move, ready to pull up the tent pegs and break camp. In 1 Peter 1, 17 we read of how the believers should live "while passing the time of your sojourning here." In the Russian translation of the Bible this is rendered "during that time while you are wandering" *(stranstvovanie)*. Hebr 11, 13 speaks of those who have died in the faith as "strangers and pilgrims on the earth" who have found their fatherland. Further: "For here we do not have an enduring city, but we are looking for the city that is to come" (Hebr 13, 14). "City" must here be taken to comprehend all manifestations of human civilization. The ideal of

[1] Implicit in the idea of the wanderer is the idea of the pilgrim/wanderer as an outsider, a foreigner – there is an etymological connection between *strannichestvo* and the Old Church Slavonic word *strannyi*, which means a stranger or a foreigner. The notion of *strannichestvo* thus has important ecclesiological implications not found to the same extent in the term *palomnichestvo*. The wanderer stands as living testimony to the fact that all God's children are pilgrims journeying to another destination. The Christian is but a "stranger" on this earth, underway to his true home, which is the Kingdom of God (see, e.g., V. Troitskii 1891, 2, 337–68). Thus, *strannichestvo* is an eschatological type of piety and devotion.

wandering thus has a clear culture-critical element: The Christian is not to settle down and accept life on earth – only find rest in the same way as, on the march, the foot rests momentarily against the ground.

Augustine is the Church Father who dealt most consistently with these ideas. In *De civitate Dei (The City of God)*, he seeks to show how humanity can be divided into two – the children of Satan, and the children of God. The former have Cain as their forefather, while Abel prefigures the Christian Church. In Genesis 4, 17 we read that Cain founded the first city on earth, whereas Abel, according to Augustine, was "a pilgrim and a stranger on earth" (Augustine 1981, 595–60: book xv, ch. 1). And, like Abel, also the Church wanders "like a pilgrim between the temptations of the world and God's salvation" (Augustine 1981, 835: book xvii, ch. 5).

Augustine's dynamic church model flourished in medieval times, in both literature and theology. In Dante's *Divina commedia* (1300–20), which in many ways recapitulates the entire medieval worldview, the Church is portrayed imaginatively as a wanderer. The journey in space – through Hell, Purgatory, and Heaven – is at the same time an educational process, morally and mentally. Also in the legend of the Holy Grail, search and wandering are central metaphors of the Christian life. In 1259, Bonaventura wrote a theological travel handbook (*Itinerarium*) for the soul's wandering in God. However, during Counter–Reformation, these ideas were gradually replaced by a more static conception of the Church as a *societas perfecta* characterized by its hierarchical structure. Also in the Eastern Church this model became increasingly common, but without ever gaining complete ascendancy. The restless, rootless attitude survived, as an underground current.

Eastern theologians took over the basic distinction of Western ecclesiology between "the struggling church" and the "triumphant church" – *ecclesia militans* and *ecclesia triumphalis*, but attached it directly to the motif of migration: The struggling Church on earth is the one that is on its way. It includes all Christ-believers, regardless of confessional attachment, as they participate in the wandering toward heaven. But only those who endure all the way to the final destination will inherit the Kingdom. "Therefore, we do not in any way confuse the wandering Church with the Church that has reached the Fatherland" (*Poslanie,* no year given, 17).

The wanderer has fascinated also many Russian thinkers. In Russia, the wandering motif was linked to a "nostalgia for space," claims Nicholas Arseniev ([1964] 1975). He explains the spread of *strannichestvo* in Russia as the result of theology and topography pulling in the same direction. The endless steppes of their country predisposed the people of Russia to the nomadic life of breaking camp, of wandering on and on (Arseniev 1975 [1964], 15–17). We find a similar view expressed by Grigorii Trubetskoi:

> Holy wandering – this is a form of folk-religiosity especially characteristic of the Russians. In religion, the Russian feels himself more of a wanderer than a settled dweller on this earth. He cares little for the externalities that earthly realities have to offer. For him, this world is one of evil and tribulation. He searches for God's Truth *(Pravda),* through prayer, asceticism and renunciation. (G. Trubetskoi 1931, 20)

Arseniev and Trubetskoi did not see the Russian wanderer as a deviant or oddity in society – on the contrary, in their view he represents a highly widespread way of thinking and acting. This was also the view of Nikolai Berdiaev, who in *The Russian Idea* described *strannichestvo* as "an extremely characteristic Russian phenomenon." This he interpreted in light of an alleged eschatological longing of the Russian people, with its millennial chiliasm and messianism, a longing that Berdiaev found also among the intelligentsia. In addition to the "physical wanderers" among the common people, Berdiaev speaks of "spiritual wanderers," "who lack the ability to resign themselves to the finite, and strive instead toward the infinite," searching for the Kingdom of God and the "distant things" (Berdiaev 1971 [1946], 199).

Most Russian scholars who have dealt with holy wandering have primarily been cultural historians, not theologians. A central work on holy wandering is *Wandering Russia, for the Sake of Christ* (1877), by the ethnographer Sergei Maksimov. For Maksimov it is important to demonstrate the considerable variety among Russia's wanderers and wayfarers. He shows that there could be widely differing reasons underlying the decision to set off for the open road. Some wanderers were *pogoreltsy* – victims of fire; others had been driven from house and home by creditors. Some were blind or had some other handicap that made normal work impossible. And yet others opted for the beggar's life of their own accord, simply because they enjoyed the lifestyle of a vagabond (Maksimov 1877, 271).

But there were also many who chose the wandering life as a way to salvation – and these were wanderers in the strict sense of the term. Also within this category there were many subgroups. Some aimed only at visiting one or two holy places before returning home, whereas others would keep on going until their legs could no longer carry them. There were wanderers who had sworn an *obet,* a voluntary, sacred oath, to dedicate some years of their lives to God. Others had gone on pilgrimage as penance. The wanderer's life was a "God-pleasing holy feat (*podvig*)" (Maksimov 1877, 299). Somewhere in-between the religious wanderer and the worldly mendicant was the so-called *proshak,* who begged partly to sustain himself, but also in order to collect funds for a religious purpose – perhaps for building a new church. Often the *proshak* had been sent by his congregation, with the bishop's blessing (Maksimov 1877, 5–48).[2]

In nineteenth-century Russia, religiously motivated wandering had become a mass movement. Maksimov estimates that in the 1860s over 170,000 came to the Monastery of the Caves in Kiev every year, but he also observed that the numbers had been declining and thought that these pilgrimages might soon become a thing of the past. According to the German church historian H.-D. Döpmann, these wayfarers were actively opposed by the authorities, state as well as ecclesiastical. Wanderers were seen as an untidy, undesirable and disturbing element who, with their restless behavior and freedom from worldly cares and responsibilities, called in question the existing structures of society (Döpmann 1981, 167).

In another book, *Siberia and Penal Servitude* (1891), Sergei Maksimov tells of a *wanderer* arrested by the police in 1835. The wayfarer stated that he had taken a holy vow not to reveal his home or his name, and that he was answerable solely to God. The man was judged to be a vagabond and received thirty lashes of the whip, before being dispatched to Enisei in Siberia. Here he called himself only "one who wanders in this world" (*stranstvuiushchii v mire*). His was no city of man – what he sought was yet to come. Not until eighteen years later did he reveal his identity: He proved to be a former lieutenant with a regiment of the Guard, fluent in both French and German. At the age of twenty-eight he had decided to take up the life of a wanderer, and had been on his way to Jerusalem when he was arrested. Maksimov adds that this wanderer had accepted his fate without protesting (Maksimov 1891, 311–14). Reading this story in 1906, Tolstoi said that it had a "wonderful subject" that he wished to use (Tolstoi PSS 55, 182). However, Tolstoi never did write a story with that theme. On the other hand, already in the final chapters of *Resurrection* (1899) he had described a nameless, wandering old man who presented himself in this way: "'I have renounced everything: I have neither name nor home nor fatherland – nothing. What is my name? Man." For twenty-three years this person had been brought before the courts and examined

[2] Vera Shevzov (Shevzov 2004, 62–64) emphasizes that itinerant collectors were required to obtain a special collection book from their diocesan consistory, containing a declaration of his or her identity, the stated purpose of the collection and a record book of the amounts they collected. However, she adds that despite attempts to control the number of collectors the practice of persons setting out "on their own" to collect funds was common and often went unreported.

by priests, but he accepted his fate without opposition, knowing that also Christ had been persecuted (Tolstoi PSS 32, 419).

During 1861–64, the folklorist Petr Bessonov (1828–1898) issued a two-volume work on *Wandering Pilgrims*, in which he presented a large selection of the hymns sung by the religious wayfarers. From many of these songs it is apparent that the *wanderers* expected their just rewards to come only in the afterlife. A central biblical text here is the description of the Day of Judgment in Matt 25, which Bessonov relates as a tale in prose. On this day, the Devil will read aloud from the Book of Life and reveal the sins of the souls of the intractable. Jesus will reply that it was not for those who have failed to live by His laws on earth that he suffered and died, and that they shall be cast out into the utmost darkness. Then, in an almost Brechtian manner, Jesus turns to the people listening to this tale. And here He explains that He would long since have destroyed them, had not His Mother and the angels interceded for them.

> But I expect you to repent and turn from your wicked deeds, that you senseless beings begin to live according to the ways of righteousness and truth (*pravda*), remembering the poor and the wretched, and welcoming wanderers into your homes. (Bessonov 1861–64, 2, 74–75)

From this we see that although the wanderers may have directed their gaze primarily toward heaven, they also dreamed of social justice here on earth. Further, the narrator reminds his audience how it is easier for a camel to pass through the eye of a needle than for a rich man to enter into the Kingdom of Heaven. Tolstoi read Bessonov's book in 1884, underlining much of the text as he went – especially the tale of the Day of Judgment (*Biblioteka* 1972, Ia, 89–91).

Russian literature abounds in depictions of the life of the wanderers. In his poem "The Wanderer" (*Strannik*), Aleksandr Pushkin told of a crestfallen and broken man who breaks up from wife and children to find "the true way of salvation and the narrow gate" (Pushkin 1974, II, 366). More familiar to Western readers, perhaps, is Nikolai Leskov's story of *The Enchanted Wanderer*, where the main motif is that "human life is a pilgrimage through the sinful labyrinth of this world" (Børtnes 1988, 5). For many Russians, their first encounter with the spirituality of the wanderers has been through the poem "Vlas" by Nikolai Nekrasov. Vlas is an incorrigible, hardened peasant who in a fever-dream sees the torments awaiting him in Hell. He then sells his peasant hut and vows a holy *obet*: His body in chains, he begins to wander about, collecting money for a chapel. Also the works of Maksim Gorkii feature various *wanderers*, the best-known being old Luka in the play *The Lower Depths* (*Na dne*), who is presented as a wise man of the common people and a visionary. *The Lower Depths* shows that the religious wanderers did not belong to the countryside only, but were known also in the towns and cities of Russia.

For an understanding of the religious side of the phenomenon of wanderers, *A Wanderer's Plainspoken Stories to his Spiritual Father* (or "*The Way of a Pilgrim*" as is the standard English translation) is particularly important. This book, published in 1884 in Kazan, quickly became a classic within its genre. The author is anonymous, and while it has been conjectured that it was written by either the elder Amvrosii at Optina Pustyn or by Feofan Zatvornik (Govorov) ([Kazan' 1980–84] Paris 1973, 6), recent research has concluded that that is highly unlikely (Pentkovsky 1999).

The wanderer in *The Way of a Pilgrim* is a young man who is driven out on the open road in search of someone who can explain to him how it is possible to "pray incessantly" as we are encouraged to do in the New Testament (1 Thess 5, 17). He finds an elder who teaches him the Jesus Prayer, a prayer of the heart that prays itself in pace with the heartbeat. Although the wanderer has now found the answer to his question, he does not return to his village, but continues his journey through the vast spaces of Siberia. Around his neck he carries a copy of *Dobrotoliubie*, which gives him answers to practical as well as spiritual questions.

Another, less fictionalized tale of a wanderer from the nineteenth century is *The Story of the Wanderings and Travels of the Monk Parfenii*. When Parfenii set out on his life of wandering, he was an Old Believer, but underway he converted to the official Russian Church and took monastic vows at Mt Athos. Parfenii's journeys brought him to Moldavia, Turkey and the Holy Land. The book's typical blend of Old Church Slavonic with everyday expressions gives it a particularly authentic character.

Parfenii introduces himself as "a wanderer." "I do not have an enduring city in this rebellious world of vanity" (Parfenii 1855, 1, 1). At the same time, he presents his wayfaring life as filled with suffering and renunciation. As a wanderer, he journeyed about, without money or destination, with not even a place to rest his head. "I cannot think back to that time without tears" (Parfenii 1855, 1, 280). Parfenii searched for a starets for succor and advice and came to Optina Pustyn', where he spoke with elder Leonid, but left only one week later. After stopping at a monastery in Saratov guberniia, he continued to Troitse-Sergiev Lavra, where he stayed for two weeks – and so on. He led this vagabond-like life even though he was a monk.

Tolstoi ordered a copy of Parfenii's book through Nikolai Strakhov in 1877 (Tolstoi PSS 62, 343). His copy is filled with underlinings, and there can be no doubt that this book was among those that provided him with inspiration for the tale *Two Old Men* (Tolstoi PSS 48, 69). The book apparently was one of several factors that convinced him of the importance of wandering as a mark of true faith.

In Tolstoi's *Gospel Translation,* the true Christian life is portrayed as the life of a vagabond, and the Greek word *ptochos* – which was in fact an honorary title among the first Christians – is regularly translated as *brodiaga,* or "tramp" (Tolstoi PSS 24, 198, 200, passim). Most other translators render "ptochos" as "poor." Tolstoi often linked together the concepts of poverty and wandering: "Poverty and journeying (*brodiazhnichestvo*) is the only way that lead to the true life," he asserted (Tolstoi PSS 24, 286). To enter the Kingdom of God, one must be "freed from all forms of life."

A central scriptural reference for Tolstoi was Matt. 8, 20: "The foxes have holes, and the birds of the air have nests; but the Son of man hath not where to lay his head" (see, e.g., Tolstoi PSS 48, 306). In his *Gospel Translation* he paraphrased this with these words: The animals have a home, but "the person who lives in the spirit has no place that he can call 'home'" (Tolstoi PSS 24, 419). "The homeless" (*bezdomovnik*) can therefore be set up as a third synonym next to "poor" and *brodiaga.*

The ideal of the vagrant that runs like a red thread through Tolstoi's *Gospel Translation,* is also found in *What I believe* (Tolstoi PSS 23, 427). Tolstoi's secretary Nikolai Gusev claims that "what particularly attracted Tolstoi about the character of Jesus at the time when these books were written was precisely his life as a wanderer" (N. Gusev 1963, 597). When Tolstoi conversed with Bishop Nikandr and the priest Ivanov in Tula in December 1879, pilgrimage (*palomnichestvo*) was one of the topics he most wanted to discuss (A. Ivanov 1901a, 262). Another metaphor within the same cluster of themes that Tolstoi found intriguing was "mission" (*poslannichestvo*). The concept goes back to the Johannite literature in the New Testament, as expressed in Jesus's High Priest's prayer: "As thou hast sent me into the world, even so have I also sent them [the disciples] into the world." "The World" is a foreign country in which the Christian takes up temporary abode only in order to carry out the mission of the Lord. Tolstoi returns to this idea in his diary several times (Tolstoi PSS 52, 128; 53, 137, 143, 179). He compared himself, for instance, with the Tsar's ambassador to Turkey – a country that, to many Russians, was the epitome of a foreign culture. A messenger in such a country must always bear in mind that he must not bring shame on the one who has sent him.

This applies equally to those who are "God's ambassador in the world" – as Tolstoi himself wanted to be (Tolstoi PSS 52, 98). "I feel my mission, though the results are meagre" (Tolstoi PSS 52, 124).

The last major work Tolstoi managed to finish before his death was a calendar of edifying stories that he gave the title of *The Way of Life – Put' Zhizni*. In his preface to the book of popular-religious stories *Tsvetnik (Flowerbed)*, Tolstoi claimed that "the truth (*pravda*) is a path – a *put'*." There is only one path, full of thorns, that leads to life – to follow the will of God (Tolstoi PSS 26, 307–08). This identification between the Truth and the Way can be traced back to John 14, 6, where Jesus uses these two metaphors about Himself along with a third – Life. The understanding of Christian life as a road Tolstoi found confirmed also in the ancient (first century AD?) Christian text *Didake* or *The Teaching of the Twelve Apostles*, which is structured around the contrast between the Way of Life and the Way of Death. Tolstoi read *Didake* in 1885, and was so excited that he made his own translation of it from the Greek (Tolstoi PSS 25, 416).

Tolstoi's Encounters with Wanderers

Even as a child Tolstoi became well acquainted with wandering pilgrims. He grew up with his aunt, Tat'iana Ergol'skaia, who liked to give them shelter (Biriukov 1905–1923, II, 289). Also his mother, Mariia Tolstaia (née Volkonskaia), had had a special fondness for *bozh'i liudi* – the people of God, as the wayfarers were often called. She died when Tolstoi was less than two years old, but throughout his life he maintained a deep love for her and tried to find out as much as possible about her life. In his diaries he spoke of her as a "holy ideal" (Tolstoi PSS 56, 133).

Tolstoi's mother was the model for the extremely devout Mariia Bolkonskaia in *War and Peace* – even the name is the same, except for one letter. Mariia lives alone with her tyrannical father, who knows no other way of expressing his love for his daughter than by tormenting her. Only in her *bozh'i liudi* can she find comfort and hope. They are the only ones who have understood that this life on earth lasts but a moment. This despised people become her ideal.

> To leave one's family, home, all worries about earthly goods; to wander about, clothed in hemp rags, under an assumed (*chuzhoi*) name, going from place to place, without harming people but instead praying for them; praying both for those who persecute you and those who protect you: surely there is no higher truth and no higher life than this! (Tolstoi PSS 10, 235)

Mariia decides to become a wanderer herself and receives the blessing of her confessor to do so. "I wish to go to a place and pray, and before I get accustomed to this and grow attached to it, I will wander on, walking until my legs give way beneath me." In fact, she does not manage to carry through her intentions. She realizes that she loves her earthly father more than she loves her Father in Heaven, and this she recognizes as a sin.

During his religious crisis in the late 1870s, Tolstoi began to take regular contact with wanderers wherever he could find them. His estate was located by the main thoroughfare to Kiev, and in springtime every year the road was filled with wayfaring men and woman headed for Kiev and its many holy places. Tolstoi would don his peasant's smock and go out to talk with them, jotting down brief accounts in the notebook he brought with him (see, e.g., Tolstoi PSS 48, 308 and 311).

In July 1879, Tolstoi set out in the wanderers' footsteps to Kiev, together with his friend Afanasii Fet. Tolstoi wore a simple grey coat, to avoid being recognized as the world-famous writer. All day long he wandered about in the cathedrals, museums and monastic cells of the city. At night he slept in the gatekeeper's room at the Monastery of the Caves, as the pilgrim hostel was full. After two days he returned home, disappointed: "It wasn't worth it," he wrote to his wife (Tolstoi PSS 83, 270). One hermit to whom he had turned in hopes of discussing his crisis of faith had dismissed him brusquely, saying he had no time. Tolstoi's best memories were of his talks with the lay gatekeepers at the Monastery of the Caves (Makovitskii 1979, I, 375).

Despite his break with the Church, Tolstoi in 1881, as noted in Chapter 5, went to the famous monastery of Optina Pustyn', not far from Iasnaia Poliana, to visit the elders there. On this occasion, he identified himself to an even greater degree with the role of the wanderer than on his trip to Kiev two years previously. He was accompanied by his servant Sergei Arbuzov, who in his memoirs relates how they set off on foot, wearing peasant jackets, bast shoes filled with rags, knapsacks on their backs, and each with a wanderer's staff. As they walked, they fell into conversation with other wayfarers. At one point, Tolstoi was asked whether he intended to stay on in Optina Pustyn', to which he replied that he did not know – "perhaps" (Arbuzov 1904, 68).

The first night they slept on straw in a peasant hut, while the stench of manure outside filtered in through the thin walls. They set off again before dawn, four o'clock, so as to avoid the worst heat of the day. On the third day, they were overtaken by a mighty thunderstorm on the open steppe. With the water sloshing about in their shoes, they trudged on to the nearest house. This proved to be a mill, where the miller would not admit them, even for five silver rubles. Tolstoi came down with a cold after this experience.

On the fourth day they reached Optina, where they were received as beggars. They did not belong in the dining hall for the best class of guests – instead they ate together with other wanderers in the hostel. Writes Tolstoi's biographer Henri Troyat:

> Tolstoy was in seventh heaven. At last he was a muzhik among muzhiks. Men and women were sitting together around a long table, elbow to elbow in the dim light, gulping down food and drink and breathing heavily in a fog of cabbage, sweat and dirt. Pulling a notebook from his pocket, Tolstoy jottet down an aside: "Borscht, kasha, kvass. One cup for four people. Everything is good". (Troyat 1980, 566)

That night Tolstoi was shown to a room so bug-infested that he could not sleep. Then the next morning he was recognized by one of his former serfs, who had become a monk: The "wretched beggar" was revealed as none other than the aristocrat and famed writer, the Count Tolstoi. Despite his protests he was now moved to a velvet-draped chamber, and without further ado was granted an audience with Amvrosii. Tolstoi returned home by train – third class, true enough . . . the unaccustomed peasant footgear had given him blisters (Biriukov 1905–23, 384–89).

This episode illustrates both Tolstoi's strong desire to enter into the role of a wanderer, and the difficulties involved. After this attempt he generally stayed quietly at home at Iasnaia Poliana, but both in his diary and in conversations with the family he frequently expressed the wish to leave, to get away from it all. On June 17, 1884, he packed a rucksack and wandered off, after a quarrel with his wife. He said that he intended to go to America or to Paris, but before he had got halfway to Tula, his conscience drove him back (Troyat 1980, 613). A month later Tolstoi wrote in his diary: "There was no point in me not leaving. It is probably inevitable" (Tolstoi PSS 49, 113).

On July 14, 1910, Tolstoi prepared his last will and testament. He also wrote to Sof'ia Andreevna, threatening that, unless she accepted his conditions for how they could live together in peace, he would take back his promise not to leave (Tolstoi PSS 84, 400). Time passed, and, in Tolstoi's opinion, his conditions were not met. On the night of October 28, that year he set off, under cover of darkness, accompanied only by his physician, Dushan Makovitskii. Despite his earlier warnings, this move came as a surprise to most, and the message he had left behind could be interpreted variously. Speculations flourished as to his "real" reason for leaving. This immediately became a world sensation, front-page stuff in newspapers in Russia and abroad. The Soviet scholar Boris Meilakh compiled the following summary of hypotheses initially put forth in the Russian press:

- presentiment of his own death
- desire for a "simpler lifestyle"
- family conflicts
- flight from the emptiness and pressures of the world
- pressures from Tolstoians
- break with Sof'ia Andreevna
- realization that his creative powers were exhausted
- old-age feebleness
- wish to bring his life into correspondence with his own teachings
- repentance of his socio-critical activities
- desire to return to the Church
- wish to enter a monastery
- exhausted by the countless stream of visitors to Iasnaia Poliana.

(Meilakh 1979 [1960]), 25)

These many speculations can be divided into two main categories. Some focused on causal explanations, concentrating especially on Tolstoi's extremely difficult personal situation of the past few years. His relations with Sof'ia Andreevna had become increasingly strained, with violent outbursts of rage followed by fragile truces. But it was also possible to see Tolstoi's action in a finalistic perspective, where the main point was not what he was trying to *leave* as what he was *striving to achieve*. For those who saw this as the main explanation, it became essential to find out where the wagon with the two escapees was headed. A fact of major importance was that their first night stop was the monastery hostel at Optina Pustyn'. For the modern Russian Orthodox researcher Georgii Orekhanov, Tolstoi's route was "not coincidental": "Prior to his death, he went to a place where people knew, remembered, and were willing to listen to him" (Orekhanov 2016, 126). This conjecture is as good as any other, but remains a conjecture. In any case, the fugitives did not remain in Optina but proceeded to Shamardino, seven *verst* distant, where Tolstoi's sister Mariia was a nun. Shamardino was the nunnery attached to Optina, built on the initiative of elder Amvrosii. Here Tolstoi expressed the wish to stay, and even arranged with a peasant to rent a small *izba* or peasant hut in the village just outside the nunnery walls. It was agreed that he would move in the next day (Tolstoi PSS 58, 270).

Tolstoi's decision to rent a peasant cottage just outside Shamardino was deeply symbolic: Just as he had, in spiritual terms, spent his entire life "just beyond the walls of the Church" (to borrow Vasilii Rozanov's phrase), so would he now settle down physically on its periphery. Not that this should be taken as the "real" motive behind his move – it was more of an impulsive decision, taken once he had arrived at the monastery. But nothing came of the plan. When his daughter Aleksandra managed to trace him the very next day, Tolstoi realized that it would be far too easy for people to find him at Shamardino. Once again, he packed up and set out on a new, unplanned wandering. Only ten days later, Tolstoi died, in the little station town of Astapovo.

On November 4, the journalist and former Tolstoian Mikhail Men'shikov wrote an article in *Novoe vremia,* discussing holy wandering as a possible explanation of Tolstoi's runaway move. But he concluded that this hypothesis was not tenable: Tolstoi was not created for the solitary life. Moreover: If one were to undertake a successful break with the "world," this would have to be taken while one was still young. Nor did Tolstoi have any possibility whatsoever to conceal himself as an anonymous wayfarer – he would be recognized immediately (Men'shikov 1910). Menshikov's article treats holy wandering as a possible role for Tolstoi in totally concrete terms. Most others who discussed this form of piety in connection with Tolstoi employed a more metaphorical perspective. By emphasizing the spiritual content of wandering rather than its external attributes, they have been able to uncover many points of similarity.

In its interpretation of Tolstoi's break, the church paper *Moskovskie tserkovnye vedomosti* stressed that his first stopping place had been a monastery and queried whether "the famed writer" now sought to "bring repentance for his suffering soul." All the same, the paper was not convinced that the prodigal son was really headed back into the fold, and launched holy wandering as an alternative explanation. Out in the desolate steppes, without any shelter, surely Tolstoi would have felt himself linked by bounds of blood to "those poor, naked, unfortunate ones who are doomed to wander about without any home." The only difference was that instead of "the poverty of the flesh" Tolstoi sought to direct all his attention to "the poverty of the spirit" (V. D. 1910, 45, 809–14).

On November 1, 1910, the proletarian writer "Skitalets"[3] (the psueudonym of S. G. Petrov) published an article in which he interpreted Tolstoi as "a bright wanderer." Skitalets was full of sarcasm toward those who sought to reduce Tolstoi's break to a simple escape from an intolerable spouse.

[3] "Skitalets" means "wanderer."

> Neither the luxury of life on the estate nor the disagreements with his family can provide a full explanation of what led him to set out on his puzzling journey . . . . His home is not Iasnaia Poliana and his family, but all mankind . . . . So, make way for the bright wanderer. Let him go where he wishes, so that his chosen stopping places can rejoice. May Russia prove great enough for him! (Quoted from Meilakh 1979 [1960], 29–31).

This rhetoric-laden article should be understood as a countermove against the attempts of the Church to capitalize on Tolstoi's dramatic move – but then it is all the more striking that Skitalets chose to interpret this action in terms of the religious context inherent in the role of the wanderer.

Nikolai Berdiaev saw Tolstoi's departure as an eschatological action, an expression that Tolstoi was seeking to step out of history and over into the divine life of Nature. "Like a spiritual wanderer Tolstoi was striving toward the End, toward the Kingdom of the Millennium" (Berdiaev 1971 [1946], 202). Many years before the death of Tolstoi, Maksim Gorkii had written in his notebooks how Tolstoi reminded him of those wanderers who are "terribly homeless and alien everywhere and to everyone, chased from one end of the earth to the other, never knowing why" (Gor'kii 1919, 10).

Between "Tolstoi the wanderer" and the age-old Orthodox wanderer tradition there is clearly both continuity and rupture. It would be misleading to say that Tolstoi simply took over a "form" and filled it with his own content. He was also concerned with and fascinated by the "content side" of *wandering* – the restless, seeking attitude that spurns the security of house and hearth and trusts that God will provide sustenance and guidance.

When Tolstoi decided to walk to the Optina Pustyn' monastery, he was not simply searching for spiritual guidance from the elders there – in fact, as we saw in Chapter 5, there is much to indicate that he was not very impressed by the kind of advice they offered. Instead, identification with the "simple Russian religious seekers" was crucial to him. In a direct sense this identification was a failure: In Optina, Tolstoi was "exposed" as the famous rich writer, was installed in a velvet-draped chamber, and took the train back home. In any case, the identification attempt was flawed from the outset: Few if any "real" wanderers would bring along a footman on their wanderings.

However, to write off this episode as a "stunt" or "performance act" would be to miss the point. Rather, it can be regarded as a kind of "preaching through action." Acts are always far more multivalent than words; and while many commentators have pointed to the link between the wanderers and Tolstoi, they have interpreted it in often radically different ways.

Tolstoi formulated a religious message that was explicitly a criticism of Orthodox theology and an alternative to the teaching of the Church. Even so, he consciously drew upon the spirituality of the same religious tradition in ways that illustrate an important point made by Lotman and Uspenskii (1985): The old continues to live on after the rupture, even in its negation.

CHAPTER 7

Tolstoi and the Ideal of "the Holy Fool"

The idea of the Christian truth as a "folly of the world" goes back to 1 Cor 1, 17–31. Paul teaches here that "For the preaching of the cross is to them that perish foolishness"; therefore, God decided to save those who believe by the "foolishness" which he preached. This notion has to varying degrees and in various ways been taken up by the Christian denominations. The Western Church had its Tertullian who preached *credo quia absurdum* – "I believe because it is absurd" – and even the sober-minded Erasmus of Rotterdam wrote a "praise of folly." But especially in the Eastern Churches, *holy fools Khrista radi* – fools for the sake of Christ – have become a distinct concept.[1] The standard English translation "holy fool" captures one aspect of this peculiar form of spirituality – the simulated insanity – but misses many others, such as their asceticism and social criticism. In deference to convention and for lack of a better alternative I will use this term below.

The contemporary Russian scholar Sergei Ivanov (S. Ivanov 2005, 9) defines a holy fool as a person who "publicly simulates madness, pretends to be a fool or shocks his or her surroundings with deliberate licentiousness." Conspicuously absent from this definition is the *religious* dimension. Ivanov describes some important features of holy foolishness, but fails to capture the concept of *holy* fools, fools *for the sake of Christ, "Khrista radi."* As Timothy Ware explains, folly for the sake of Christ is a mode of "sanctity": It was found in Byzantium, but was particularly prominent in medieval Russia:

> the "Fool" carries the ideal of self-stripping and humiliation to its furthest extent, by renouncing all intellectual gifts, all forms of earthly wisdom, and by voluntarily taking upon himself the Cross of madness. These Fools often performed a valuable social rôle: simply because they were fools, they could criticize those in power with a frankness which no one else dared to employ. (Ware 1978, 118)

[1] The Russian word for "holy fool" "*iurodivyi*" (plural: *iurodivyie*) is a derivative of "*iurodstvo*," the word for "foolishness" used in the Russian Bible translation of the verses quoted above.

Their "folly" was not due to being slow-witted: It was usually a feigned madness, a peculiar form of penitence. George Fedotov underlines that, in addition to the anti-intellectual side, this "foolishness" often gave rise to immoral and asocial actions. The holy fools deliberately ignored accepted norms and social conventions, shocking his fellow human beings by eating sausages on Good Friday, destroying market stalls in the square, dancing with prostitutes, and so on (Fedotov [1966] 1975, 2, 317–18).

A classic study of *holy foolishness* in the Orthodox-apologetic tradition is *Holy foolishness in Christ and holy fools for the Sake of Christ in the Eastern and Western Churches*, by the priest Ioann Kovalevskii (1895). In Kovalevskii's view, the supreme goal of holy foolishness is to lead people to moral perfection. It is a compact protest against man's inclination toward worldly, secular pursuits – a living and visible reminder that the goal of life lies beyond this world. When the holy fools consorted with prostitutes, for example, it was never for carnal enjoyment, but rather with the aim of getting them to renounce their sinful ways. And if holy fools broke the regulations concerning fasting, this was meant not to demonstrate disobedience to the Church, Kovalevskii asserted. It was a symbolic act: True piety lies not in external obedience, but in inner purity of heart. Jesus himself was accused of being a friend of sinners and money changers, as well as of setting himself above the laws of the Sabbath.[2] In that sense, holy foolishness can be regarded as an *Imitatio Christi.*

Similarly, according to Kovalevskii, the irrational behavior of the holy fools was only superficial: It was merely an external disregard for the use of reason – not an inner, total rejection. The holy fools renounced the "natural" rationality of society, not in order to be reduced to dumb beasts, but so as to become filled with the higher rationality of Christ. By this, Kovalevskii did not mean something radically different from natural rationality: It is a matter of the same natural quality, but further enlightened by the truths of heaven (Kovalevskii 1895, 52–55).

Both the apparent immorality and the outward irrationality can be perceived as a consequence of the holy fools' asceticism. When they discarded their clothing and wandered around naked, it was not intended as indecent exposure, but to harden their bodies by enduring both cold and heat. Equally important, these actions were aimed at invoking ridicule and mockery, thereby training themselves in the school of humility. Also the assumed insanity of the holy fools must, up to a point, be regarded as an exercise in humility and self-denigration. As intelligence is the highest

[2] "A man gluttonous, and a winebibber, a friend of publicans and sinners" – Matt 11, 19.

hallmark of men, what elevates them above the beasts, renunciation of it is the utmost form of asceticism.

According to Kovalevskii, the way of holy foolishness is a path for the few chosen, and experienced elders warned all who wanted to enter it. Many of those who nevertheless took it up had first lived several years as monks and had trained themselves in ordinary monastic asceticism. This form of piety can therefore be regarded as an extension of the monk's life in a potent form. However, there is an important difference. While the Orthodox monk lives secluded from the world, holy foolishness is always performed *v miru*, "in the world" (Kovalevskii 1895, 76). We could say that holy foolishness supplements the monastic ideals with ideals derived from holy wandering. Like the wanderers, the holy fools walked about, with no place they could call "home." Often they established a sort of hangout on the church steps or somewhere else in the immediate vicinity of a church.

The reason why holy foolishness can be lived only in society is that the foremost task of the fool is to serve other people (Kovalevskii 1895, 66). The anchorite works on the salvation of his own soul: The holy fools endeavor to save their neighbors. In this service, they employ various tools, depending on the situation – the holy fool Serapion, for instance, even sold himself as a slave in order to convert his pagan buyer. Others rebuked the wicked in authoritative and fearless words, invoking the wrath of heaven upon those who did not repent. Such castigations were first and foremost directed against the mighty in society. During the *oprichnina* – Ivan the Terrible's reign of terror in the sixteenth century – the holy fool Nikolai made the Tsar leave Pskov without sacking the city (Kovalevskii 1895, 72).

In addition to such direct, individual manifestations of the chastisement of the holy fools, their way of living was an indirect, generalized criticism of society's institutions and conventions. They acted as if they were "strangers" from another world who did not know and therefore did not heed the established norms (Kovalevskii 1895, 4). Thus, they questioned the validity of these standards. It is tempting to see a parallel here between Kovalevskii's interpretation of holy foolishness and the technique of "alienation," *ostranenie,* which Tolstoi employed in his criticism of religious and social institutions.

Some holy fools were recruited from among the monks, but there were also many lay people among them, especially in Russia. They hailed from all walks of life, but Kovalevskii stresses that holy foolishness was first and foremost a spirituality found among the *common people*. The ragged, malodorous "fools" were often unceremoniously ejected from palaces and manors, but they were welcomed with love and respect by the simple populace. No less than thirty-six holy fools were officially canonized by the Russian Orthodox Church between the thirteenth and the seventeenth centuries. Then the great national synod of 1665–66 adopted a ban on wandering holy fools, and after the time of Peter the Great the authorities began to persecute them. For a while, they were arrested and put to a lifetime of forced labor in the monasteries (Kovalevskii 1895, 151–52).

Another Russian-Orthodox authority on holy foolishness, the priest-monk Aleksii (Kuznetsov), underscores that the holy fools embody virtues that all Christians ought to strive for at all times. Like Kovalevskii, he emphasizes that holy foolishness is a kind of asceticism. The holy fools train themselves to withstand all kinds of pain; they practise the standard ascetic exercises of monasticism by denying themselves food, sleep, clothing and shelter. They do not own anything of value, and in that way they escape attachment to this world. For the same reason, they lead peripatetic lives: By constantly wandering about, they preach that this world is just a place we are passing through (Aleksii [Kuznetsov] 1913, 106).

In addition to their physical deprivations, the spiritual pains that the holy fools suffer are severe. As Aleksii explains, they endured scorn and humiliation from other people – which they have in common with Christ: "Through this remarkable idea of voluntary suffering inflicted by others, the feat of holy foolishness in a sense approaches the Saviour's innocent suffering for mankind" (Aleksii [Kuznetsov] 1913, 131). A major aspect of holy foolishness is its concealment or *skrytnost'* (Aleksii [Kuznetsov] 1913, 102–3). The virtues of the holy fools are hidden from others, who see only their apparent indecency and insanity, and despise them.

The aim of holy foolishness, Aleksii goes on to explain, is moral perfection: "Through their lives the holy fools eloquently preached precisely this: In an unsightly, simple life in this world it is possible to keep the soul clean and achieve the perfection (*sovershenstvo*) which every person is required to strive after." Since God is perfection, this means that the aim of the holy fools is nothing less than *bogopodobie*: To achieve the likeness of God. "Created in the likeness of God, man naturally ought to strive towards his Prototype (*Pervoobraz*), and assimilate to Him" (Aleksii [Kuznetsov] 1913, 118). Similarly, Tolstoi regarded the life of a Christian as a path toward a restoration of man's original self-understanding as a "divine spark" and "the son of god" (Tolstoi PSS 28, 85).

Further, Aleksii teaches that the godlike perfection of the holy fool has two aspects – one external, directed against other people, and one internal, directed against ourselves. In its outward relations, this is expressed through love, as it was for Tolstoi. The holy fool loves his fellow men and wants them to attain the same degree of perfection as himself. In order to become a model for others, he must incessantly work on his self-perfection. His life becomes a constant fight against carnal, as well as spiritual, passions and temptations. The goal of this fight is *apatheia*, which is the highest expression of true holy foolishness.

> The holy fools tried to achieve a state in which they did not hear or feel any movement, neither with their internal nor with their external nature, except this one thought, which, like a ray of light, is the immovable striving towards God, in other words, the state of *apatheia* (*bezstrastie*). (Aleksii [Kuznetsov] 1913, 217)

The holy fools "enthral all their feelings" in order to "ascend to the mountain of apatheia." Using the same metaphor as Callistus and Ignatius in *Philokalia*, Aleksii describes *apatheia* as "the resurrection of the soul before the resurrection of the body" (Aleksii [Kuznetsov] 1913, 223–24). Aleksii's anthropology, then, is characterized by the same kind of dualism as we find in both the *Dobrotoliubie* and in Tolstoi's teaching.

The holy fools achieve *bezstrastie* by mortifying their flesh through great acts of asceticism, Aleksii explains. As an illustration, he points to the holy fool Andrei in tenth-century Constantinople. Andrei went about clad in "some indecent rags" (*rubishche nekoe nepotrebnoe*) that were barely enough to conceal his nakedness. He spent the nights in prayer and wandered about during the day. He "had nowhere to rest his head" because the poor chased him away from their shelters and the rich never let him past their gates. Occasionally, he would lie down to sleep among the dogs, but even they refused to accept this servant of God. Even in this miserable bodily state – or, rather, as a result of it – Andrei experienced a mystical rapture and was carried into "the third heaven" (*Kniga zhitii sviatykh*, IV, 1859, 28b). Tolstoi owned a copy of *The Lives of the Saints* that contained a version Andrei's *Vita*, and had apparently read this story with particular attention and interest. In this text, Tolstoi made notes on eight out of thirteen pages, sometimes underlining an entire page (*Biblioteka* 1972, 1a, 366).

Like the monks, the holy fool renounces all worldly goods, but unlike them he continues to live in the world, Aleksii notes. Whereas the hermit solves the problem of temptations by isolating himself physically from them, the holy fool must rip desire from his heart and vanquish all passions within him. Aleksii relates the story about the holy fool Serapion the Sindonite to demonstrate this contrast between monastic and worldly asceticism. Serapion visits a nun who has lived in solitude for twenty-five years and is famed for her piety. She tells him that she is dead to this world – but Serapion doubts this. As a test, he proposes that they should stroll naked through the streets of the town. This the nun will not do – thereby revealing that she is still concerned about what other people think of her. Serapion, by contrast, has left behind not only the desires of the flesh but also any care for what others may say. He has achieved full *apatheia* (Aleksii [Kuznetsov] 1913, 223–26). Thus, a true holy fool can surpass monastic asceticism: His form of piety proves itself more complete.

Since God Himself is eternal, immovable and dispassionate, the person who manages to rid himself of his or her passions approaches a state of divinity (Aleksii [Kuznetsov] 1913, 218–19). "*Apatheia* is a struggle for *bogopodobie*, through which all passions subside" (Aleksii [Kuznetsov] 1913, 219). The closer a holy man (*podvizhnik*) approaches godlikeness, the more he shows himself to be an ascetic (*asket*), Aleksii explains.

Aleksii acknowledges an apparent similarity between the Christian ideal of *apatheia* and the teaching of the Stoics. This resemblance, however, is superficial and spurious, he claims: The Stoics sought supreme perfection in "cold indifference" and "severe insensibility" – whereas in the life of the holy fools, *apatheia* was linked to a strong faith in God, deep love and devotion to Christ (Aleksii [Kuznetsov] 1913, 140). This linkage between love and the fight against the passions we also find in Tolstoi's asceticism.

It is debatable whether father Kovalevskii's and priest-monk Aleksii's theological interpretations give a correct representation of the historical holy foolishness as practised in the Early Church and the Middle Ages. Holy fools generally conveyed their message not by words, but through actions, and these were highly ambiguous. They could, with equal right, be perceived as sacrilege and histrionics and as expressions of piety and virtue. Often, the holy fools were condemned by their contemporaries, to be appropriated by the Church only after their death.

"The historical holy fool" may prove to be just as inaccessible to research as "the historical Jesus." What Kovalevskii and Aleksii convey is the ecclesiastical, canonized version as embodied in the Calendar of Saints. On the other hand, it is precisely this canonized version that is of interest to us, for it is this that has formed later perceptions of the phenomenon. The holy fools of Tolstoi's time understood themselves in light of this version, which is also the one Tolstoi himself was concerned with when he developed his own concept of holy foolishness.

Tolstoi had experienced holy fools long before he read the *Lives of the Saints*. To his biographer Pavel Biriukov he said, "[M]any holy fools came to our [childhood] home. I am very grateful to my educators for that, and I got used to regarding them with great respect" (Biriukov 1905–23, II, 287; see also the fragment *What am I?*, Tolstoi PSS 23, 509). When the adult Tolstoi thought back on these strange guests, he focused especially on their desire for humility and self-degradation.

> They did what Marcus Aurelius speaks of: There is nothing higher than being despised for one's good life. So damaging and insurmountable is the temptation of human glory which always gets mixed in with good works, that one can only sympathize with the attempts of not only avoiding praise, but even evoking the contempt of men (Tolstoi PSS 31, 395; Biriukov 1905–23, II, 288–89; see also Biriukov 1905–23, I, 75).

In his autobiographical debut work *Childhood* (1852) Tolstoi describes how the main character, Nikolen'ka Irten'ev, together with a friend, secretly witness the ascetic practices and ecstatic prayers of the holy fool Grisha.

> He prayed for himself, asking God to forgive him his grievous sins, and he kept repeating: "Oh God, forgive my enemies!" He rose to his feet with a groan and repeating the same words again and again, fell to the floor and again got up despite the weight of his chains, which knocked against the floor every time with a dry harsh sound. . .
>
> Much water has flowed under the bridges since then, many memories of the past have lost their meaning for me and become dim recollections; even the pilgrim [*strannik*] Grisha has long ago completed his last journey; but the impression he made on me and the feeling he evoked will never fade from my memory. (Tolstoi *PSS* 1, 34–35)[3]

Grisha, Tolstoi explains, is a fictive character, based on his impressions of many different holy fools (Tolstoi *PSS* 34, 395). Grisha is, in a way, an incarnation of the very concept of holy foolishness as Tolstoi understood it. In the quotation, the holy fool Grisha is also described as a holy wanderer, a "*strannik*": Thus, Tolstoi perceived these two forms of piety as variants of the same invariant. The quote also describes death as "the last journey" (*stranstvovanie*). This might be seen as a word-play that the concept of the "*strannik*" almost invites – but it is also an accurate expression of the theology behind holy wandering. Tolstoi's first biographer and close friend Pavel Biriukov considered Tolstoi's early encounters with holy wanderers and holy fools as being among the most significant

[3] Translation by Rosemary Edmonds, in Leo Tolstoy's *Childhood, Boyhood, Youth* (Harmondsworth 1964), 44.

experiences of his formative years, an important source for understanding the religious focus of his later years (Biriukov 1905–23, II, 287–90). "Perhaps we might say that [Grisha] was Tolstoi's first teacher in the people's faith, the faith that captivated his soul after its futile wanderings (*skitanii*) through the impenetrable forest of theology, philosophy and positive science?" (Biriukov 1905–23, I, 75). Here, ideas from holy wandering, eldership and holy foolishness are woven together into one picture: Tolstoi's soul is presented as a "wanderer" who finally finds rest with the "elder" Grisha. Tolstoi had read through Biriukov's biography and partly corrected it before it went into print. It can therefore to a greater extent than the later biographies be seen as a representation not only of Tolstoi's life, but also of his own self-understanding.

***

Most people who had known Tolstoi in the 1850s and 1860s shook their heads at his religious ruminations in the mid-1870s, which they tended to perceive as sheer nonsense. In Moscow, it was rumored that Tolstoi had become completely unhinged. In May 1880, for example, Fedor Dostoevskii wrote to his wife, with Dmitrii Grigorovich as source, that Tolstoi was supposed to have become almost mad, "or perhaps totally mad" (Dostoevskii 1959, IV, 154). When it became clear that this "madness" was of a religious nature, it was often characterized as holy foolishness. "But this characteristic could not embarrass Tolstoi, rather, he was ready to acknowledge it as correct," claims Boris Eikhenbaum (Eikhenbaum 1960, 258). Eikhenbaum regarded the renunciation of all amenities of life, the exposure of all lies and the proclamation of nonviolence as typical elements of holy foolishness and was thus able to establish an ideational relationship between holy foolishness and Tolstoianism.

In *Notes of a Madman* (1880), Tolstoi himself presented his new religion as "madness" (Tolstoi PSS 26, 474). Similarly, in a letter to his brother Sergei dated December 20, 1879, he called his new worldview "madness," apparently because Sergei had used that term about his brother's state of mind during a previous conversation, referred to in the letter (Tolstoi PSS 62, 507). Tolstoi provided a more explicit reference to the holy foolishness tradition in a letter to Nikolai Strakhov in the crisis year of 1877. Here he wrote that "if I had been alone [= had had no family. P.K.], I would not have become a monk, but rather a holy fool, that is, I would have disdained all things in life, and not hurt anyone" (Tolstoi PSS 62, 347). Here it is holy foolishness as compassion and renunciation of the world that appealed to him.

As pointed out above, the holy fools in Russian history had a special license to criticize authorities and Tolstoi's biographer Rosamund Bartlett writes that holy foolishness was a strategy adopted by Tolstoi when he wrote to Alexander III and asked for clemency for Alexander II's murderers. For Tolstoi, foolishness was a "fundamental medium for the communication of his message" (Bartlett 2010, 333).

In *Circle of Reading* from 1904–08 Tolstoi wrote that,

> What is called holy foolishness, that is, a behaviour that evokes condemnation and attacks from other people, cannot be defended to the extent that it causes bad actions by other people, but is understandable and desirable as the only possible test of one's love for God and one's neighbour. (Tolstoi PSS 41, 331)

Vladimir Chertkov believed that Tolstoi was here referring to himself (Chertkov 1922, 27). Having begun to preach the ideal of renunciation of all property and the necessity of a simple, Spartan life, Tolstoi continued to live at his Iasnaia Poliana estate, surrounded by servants and luxury. Although he did so for the sake of the family, who for the most part did not share his beliefs, this created a disjoint between his life and teaching that was condemned by many of his opponents and even some of his followers. It is this scorn Chertkov believed that Tolstoi was comparing to the denunciation of the holy fools. This interpretation is supported by Tolstoi's daughter Tat'iana (Sukhotina-Tolstaia 1981, 395–96). Such an application of the idea of holy foolishness is also found in Tolstoi's unfinished play *The Light Shines in the Darkness* (1900). This work is strongly autobiographical. The protagonist, the squire Nikolai Ivanovich, loathes his aristocratic upper-class life, and threatens to break free from home and family and take to the roads. After a harrowing scene with his wife, he nevertheless promises to stay. In his despair, he prays to God:

> ... You want me to be humiliated, that everyone shall be able to point their finger at me and say: He does not live as he teaches. Let that be as it may. You know best what you need. Humility, holy foolishness. Yes, if only I could rise to that. (Tolstoi PSS 31,181)

Tolstoi's diaries have numerous references to holy foolishness. In 1863, he had recently married Sof'ia Behrs and sought happiness in family life. Suddenly, however, he found himself struck by doubts as to whether this life was capable of giving meaning to human existence. On June 18, he noted in his diary:

> It is terrible, frightening and meaningless to tie one's happiness to material conditions – wife, children, health, wealth. The holy fool is right. One can

> have wife, children, health, etc., but that is not what matters. Lord, have mercy on me and help me. (Tolstoi PSS 48, 55)

Here the holy fools' deliverance from all earthly ties is held forth as an ideal. Ten years later, in 1873, Tolstoi jotted down two isolated words linked together with a dash: "Perfection – holy fool" (Tolstoi PSS 48, 99).

However, it was not until his "Tolstoian" period that the references to holy foolishness in Tolstoi's diaries became frequent. On December 4, 1888, he noted: "On the way, I thought: . . . [We should try to] await, get used to, and desire derision and offenses from the people we meet (to test ourselves and to destroy our abominable individuality) to wish to be humiliated, insulted and misunderstood (holy foolishness)" (Tolstoi PSS 50, 9). Again, the ideal of humility is in focus. In 1890, several diary entries were devoted to holy foolishness. On August 13, Tolstoi wrote:

> Holy foolishness is of course an unnatural ideal: an unchanged attitude and full *ravnodushie* whether you are met with praise or condemnation from people. But in this world we (or at least I) to such a degree have become accustomed to living solely for vanity – to attain human praise – that it is necessary to consciously train ourselves to endure the condemnation of men. From one extreme we have to go over to the other extreme in order to get it right. (Tolstoi PSS 51, 75)

Here Tolstoi, like priest-monk Aleksii, linked the idea of holy foolishness to the *ravnodushie* or *apatheia* ideal. However, it is paradoxically presented as both a necessary ideal for imitation and as an unnatural exaggeration. Tolstoi was always in doubt as to whether this medicine was too strong for the patient and might cause undesirable side effects. He ultimately decided against prescribing it for himself, because he was too spiritually weak:

> Today, during prayer, I thought about the temptation of human fame, and that we should rejoice when men despise us. I thought about holy foolishness and how I could apply it myself. I felt how dangerous holy foolishness is to such a weak person as I am.
>
> If a person tears himself completely away from the perceptions of men and even begins to seek out condemnations, then he is deprived of the moderating power of the popular opinion which a weak person needs. This, I think, is the Achilles' heel of holy foolishness. (Tolstoi PSS 51, 113)

Yet, even though Tolstoi did not dare to take the final step into holy foolishness, he never could stop thinking about it. In 1899, he noted that "involuntary holy foolishness is the best school of goodness" (Tolstoi PSS

53, 218). Some years later, he elaborated on this idea: In order to lead a good life, he wrote on March 22, 1905, is it necessary "to be guided in life (in addition to the bodily demands) only by the will of God, whatever people might think, even to practice holy foolishness (unnoticed)" (Tolstoi PSS 55, 130). That same year, he made some notes on several stories he wished to write – and one of these was to be about "the joy of holy foolishness" (Tolstoi PSS 55, 301). That idea was never realized, but that fact that he had made a note of it shows that holy foolishness for Tolstoi also had its bright sides.

Also in 1908 and 1909 he returned to the holy foolishness ideal, calling it "a great thing" (Tolstoi PSS 56, 97; 57, 94). The next year, he wanted to a find a criterion to distinguish between "open and secret holy foolishness" (Tolstoi PSS 55, 350). The first is the "recognized professional holy fool," whereas the other's involuntary holy foolishness is "unknown to everyone," and "only the latter is pleasing to God" (Tolstoi PSS 55,213). Tolstoi's categories seem to coincide to some extent with Kovalevskii's distinction between genuine and false holy foolishness, but for Tolstoi the true holy fool operates incognito and therefore seems closer to Aleksii's teaching on the *skrytnost'* or hiddenness of holy foolishness. Holy foolishness should be internalized, becoming a way of life that all people can follow. In this way, it became possible for Tolstoi, who lacked all the external attributes of holy foolishness, to associate himself with this type of spirituality.

Tolstoi was fascinated by the holy foolishness tradition throughout his life, as these many quotes clearly show. His assessment was predominantly positive, and he focused on several aspects of the phenomenon: Renunciation of the world, passionlessness, love for your enemies, its relationship with holy wandering and, not least, humility and being able to endure the contempt of others. On the other hand, he never commented on holy foolishness as an expression of anti-intellectualism.

Tolstoi never wrote any longer exposé of his views on holy foolishness. When he touched upon this concept, it was usually in private situations such as diaries, letters and confidential conversations. In none of his published writings did he draw any direct line from holy foolishness to his own person. However, Tolstoi was identified with this form of piety very early, and in the Russian press there were discussions on this point.

In 1885, literary historian Orest Miller wrote, "it is as if we hear someone from the people say: The count is no fool, but he behaves like a holy fool (*iurodstvuet*)." Miller himself was very critical of Tolstoi's activity as a religious preacher, and added that even if someone might call him a holy fool, no one would regard him as a holy fool "*Khrista radi*," "for the sake of Christ" (Miller 1886, 441). Miller, then, placed Tolstoi in precisely the category he wanted to avoid at all costs – the false holy fool, the holy fool as a performer who lacks the deeper spiritual message of holy foolishness.

The comparison between Tolstoianism and holy foolishness must have caught on fairly quickly, because already in 1886 S. Rozenberg deemed it necessary to defend Tolstoi against this accusation. In an article titled "Holy foolishness and phariseeism. On the occasion of the controversy against Count L. N. Tolstoi," Rozenberg sought to show that Tolstoi's teaching on nonviolence should not be characterized as such. For Rozenberg, "holy foolishness" was a purely negative term, connoting impracticability and removal from real life. He therefore tried to show that this label was more applicable to Tolstoi's ostensibly pragmatic critics than to the great writer himself (Rozenberg 1886, 63–82).

The best-known identification between Tolstoianism and holy foolishness is probably Vladimir Lenin's analysis of Tolstoi as a "Mirror of the Russian Revolution." Lenin regarded Tolstoi as an ideologue of the patriarchal Russian peasantry during the transitional period between the emancipation of 1861 and the First Russian revolution in 1905. At that time, the masses "had already begun to hate their masters in this life, but had not arrived at a conscious, resolute, consistent and uncompromising struggle to the bitter end against them" (Lenin 1973, 16). Therefore, the peasant consciousness contained various contradictions, which were reflected in Tolstoi's teaching. On the one hand, it was "a remarkably strong, direct and sincere protest against social lies and falsehood"; on the other hand, Tolstoi was "a landlord acting as a holy fool in Christ" (*iurodstvuiushchii vo Khriste*). The doctrine on nonviolence Lenin singled out as especially "holy-foolish" in spirit (Lenin 1973, 4). For the Marxist leader, holy foolishness was a *perezhitok*, a remnant of the past that would have to be removed before the Russian peasantry could rise to true class consciousness. Lenin's language leaves the impression that holy foolishness was for him simply a synonym for religion, something which he considered "one of the vilest things in the world" (ibid.).

Several Orthodox writers of the time also characterized Tolstoi as a holy fool. Shortly after Tolstoi's death, Sergei Bulgakov wrote an article titled "Simplicity and Simplification." Bulgakov had a background as an economist, and was as much concerned with Tolstoi's social theories as with his religious message. Tolstoi's social and cultural criticism, in Bulgakov's opinion, could be summed up under the heading "Back to the simple," and in this he saw a strong ascetic impulse. Asceticism was the point where Tolstoi came closest to a Christian worldview – but, Bulgakov maintained, a deeper analysis would show that precisely here Tolstoi's philosophy parted ways with the Christian teaching.

To illustrate the contrast, Bulgakov related the story about the holy fool Aleksei in ancient Rome, who, like Tolstoi, hailed from a very rich family. Aleksei left his wife on the wedding night and roamed about for many years as a penniless beggar before returning home without revealing his true identity to anyone. Only on his deathbed did he disclose who he was. According to Bulgakov, Aleksei was able to thwart all human inclinations in himself by means of a natural simplicity as a true holy fool.

> All holy fools renounced their entire spiritual personality and rejected the world without compromising on it. They incarnated the commandments of the Sermon on the Mount, not as terrible and exhausting maximum demands, but as the natural consequence of a decision made once and for all. (S. Bulgakov 1978b, 126)

For the holy fools, external asceticism was only a *method*: The deeper aim was deliverance from the world in order to discover the simplicity of the soul and the purity of the heart. For Tolstoi, on the other hand, asceticism acquired a significance of its own, accompanied by pretensions of being the only solution to the problem of culture, Bulgakov claimed. "The liberation of the soul from earthly ties is imperceptibly transformed into a means to solve of all of society's problems" (ibid.). For Tolstoi, asceticism was not natural simplicity – as it was for the genuine holy fool – but affected simplification.

Western scholarship on Tolstoi and his religious teaching has paid little attention to his fascination with holy foolishness. Typical in this respect is G. W. Spence, who does not comment upon it at all, even though he explicitly defines Tolstoi's religious philosophy as ascetic (Spence 1967).[4] Biographer Henri Troyat cites a diary entry from 1863 in which Tolstoi sets up holy foolishness as an alternative to a life of happiness based on family and wealth. Troyat, however, cuts off the quote just before Tolstoi refers to holy foolishness, indicating only with ellipsis points that there is a continuation (Troyat 1980, 371). Troyat probably did this because his

[4] This can partly be explained by Spence's deliberate decision to focus only on Tolstoi's written works and ignore his private reflections in diaries and elsewhere. As noted, Tolstoy's fascination with holy foolishness comes across most clearly in such private settings.

Western audience could be expected to have such vague notions of holy foolishness that including it would have only led to confusion.[5]

Some newer studies of Tolstoi do discuss his interest in holy foolishness. In a short but informative article on the motif of the holy fool in Tolstoi's fiction and personal life, Per-Arne Bodin points out the writer's strongly ambiguous attitude toward this form of piety. Bodin underscores – and, I feel, exaggerates somewhat – the element of irrationality in the holy fool tradition, seeing this as a contrast to Tolstoi's rationalism – which he also, in my view, exaggerates slightly (Bodin 1995, 35–46). The strong similarities between Tolstoi's asceticism and the ethos of holy foolishness are less emphasized by Bodin.

Daniel Rancour-Laferriere has developed a psychoanalytic reading of Tolstoi's teaching, seeing Tolstoi's yearning for holy foolishness as an expression of his "masochistic needs," similar to the Shiite Muslim who engages in public self-flagellation, or the affluent American analysand who always manages to find himself or herself in humiliating situations (Rancour-Laferriere 2007, 96–98). I do not find this interpretation very helpful. Rancour-Laferriere explicitly attempts to translate the culturally circumscribed phenomenon of holy foolishness into a cross-culturally applicable concept. In my reading, however, it is precisely the specifically religious culture of Orthodox Christianity that provides the key to understanding Tolstoi's fascination with holy foolishness.

[5] In his monumental work on Tolstoi's religion, which specifically explores its connection to Orthodox theology, Richard Gustafson pays a brief visit to holy foolishness. He notes that for Tolstoi "the fool for Christ's sake is the one who seeks humiliation from others to test and perfect his love for those others" (Gustafson 1986, 183). While this was certainly part of Tolstoi's idea, Gustafson fails to explain the crucial role that the extinction of passions, or *apatheia*, plays in this endeavor.

CHAPTER 8

Father Sergius: Kasatskii's Spiritual Journey to Holy Foolishness

In his fictional writings, Tolstoi portrayed many representatives of the Russian Church, with varying degrees of sympathy and antipathy. However, only in one major work is Orthodox faith a major topic. This is the story of *Father Sergius* – the court officer Kasatskii who became a monk and an elder, only to discard the monk's robe later.

Tolstoi started working on the short story in 1890, but then set it aside. He returned to it in 1895 and 1898, but without completing it. Only after Tolstoi's death was it published, along with some other posthumous works. Although he did not regard *Father Sergius* as finished, the story that we now have is no torso. It has a complete, rounded form; only a few minor corrections might have remained before the author would have been satisfied with it (Christian 1969, 235).

The story rightly bears the name of its protagonist. All attention is directed to his person and the story of his spiritual and psychological development. As Tolstoi himself wrote in his diary while he was working on *Father Sergius*: "The entire interest lies in the psychological stages he is passing through" (Tolstoi PSS 51, 47). The drama unfolds on the inner plane, but is reflected in three incidents when he suddenly breaks away from his former life and finds new meaning in an existence that coincides with four traditional forms of Orthodox piety; monasticism, *eldership, holy wandering* and *holy foolishness.*

Kasatskii in the World

In chapters 1 and 2, we follow Kasatskii's path to the monastery gate. What is it that makes a young, handsome and relatively wealthy court officer abandon a promising career and break with the "World"? Kasatskii is presented as an exceptionally goal-oriented and ambitious person. He always sets himself concrete aims and does not give up until he has achieved them. He follows this rule of life when he learns to converse in fluent French, play chess, or show off his bookish erudition. As soon as he is counted among the first and foremost in one field, he puts all his energy into perfecting something else. This is the same urge for perfection that Tolstoi had described from his own life in *A Confession*. Basically, as Tolstoi sees it, this is a healthy attitude of life, but for Kasatskii it has been misdirected. He has chosen a wrong measure of perfection: Human recognition rather than the recognition of God. The urge to perfection therefore becomes a pursuit for success. Even when Kasatskii proposes marriage, he is not acting out of love, but for career reasons: His chosen one can lead him higher up the social ladder. He wants to use her as a thing, an ends to his means. Among Kasatskii's main character traits, Tolstoi emphasizes pride, honor and self-love.

Nevertheless, Kasatskii is not presented as a pure cynic. His striving for perfection is also reflected in an urge to live a moral life. Kasatskii neither drinks nor visits prostitutes like his fellow officers, and is "remarkably truthful" to himself and others. An important flaw in his character, however, is the fierce, uncontrollable anger that at times can overpower him. These outbreaks of rage result from his thin-skinned self-esteem, but they also indicate passionate depths within him that do not fit with the role of a one-dimensional careerist.

Kasatskii is indeed able to love passionately. He becomes deeply enamored of his fiancée, whom he perceives as the embodiment of female purity and innocence. His ability to love is also directed toward Tsar Nicholas I, for whom he wants to sacrifice himself completely. All too soon, he gets the opportunity to do so, but in a bitter, twisted way: It emerges that his fiancée is the tsar's former mistress whom someone had found it convenient to marry off to the young officer. Kasatskii the cynic has become the victim of the cynical games of others. The "sacrifice" required of him is his very pride, his self-esteem, and he is not prepared to renounce these – not yet.

Kasatskii's painstakingly constructed position in society falls in ruins to the ground. He, who strove to be counted among the first, at whatever cost, has become one of the last, a laughingstock. The only way he can save his self-image is by giving the impression that he now disdains the values he had lived for – worldly honor and fame. Precisely the monastery stands as the ultimate expression of contempt for the world, the renunciation of temporal pleasures.

Also Kasatskii's entry into the monastery at first glance seems to be guided by sheer cynicism, but Tolstoi introduces more complex motives. In the first drafts of the story, it is explained as an act of repentance for the injustice he has committed against his fiancée, who was also a pawn in the games of others. In the final version of *Father Sergius*, this motive is abandoned; instead, we are told that Kasatskii is driven by a "true religious feeling" that "merges with pride" (Tolstoi 31, 11). Disillusionment over his fiancée leads him into despair, and from that condition there is only one way – to God, through the childhood faith that he had never really lost.

Sergius in the Monastery

Why, then, can Kasatskii not find a lasting, new meaning of life in his new identity as Father Sergius in the monastery? In the third chapter, Tolstoi attempts to provide insights into the sociology and psychology of coenobitic monasticism, conveyed through the experiences of a sincere believer and truly struggling monastic.

It emerges that the living conditions the monastery can offer Sergius are not essentially different from what Kasatskii had in the "World." Also in the monastery he has ample opportunities to unfold both his positive and his negative character traits – the thirst for perfection, pride, and irritability. The difference is only that these qualities now assume more refined, spiritualized forms. "Just as he in the regiment had been not just an impeccable officer but had done more than was demanded of him and had broadened the scope of perfection, he now sought to be a perfect monk" (Tolstoi PSS 31, 11–12). He strives to achieve diligence, total abstinence, chastity in thoughts and deeds, and, importantly, obedience and humility. He donates his estate to the monastery, he finds it easy to overcome the temptations of gluttony and lust, and humility now gives him true joy. All his concerns are focused on the inner life, and he gains a high degree of peace of mind. On hearing that his mother has died and that his fiancée has married, he receives the news *ravnodushno* – with indifference or equanimity of mind.

But also the fulfillment of monastic ideals can be distorted into a desire to outdo other people. Sergius's yardstick remains human recognition – only he has now replaced his fellow officers with his monastic brethren. In humility, his conceit finds new and more refined forms, such as pride in how far he has progressed on the path to submission. But, because he manages to achieve the goals he has set himself as a monk, in the end he has nothing more to strive for, and falls prey to "boredom" and dullness (*usyplenie*). Sergius has not managed to eradicate his passions – he has only suppressed them. Then, consecrated as a priest, he is offered a leadership position in another monastery – and the dream of a career is reawakened. In this new monastery, he is also exposed to sensual temptations in the form of bigoted, importunate ladies.

Beneath Sergius's obedience to the abbot a deep aversion is simmering that erupts into a new temper tantrum: In the midst of a vesper, he is called up to the chancel to appear before a visitor, "like an animal." Sergius later asks forgiveness for his pride, but shortly afterward moves out of the monastery and into a hermit *skit* in another province to escape the temptations. But himself he cannot run away from.

Sergius as an Elder

The main part of the story about Father Sergius deals with his career as an elder. Yes, also eldership can be transformed into a career. Sergius becomes an elder in the full sense of the word. He is a holy man with an ascetic way of life and supernatural powers of healing. People come from afar to get his advice and blessing. Tolstoi explicitly places Sergius in the Hesychast tradition of the Optina monks: Sergius's confessor and tutor in the first monastery is a student of elder Amvrosii. Sergius also practices the Jesus Prayer, the inner prayer of the heart, an essential element in Hesychasm.

In the elder hermitage, the *skit*, Sergius continues to fight temptations and troubles. He begins to be tormented by thoughts of unbelief. A nagging doubt arises: Why has God created this world, with its strong attractions, if it is totally sinful? This point, however, is not followed up. It remains a dangerous question that threatens to undermine not only Orthodox monastic ideals, but also Tolstoi's own teaching of asceticism. Instead, attention is focused on the vices that constantly tempt Sergius: The spiritual passion – pride and the carnal – attraction to the other sex.

Twice his chastity is put to the test. After six years in the skit, he is approached by a frivolous, rich beauty who has wagered that she will be able to seduce the famous elder to admit her into his hut and stay overnight with him. Sergius is convinced that it is the devil incarnate who has come to tempt him to fall, and cuts off a finger with an axe to subdue the lust with physical pain.

Rumor of this feat (*podvig*) spreads rapidly, and the hermit finds himself beleaguered by monks and wanderers who want to be blessed by the holiness of this elder. He is forced to lay his hands on the sick and ailing, and is shocked when some of them are actually healed. Word of his powers spreads throughout the Russian Empire, and even to Europe.

Sergius's fame engenders vanity and arrogance, and he begins to compare his own achievements with those of the saints and even Christ Himself. At the same time, with his "remarkable truthfulness" he is able to study himself critically. "Others I may fool, but not myself or God." Sergius restricts his ascetic diet to dark bread and water, but recognizes that "the source of living water" is about to dry up within him. He has less and less time for meditation and prayer: "the inner" is replaced by "the outer" (Tolstoi PSS 31, 29). Sergius discovers that he is once again being subjected to the cynical exploitation of others: The monastery that he is affiliated with has made a thriving business of his activity. Even so, he continues to live up to what is expected of him, while constantly asking himself: Do I do this for God or for men?

The second woman who seduces him is a simple merchant's daughter. This time Sergius yields to the sin of the flesh without resisting. The woman is voluptuous, but slow-witted: It is a purely animal sexual instinct that leads him to the fall.

Kasatskii as Holy Wanderer

The next day, Sergius cuts his hair, dons a peasant shirt, and goes out on the road. He has once again embarked upon a new identity, as a wanderer. While his *podvig* when confronted with the first temptress had given new nourishment to his pride, his fall in the second case finally shook him out of his arrogance. He has been set free to see himself, unvarnished, as the sinner he is.

To Vladimir Chertkov, Tolstoi wrote in February 1891 about *Father Sergius*: "The fight against the flesh is here only an episode, or rather a step (*stupen'*). The main struggle is against something else, against the honour of men" (Tolstoi PSS 87, 71). The defeat in the fight against the flesh becomes a prerequisite for being able to overcome the more basic flaw – vanity. In his diary, Tolstoi noted:

> It is necessary that when [Sergius] fights against pride, he ends up in a vicious circle where humility turns out to be pride. He felt how hopeless it was to free himself from this pride. Only after his fall and the shame did he feel he could break out of the vicious circle and become truly humble. (Tolstoi PSS 52, 57–58)

As was the case after the break with his fiancée, Kasatskii/Sergius is led into despair after his fall. The first time he had found a way out that led to God – but now that path seemed closed. "As always when he was in despair, he tried to pray. But there was no one to pray to" (Tolstoi PSS 31, 37). And yet, there was a way back to Him after all – through the people, embodied for Kasatskii in his relative Pashenka. She shows him that service to God or service to man is a false dilemma: Only by living for man is it possible to live for God.

With Pashenka as a role model, Kasatskii takes to the road along with other wanderers "to search for God." He helps those whom he meets with advice and deed – but, because he is now at the very bottom of the social ladder, there is no longer any danger that anyone will honor or revere him.

However, the portrayal of the holy wanderers in *Father Sergius* is not entirely positive. As elder, Sergius had met multitudes of them:

> Among them were the female wanderers who went from one sacred place to the next, from elder to elder. Every new sanctuary and every new elder touched them deeply. Father Sergius knew this common, highly irreligious, cold, and conventional type. There were also wanderers . . .who drifted from monastery to monastery just to be fed; as well as simple peasants and peasant wives with selfish demands to be healed or to have highly practical questions cleared up: Should they marry off their daughter, rent a shop, or buy a plot of land . . .? (Tolstoi PSS 31, 31)

Kasatskii as Holy Fool

Holy wandering proves to be a yet another form of piety that can be filled with various kinds of content. Why, then, does it seem to work for the best for Kasatskii? – because it teaches him true *apatheia*. We are not told much about Kasatskii's life on the road, a single episode expresses the change that has taken place in him. One day he and his fellow wanderers are stopped by a group of tourists: A squire and his family are showing a visiting Frenchman the Russian countryside, and Kasatskii is stared at and quizzed as a choice ethnographic specimen. The scene has clear parallels to the episode in the monastery church, when the abbot called on Sergius to exhibit him to a general. Objectively speaking, the treatment on the road is far more degrading. But Sergius reacted with rage in the church, whereas Kasatskii reacts with utter peace of mind toward the French-speaking tourists:

> Kasatskii found this meeting particularly pleasing, for he scorned the opinions of men and did the easiest thing the world: humbly he took the 20 kopeks [which he had been given] and handed them to his travel companion, the blind beggar. The less that man's opinions meant to him, the more strongly did he feel God. (Tolstoi PSS 31, 46)

R. F. Christian finds this key scene unconvincing: There is no reason why this action should not impress those present and thereby feed Kasatskii's self-esteem (Christian 1969, 236). However, there can be no doubt that Tolstoi's intention here was to depict true *apatheia* translated into practice. His diary entry for June 10, 1891 reads:

> About *Father Sergius*: He learned what it means to rely on God only when he was irrevocably lost in people's eyes. Only then did he learn firmness and fullness of life. He achieved complete *ravnodushie* towards people and their deeds. (Tolstoi PSS 52, 39)

In Chapter 7 we saw that one of the *topoi* where the *apatheia* ideal most clearly meets popular Russian religiosity is holy foolishness. In this form of piety, the role of the holy wanderer meets the monks' asceticism and struggle against the passions. Tolstoi emphasizes the ability of the holy fool to endure human contempt as particularly valuable. This he regards as a safeguard against vanity and a test of the degree of passionlessness and detachment. In *Father Sergius* we find no explicit references to holy foolishness, but this form of piety resonates as an undertone. It is suggested, *inter alia,* by Kasatskii's holy role model Pashenka being depicted as "dumb." This interpretation also finds support in Tolstoi's own notes for the story:

> I have often thought and written that holy foolishness (in Christ), that is to say, to present yourself intentionally as worse than you are, that is the highest characteristic of virtue. Now I see that this is not only the highest characteristic of virtue but the necessary first (or rather, second) precondition for any good life. As soon as a man manages to free himself ever so little from the sins of the flesh, then he departs from the right path again and fall into an even worse pit – the praise of men . . . . This theme I must develop further in *Sergius*. It is worth it. (Tolstoi PSS 52, 81–82)[1]

In the Jubilee edition of Tolstoi's collected works, the publishers claimed that the final scenes of *Father Sergius* reflect "one of the writer's most dangerous tendencies": "the exaltation of *holy foolishness*, the reactionary preaching of meekness and humility" (Tolstoi PSS 31, ix). Although Soviet-era scholars had only contempt for Tolstoi's religious ideal, they nevertheless managed to see clearly the message he sought to convey in *Father Sergius*.

[1] Andrei Zorin (Zorin 2020, 187) quotes this passage but starts after the reference to holy foolishness. Another missed chance to understand the attraction this form of spirituality exerted on Tolstoi.

The life of Kasatskii alias Father Sergius is a circular motion. He starts in the world, withdraws from it, and finally returns to it. However, he has not come back to the starting point, for he is now equipped with new insights about God and life. Along the way he has taken up several Orthodox forms of piety – coenobitic monasticism, *eldership* and *holy wandering*. He ends up in *holy foolishness*, which combines elements of them all, as a life *in* the world, but not *of* the world.

These varieties of piety prove to be, with the words of Søren Kierkegaard, "stages on the path of life," hierarchically arranged, rising from lower to higher forms. Despite the abrupt breaks between them, they must be understood as parts of a developmental process, all contributing to a cumulative maturation. From each stage, Kasatskii is able to gain new wisdom.

Margaret Ziolkowski sees "hostility towards monasticism" as an important ingredient in the message of *Father Sergius* (Ziolkowski 1982, 74–75). Up to a point, I think this is correct, but Sergius's years in the monastery should not be regarded as completely wasted. He was on the right track when he managed to be increasingly content with his life on the inner plane, but coenobitic monasticism could not take him all the way. Despite the clear criticism of the institution of the monastery in this short story, the monastic way of life is nevertheless given partial redress: Sergius's first temptress takes the veil after having caused his mutilation. With this piece of information, Tolstoi evidently wants to say that she has chosen a better and truer life: Thus, the monastic life may be a viable way for some, for those who have a less obdurate personality than Kasatskii. This conclusion is substantiated by notes that Tolstoi made in his diary in the years just before he began writing the story. In October 1890, he commented on the emergence of monasticism under Constantine the Great: "The Christians became monks, the non-Christians remained" (Tolstoi PSS 51, 93). One year earlier, Tolstoi had maintained that "the life of a monk has many good aspects." The most important, he believed, was that the monks keep the temptations at a distance and spend time in prayer. Even if the prayers prescribed by the Church are often quite confused and meaningless, at least they are not harmful, he argued (Tolstoi PSS 50, 95).

Several Orthodox writers have held that Tolstoi in *Father Sergius* reveals poor knowledge about the monastic environment he is trying to portray (e.g., Ioann [Shakhovskoi] 1939, 87–89; Kontsevich 1960, 49). Indeed, *Father Sergius* is probably not correct in every detail, and whether Tolstoi was able and willing to understand the monks on their own terms can probably be discussed. However, he did undertake a thorough investigation of the monastic milieu before starting to write this story. His third visit to Optina Pustyn', in 1890, was motivated largely by the desire to collect material for *Father Sergius*. Like a sociologist of religion on a field trip, he walked around on the monastery premises with a notepad and a pencil. The portrayal of the irreligious peasants with mundane requests in *Father Sergius* is direct transcripts of the conversations he overheard outside elder Amvrosii's hut. Further, Sergius' healing abilities as an elder were modeled on the narratives of miracles that circulated about the Optina monks (Tolstoi PSS 31, 260).

After visiting Optina in 1880, Tolstoi returned home with predominantly negative impressions. In his notes he described monasticism as "spiritual self-indulgence" (Tolstoi PSS 51, 23). In isolation, this statement may seem paradoxical and incomprehensible. The remark makes more sense, however, in the context of *Father Sergius*: By suppressing the carnal passions, the monastery gives greater leeway for spiritual sins. The monastery can function as a greenhouse where certain refined passions are cultivated, while only the coarse, carnal ones are weeded out.

Nevertheless, the depiction of eldership in *Father Sergius* is by no means solely judgmental. Sergius' confessor and elder, of whom we admittedly get only a few glimpses, is portrayed as a good person with deep spiritual wisdom. He is the first to make a diagnosis of Sergius' case, a diagnosis Tolstoi undoubtedly regarded as correct (Tolstoi PSS 31, 16). However, not even this elder could prescribe a sufficiently strong cure for his spiritual patient.

The last diary entry Tolstoi made about *Father Sergius* dates from 1898:

> There is no peace (*uspokoeniia*) for those who live for worldly purposes among people, nor for those who live alone for spiritual purposes only. Only the man who lives to serve God among men can find peace. (Tolstoi PSS 53, 204)

CHAPTER 9

Tolstoi and the Social Ideal of the Eastern Church: John Chrysostom

In *What I Believe* (1884), Tolstoi refers to several Orthodox writers from early Christian times as well as the early Byzantine period. Some of them he mentions only in passing, and had apparently found their names in secondary literature without reading them in the original.

However, two of the Church Fathers whom he mentions – Origen and John Chrysostom – Tolstoi had apparently consulted more deeply, as he refers to specific chapters in their works. Of Origen's works, he cites *Against Kelsos* (*Contra Celsum)*, an apology directed at the pagan critic of Christianity, Kelsos; from Chrysostom, he cites *Commentary on Matthew.*

In *What I Believe*, Origen and Chrysostom serve as hero and villain, respectively. They lived on either side of the great watershed in ancient Church history – the Constantine Revolution – when Christianity passed from being a persecuted sect to the official religion of the Empire. As we have seen, Tolstoi considered this to be the "fall from grace" in the history of the Church, and as something that he saw reflected in the writings of these two theologians. While warmly embracing Origen, he contemptuously rejected Chrysostom's Bible exegesis. Even so, it is easier to find positive impulses that Tolstoi received from the latter than from the former.

Origen (184–254) was one of the most influential Eastern theologians (Hägglund [1956] 1975, 47), even though the Orthodox Church does not recognize him as a "Church Father." At the end of the fourth century, a dispute over him erupted, and some of his ideas were declared heretical. What endeared Origin to Tolstoi was primarily his pacifism. In *Against Kelsos*, Tolstoi could read that Christians of Origen's time refused to do military service, even when forced to do so (Tolstoi PSS 23, 367). Nor did they take part in litigation, but persistently endured the sufferings imposed on them by the courts (Tolstoi PSS 23, 324). This, Tolstoi says, shows that Christians in the first centuries understood the Sermon on the Mount in the same way as he did, and not as later distorted by the Church.

John Chrysostom was a somewhat less astute theologian than Origen, but has become one of the most popular saints in the Orthodox Church. In his youth, Chrysostom had studied under the famous pagan orator Libanius and had good prospects of making a career in the Byzantine state service. Instead, he chose to settle down as a hermit in the Syrian Desert, where he practiced very strict asceticism. In 386, he was called as a presbyter to his home town of Antioch, and was later installed as archbishop in the imperial city of Constantinople. He was given the nickname of *Chrysostomos* – "golden-mouthed" – because of his well-structured, fiery sermons. The bulk of his extensive production consists of stenographic records from these sermons, as was the text Tolstoi read, the *Commentary on Matthew*.

Chrysostom's homilies are infused with strong indignation against moral dissipation and social injustice in Byzantine society. Almost irrespective of the topic at hand, he touched on socio-ethical questions. He did not present his criticism in general terms only, but specifically rebuked the Court and, in particular, the Empress Eudoxia, whom Chrysostom reportedly referred to as "Adoxia," "the ignominious." He also provoked many of his colleagues in the higher clergy by serving them a simple monk's menu when they were visiting, instead of the lavish dinners they were accustomed to from the time of his predecessors. In the end, he was deposed and sent in exile to Armenia, under strong protests from Constantinople's poor masses, who saw him as their spokesperson. All this makes it difficult to see in Chrysostom a typical representative of the Byzantine ecclesiastical hierarchy and its ideology, as Tolstoi portrays him in *What I Believe*.

As an example of the Church's falsification of Jesus' message, Tolstoi singles out Chrysostom's interpretation of the Sermon on the Mount. Even though Jesus taught "Judge not, that ye be not judged" (Matth 7, 1–5), Chrysostom defends the right of Christians to pass legal verdicts by referring to the example of the Apostles (Chrysostomus 23, I: 1915–16, II, 67–69, quoted by Tolstoi PSS 23, 325). However, Tolstoi does not mention that Chrysostom here especially notes that this interpretation of the Gospel is his "assumption," something that he "believes."

Tolstoi also quotes a long paragraph from *Commentary on Matthew* to show that the Church juxtaposed the Law of Moses "an eye for an eye and a tooth for a tooth" with Jesus' command of non-opposition to evil, and regarded them as equally valid. In this paragraph, Chrysostom also claims that the Law of Moses comes from God and is an expression of His love for mankind. The opposite of the Law of Moses would be lawlessness, the archbishop argues (Chrysostomus 16, 6: 1915–16, 1, 285–6; quoted by Tolstoi PSS 23, 334–35). Tolstoi, however, holds that one must choose either the Law of Moses or the Sermon on the Mount: To claim that both come from God would be a contradiction in terms.

In fact, Tolstoi's excerpts from the *Commentary on Matthew* give a rather skewed picture of Chrysostom's view on the law of the ancient Jews. Admittedly, Chrysostom strongly insists that it is the same God who is acting in both the Old and the New Testament, something that many Gnostics had denied. However, he adds that God does not act in the *same way* in both Testaments, for the people under the Old and New Covenants are at different stages of development.

> If you consider what kind of people to which this rule [= 'an eye for an eye', P.K.] was given, what disposition they had and which times they were living in, then you will fully recognize the wisdom of the lawgiver. (Chrysostomus 18, 1: 1915–16, 1, 323)

The eternal law must be adapted to man's ability to understand and acquire it. Chrysostom's view here is surprisingly similar to one of Tolstoi's basic ideas: That the religious message must be adjusted to the spiritual development of the society in which it is preached, in order to become genuinely true.

In *The Kingdom of God Is Within You* (1890–93), Tolstoi claimed that a religion that was true when first preached may later become false if the people's collective knowledge is expanded without the religion taking that into account. Conversely, a religion may be too advanced for the society in which it is preached, if it presupposes a level of enlightenment and a moral consciousness that the people of this particular society have not yet achieved.

> If a religion establishes a relationship between God and man, but does this with claims that contradict reason and *human knowledge (*znaniia*) at this time*, so that man cannot believe in these claims, then this is only a likeness (*podobie*) of a religion. (Tolstoi PSS 35, 162, emphasis added)

The same idea was expressed in rudimentary form already in *What I Believe*. In this work Tolstoi asserted that the Church played a historically conditioned, temporarily positive function as long as humanity was at a spiritual "embryonic stage." This he compared to a placenta that is discarded after birth (Tolstoi 23, 448). Chrysostom used another analogy, likewise taken from the beginning of human life: Man under the Old Covenant was like an infant. Only after the coming of Jesus it was ready to accept solid food, and had to be weaned from the mother's breast, even though this can be a painful process (Chrysostomus 17, 5: 1915–16, 1, 316; see also 1 Cor 3, 2).

Chrysostom also drew the same negative corollaries of this perspective as did Tolstoi: An overly advanced religion would be *detrimental* if preached to a society that was not ready for it. As Chrysostom put it: A child who has to wear an adult man's clothes can easily trip over and fall when trying to move about (Chrysostomus 17, 6: 1915–16, 1, 318). Tolstoi used this line of reasoning to explain why Christianity, in his opinion, had become more distorted than other religions: When Christ lived and preached among men, his teachings were too advanced for the times – in a sense, better than good, more than optimal (Tolstoi PSS 37, 152).

In order to make Chrysostom a representative of the ecclesiastical dilution of the absolute commandments of Christ, Tolstoi had to suppress much of Chrysostom's message. The injunction not to take oaths Chrysostom understands just as literally as did Tolstoi (Chrysostomus 17, 5–6: 1915–16, 1, 3, 5–7). The most important verse in the Bible, as Tolstoi saw it, is the words of Jesus that we shall not resist evil (Matt 5, 39). It is from the standpoint of this commandment that he separates the chaff from the wheat among those who profess to be Christians. At this crucial point, too, Chrysostom's interpretation coincides with that of Tolstoi:

> Shall we then really not resist the evil? Indeed we shall, but not in that way, but as He commanded us. We shall willingly endure the wrong, for in that way you will master it. One does not extinguish fire with fire, but with water . . . . Nothing restrains the wicked as effectively as when one meekly accepts the wrongdoing. (Chrysostomus 18, 1–2: 1915–16, 1, 324, 326)

Chrysostom's form of "resistance to evil" is strikingly similar to Tolstoi's nonresistance. Both thinkers distanced themselves from what they perceived as wrongly understood fatalism, and believed they had found a powerful means to master wickedness. Chrysostom believed that actions are contagious: Good actions have a positive "infectious effect." For instance, he referred to Jesu words that true disciples are like the salt of the world (Matt 5, 13; Chrysostomus 18, 3: 1915–16, 1, 328). Chrysostom also claimed that if you give your robe to the one who has taken your shirt, he will be so ashamed that he will hand it back. If, contrary to expectation, he does not do so, other people will be so moved by observing your good example that they will give you what you need. However, even if nonresistence to evil should result in your being naked, there is no reason to despair. Adam and Eve were naked in Paradise without feeling ashamed, and in your nakedness you will be more decently clad than all gaudy people who adorn themselves with costly attire (Chrysostomus 18, 2: 1915–16, 1, 1, 327).

Like Chrysostom, Tolstoi strongly believed that actions – good as well as bad – are contagious, and this idea occupied a central role in his social theory. According to this thinking, all human actions, the evil as well as the good ones, are surrounded by a power field, as it were, like magnets.[1] Evil fields are charged with negative energy and good ones with positive energy. Those who enter one of these fields are affected or "infected" (Tolstoi PSS 41, 552). Since all power is based on violence or the threat thereof, all exercise of power (*vlast'*) is to Tolstoi acts of evil. Tolstoi's theory of contagion provides an important part of his explanation why violence has become so widespread in modern society. The rulers' violent treatment of their subjects makes them treat each other equally badly. Next, each new generation is taught violent behavior by their parents. But, luckily, also good deeds are surrounded by a strong magnetic field and have the ability to affect the actions of other people who come under the influence of them. It is possible for some individuals to escape from the vicious circle of violence and create new benevolent circles. "What makes actions of love so important is that they are contagious. . . . And since they are contagious there are no limits to their repercussions" (Tolstoi PSS 29, 113). Both for Tolstoi and Chrysostom the theory of contagion was crucial to avoid the charge that their theory of nonresistance to violence would lead to the inevitable victory of the wicked in this world.[2]

In 1894, the Orthodox theologian Timofei Butkevich cited from Chrysostom's *Commentary to Matthew* in order to show that the Church has always taken Jesus' words of nonopposition to evil seriously and understood them correctly. Butkevich reminded his readers that Tolstoi had a number of references to Chrysostom and wondered why he never referred to the archbishop's teaching about nonviolence. Instead, Tolstoi pretended not to know it (Butkevich 1894, 5–7).

In *What I believe* Tolstoi claimed that a Christian life characterized by nonviolence and abstention from property does not lead to martyrdom; on the contrary, it is "the people of the world" with all their self-inflicted

[1] Tolstoi vacillated between biological metaphors like "contagion" and metaphors from physics, like "magnets."

[2] Tolstoi's concept of infection lies at the heart not only of his social theory but also of his understanding of the workings of art. See Tolstoi PSS 30, 27–203; Robinson 2007; Pickford 2016, especially chapter 4.

concerns who are the true martyrs. This view we can find also in Chrysostom's book.

> But you will perhaps object: What is more difficult than not owning anything, than to turn the other cheek and not strike back when you are hit, indeed, even having to suffer a violent death? And yet, when we consider the matter properly, all this is insignificant and immaterial and a source of joy . . . . Tell me, what is more difficult: . . . Being dressed in just one garment without demanding anything more or having the house full of clothes, and day and night worry about them and tremble for fear that they may be eaten by moth or stolen by your servant? (Chrysostomus 38, 3: 1915–16, 2, 323)

The rich becomes a slave under his belongings, he loses control over his life and becomes like an obsessed. Love of money conquers the mind and leads to all kinds of injustice (Chrysostomus 21, 1: 1915–16, 2, 43). This passion is all the more incomprehensible since greed is "vanity and vexation of spirit" (cfr. Eccl 1, 14). A handful of money is less useful than a heap of dung, since the dung can at least be used to fertilize the soil. Chrysostom, however, was not completely satisfied with this metaphor: Money, he believed, is not just useless, they are positively harmful. For their sake, houses are brought to ruin, terrible wars are started, people are sent to death. The avaricious proceeds directly to hell. It is impossible for a rich man to enter the Kingdom of Heaven (Chrysostomus 63, 4: 1915–16, 3, 303–5).

In *What Can We Then Do?* (1886), Tolstoi presented a socioeconomic theory according to which money was the foundation and premise of modern forms of exploitation. He developed this theory after he had visited the slums of Moscow and observed the squalid living conditions of the city's *lumpenproletariat.* "I felt that in the possession of money, in money itself, something repulsive and immoral was attached" (Tolstoi PSS 25, 247). To be sure, Tolstoi's socioeconomic theory was more detailed and speculative than Chrysostom' thoughts on the subject, but they shared the general perception of money as something dirty (Tolstoi PSS 25, 290–91).

Like Tolstoi, Chrysostom directed his attacks not only against the luxury and extravagance of the rich, but also against the very foundation of their wealth: ownership rights. Chrysostom was not content with encouraging wealthy people to share some of their plenty with the poor: He also argued that private property came into the world as a result of the Fall, and therefore has a highly dubious legitimacy (Chrysostomus 28, 49: 1915–16, 2, 155–70; 3, 82–141). All property is unjust, even if you have inherited your wealth, even if you have received your property in compensation for something else (see Nyström 1911, 74). Henry Chadwick calls Chrysostom's view of property "socialist" (Chadwick 1978, 188). In particular, the archbishop fulminated against the landowners' possession of land:

> Can there be any more unrighteous people than those who possess land and gain their wealth from the earth? When one examines how they treat the poor and miserable farm workers, one is convinced that they are more inhuman than the barbarians. They place heavy corvée duties and unfulfillable tasks on the shoulders of people who their whole life go hungry and suffer need. They exploit them as donkeys and mules, yes, like stones. (Chrysostomus 61, 3: 1915–16, 3, 271)

This description could just as well have been taken from one of Tolstoi's pamphlets against conditions in the Russian countryside of his times.[3]

As a positive alternative to money and wealth, Chrysostom singled out physical work. He reminded his audience that the first disciples were poor fishermen, and regarded this as a "no small evidence of their high morals" (Chrysostomus 14, 2: 1915–16, 1, 231). Also on this point, Tolstoi followed closely in the footsteps of the Greek prelate.

In this review of Chrysostom's social ethics, I have drawn solely on quotes and examples from his *Commentary on Matthew*, the only work we can safely say that Tolstoi had read. We have no guarantee that he ploughed through this 1,000-page work, cover to cover – but that was not necessary. Chrysostom returned to the same thoughts in sermon after sermon, so even a random reading of the *Commentary* should have sufficed to convince Tolstoi that here was a kindred spirit. One can ask why Tolstoi then treated Chrysostom so poorly as he did in *What I Believe*. There is reason to believe he opened the *Commentary* for one purpose only: to find evidence to support conclusions he had already drawn. Occasionally, Tolstoi found something he thought he could use, but everything contrary to his thesis was removed from his field of vision by some kind of selective perception. Nonetheless, some ideas of this Church Father seem to have made sufficient impression to leave a trace on Tolstoi's own thinking – such as the idea of timeliness as a criterion of truth.

[3] Shortly after Tolstoi had finished writing *What I believe*, he became acquainted with Henry George's book *Progress and poverty* in which this American social reformer proposed the abolition of private property of land altogether, instead, all land should become common property. For a while Tolstoi was strongly fascinated by this idea (Wilson 1988, 476; Bartlett 2010, 318), but his radical views on private land property placed him much closer to Chrysostom than to George.

In any case, we can find several far more positive statements about Chrysostom in Tolstoi's works than what is expressed in *What I Believe.* In 1879, he mentioned, with appreciation, the sermons of Chrysostom that he had read in the Orthodox text compilations *Prolog* and *Chet'i-Minei* (Tolstoi PSS 23, 52). In 1888, the Tolstoian publishing house *Posrednik* published L. P. Nikiforov's *The Exhortations of the Holy John Chrysostom,* which Tolstoi had read in manuscript and recommended for publication (Tolstoi PSS 86, 20–21). This book consists of excerpts from Chrysostom's *Commentary on John,* and there too, the Greek prelate constantly discussed social questions. Among other things, he claimed that the desire to possess wealth is contrary to human nature. "The desire for money (*srebroliubie*) is a terrible disease . . . it clogs up our eyes and ears and makes us more frantic than predators" (Nikiforov 1888, 24). In 1908, Tolstoi claimed that "Chrysostom always speaks well" (Makovitskii 1904–10, I, 257). Several quotes from Chrysostom found their way into Tolstoi's compilations of devotional texts, such as *Circle of Readings, For Each Day* and *The Way of Life* (Tolstoi PSS 41–45, passim).

Many Russian Orthodox believers were apparently ambivalent toward this popular fifth-century saint. Evidence of this can be found in Aleksandr Orfano's *What Should Constitute the True Faith of Every Human Being? (A Critical Analysis of Count L. Tolstoi's Book* What I Believe*)* from 1890. Orfano had known Tolstoi personally in the 1870s, but was not particularly impressed by his teaching (see Tolstoi PSS 45, 12). In his book, Orfano reproduced lengthy excerpts from Chrysostom's *Commentary on Matthew* to show that Tolstoi's interpretation of Matt 5, 39 ("But I say unto you, that ye resist not evil") only repeated what the Church had always held and preached:

> One must ask: If Tolstoi understands this commandment in such a way that instead of setting yourself up against evil, you shall do well toward the evil-doer, and in this sees the meaning of the commandment, what is then the new thing he has discovered in this commandment? What does it mean when he claims that this gave him a "momentary enlightenment"? We see that this is the way which the holy John Chrysostom understands the commandment, and this is the way the entire Church of Christ has understood it throughout all the centuries Christianity has existed. (Orfano 1890, 55)

Several ecclesiastical writers stated explicitly that they wished to spread knowledge about Chrysostom's social message as a counterweight to socialist and communist propaganda in Russian society. In Chrysostom, the Church had a saint who, to the highest degree, took social need and injustice seriously, but who "avoided all fallacies and exaggerations" (Goviadovskii 1906, 4, 612; see also Kudriavtsev 1907, 786). It therefore caused great consternation in church circles when Vasilii Ekzempliarskii, a professor of patristics at Kiev Theological Academy, in a lecture on "the importance of the commandments of Christ for life" ventured to compare the Saint with the "anarchist preacher" Lev Tolstoi, finding a remarkable congruence of ideas, as exemplified by their understanding of private property rights, in particular the view that land should not be privately owned. "Furthermore, both reject oath-taking in the life of a Christian and agree that poverty is a positive good. Both consider city life unnatural; emphasize the significance of physical labour; regard the life of the Christian on earth as a pilgrimage, and so on" (Ekzempliarskii [1912] 1978, 109). Ekzempliarskii acknowledged that there were also some real differences between the views of the Greek prelate and the Russian author, but believed that these did not undermine their fundamental agreement. He also claimed that all the most important Church Fathers had been in agreement with Chrysostom – thereby implying that, fundamentally, Tolstoi's social message coincided with the social teachings of true Orthodoxy.

Ekzempliarskii had in particular done research on the Church Fathers' attitude toward property and property rights. In addition, he had for several years given lectures to his students about Tolstoi's teaching. The professor therefore ought to have particularly good qualifications for his discussion of the topic at hand. Large parts of Ekzempliarskii's article consisted of excerpts from Tolstoi's and Chrysostom's writings juxtaposed, so that readers could make up their own opinions. But Ekzempliarskii himself also drew some conclusions from the material. He noted that while Tolstoi with great magnanimity had overlooked fundamental contradictions between his own religious system and what had been proclaimed by Confucius, Lao-tse, Zarathustra, Socrates, and Epictetus, his attitude toward the early Christian theologians was marked by harsh intolerance. Tolstoi became wildly agitated when the Church Fathers' views of some verses in the Gospels seemed to deviate from his own ideas. However, this was often a matter of "non-existent disagreements," Ekzempliarskii claimed. In reality, the old Church Fathers were precursors of Tolstoi, far more than the Asian sages he had referred to (Ekzempliarskii [1912] 1978, 77).

Even so, Tolstoi had not found Christ's true message in the Church – and Ekzempliarskii placed the blame for this primarily at the door of Russian theology. On important points it had deviated from the social teaching of the universal Church. "Our Russian theological thought has besmirched itself by attempting to prove that the teaching of the Gospel sanctions serfdom and corporal punishment, the opulence of the rich, capital punishment, coercive measures against people's conscience, and many, many other things." In attacking Tolstoi's teachings, Russian theologians thereby contributed to cementing a commonly accepted but misconceived understanding of what the Church really teaches on social matters, Ekzempliarskii concluded.

This broadside was more than the Russian Church establishment could take. Ekzempliarskii was accused of "anti-Orthodox activity" and given a dishonorable discharge from his position at Kiev Theological Academy. Refused the right of defense, he chose instead to present his case before the Russian public. In his published apology he emphasized that his intention had not been to elevate Tolstoi to the status as a new doctor of the Church – he fully realized that Tolstoi's religious ideas placed him well beyond the pale of the Christian community. Even so, Ekzempliarskii insisted that Tolstoi's teaching was a path "to the Promised Land." Indeed, "after St. John Chrysostom, not one of our moral theologians has explained the significance of the Gospel message for this life in such a lucid, determined, and straightforward way as the late L. Tolstoi did" (Ekzempliarskii 1912, 10–11).[4]

The Ekzempliarskii case became a *cause célèbre* and widened the schism between the liberal and reactionary camps in the Russian Church. Sergei Bulgakov, a former Marxist who later became an Orthodox theologian,[5] was one prominent Russian intellectual who publicly defended the expelled professor. It was most peculiar, he noted, that the Church leadership should suddenly exhibit such zeal for the correct teaching when it for such a long time had tolerated the antics of the religious charlatan Grigorii Rasputin (S. Bulgakov 1912a).

[4] Philip Gorski also notes that "Tolstoy's resounding denunciations of inequality and the lifestyles of the Christian wealthy stand directly in the tradition of St. John Chrysostom's well known homilies" (Gorski 2019, 42).

[5] See Chapter 11.

CHAPTER 10

The Church Mounts a Counterattack: Threat Perceptions and Combat Strategies

Leading figures in the Russian Orthodox Church were quick to identify Tolstoi as a formidable adversary, and for several decades bishops, theologians and lay Christians fought a fierce struggle to combat his influence over the hearts and minds of Russians. This massive and multifaceted anti-Tolstoian campaign was one of the Orthodox Church's most desperate attempts to stem heretical thought in the nineteenth and early twentieth centuries.

At the time, many observers found it odd that the men of the Church should be so preoccupied with this particular freethinker – aggressive critics of the Church were hardly in short supply in Russia then. However, the massive Orthodox counterattacks against Tolstoi's teaching must be understood against the background of the general position of the Church in Tsarist society. By the end of the nineteenth century, the Russian Church found itself in a paradoxical situation: It was at the same time powerful and impotent. It continued to be the empire's only state church and enjoyed the full support of the tsarist powers. Until 1905, it was strictly forbidden for members of other denominations to perform missionary work in Russia. The only non-Orthodox confessions that were tolerated were those that had a history connected to some nations abroad, such as Lutheranism and Catholicism in the Baltics and Islam in Central Asia. These religious communities were allowed to serve their own adherents, but not to recruit Russian members (Werth 2014).

But, despite its privileged position, the Orthodox state church was in many ways paralyzed. It was not even master in its own house: In several purely internal matters, such as the appointment of bishops, it had to bow to the will of the tsarist authorities (Curtiss 1940; Szeftel 1978; Döpmann 1981).The Church had reason to believe that when the state had given it a privileged position among the faiths, this was not primarily due to a deep concern for the well-being of Orthodoxy, but because it needed support in the fight against the radical intelligentsia that sought to topple the regime.

Not least as a result of its forced alliance with increasingly unpopular tsarism, however, the Church was rapidly losing its grip among ordinary Russians. Their identity as Orthodox believers was undermined from two directions. In the intelligentsia and the upper classes, atheism, agnosticism and indifference grew increasingly stronger; among the peasants and workers, more and more people were drawn toward the outlawed sects. The Russian Church tried various means for curtailing both of these tendencies, often with little success.

In the nineteenth century, the Russian dissenter movement was far from a negligible phenomenon. Unfortunately, official statistics are hopelessly incomplete and unreliable, but it is clear that in addition to those belonging to "foreign faiths" such as Catholicism, Protestantism, Islam and Judaism, many million of the tsar's subjects stood outside the Russian Orthodox Church.[1] The most important forms of Russian religious nonconformism had arisen already in the seventeenth and eighteenth centuries, some with roots dating back to fifteenth and sixteenth centuries. The *starovery* (or *staroobriadtsy*) – Old Believers or Old Ritualists – had broken off from the official Russian Church in the 1660s and represented perhaps as much as two-thirds of all Russian dissenters.[2] This underground church had split into several branches: The largest by far, the "priestly" Old Believers, differed little from official Russian Orthodoxy in theology and practice. They saw themselves as the true Orthodox Church, and had achieved a live-and-let-live understanding with the official Church. One group within the priestly branch, the *edinovertsy*, had even taken the step of acknowledging the supremacy of the state church as a precondition for being officially recognized and allowed to practice their old rituals (De Simone 2019).

The relationship between the Russian state church and the non-Orthodox dissenters, the "sects," was far more strained. The mystical-ecstatic movements of *khlysty* and *skoptsy* were exposed to systematic and brutal persecution, even though they were only marginal phenomena and did not pose any real threat to the Church's position of power (Buss 2003, 73–82). Also the spiritualistic communities of *dukhobory* and *molokane* were actively persecuted (N. Nikol'skii 1983; Donskov 2019). In some cases, the children were taken from *dukhobor* parents who had not married

[1] According to official statistics, there were more than 8 million dissenters in Russia in 1863, not counting the unbelievers (Miliukov 1909; Bolshakoff 1950, 15–16; Donskov 2019, 3).

[2] Richard Charques (Charques 1958, 43) speculates that the Old Believers alone may have been as many as "anything between fifteen and twenty million."

according to the Orthodox ritual: Their offspring were deemed born "out of wedlock." At other times, young men from these sectarian movements found themselves enrolled in penal battalions, since they refused to do ordinary military service. Entire Dukhobor communities were also exiled to desolate areas in order to isolate them from the Orthodox peasants. Only to a limited degree did the official strategy toward the sectarians consist of missionary measures to win them back into the fold. First and foremost, it had a defensive purpose: To prevent their doctrines from spreading. The harshest reactions were reserved for sect members who evangelized among the Orthodox. Some of them languished for decades in special Church prisons (Prugavin 1906; Shubin 2001).

In the last third of the nineteenth century, a new wave of religious nonconformism, with roots in West European Protestant denominations, swept over Russia (Blane 1975; Byford [1912] 2012). German settlers on the Volga and in Ukraine had brought their faith with them when they came to Russia and the Tsarist authorities did not interfere with their worship as long as it was purely an internal matter for these communities. Around 1870, however, German Baptists and Mennonites began to baptize Slavic peasants, and these passed the Gospel message on to their neighbors and friends. Soon, entirely Russian and Ukrainian evangelical congregations were formed, usually under the name of "*Stunde*," after the German word for "hour" (also "Bible instruction") (Nikol'skii 1983, 384–86). While the *Stundisty* preached the same religious message as the German settlers, the authorities treated them very differently (Werth [2014] 2016, 103). Even if ethnic Russians (a concept that included all Eastern Slavs) who switched to another religion than Orthodoxy were liable to persecution, the *Stunde* movement spread remarkably fast, for several reasons. Firstly, its adherents were known for their high moral standards, including low alcohol consumption and stable marriages. Second, they knew the Bible far better than most Orthodox believers and could argue convincingly for their interpretation of its message. And most importantly, the *Stundisty*, in contrast to most other sects in Russia, actively set about proselytizing (Blane 1975, 277). They considered it their Christian duty to bring the Gospel to the unsaved and to rescue as many as possible from perdition. At the same time, Western media were monitoring developments, making it difficult for the Russian authorities to persecute these evangelizers. Faced with this new and hitherto unknown challenge, the Orthodox authorities were at a loss.

At this time, Protestant preaching found its way also into certain circles among the upper classes. The Irish preacher Lord Radstock recruited many new disciples at his series of revival meetings in St. Petersburg in 1874. One of his converts was Colonel V. A. Pashkov, who in turn became a successful preacher himself (Blane 1975, 275–280). His activity gave rise to a considerable sect movement colloquially referred to as *pashkovshchina* (Heier 1970).

Tolstoianism as a Sect Movement

When Tolstoi started his preaching in the early 1880s, many Orthodox feared that they were faced with a new Pashkov, only of a far more awe-inspiring format. There were, in fact, some lines of connection between the Irish preacher and Tolstoi. Lord Radstock had been invited to Russia by Madame Chertkova, the mother of Tolstoi's close collaborator Vladimir Chertkov. Tolstoi, however, was not particularly impressed with Radstock's piety, as evident in the sarcastic account given in *Anna Karenina*. It soon became clear that Tolstoi and Vladimir Chertkov represented a very different kind of religiosity than Radstock and Pashkov. However, there were other Russian sectarians with whom Tolstoi had much closer relations. In 1881, he visited the sect leader Vasilii Siutaev, who was often regarded as a *Stundist* (N. Nikol'skii 1983, 387–90). Later, Tolstoi claimed that few Russians had influenced his own thinking as much as this unlearned, freethinking peasant (Tolstoi PSS 25, 834).

Many Orthodox feared that Tolstoi's preaching might lead to even more widespread apostasy among Russians than what had followed in the wake of other heretics. With his worldwide reputation and elegant form of expression, Tolstoi could arouse interest among social groups that would otherwise have difficulty identifying with sectarianism. While most of the new sects had originated among simple, uncouth people and had a fairly limited spread, Tolstoianism threatened to become a nationwide movement. Already in 1886, the Church writer Ivan Palimpsestov feared the worst:

> Look at the speed with which Stundism is spreading! How many of the children of the Orthodox church have not been torn worn away from their [spiritual] mother over the two or three last years! And Stundism did not emanate from such a highly praised authority as our writer Count L. N. Tolstoi. (Palimpsestov 1886b, 803)

The sect with which Tolstoi had the closest contact, however, was not Stundism, but the Dukhobors. In 1895, he learned that Dukhobor communities, which had been expelled to the Caucasus in the 1840s, were exposed to a new round of harassment and persecutions, since they refused to take an oath to the Tsar and do military service, and he sent his close collaborator Pavel Biriukov to look into the matter. Biriukov concluded that if nothing were done, the Dukhobors would succumb to hunger and cold – whereupon Tolstoi took the initiative to a large media campaign to get the state authorities to let the Dukhobors emigrate. The campaign succeeded, and when a group of the sectarians left for Canada in 1898, Tolstoi covered much of their travel expenses. He also conducted an extensive correspondence with the leader of the Dukhobor colony, Petr Verigin, and discovered that they held several beliefs in common (Donskov 2019; L. N. Tolstoi 1902).

The lines of influence between Tolstoi and Verigin went both ways; indeed, many contemporary observers saw Tolstoianism and *dukhoborchestvo* as two branches of the same movement. In 1900, a leading Orthodox expert on sectarianism, Vasilii Skvortsov, inspected some of the Dukhobor villages in the Caucasus at the behest of the Holy Synod. He concluded that Tolstoi had been one of their "heretical ringleaders" (V. Skvortsov 1900, 12). The branch of the Dukhobor sect that had emigrated to America, Skvortsov referred to as "Dukhobors, aka Tolstoians" (V. Skvortsov 1900, 5).

Vasilii Skvortsov (1859–1932) was one of the most remarkable and influential figures in the Russian Church around the turn of the nineteenth and twentieth centuries. He held a position as a privy councillor and was attached to the Synod as a special advisor in sectarian matters. Here he functioned as what we today could call a "lobbyist" for strict reactions to sectarianism. Skvortsov consistently opposed the introduction of religious freedom in Russia, arguing that Orthodoxy was linked to the autocratic state in a "mystical" connection (V. Skvortsov 1902b, 798). As expressed by Skvortsov's biographer and admirer, Vladislav Maevskii, he would fight religious deviations "with the efforts of missionaries, doctors, and lawmakers" (Maevskii 1954, 190). In Skvortsov's opinion, admission to a psychiatric ward could be an efficacious remedy against sectarian inclinations.

Skvortsov's interest in the sects had been awakened already when he studied at the theological academy in Kiev. Here he had "infiltrated" the local Stundist congregation in order to study it from the inside. He organized a series of Congresses for Orthodox Home Missionaries – in 1887, 1891, and 1897 – and also founded the theological journal *Missionerskoe obozrenie*. The journal later moved its editorial premises to

St. Petersburg and became the leading organ of home mission in Russia (Coleman 2014, 67–69). It regularly published attacks on Tolstoi and his teachings.

Skvortsov was constantly on the lookout for signs that Tolstoianism was about to develop into a regular sect. In particular, he was worried that the Tolstoians would start evangelizing among the Orthodox. As Tolstoi himself was a Russian and had an Orthodox background, the danger seemed imminent. At the Third Russian Congress for Orthodox Home Missionaries, held in Kazan in 1897, Tolstoianism was among the main themes discussed. Reports presented at the congress documented that this heresy had taken root among the Orthodox population in several provinces (*gubernii)*: Khar'kov, Kursk, Poltava, Voronezh, Ekaterinoslav, Kiev, Don and the Caucasus. It was reported that among the worst affected areas was Voronezh, where the wealthy squire and Tolstoian Vladimir Chertkov had his estate. A local diocese missionary claimed that Chertkov bribed simple Orthodox peasants in order to recruit them to his faith ("Tolstovstvo, kak sekta" 1897, 826).

The keynote speaker at the congressional session devoted to Tolstoianism was the priest Timofei Butkevich from Khar'kov, who had studied Tolstoi's teachings thoroughly and already published two thick books against him (Butkevich 1893; Butkevich 1894). The priest regarded the 1892 famine as a turning point. In that year, active Tolstoians had established soup kitchens for the needy in several places in the Khar'kov area. Under the guise of this philanthropic activity, they had conducted an intense and successful Tolstoian propaganda campaign, Butkevich claimed. To his relief, he saw clear signs that these rabble-rousers were now coming under control. In the last few years, the Tolstoians had become less aggressive and proselyting. Their relations with the secular powers had improved, and they also behaved more politely toward the priests. The reason for this, Butkevich explained, was that Khar'kov had a new governor who had made determined efforts to eradicate this movement. The ringleaders were banished from the region, and Tolstoians who refused to perform their civic duties, were heavily fined. However, Butkevich warned against rejoicing prematurely. Many Tolstoians were still brimming with self-confidence, in conversations with Orthodox declaring that "in five years' time, you will have become Stundists just as we are." Butkevich concluded his report with a clear warning: "*If circumstances change or the vigilance of the secular authorities lets up*, then Tolstoianism may again rear its head ... [The current situation may] be just the lull before the storm" (Butkevich 1897, 182, emphasis in the original).

Following this lecture, Vasilii Skvortsov declared that they had enough information to conclude that the Tolstoian movement had by now become established as a separate sect. There existed separate Tolstoi communities and congregations, and they had their own Tolstoian doctrine. Skvortsov also claimed that this sect had its own statement of doctrine, namely, "The catechism of the evangelical brotherhood of Jesus (the *Stundists*)," often referred to as "the Tolstoian catechism for the people." (This text is reproduced in its entirety in Butkevich 1910, 580–98; and Weisbein 1960, 490–505.) Skvortsov admitted that it was still an open question whether the heretic of Iasnaia Poliana had authored the catechism himself. However, the substantive coincidences between that text and Tolstoi's writings were so striking that "it provides ample grounds for concluding that the publication of the catechism cannot have taken place without Tolstoi's active cooperation" ("Tolstovstvo, kak sekta" 1897, 829). Thus, Skvortsov felt that he had established that Tolstoianism exhibited one of the standard features needed to characterize something as a religious sect – a sect leader.

On this basis, the Missionary Congress adopted a resolution with the following wording:

> Tolstoianism preaches heretical anti-Christian views on religion. Its condemnation of the Church coincides with Stundism. At the political level, this doctrine contains criminal, anti-state tendencies (which only pretend to be a religion). It therefore constitutes a religious-social sect. In order to combat it, spiritual admonitions are not enough: resolute action from the state is needed to limit the damage. These measures must be implemented not only against those who propagate the sect, but also against its followers. They must bear criminal responsibility for the fact that they belong to Tolstoianism. ("Tolstovstvo, kak sekta," 1897, 831)

Nevertheless, debate on whether Tolstoianism was a sect in the full sense of the word continued. In 1910, Timofei Butkevich published a revised version of his lecture from the missionary congress. Now he admitted that the Tolstoians had never developed their own religious cult or their own rituals. Further, they did not hold regular services or liturgy, nor did they sing hymns. "At present, it would hardly be correct to call them sectarians. They are simply atheists and coarse disbelievers" (Butkevich 1910, 597). However, this assessment was presented in a book which Butkevich titled *A Survey of Russian Sects and their Teachings,* where the discussion of Tolstoianism covered no less than twenty-four pages.

Orthodox writers who lumped Tolstoianism together with sectarianism recognized that Tolstoi's message contained certain aspects that distinguished it from other doctrines. This, however, made it no less dangerous, they believed – quite the contrary. In 1911, the year after Tolstoi's death, a priest from Saratov, S. Il'menskii, claimed that Tolstoianism was far more aggressively anti-Church than all other sect movements. Condemnation of the official Church had been an integral part of Tolstoi's activity. Il'menskii reported that for more than twenty years he had been working as a home missionary and had met a large number of rabidly fanatical sectarians. "But not from a single one of them have we heard such satanic profanities of our true Christian faith than what is spewed out by the blasphemous mouth of Tolstoi the God-denier" (Il'menskii 1911, 19). There can be no doubt that Tolstoi's fierce attacks on the Orthodox faith were a major reason why the apologists of the Church singled him out as one of their fiercest opponents.

Tolstoianism as an Intelligentsia Movement

A consensus view developed among Orthodox apologists that Tolstoianism was probably a sect, but it was also something far more than a sect: It appeared as an ideological current within the radical intelligentsia. Like Anarchism, Socialism and *Narodnichestvo,* Tolstoi directed blistering criticism against all social institutions (Christoyannopoulos 2020). His attitude toward the tsarist regime was just as uncompromisingly negative as that of the revolutionaries. Some among the Orthodox hoped that this aspect of Tolstoianism might in fact have some positive side effects for the Church. To the extent that Tolstoianism appeared as a direct threat not only to the Church but also to the state power, they could hope that the secular authorities would contribute more actively in the fight against this heresy than they would otherwise do.

The Russian intelligentsia had arisen in the first half of the nineteenth century, and had undergone a noticeable radicalization since the 1860s (Billington 1970; Szamuely 1988). The reforms introduced by Alexander II between 1861 and 1864 did not meet the expectations that had been placed in them, and many had stopped believing that tsarism could be reformed from above. More and more people concluded that the established social order would have to be overturned by violence, and various conspiratorial societies were formed. In 1874, large crowds of students and other intellectuals went out into the countryside to arouse the peasant population. Partly, they would do educational work in order to open the peasants' eyes to their "true interests," and partly to incite them to armed rebellion. However, the great "march to the people" proved to be a formidable failure (Ulam 1977, 203–33; Billington 1970, 385–400). Most peasants nurtured a deep distrust of their self-proclaimed liberators, and simply denounced them to the secret police – largely because they rejected the atheism of the intelligentsia.

Confronted with this defeat, some revolutionaries chose to change their strategy. If the people would not contribute to the liberation from the tsarist regime, they would have to rely on their own resources. Since they were so few, the revolutionaries fell back on acts of terrorism as one of their most important means. Urban guerrilla actions against Russian officials and politicians, a feature of Russian society ever since 1866, now escalated into a veritable epidemic (Ulam 1977). After several unsuccessful attempts, they managed to kill Tsar Alexander II, in March 1881. This event in many ways marked the high tide of the revolutionary movement but also the beginning of its downturn. As the Marxist Gennadii Plekhanov later noted, the assassination had resulted only in the addition of another "vertical line" after the name of the tsar – Alexander II was replaced by Alexander III. The new tsar was deeply reactionary. He resolutely stepped up the fight against the revolutionaries with all available means, and in this he largely succeeded. Between 1885 and 1900, the Russian urban guerrilla was forced to suspend most of its activities.

In this situation characterized by triumphant reaction, Tolstoi stood forth with a message that many perceived as a continuation of the struggle of the radical intelligentsia in a new guise. During the debates on Tolstoi's teachings at the 1897 Kazan Congress of Home Missionaries, Archimandrite Tikhon reminded his audience that the anarchist preaching of the *Narodniks* among the peasants in the 1870s had been a failure. Now, however, the intelligentsia had concocted a new strategy for a "march to the people" – this time as sectarianism. Of the various sects, Tolstoianism was best suited as a conduit for incendiary social preaching. In contrast to, for instance, the Stundists and the Pashkovians, the religious content of the Tolstoian doctrine was extraordinarily vague, while its social message was simple and alluring: It promised nothing less than "The Kingdom of God established on earth." Archimandrite Tikhon therefore concluded: "Tolstoianism is even more dangerous to the state than to the Church, and represents in this regard an even greater danger than undisguised anarchism" ("Tolstovstvo, kak sekta" 1897, 831).

However, the problem for the Church was that few persons in the tsarist state apparatus shared this view. In 1892, it was rumored that the Synod intended to issue an official condemnation of Tolstoi, but nothing came of this. According to one Soviet researcher, the tsar would not have it:

"Alexander III kept his promise not to 'add to Tolstoi's fame the wreath of martyrdom'" (Petrov 1978, 23). While Church leaders tried to draw the attention of the tsarist state to the subversive potential of Tolstoian *anarchism*, most state leaders focused on Tolstoi's *pacifism*, and took comfort in it.

Thus, despite the proddings of the Home Missionaries and other clergy, the state authorities did little to combat Tolstoianism. They harassed many of Tolstoi's disciples, but left the fountainhead of this new "sect" in peace. The archives, it is true, show that a police agent monitored Tolstoi's movements in Moscow from February 7 to 12, 1897 (Sreznevskii 1923, 191). However, even most of the surveillance of the famous writer seems to have been conducted by men of the Church. The Bishop of Tula, for instance, received reports from the priest in the village in Iasnaia Poliana that he passed on to his ecclesiastical superiors in St. Petersburg. In his annual report from 1899, the bishop announced that the count was no longer infecting the peasants with his subversive ideas, but had instead cloistered himself in his study.[3] That Tolstoi might possibly do more damage from his study than among the peasants does not seem to have occurred to the bishop. Seated at his desk at Iasnaia Poliana, the recluse was most likely busy writing the sharply anticlerical novel *Resurrection.*

The home missionaries' analysis of Tolstoianism contained elements of a conspiracy theory: All who are against us must be in league with one another. However, the basis for this theory was relatively thin. In general, the distance between the sectarians and the intelligentsia was probably as great as their respective distance to the Russian church. Nevertheless, that analysis cannot be dismissed as sheer paranoia. In many sects, rejection of the state was undoubtedly strong, as noted for instance by the Marxist student of sectarianism Vladimir Bonch-Bruevich (Bonch-Bruevich 1914). It is also clear that some Russian revolutionaries deliberately attempted to exploit this potential for rebellion in their struggle against the tsarist regime: Bonch-Bruevich himself was a clear example of this.

Subjectively, Tolstoi would no doubt have rejected any attempts at pigeonholing him as either a sectarian or a member of the revolutionary intelligentsia. Objectively, however, there was a certain basis for the fears/hopes that some people nurtured at the time: That Tolstoi was the man who could bring the religious and secular opposition in Russian society together in one strong, unified movement.

[3] RGIA, f. 796, op. 442, d. 1811.

When it came to atheism, it was not difficult for the Church to draw the line. The atheists rejected the entire Christian tradition, willingly accepting the Church's exclusive claim to represent it. Tolstoi, on the other hand, denied that the Church represented true Christianity. Unlike the atheists, he challenged the Church head-on over the interpretation of specific points of Christian doctrine, forcing the apologists of the Church to rebut him, detail by detail. With his alternative interpretation of the message of Christ, he and the priests became competitors on the same market. To a far greater extent than the secular intelligentsia, Tolstoi catered to the religious needs of the people, and could appeal to Russians who previously had had this need met through the Church. Discussing the spread of unorthodox religious movements in urban areas of Russia around the turn of the last century, Mark Steinberg suggests that they "represented more complex, and perhaps more troubling, challenges to religious orthodoxy than secularization." Among these movements, he includes "widespread sympathy for Tolstoy's religion of ethics and spiritual feeling but shorn of Church dogma and ritual" (Steinberg 2007, 307).

In 1901, Bishop Amvrosii (Kliucharev) of Khar'kov, writing in the Synod's official journal *Tserkovnye vedomosti,* highlighted this circumstance as an important reason why Tolstoi was one of the "most dangerous enemies" of the Church, more dangerous than most *intelligenty*. Tolstoi did not demand from Christians that they should replace their faith with science or the like, but approached them in the name of Jesus Christ and with words from the Gospel, the bishop pointed out. Tolstoi equipped his stories with epigrams from the Holy Scriptures, interweaving "his false thoughts with the people's beliefs" (Amvrosii [Kliucharev] 1901, 528).

In 1887, the priest Sergii Bogoslovskii claimed that not even Russia's worst enemies could inflict so much damage to the country as Tolstoi had done. Tolstoianism was dangerous both to Christianity and to the state. Ruefully, Bogoslovskii had to observe that this doctrine was spreading "with the speed of an epidemic over the lands of Russia, threatening to overthrow everything that for Russians is holy, near and dear" (S. Bogoslovskii 1887, 48–49).

It is against the backdrop of such perceptions we must understand the reactions of Orthodox believers toward Tolstoi. Faced with enormous challenges of the late nineteenth and early twentieth centuries, the Russian Church could often seem paralyzed. A common attitude of the men of the Church was to insist on its prerogatives; relatively few Orthodox felt the urge to pursue apologetic work among doubters and apostates. It seemed as if the Church tried to shut the outer world out as much as possible, simply ignoring the rapid changes in society around it.

If this impression is correct, then the anti-Tolstoi campaign represented a clear exception. Many hundreds of Russian clergy and ordinary believers held sermons, wrote pamphlets, arranged meetings, and so on aimed at stemming his teaching. At the same time, the Orthodox who participated in this campaign often held highly differing perceptions of what Tolstoi actually stood for and used so contradictory a means to fight him that their various initiatives often worked at cross-purposes.

Individual Orthodox Reactions: Scope and Motives

The Church leadership as well as individual Orthodox believers relied heavily on public polemics in their anti-Tolstoian endeavors. Tolstoi's social-religious preaching unleashed a considerable writer's itch among Orthodox believers. Privy councillor Vasilii Skvortsov wrote ten anti-Tolstoian articles and edited a 500-page book with analyses-cum-denunciations of Tolstoianism. Nor was Skvortsov the only Russian Orthodox believer who tried to use Tolstoi's own weapon, the pen, against him. Hundreds of articles and dozens of books and booklets were written about the new prophet at Iasnaia Poliana by persons who wanted to defend the position of the Church. While much of this literature was run-of-the-mill stuff of no lasting interest, some of the finest Orthodox thinkers of the time also contributed, including luminaries such as Vladimir Solov'ev (1853–1900), Sergei Bulgakov (1871–1944) and Bishop Antonii (Khrapovitskii, 1863–1936). Indeed, it seems that few issues agitated the minds and pens of Orthodox believers as much as Tolstoianism did.

Tolstoi scholars have paid scant attention to the Orthodox contributions to the Tolstoi debate. Insofar as they have shown any interest at all in the Russian Orthodox Church's relationship with Tolstoi, they have tended to focus almost exclusively on the *Circular Letter* issued against him in 1901, as if that one document expressed the attitudes of all Russian Orthodox believers. This was far from the case. Many Orthodox believers contradicted each other – and, occasionally, also the official position of the Church – in their writings on Tolstoi and Tolstoianism. Sometimes the various authors presented Tolstoi in such different ways that one wonders whether they were writing about the same person. Most Orthodox writers who defended viewpoints in conflict with the *Circular Letter* expressed more moderate stances than those of the Church leadership, but some represented more uncompromising, strident positions. These writings, then, should be regarded, not as a centrally orchestrated anti-Tolstoian campaign, but rather as the result of numerous uncoordinated initiatives by individual Orthodox believers. Taken together, they bear witness to both the breadth and vitality of Orthodox public opinion, and to its strong polarization.

I have been able to identify more than 350 larger and smaller titles about Tolstoi, including more than eighty-five books and brochures, in which the author clearly adhered to the Orthodox faith.[4] To this considerable library more than 250 authors contributed – newspaper articles are not included in this estimate.

The Orthodox literature on Tolstoi ranges from heavy tomes to journal articles and small, popular pamphlets. In 1915, the signature M. B. claimed that "no religious or philosophical teaching has been met with such a broad-based polemical Orthodox literature as Tolstoianism" (M. B. 1915, 216). While I have not made any quantitative comparisons, this assertion seems reasonable. Furthermore, a number of these anti-Tolstoian texts were printed in several issues and editions, often first as an article in an Orthodox journal and later as a separate brochure.

It is a common impression that in the Orthodox Church the hierarchs set the agenda alone, while the believing lay people more or less willingly or reluctantly embraced the message they received from above. This impression is not confirmed by the campaign against Tolstoi. Not only priests and church officials, but also a great number of laymen (and a few laywomen) joined the fray. This debate serves as a reminder that the Church was not identical with its hierarchy. In order to understand Russian Orthodoxy in the synodal period, we must move beyond the bifurcated image of an official versus a popular Church. The Russian Church at the end of the nineteenth century was indeed polarized – but the divisions followed political and theological lines, not social or hierarchal ones (Shevzov 2004). Several lay believers demonstratively signed their articles against Tolstoi as "layman," "peasant," "doctor," and so on apparently to show that people from all walks of life contributed massively in condemning the new heresy. It is quite another matter that this popular literature on the average maintained a lower quality, stylistically and theologically, than what was written by educated theologians.

[4] A complete list of the titles I have identified can be found in Kolstø 1997, 480–510. This figure may well be somewhat too low, as the prerevolutionary bibliographic literature is faulty. Bitovt (1903) stops eight years before Tolstoi's death and contains significant gaps also for the earlier periods (Zaidenshnur 1981, 132–34). A few titles that I had not detected are given in Nickell 2006, 49–51.

Only fourteen of the Orthodox writers I have found who wrote about Tolstoi can be safely identified as representatives of the "black clergy" (monks, priest-monks, bishops and metropolitans). The most active group was the "white" or married clergy. This category included village priest and diocesan missionaries as well as professors at theological seminars and academies (some of whom were not ordained priests). Many of them displayed considerable erudition in philosophy and philology, history and law, in addition to their own discipline, theology.

In the late nineteenth century, an impressive number of Orthodox periodicals were published in Russia, both scholarly and semi-scholarly journals and popular devotional magazines. As Heather Coleman argues (Coleman 2014, 66), this vast Orthodox publication effort "represents a valuable and still underutilized source not just for the intellectual and cultural history of the Orthodox Church, but also for major themes in late imperial Russian thought." This holds true also for the contemporary debates on Tolstoianism. A very high number of articles on and against Tolstoi were published in these journals.

A striking feature of the ecclesiastical anti-Tolstoian literature is the significant role played by the provinces. Out of what was produced before 1917, approximately 100 titles were published in cities other than St. Petersburg and Moscow, including several of the longest and most ambitious works. In particular, Kazan', Ryazan' and Khar'kov had active anti-Tolstoian milieus. For example, *Bogoslovskii vestnik,* published by the Moscow theological academy, contained just half a dozen articles on Tolstoi, while *Vera i razum* at the corresponding institution in Khar'kov produced twice that number. Up to a point, this can be explained by personal interests of the publishers: *Vera i razum* had been started by Bishop Amvrosii (Kliucharev), one of the hierarchs who most insistently pushed for the excommunication of Tolstoi. Similarly, the journal *Missionerskii sbornik* in Riazan' was edited by a resolute anti-Tolstoian, N. Ostroumov, who kept the columns of his journal wide open to virtually every kind of counterattack against Tolstoi.

But the strong involvement of the provinces should probably also be understood in sociological terms: In the Kazan' *guberniia*, a large proportion of the population were non-Russians and non-Orthodox, and the city had long been a center of Orthodox missionary activity. The general expertise and interest in apologetics at the Kazan theological academy was transferred to the case of Tolstoi and his preaching. Similarly, in the Khar'kov *guberniia*, several sects had made significant inroads into the ranks of the Orthodox believers, which had stimulated the local priests' engagement in home mission.

Between 1887 and 1910, not a single year passed without a new article or book appearing with Orthodox refutations of Tolstoi's teachings. The Orthodox counterattacks against Tolstoi followed the releases of his books and pamphlets step-by-step as they appeared; since he was so active, the apologists of the Church were similarly productive. As Tolstoi's interests ranged widely, from social sciences to vegetarianism and to sexual morals, all could find an aspect of Tolstoianism that fell within their special interest or expertise. Orthodox educators rejected his pedagogical theories and his Christian catechism for children (Makkaveiskii 1902, 1909; Nikanorov 1900); exegetes dealt with his Gospel translations (Sollertinskii 1887; Elconskii 1889; Alfeev, a series of twelve articles between 1907 and 1911); believers with literary interests analyzed his novels and short stories (Solonikio, eight articles in 1901 and 1902; Bronnitskii, three articles in 1901; Palimpsestov 1886a, 1886b, 1887); liturgists defended the Church rituals against his ridicule (Sokolov, two articles in 1904), various morality teachers explained the exalted meaning of the Christian marriage, and so forth.

It is noteworthy that the steady stream of anti-Tolstoian literature did not stop at Tolstoi's death. For the period 1911–16, I have registered more than sixty titles, obituaries not included. This is a clear indication that Tolstoianism retained much of its fascination in Russian society right up to the Revolution of 1917.[5] In 1914, one Orthodox writer admitted that "precisely in our times" Tolstoianism seemed attractive and alluring to the people (N. Ostroumov 1914, 175).

Orthodox writers could have diverse ulterior motives for sharpening their pens against Tolstoi. In 1894, A. Ponomarev, a professor at St. Petersburg's Theological Academy, wrote an article in the journal *Strannik* in which he compared the Orthodox popular legend "On God's inscrutable judgements" with L. N. Tolstoi's story "What men people live by." Here, the theologian quickly passed on from a discussion of Tolstoi's short story to explain in detail the nature of Orthodox folklore (Ponomarev 1894). It seems almost as if the reference to Tolstoi in the title of the article only served as a pretext for taking out of the desk drawer a piece of research on Russian folk tales that would otherwise not have attracted many readers. The same tendency was evident in the article "Count L. N. Tolstoi's view on the historical life of the Church of

[5] Even if one Orthodox writer of this period (Seludiakov 1913) tries to convince us of the converse.

God," by the distinguished Church historian A. P. Lebedev. Lebedev's starting point was Tolstoi's legend "The destruction and recreation of hell," one of his most coarse and burlesque lampoons against the Christian church. Here Tolstoi tells of how hell was almost emptied of sinners and deserted after Jesus had appeared on earth and preached his glad tidings. People began to live together in peace, happiness, and congeniality. However, after a few centuries, an imaginative devil succeeded in spreading discord among Christians by letting them clash over ritualistic and dogmatic questions. Eventually, he got them to invent the concept of "church," and victory was secured. From then on, hatred and enmity ruled among Christians. Soon, virtually any crime could be committed in the name of Christ, and hell was filled up, more than ever before. The story ends with the demons dancing around Beelzebub, celebrating their victory (Tolstoi PSS 34, 100–15).

Few if any would take this travesty seriously as an exposé of Church history, but that is precisely what Lebedev did. Painstakingly, he refuted Tolstoi's version point by point, and gave a thorough account of how the history of the Church actually had been. In a footnote, Lebedev explained that his article was based on a lecture he had held at the Moscow University, and added that "it is no secret, ladies and gentlemen, that at the universities, Church history is not among the most thriving or favored studies" (Lebedev 1903–4, 394). Even a scholarly capacity like Lebedev clearly had difficulty in filling the auditorium without latching onto the interest in Tolstoi among his students. Lebedev found Tolstoi's teaching utterly inane, as he pointed out explicitly.

The cases of Ponomarev and Lebedev were by no means unique. In some articles, we find Tolstoi's name in the title, while he is not mentioned at all in the text (Olesnitskii 1892, 1895; *Tsarskoe dostoinstvo* 1889). In all of these cases, Tolstoi apparently served only as a bait to catch the interest of the readers. In that way, these articles serve as testimonies to the outstanding popularity Tolstoi enjoyed in Russian society around the turn of the nineteenth and twentieth centuries.

Even so, the vast majority of Orthodox anti-Tolstoian writers had indeed studied Tolstoi's writings thoroughly before entering into close combat with it. Some of them provided explicit reasons explaining why they had produced their various publications, thereby giving us insights into some of the motives behind the anti-Tolstoian campaign. Roughly, the writers can be divided into two categories: There were those who did their utmost to try to help Tolstoi back into the community of believers in the Orthodox Church; for many, however, it was more important to shield the children of faith from his pernicious influence. The priest G. Bogoslovskii, for example, explained that the purpose of his article was to "crush the fascination which Tolstoi wields over the hearts and minds of men" (G. Bogoslovskii 1913, 37). Another priest pointed out that Tolstoianism could be seductive not only for impressionable souls; even Orthodox believers were sometimes carried away by it – because many Orthodox had a rather flimsy understanding of what the Church taught and what Tolstoi taught (Pospelov 1898, 1).

While some anti-Tolstoian writings were intended mainly as an antidote to Tolstoi's writings among members of the Church and therefore served a defensive purpose, others were more aggressively directed at Tolstoi and all those who were enthusiastic about his teaching. In 1914, the retired school principal L. Anninskii delivered a series of lectures in Moscow and Riazan' about *Count Lev Nikolaevich Tolstoi as a moralist*, later published in book form. In the first lecture, he pointed out that he primarily wanted to influence Tolstoi's "many admirers." A large number of them were poorly informed about Tolstoi's teachings, knowing them only "by word-of-mouth, under the influence of other people," he claimed (L. Anninskii 1914, 7). However, if *that* was the problem, Anninskii should probably have referred his audience to Tolstoi's own writings, instead of producing yet another second hand presentation of his teaching.

Another Orthodox writer, Zosima Tsvetkov, noted in the introduction to his anti-Tolstoian article that the Gospels need no defense, they are fully capable of fending for themselves. When he nevertheless had taken up the pen to refute Tolstoi's ungodly attacks, it was not intended as an apology, but as an attempt to establish a dialogue with the apostates, he explained. Perhaps some of his readers might be moved to reconsider how transient their cocksure, anti-Christian beliefs were (Tsvetkov 1892, 1218). Tsvetkov wrote in the Orthodox devotional magazine *Blagovest'*, so it is doubtful whether his article was read by many Tolstoians.

Some Orthodox anti-Tolstoian writers had primarily one particular reader in mind: Tolstoi himself. In 1888 N. Ryshkovskii wrote "A fraternal word to L. N. Tolstoi," and explained that he would never have a quiet moment in life if he had seen a man like Tolstoi walk toward the abyss without trying to stop him (Ryshkovskii 1888, 3). Also other Orthodox believers approached Tolstoi directly in their pamphlets, addressing him either in the polite "*Vy*"" or by the familiar "*ty*""-form. Several of these articles were formulated as open letters. In a kind of "direct mail" campaign, large numbers of Orthodox brochures were sent to Iasnaia Poliana, usually with the author himself as the sender. The monk Silvestr sent two of his brochures, one about matrimonial law and another on religious freedom, equipped with the urgent plea: "The author prays to the merciful God that He bring his servant Lev back to the fold of the holy Orthodox Church." The priest D. Silin sent his article "The tragedy of Tolstoianism and the peace of the Gospel" to Tolstoi "as a token of my deep and compassionate love" (*Biblioteka* 1972, Ib, 230). But not all dedications were so deferential. The priest N. A. Eleonskii dedicated a copy of his *Count Tolstoi's "new gospel"* to "the wretched maniac Tolstoi" (*neschastnomu man'iaku*). Those who sent Tolstoi the reactionary priest Ioann Vostorgov's anti-Tolstoian brochure *The signs of the time* (1909), asked him to read it closely:

> It is time for you to collect yourself and repent. For you shall not live much longer and judge [others. Instead], you shall be judged yourself and will have to answer for how many deceived followers you have led astray and dispatched to the gallows. (*Biblioteka* 1972, Ia, 162)

Tolstoi read some of the Orthodox anti-Tolstoian literature he received, including Vostorgov's pamphlet, in spite of its disrespectful greeting. Bishop Nikanor's anti-Tolstoian sermons were read aloud at the dinner table at Iasnaia Poliana, and allegedly gave Tolstoi a good laugh (N. Gusev 1958, 766). In 1909, a theology student in Riazan' sent Tolstoi an issue of *Missionerskii sbornik,* which contained anti-Tolstoian articles by N. Ostroumov and P. Alfeev. Tolstoi read them and wrote the following response to the sender: "I have looked through the articles about me that you sent me. Such articles are always of interest to me in the hope of finding something that can show me my mistakes." However, Tolstoi claimed that he had not found anything of interest in this material. It discussed only his criticism of the faith of the Church, and not the most important thing: His own religious worldview (Tolstoi PSS 79, 160).

Tolstoi sometimes expressed the view that the Orthodox anti-Tolstoian literature was useful as it prevented the veil of oblivion from descending over his writings. The criticism it was met with in "worldly" circles was primarily concerned with his fictional production, and often completely ignored his socio-religious message. For example, only Orthodox believers wrote about two such central works as his *Gospel Translation* and *The Kingdom of God Is Within You* (Bitovt 1903, 226–27). Some Orthodox believers were concerned that the apologetic literature against Tolstoi might have the unintended effect of making advertisement for his books. S. D. Romashkov opined that "far too much fuss has been made about Tolstoi. By attempting to refute all the stupidities emanating from his pen, one has done him too much honor" (Romashkov 1902, 2). In spite of this insight, Romashkov sent his own anti-Tolstoian brochure to the printing press!

But if the Orthodox polemics against Tolstoi could whet the appetite for Tolstoianism among the reading public, the effect could also be the opposite. Aleksandr Rozhdestvin noted that Tolstoi's teaching was beneficial to the Church in one sense: It had motivated many Orthodox believers to learn more about the dogmas of their religion. After Tolstoi had stood forth as a preacher, Russian theological literature had been enriched with many valuable articles and treatises on various aspects of the faith. Particularly important was the fact that some of these texts were also read by persons who had previously been indifferent to theological questions, Rozhdestvin maintained (Rozhdestvin 1892, 126).

Some Orthodox complained that much of the anti-Tolstoian literature did not match up to professional standards; moreover, it was written in an unchristian and unkind tone. The Tula priest Dmitrii Troitskii wrote that such writings

> occasionally have been filled with direct reproaches and abuse against Tolstoi. They have therefore failed to calm sincere believers who have been confused by Tolstoi's preaching, and to Tolstoi himself and to the Tolstoians they have only been irritating. (Troitskii 1913, 9)

As an indirect confirmation of this, the signature "layman, M" ended his pamphlet on Tolstoi's book *What I Believe* by declaring that as a believer he was conscious of his many sins and regretted that in his brochure "there is much venom and much indignation over Lev Tolstoi's work" (M. Mirianin 1888, 61). But since the pamphlet was already written, he nevertheless dispatched it to the print shop.

One institution that early on launched a counterattack against Tolstoi's new teaching was the Kiev Theological Academy. In November 1887, the Academy announced a prize competition for the best refutation of Tolstoi's *What I Believe*. The prize money was 1,000 rubles (*Konkurs* 1887, 3). What the Academy had been looking for must have been solid scholarly theological dissertations, since the prize went to Aleksandr Orfano for his 300-page treatise, *What Should Constitute the True Faith of Every Human Being? (A Critical Analysis of Count L. Tolstoi's Book* What I Believe, 1890*)*. This and similar theological tomes had a relatively small potential readership (although Orfano's book was printed in 1,200 copies). The same applies to the theological journals. The numerous anti-Tolstoian articles printed here often had significant theological pretensions and gave in-depth analyses of Tolstoi's works, but their message rarely reached beyond the narrow circle of theologians and some educated lay believers from the upper classes (see, e.g., Palimpsestov 1886b, 801) – although one author insisted that he had "repeatedly encountered people on whom the theological articles on Tolstoi's works have made the necessary impact" (Rozhdestvin 1889, 11).

In any case, there was clearly a market also for more accessible Orthodox literature on Tolstoi for those wanting a quick introduction to what this heretic preached. Most of the anti-Tolstoian literature belonged to this category. However, it is not clear to what extent even this counterpropaganda reached the common people. After the Synod had promulgated its *Circular Letter* against Tolstoi in 1901, one concerned Orthodox lay believer wrote to Metropolitan Antonii in St. Petersburg that many Russians, even priests, had difficulty understanding why it had been necessary to move against Tolstoi. This confusion could have been avoided, he thought, if the Synod had commissioned one of the theological academies to prepare a simple and clear refutation of Tolstoi's heresy. The author was aware that there already existed many thick, academically heavy books on the subject, but they were so expensive that nobody could afford to buy them. The type of anti-Tolstoian literature he had in mind should cost no more than 25 kopeks.[6] This letter showed that even an Orthodox believer who took the trouble to write to the metropolitan had not discovered that dozens of anti-Tolstoian pamphlets in the price range he desired were already available.

Censorship

Orthodox individuals who wanted to defend the faith against Tolstoi's attack could take resort only to the weapon of the word. The Church authorities had a larger register of possible reactions, from public pronouncements and denial of ecclesiastical services, to censorship and incarceration. Since Tolstoi approached the Russian public almost exclusively through the written word, a very natural response from the authorities was censorship. Censorship was a well-established institution in Russian social life; it had been practiced as long as book printing. At the end of the nineteenth century, there were several different censorship organs and a varied system of censorship forms. Books below a certain size that were sold at low prices were subject to prior censorship: Such literature was

[6] St Petersburg Public Library, Otdel rukopisei, A, I, 289, no. 12.

considered potentially very dangerous as it could reach a large audience (Balmuth 1979). Thick books could be published without prior permission, but the entire print-run could be confiscated later, if it displeased the authorities (Møller 1983, 60–82).

Russian censorship was a maze of complicated rules, with unclear levels of competency among the various institutions. There were separate offices for secular and ecclesiastical, so-called spiritual, censorship. The church censors dealt with not only theological and other explicitly religious literature – in principle they were to check all printed material that could undermine "important truths of faith and the regulations of the Orthodox Church," according to Article 237 in the Statutes on Censorship (*Svod zakonov* 1857, 14, 42). Two ecclesiastical offices – at the theological academies in Moscow and St Petersburg – had nationwide competence; the academies in Kiev and Kazan' had local competence (Lialina 1989, 464). Chief procurator Konstantin Pobedonostsev himself headed the central office of the spiritual censorship.

Practically everything Tolstoi wrote after 1880 met objections from the censors, but the individual works often had highly differing fates. Several of his writings were banned entirely, and in many cases Tolstoi and his publishers did not even try to steer them through the censorship. Instead, they were printed abroad and smuggled into Russia. Some writings circulated in various hectographed and lithographed transcripts; others passed through the censorship on special conditions. *The Kreutzer Sonata* was completely banned at first, but when Sof'ia Andreevna achieved a personal audience with the Tsar, permission was given to print the story in her edition of Tolstoi's *Collected Works* (Møller 1983, 76–95). *The Power of Darkness* went the other way, from full approval to restrictions. When this play was already available in book form, Chief Procurator Konstantin Pobedonostsev instructed that the play should banned from being staged on Russian scenes (Tolstaia 1975, 284, 297). Another play, *The Fruits of Enlightenment*, could be performed on stage – but only if the actors were amateurs! This restriction was lifted only in 1894 (Tolstaia 1975, 307; Troyat 1980, 672).

A general feature of the censorship policy was to allow Tolstoi's writings to be printed in journals and books with a high retail price (collected works, etc.), but to deny publication as separate texts in cheap booklets (Apostolov 1929, 221). For example, The *Godson* (*Krestnik*) was allowed to be printed in the journal *Knizhki nedeli*, whereas the publisher *Posrednik* (The intermediary) was banned from publishing the same story in a cheap edition. However, this line was not followed consistently. In 1886, *Ivan the Fool* passed the censorship both in the twelfth volume of Tolstoi's *Collected Works* and in *Posrednik's* popular edition (Breitburg 1924). Two years later, the authorities regretted their lenience, and the Central Authority on Censorship issued a circular that prohibited reprint of this story (Apostolov 1929, 224). Not until 1905 were the censorship rules substantially liberalized (Balmuth 1979, 129–32). Several of Tolstoi's books previously available only in foreign editions could now be printed in Russia.

The Church authorities were for the first time confronted with Tolstoianism when the editorial staff of the journal *Russkaia mysl'* presented the May issue 1882 for censorship. The issue contained Tolstoi's *A Confession*, and the ecclesiastical censors at the Troitse-Sergiev monastery were obviously at a loss as to how to deal with it. After some time, the delicate matter was sent to the Metropolitan of Moscow, Makarii (Bulgakov). According to the editorial secretary of *Russkaia mysl'*, N. N. Bakhmet'ev, Makarii was prepared to release the issue, but hesitated to take responsibility for such an action. The case circulated in various ecclesiastical organs for a long time until the rector of Moscow's theological seminar, dean Filaret Sergievskii, came up with a solution: The journal could print the article unchanged if Tolstoi added some lines to the effect that it expressed opinions he had held previously and later abandoned. When this was rejected by the editorial staff, Filaret formulated a lengthy statement in which he, with numerous quotes from Scripture, justified why it was impossible to let the article go to print. The pages with *A Confession* were then cut out of the journal under ecclesiastical supervision before it could be sent out to subscribers, several months late (N. Gusev 1970, 147–55, where Filaret's statement is reproduced in extenso).

This episode shows how hesitantly and cautiously the Church initially proceeded toward Tolstoi. It was no easy matter to censure the country's most famous author. On the other hand, it made little sense to retain a Church censorship apparatus if *A Confession* were allowed through. The anti-Orthodox statements in this text are so open and direct that it should hardly be necessary to expose it to meticulous examination in order to show that "it undermines important articles of [the Orthodox] faith."

Also with regard to the next in line of Tolstoi's religious books, *What I Believe*, the ecclesiastical censorship experienced difficulties in making a decision. Again, Tolstoi had sent the manuscript to *Russkaia mysl'*, which, however, decided to produce a book version of it rather than publishing it in the journal. The book was printed in a minuscule print run, only fifty copies, to be sold for the hefty sum of 25 rubles apiece. With such a dauntingly high retail price, they hoped to make the book more palatable to the censors. This work ended up first in Moscow's secular censorship, where the chairperson V. Fedorov read it "with great interest." He thought it would be impossible to take legal action against such a work, and had reached this conclusion despite the fact that, in his opinion, the book "completely annihilates the teachings of the Church." The book was then passed on to the Moscow Theological Academy, where the Archimandrite Amfilokhii chaired the censorship committee. On January 29, 1884, Sof'ia Andreevna wrote to her husband that, according to rumors, Amfilokhii thought the book contained many great truths and saw no reason to stop it (Tolstaia 1936, 246). If that rumor was correct, Amfilokhii was then voted down by his own committee. In the committee's final recommendation, it was established that the book "obviously contravenes the spirit and letter of Christianity and undermines its moral doctrine." On this basis, the Central Authority for Secular Censorship in St. Petersburg decided to ban the book altogether (Tolstoi PSS 23, 551–52).

In August 1887, the Central Authority for Secular Censorship issued a circular to the effect that in the future no story from Tolstoi's hand should be accepted for publication by local censorship offices: Everything should be passed on to an office with nationwide competence. Not least in those cases when Tolstoi's religious message was presented in a fictional, positive form, and not in polemics against the teaching of the Church, astuteness and a trained eye were required to detect his heresy. A certain Elagin, who was commissioned to assess Tolstoi's short story "The Coffee House of Surat," has given us a glimpse into the dilemmas that a censor might encounter. His report about this text concluded with the following statement: "In the aforesaid piece I do not find anything harmful, nonetheless, I hesitate to let it pass through, as it stems from the pen of Lev Tolstoi and deals with religious questions, something which might lead to false interpretations" (quoted in A. Anninskii 1922, 413).

But not even the staff at the Central Authority for Secular Censorship had the necessary theological expertise to pass judgment on the religious message in Tolstoi's writings, so most of his fiction was transferred to the spiritual censorship committees. In the specific case of "The Coffee House of Surat," the manuscript finally ended up on the desk of Konstantin Pobedonostsev personally, who concluded: "[I]n truth, I do not see any reason to prevent the printing of this article by Count Tolstoi" (quoted in

A. Anninskii 1922, 412). This incident shows that the spiritual censorship authority studied the actual content of Tolstoi's religious texts, and not only checked the name of the author.

The decision to centralize the censorship of Tolstoy's writings testifies to the importance that the Church leadership attached to this instrument in its fight against Tolstoianism. However, several Orthodox writers expressed the view that censorship could be counterproductive. The priest M. I. Spasskii (pseudonym) claimed that *The Kreutzer Sonata* raged like a steppe-fire across Russia despite, or rather as a result of, it having long been forbidden (Spasskii 1901, 5). The secrecy around the book greatly helped to whet the curiosity of the readers – a view shared by Tolstoi himself. In a letter to Vladimir Chertkov in 1886, he wrote that censorship, like any kind of violence, leads to the opposite of what it is intended to achieve. This is just as certain as that the fire will flare up in the stove when the door is closed (Tolstoi PSS, 85, 421). In 1916, a lapsed Tolstoian, now active Orthodox believer, wrote that the Tolstoian movement had benefited from the sequestration of Tolstoy's publicist works: On the basis of these texts it would have been very easy to document that Orthodoxy is superior to Tolstoianism. "For the apologist of autocracy and Orthodoxy, the confiscated works could have served as an excellent springboard" (Khilkov 1916, 229).

In 1905, Vasilii Skvortsov admitted that many village priests were embarrassed when they tried to clarify to their spiritual children why the Church was so scathing in its condemnation of Tolstoi (Skvortsov 1905a, x). He assumed that many people would explain this by referring to the village priests' alleged obtuseness and lack of education, but Skvortsov had a different theory: Russians in general had a completely erroneous understanding of what Tolstoi actually stood for. Those of his works that passed through the censorship looked so innocuous that many could not understand how they could evoke the wrath of the clergy. Skvortsov went so far as to claim that Tolstoi "hid" behind the censorship, to portray himself as less anti-Orthodox than he actually was:

> The reading public knows and judges one-sidedly about Tolstoi as a great author and artist, the exhibited Tolstoi, as it were, the *censured* Tolstoi, but they do not know and will not know the *underground* Tolstoi who is hiding his head like an ostrich behind the back of his militant followers and agents, the destructive and terrible Tolstoi with his religious nihilism and state anarchy. (V. Skvortsov 1901c, 244, emphases in the original)

This strange and twisted argument turned the matter upside-down, but shows that the institution of censorship could indeed be a two-edged sword in the Church's struggle against Tolstoi. The highly intelligent and strategy-conscious Skvortsov no doubt understood this, and his statement might perhaps be read as a veiled, indirect criticism of the censorship practiced by the state authorities.

CHAPTER 11

Between "Almost Orthodox" and "Antichrist": Images of Lev Tolstoi in Russian Orthodox Polemics

Among the Orthodox writers who engaged in polemics against Tolstoi, assessments of his thinking and activities differed wildly. Attitudes covered the entire spectrum from admiration, via balanced discussions and matter-of-fact refutations of specific points in his teaching, to outright denunciations. In this chapter, I focus on those who expressed the most sweeping evaluations and moral judgments, whether positive or negative.

According to one group of writers, Tolstoi was definitely not a true Orthodox believer, but many of his philosophical ideas were nevertheless remarkably comparable with the teachings of the Church (or what these writers felt *ought* to have been the teachings of the Church). Some noted his emphasis on personal self-perfection and his preaching of poverty and asceticism – ideas that, they felt, brought him close to the message embodied by the Orthodox monks. Others praised his social gospel and his message of nonviolence as genuine Orthodox concerns. Some even held that Tolstoi had expressed the Orthodox position in a clearer and truer form than the Russian Church itself did – as Vasilii Ekzemplarskii claimed about Tolstoi's relationship to St John Chrysostom (see Chapter 9). In their writings, Tolstoi was presented not as a threat to the Christian faith but as a positive figure with a wholesome influence on Russian society. At a time when the Russian people were sinking deeper and deeper into the quagmire of materialism, Tolstoi had proclaimed that the truly important matters in life are spiritual. He had asked crucial questions and pointed in the right direction – but had, unfortunately, given wrong or misleading answers. Luckily, the Orthodox Church could provide better answers, thereby reaping the harvest that Tolstoi had sown. This position was eloquently summed up by Bishop Antonii (Khrapovitskii) and the philosopher Sergei Bulgakov. Both pointed out that some of the early Church Fathers had regarded virtuous pagan sages like Plato and Virgil as *paidagogoi eis Christon*: Good people who, while not Christians themselves, nevertheless guided others to Christ (see below).[1]

Other Orthodox writers agreed that Tolstoi's message often bore a strong resemblance to Orthodox teaching, but also insisted that whatever elements of truth and virtue might be found in his beliefs he had purloined from the Church. They saw Tolstoi as a plagiarist who had "stolen the pearl of the Gospel"; he was "a peddler of contraband" (A. Nikol'skii 1912, 4, 316). All the true or seemingly true ideas in his teachings had been taken out of context and could therefore no longer be deemed genuinely Orthodox. The task of the Orthodox apologist was to expose this twofold nature by "separating the wheat from the chaff, and the grain of truth from the glitter of tinsel" (Amicus 1899, 1, 73). One priest admitted that Tolstoi's teachings were marked by "high moral beauty" – and then hastened to add that there was a "but": "This 'but', gentlemen, is extraordinarily important: this entire beauty Tolstoi has stolen from us, from the Christian Church – all of it is lifted from the Gospel! Tolstoi plundered Christ, he robbed him. Then he threw Christ aside in order to shine before the world with the treasures he had taken!" (Dmitrievskii 1912, 11, 627)

Some Orthodox polemicists denounced Tolstoi as not only a heretic, but indeed the incarnation of evil on earth, an accomplice of Satan. He was the sworn enemy of Christ and the Church (no distinction was drawn between the two), a godless blasphemer, a liar and depraver of the youth, the devil's standard-bearer, a demon. His apostasy and the enormous success that his teaching enjoyed in Russian society signaled that the end of the world was near. Some found proof in the Bible that Tolstoi was Antichrist. The New Testament tells us little about this ominous eschatological figure, but the very vagueness of biblical information on the Antichrist made him amenable to fanciful interpretations. In Russian history, several individuals had been identified as Antichrist, without Doomsday having manifested itself.[2] Now, many believed, Tolstoi fit the bill better than anyone else before him. A weaker version of the same conjecture claimed that Tolstoi was not the Antichrist himself, but his herald or precursor.

Finally, elements of the two most extreme positions – Tolstoi as "almost Orthodox" and as the Antichrist – could be combined into a third version,

[1] *Paidagogos eis Christon* refers to Galatians 3, 24: "our schoolmaster to bring us unto Christ" (KJV).

[2] Ivan IV, Peter the Great and Napoleon were all interpreted as the Antichrist by Russian believers. In the last decades before the 1917 Revolution, the number of Antichrist identifications in Russia seems to have increased. Individuals as disparate as Nikolai II, Kaiser Wilhelm and Grigorii Rasputin were all cast in this role. See Pavel Miliukov 1909–16, 2, 48–54; Bonch-Bruevich 1914, 102–15.

"the demonized double": Tolstoi was particularly dangerous precisely because his message was, in many regards, so close to true Orthodoxy. That made it all too easy for unenlightened seekers of the truth to confuse his counterfeit Christianity with the genuine Orthodox original. In the New Testament, Paul the Apostle had described Satan as "an angel of light" (2 Cor. 11, 14): The worst evil may disguise itself as the most virtuous goodness. According to the New Testament, the Antichrist will manage to lead the faithful astray precisely by successfully imitating Christ himself. The Antichrist is thus the demon double. The most eloquent and elaborate expression of this composite image was presented by the famed philosopher, Vladimir Solov'ev in his last major book *Three Conversations about War, Progress and the End of History*. This was the point on which the most extreme positions in the Orthodox debate on Tolstoi and Tolstoianism converged.

Around the turn of the nineteenth and twentieth centuries, an increasing polarization developed in the Russian Church between a conservative/reactionary and a liberal/radical wing, along political as well as religious lines. Those who supported the Tsarist Empire usually also advocated very traditional dogmatics, while many theologically liberal writers pressed for political and social reforms. This pattern was repeated also in Orthodox writings on Tolstoi. However, some important figures cannot be accommodated into this schema. For instance, the powerful prelate and influential theologian Antonii (Khrapovitskii) was both a political reactionary and an innovative religious thinker. He wrote several articles on Tolstoi, some of which were damning whereas others pointed out important similarities between the teaching of the sage of Iasnaia Poliana and true Christianity as he – bishop Antonii – understood it.

Assessments of Russian Orthodox Radicals

The new Russian Orthodox radicalism stemmed from various circumstances. Firstly, the rapid urbanization and industrialization of many Russian cities in the 1890s onward created a new indigent working class that lived in desperate squalor, and many ordinary priests, especially in St. Petersburg, saw the need to combine the preaching of salvation with a social gospel (Hedda 2018). Secondly, through the establishment of religious-philosophical associations in the northern capital and other cities, the Church had, for the first time in decades, come in close contact with the intelligentsia. However, these encounters failed to create a deep and lasting understanding between Orthodoxy and "the new religious consciousness" as religiously oriented members of the intelligentsia were called. Dmitrii Merezhkovskii, the leader of the St Petersburg religious-philosophical association, among others, saw this attempt at bridge-building as unsuccessful (Merezhkovskii 1907, 3, 32). Nonetheless, many members of the clergy were permanently influenced by their participation in these religious-philosophical associations; moreover, some in the intelligentsia took the step from a nonreligious or a nondenominational religious worldview to the Christian, Orthodox faith (Scherrer, 1973).

A third factor that contributed to the radicalization of parts of the Russian Church was the Revolution of 1905. Especially the events of "Bloody Sunday," on January 9 (O.S.), revealed that the Emperor was not the Orthodox "little father" he would like to be seen as. When masses of working people marched toward the Winter Palace, holding icons and church banners, they were mowed down by soldiers of the Imperial Guard. The revolution eased the pressure on the political opposition. The October Manifesto, which the Tsar was pressured into issuing on October 17 that year, introduced freedom of speech, press and assembly. Groups and individuals in the Church who did not march in step with the Holy Synod, could now more easily voice their views openly. In the following, I present the views of some radical Orthodox theologians and writers who expressed an interest in Tolstoi.

Otdykh khristianina. One of the journals that most clearly reflected the new radical currents in the Church was *Otdykh khristianina*, the organ of the Orthodox temperance society "The Aleksandr Nevskii Brotherhood." Contributors to this journal included the priests Konstantin Aggeev, N. Drozdov, Stefan Kozubovskii, Stefan Ostroumov, N. Smolenskii, I. I Solov'ev and Mikhail Tareev, all of whom wrote articles about Tolstoi.[3] Aggeev was a member of the important group of "32 clergymen" in St. Petersburg, who repeatedly engaged in the theological and political debates on Church issues with declarations and public appeals (Scherrer 1973, 140; Hedda 2008, 155–60).

Several radical theologians used their articles on Tolstoi as a way of shedding critical light on the Church itself. Typical in this respect was an editorial in *Otdykh khristianina* after the death of Tolstoi. The journal held that the leadership of the Russian Church and the general masses of

[3] Kozubovskii and Solov'ev also corresponded with him (Tolstoi 78, 178, 302). To Kozubovskii Tolstoi wrote, "please do not think that I want to quarrel with your beliefs, God forbid; I am only happy with people who have strong faith, such as, as far as I can conclude from your letter, you have."

Orthodox believers bore responsibility for not having managed to bring this lost sheep back into the fold. Russian Christians should examine their own consciences:

> Perhaps we, with our indifference to the principles of religious life, have created the fog that hides the bright, shining figure of the real Church of Christ from those who seek it? (*Tserkovnoe obozrenie* 1910, 734)

In the next issue of *Otdykh khristianina*, N. Smolenskii elaborated on this view. Noting how Tolstoi himself had considered the Gospels as being among the books that had meant the most to him in his youth, Smolenskii held that Bible reading had left a distinct imprint on the great writer: Only a man who had been under the direct influence of the Divine books could experience such moments of pure, religious ecstasy as Tolstoi had depicted in several novels and diary entries. The red thread in Tolstoi's writings was his quest for truth, but Smolenskii doubted whether he ever found it, because Tolstoi's teachings lacked two essential elements of true religious faith: The mysterious and the poetic. When Tolstoi broke up from his home at the end of his life, that confirmed that Tolstoianism had not given him the peace he sought.

To a considerable degree, the Russian clergy were responsible for this tragedy, Smolenskii believed. They had not been able to preach true Christianity with sufficient force to allow Tolstoi's intellect to be captured by it. The entire Russian Orthodox population bore an even greater responsibility, because they did not lead lives of *Imitatio Christi*. "We are Christians in name, but do not live in a Christian way." Tolstoi, by contrast, had verbally rejected many Christian dogmas, but in his deeds he had loved Christ and mankind. The ways of God are inscrutable: Perhaps in His eyes, Tolstoi would stand above many who honored Him with their lips while being far away from Him in their hearts. Perhaps God could even use Tolstoi as His tool among men:

> God leads people towards the good along the most diverse paths, and not infrequently He also turns evil into something good. In Tolstoi's activity, which outwardly was an attack on Christianity, perhaps much was to the greater glory of Christ and to the benefit of the Christian Church. (Smolenskii 1910, 889)

Another contributor to *Otdykh Khristianina*, the priest Stefan Ostroumov, wrote a lengthy analysis of Tolstoianism, "An assessment of the positive significance of L. N. Tolstoi's religious and moral teachings" that ran over six issues of the journal in 1916. The serial article consisted mainly of excerpts from Tolstoi's works and letters put together thematically and annotated with Ostroumov's comments. The intention, as stated in the title, was to show that Tolstoi's teachings contained far more positive elements than most Russian believers had recognized.

Most Orthodox believers who had written about Tolstoianism presented Tolstoi's ideas in a biased, one-sided way, Ostroumov claimed. Even on those points where these ideas deviated very little from the teaching of the Church, they had fiercely emphasized the minuscule differences that existed. Tolstoi's message concerning fasting, self-sacrifice, chastity, and other central matters had been passed over in silence by these Orthodox bigots; instead, they had focused on his condemnation of State power and of the Christian dogmas. They had failed to note that Tolstoi's writings had not had an equally destructive influence on everyone: While some had no doubt been shaken out of their childhood faith, others who had lost this faith a long time ago had returned to it – by reading Tolstoi.

> Also many conscious believers experienced not only grief over Tolstoi's delusions when they read the brilliant author's didactic works, but also a sense of religious communion with him in many questions of faith and morality. (S. Ostroumov 1916, 1, 116)

Ostroumov found precedents for his views on Tolstoi among the early Church Fathers, many of whom had read the Greek pagan writers with an open mind, finding brilliant confirmation of Christian truths. A cunning bee can collect valuable nectar also from poisonous flowers, they had explained. However, Ostroumov's selection of quotes from Tolstoi sometimes appears just as one-sided as the anti-Tolstoian Orthodox pamphlets he criticized: Whereas they collected only the poison, he found only the nectar. He even denied that Tolstoi had presented any fundamental objections to the Christian rituals anywhere in his writings! (S. Ostroumov 1916, 5–6, 132) Even so, several of Ostroumov's observations were quite accurate. For instance, he argued convincingly that the often-repeated depiction of Tolstoi as a pantheist was based on a misunderstanding. Anyone who, like Tolstoi, saw God as "the source of all things, a being with will, love, knowledge, and care for all," was necessarily far removed from pantheism. True, Tolstoi denied that God is *lichnyi* (personal, individual) – but so does the Church, Ostroumov noted. The Church sees God not as an individual, but super-individual: Triune (S. Ostroumov 1916, 1, 122).

Further, seeking to accentuate the teaching of Christ, Tolstoi had unfortunately downplayed the meaning of His person, but many of Tolstoi's ecclesiastical critics had fallen into the opposite trap: They preached the divinity of Christ, but sold His teaching "on the cheap" (S. Ostroumov 1916, 10, 153–54). The true value in Tolstoi's message lay primarily in that it could serve as a corrective to the one-sidedness and distortions of traditional Church doctrine (S. Ostroumov 1916, 5–6, 148).

The Put' anthology. Another group of radicals in the Orthodox Church was the circle around the Solov'ev society in Moscow, founded in 1905. This society was a counterpart to Merezhkovskii's religious-philosophical society in St. Petersburg, but had a more ecclesiastical, Orthodox profile. Even so, also the Solov'ev society was primarily a forum for the intelligentsia, and only secondarily for the radical clergy. Prominent members were Nikolai Berdiaev, Sergei Bulgakov and Evgenii Trubetskoi, all of whom were highly philosophically oriented (Zernov 1963, 111–30).

In 1910, some members of the Solov'ev society established the *Put'* publishing house, which in the years up to the 1917 Revolution issued several important religious and philosophical works, written mostly by members of the group (Scherrer 1973, 221). In 1911, they published an edited volume on Vladimir Solov'ev, a thinker who had deeply influenced many of them.[4] This was followed in 1912 by a book about another thinker, one toward whom they were far more reserved – Lev Tolstoi. They explained that they had had enough of the cheap panegyrics that had flooded the Russian press after his death. "The irreconcilable iconoclast has been canonized, with his own cult of relics, and there is obviously a desire to turn his biography into the *Vita* of a saint" (*O religii Tolstogo* [1912] 1978, I). As a motto for this *Put'* anthology, they quoted from Tolstoi's *Circle of Reading*: "About the dead it is customary to tell flattering lies, but it would not hurt to speak the whole truth." They believed they would honor his memory best by analyzing what had meant most to him: His understanding of Christianity.

Two of the contributors to *O religii Tolstogo*, Andrei Belyi and A. S. Volzhskii, had such a peripheral relationship to Orthodoxy that their articles fall outside the scope of this book. Vladimir Ekzempliarskii's article has already been discussed (Chapter 9). In the following, I concentrate on the contributions of Vladimir Ern (1881–1916), Vasilii Zen'kovskii (1881–1962), Nikolai Berdiaev (1874–1948) and Sergei Bulgakov (1871–1944).

V. F. Ern was a fervent Orthodox believer and at the same time a fierce opponent of the Tsarist state. Shortly after "the bloody Sunday" of 1905, he, together with V. P. Sventitskii, created "The Christian Fighting

[4] See also below, *The Solov'evian Synthesis: Antichrist as a Double.*

Brotherhood," to work for the dissolution of "the reactionary connection between Orthodoxy and autocracy" (Scherrer 1973, 144–45). Ern supported "the freedom of Christ and the love of Christ in all human relationships," while opposing anti-Christian socialism (Rovner 1975, 384–85). These were views he put forward in several publications during a short but hectic life.

Ern titled his Tolstoi analysis "Tolstoi vs. Tolstoi." He believed that in Tolstoi's mind there had been two opposite tendencies that struggled against each other. On the one hand, Tolstoi was a thinker and moralist who wrote dreary rationalistic treatises; on the other hand, he had received from God a brilliant talent as a writer of fiction. In this second capacity, Tolstoi had given the world several invaluable portraits of true Orthodox Christians who lived in harmony with their beliefs, such as Grisha and Natal'ia Savishna in *Childhood*. These characters made a far greater impression upon readers than the pitiful slander of the Church he was to present later, Ern claimed. Tolstoi's purely artistic recognition of Orthodoxy was more original, more genuine and significant than his pamphleteering rejection of it – and thus he ended up in the same situation as Balaam in the Old Testament: Instead of cursing, he found himself blessing (Ern [1912] 1978, 231–37).

Vasilii Zen'kovskii was a Ukrainian and studied in Kiev where he took an active part in the city's religious-philosophical society. He had wide interests within as diverse disciplines as natural science, literature and philosophy. For a brief period during the Russian Civil War of 1918–20, he was Minister of Culture in Hetman Skoropadskii's conservative Ukrainian government, before emigrating to Western Europe. From 1927 until his death, Zen'kovskii taught philosophy at the St. Sergius Orthodox Theological Institute in Paris. Here, he also published his main work, *The History of Russian Philosophy*. In 1942, he was consecrated as a priest (D. Grigor'ev 1975).

Unlike Ern and many others who saw Tolstoi's greatness solely in his fictional works, Zen'kovskii regarded his religious writings as the most important and valuable contributions. "Whoever does not know Tolstoi as a religious thinker and as a religious man, does not know the deepest and most genuine in him" (Zen'kovskii [1912] 1978, 28). Tolstoi had deduced all his teachings from his personal religious experiences – experiences of a mystical nature, Zen'kovskii claimed. Tolstoi's mysticism had resided more in his mind than in his feelings, but it would nevertheless be wrong to see him as a pure rationalist. Rationalism could be found only in Tolstoi's criticism of the Church teachings, and not in his personal religious system.

Tolstoi's main concern, as Zen'kovskii saw it, was the problem of individuality, which in turn was intimately linked to the problems of death and immortality. Always searching for a meaning of life that would not be destroyed by death, and observing that human individuality is temporal and perishable, Tolstoi concluded that salvation must consist in liberation from the individual life. In the long run, however, this collective, apersonal doctrine of immortality could not satisfy Tolstoi. In *On Life (O zhizni* 1886–87*)*, he presented a doctrine holding that human beings are in possession of a sentient "I" that survives death – thereby becoming entangled in insoluble contradictions, Zen'kovskii maintained. These could have been resolved if Tolstoi had been willing to accept the Church's doctrine of individual immortality and the restoration of the entire human being with the resurrection of the flesh. With this analysis, Zen'kovskii hoped to have demonstrated that "in the teachings of the Church, Tolstoi could have found the solution to the conclusions he drew from his mystical experiences" (Zen'kovskii [1912] 1978, 32).

Sergei Bulgakov grew up in the family of a priest; as a young boy he was sent to Moscow to study at the theological seminar there. Like so many other seminarians, he soon lost his faith and became a convinced Marxist. In the years 1901–6, however, he experienced a spiritual crisis; after studying the Bible and the writings of Vladimir Solov'ev, he returned to Orthodoxy (S. Levitskii 1975, 205–6). In 1903, Bulgakov published *From Marxism to Idealism*, which gave the name to a whole movement. However, he remained deeply interested in political and social issues also after bidding farewell to Marxism, and in 1905 launched a "Union of Christian Politics." His political views at that time were close to those of the Constitutional Democrats. In 1906, he was elected to the Second Duma as a nonpartisan deputy. Bulgakov visited Tolstoi at Iasnaia Poliana in 1902 (N. Gusev 1960, 418), and was the only contributor to the *Put'* anthology who had known him personally. He also followed the great writer to his final resting place when he was buried at the Iasnaia Poliana estate in November 1910 (S. Bulgakov 1910, 220).

In his articles on Tolstoi, Bulgakov sought to place him in relation to the Russian spiritual tradition. Although a thinker like Vladimir Solov'ev had engaged in vigorous polemics against Tolstoi, Bulgakov believed that their final ideals coincided: Both had defended the absolute-religious against the historical-relative. Also between Gogol and Tolstoi, Bulgakov found clear parallels: Both wanted to put all their writings at the service of religion. Deep down, this desire should be understood as an expression of the elementary Christian force (*stikhiia*) in the Russian soul.

Tolstoi's strong appeal to the human conscience and sense of responsibility had, according to Bulgakov, an undeniable religious value. Likewise, he saw Tolstoi's teaching of personal self-fulfillment as being fully in line with the Church. Even so, he held it would be mistaken to regard Tolstoi's religion as Christian. The only thing that Tolstoianism and Christianity had in common was their ethics. In the Church, however, ethics do not have an independent but a derived significance, as a function of dogmatics. When Tolstoi rejected the dogmas, his ethics also acquired a completely different meaning (S. Bulgakov [1912] 1978, 10).

According to Bulgakov, in Tolstoi's soul there were two opposing elements, a religious, and a nihilistic. The latter dominated, so the mysterious and metaphysical side of Christianity remained inaccessible to him. And yet, while there was strong repulsion, even mutual hostility, between Tolstoi and people of the Church, "at the same time there was an unaccountable attraction, some closeness" (S. Bulgakov 1910, 218).

> [N]o one who looks soberly on the matter, without fanaticism, can relate to Tolstoi 'the heretic' as to a "heathen and publican", that is, as to one who is completely foreign to the Church. Even as excommunicated, Tolstoi continued to stand near the Church and was connected to It with deep, invisible ties. (S. Bulgakov 1910, 219)

This assessment, which Bulgakov first expressed in a short article in *Russkaia Mysl'* in December 1910, he repeated verbatim in his contribution to the edited volume *On Tolstoi's religion* two years later (S. Bulgakov [1912] 1978a, 12). Bulgakov recalled that Tolstoi's activity had coincided with a sharp religious decline in Russian society, and believed that the thinker of Iasnaia Poliana had exercised a positive influence by awakening a greater understanding of religious issues. In Bulgakov's view, the cultural situation in Russia had so much in common with the paganism of antiquity that it was possible to regard Tolstoi as St. Paul had regarded the Old Testament law: As a "schoolmaster to bring us unto Christ" (Gal. 3, 24). Tolstoi led the children to Christ without being a Christian himself (S. Bulgakov 1910, 219; S. Bulgakov [1912] 1978a, 12).

Like Bulgakov, also Nikolai Berdiaev had been attracted to Marxism in his youth. After taking part in student disturbances in Kiev in 1898, he was arrested and sent into internal exile in Vologda for three years. He gradually found a Christian faith; before the October Revolution broke out, he had become an avowed member of the Orthodox Church, his biographer claims (Lowrie 1960, 215). However, in his own autobiography, Berdiaev wrote that his relationship with the Church always remained "painful" and was never without tensions. He wanted to be a liberal truth-seeker, and saw himself as a representative of "a new religious consciousness" (Berdiaev 1949, 188 and 154).

In the *Put'* anthology on Tolstoi, Berdiaev contributed an analysis of the place of the Old and the New Testament in Tolstoi's religious thinking. Berdiaev concluded that Tolstoi was "pre-Christian": As with the Old Testament, he knew God only as lawgiver, not as savior. At the same time, many points in his teachings were reminiscent of Buddhism. In both of these intellectual systems, salvation is equated with self-salvation, and love is replaced with compassion. Because the personal man disappeared for Tolstoi, the personal God also vanished.

Asceticism was apparently a point where Tolstoi preached the same message as the Orthodox Church. But even though Berdiaev admitted that Christian asceticism might easily be confused with Tolstoi's teaching, he thought that in reality they were essentially different. The Christian ascetics were at the same time mystics, while Tolstoi's moralism, in Berdiaev's opinion, had no room for the mysterious. His asceticism therefore became iconoclastic: He could not tolerate any kind of "sacred beauty or sacred riches" (Berdiaev [1912] 1978, 192).

Although Berdiaev could not in any way accept the answers Tolstoi gave to religious questions, he was willing to concede to him a positive, purifying role in contemporary Russia: With unusual power and radicalism, Tolstoi had entered the field of a quasi-Christian society and the lies of a quasi-Christian state. "In an ingenious way, he exposed the monstrous falsehood and deathliness of the official state (*kazennaia*) Christianity" (Berdiaev [1912] 1978, 193). Tolstoi addressed a society that was partly atheist, partly hypocritically and affectedly Christian. It was not possible for Tolstoi to destroy the religion of this society, Berdiaev claimed: It was already completely corrupted. For the purely ritualistic Orthodoxy that continued to exist in Russia solely due to inertia, it was important and wholesome to be shaken and disturbed by Tolstoi.

> Tolstoi's anarchist rebellion marks a crisis in historic Christianity, a turning point in the life of the Church. This rebellion anticipates the coming rebirth of Christianity. For us it will remain a mystery, rationally incomprehensible, why a person who was foreign to Christianity could nevertheless serve the rebirth of Christianity. (Berdiaev [1912] 1978, 194)

The contributions of Church radicals to the study of Tolstoianism did not add up to a coherent, consistent analysis. Some, such as Stefan Ostroumov, did their utmost to detect the valuable Christian elements in Tolstoianism, while others rejected them almost entirely. Zen'kovskii defined Tolstoi's religion as deeply mystical, whereas Berdiaev and Bulgakov lamented the absence of mystical components in it. When these critics nevertheless, in a certain sense, could form a united front, it was primarily because of their shared attitude toward the official Church. Although they all identified as Orthodox believers, they had strong reservations against certain aspects of its dogmatics and, not least, against Russian church life. They were not primarily concerned with combating Tolstoianism, but with promoting profound reforms in the Russian Church and Russian secular society. To that end, their analyses of Tolstoi's teachings could serve as a driving force. In his teachings, they found a religiously motivated rebellion against the same political and ecclesiastical structures to which they too objected. Although Tolstoi's rebellion did not coincide with their own, neither in its justification nor its objectives, most of them recognized his activity as positive, beneficial and pioneering.

Bishop Antonii (Khrapovitskii)

The most prominent Russian theologian to engage in "the Tolstoi case" was undoubtedly Metropolitan Antonii (Khrapovitskii) of Kiev (1863–1936). Around the turn of the nineteenth and twentieth centuries he was one of the towering capacities in the Russian Church, theologically as well as in ecclesiastical politics. Intellectually precocious, he was appointed principal of Moscow's theological academy at the age of 27. Here, he soon gained influential enemies and after a few years was sent in a kind of "inner exile" to the academy in Kazan, a provincial town (Rklitskii, xxiv). Later, he served, in turn, as bishop of Ufa, then of Volhynia and Khar'kov before being appointed Metropolitan of Kiev in 1917.[5] His ideal Church was "the 'militant church' – church understood as an active moral force for preserving and implementing God's commandments in society" (Pärt 2010, 157).

At the all-Russian Church Council in 1917, Khrapovitskii headed the most conservative faction of delegates. When the Council decided to restore the patriarchy, he was the candidate who received the most votes.

[5] William Nickell (Nickell 2006, 45) writes that Antonii signed Tolstoi's excommunication in 1901, but confuses the bishop with his namesake, Metropolitan Antonii (Vadkovskii). Antonii (Vadkovskii) was the presiding member of the Synod at the time when the Circular letter was issued.

The election procedure, however, followed Acts I, 23–26, with a lottery between the three most popular candidates, and the lot fell on Metropolitan Tikhon (Belavin). Khrapovitskii emigrated from Soviet Russia shortly afterward, and headed the Russian Orthodox Church Outside Russia (ROCOR) until his death.

Khrapovitskii's writings on Tolstoi consist of eight shorter and longer articles, most of them dedicated to one specific Tolstoian text. The first work Khrapovitskii embarked on was *On Life*, which he saw was an attempt to wrest from the hands of the Church the answers it provides to the fundamental questions of life: How to reconcile ourselves with evil and with death. These are problems that the enemies of the Church had not managed to deal with satisfactorily, as Tolstoi had excellently demonstrated in his criticism of materialism and utilitarianism (Antonii [Khrapovitskii] [1889] 1967a, 68–99). However, according to Khrapovitskii, much of Tolstoi's criticism of contemporary secular worldviews could also be directed against Tolstoi's own attempted solutions. Tolstoi had adopted a utilitaristic understanding of man as a self-seeking, selfish being, while retaining the true Christian belief that egotism is evil – and thus found himself forced to conclude that man must destroy his individuality. The Church, however, teaches that man is created in the image of God and is therefore fundamentally good. The goal is "not to lose one's individual consciousness, but to perfect it, cleanse it and raise it up to its perfect Prototype" (Antonii [Khrapovitskii] 1967a, 81). This gradual approach to God takes place through a double movement of love – love toward God and toward mankind. In Tolstoi's teaching, true love of God is not possible, since God is not perceived as a person. Nor is there any real love for mankind: In the Tolstoian solipsism, concern for our neighbor is reduced to a consequence of the individual's self-understanding, not an active driving force behind our actions.

In his next article, Khrapovitskii discussed Tolstoi's understanding of the Gospels as expressed in his Gospel translation and in *What I Believe*. Tolstoi here claimed that the inner core of the New Testament is Jesus' teaching about the meaning of life and the essence of virtue. Up to a point, Khrapovitskii agrees with the sage of Iasnaia Poliana: "There is no doubt that the Lord came down to earth also to reveal to man the true meaning of life, and equally indubitably He explained that the meaning of life consists in the fulfilment of the Commandments" (Antonii [Khrapovitskii] 1891, 12). Khrapovitskii also noted that, throughout the history of the Church, the Christian doctrine has repeatedly been perceived as precisely that: A doctrine. But with Tolstoi, this doctrine was decoupled from its originator: What Jesus did was allegedly merely clarify a doctrine already written in the hearts of men. For the Church, on the other hand, this doctrine is an integral part of Jesus' work of salvation, along with His suffering, death and resurrection.

Although Tolstoi was correct in portraying the moral struggle of man as an essential part of the Gospel message, his understanding of how this battle must be fought was imperfect. First, he did not manage to give people the support and the means they need to achieve their moral goals, Khrapovitskii claimed. In particular, he noted Tolstoi's perception of God as an *impersonal* principle of reason. Such a deity can, to a much lesser extent than a personal, all-powerful Savior-God, influence the moral will of men. In addition, the Church's conception of personal immortality serves as a stimulus in the struggle against evil, while Tolstoi's impersonal immortality could not have the same positive effect (Antonii [Khrapovitskii] 1891, 17–20).

Tolstoi was also mistaken when he identified the struggle between good and evil with the contradiction between spirit and flesh. Wickedness can also be entirely spiritual. On this point Khrapovitskii accused Tolstoi of Manicheanism, apparently without noticing that this criticism could equally be directed against the monastic tradition he himself represented. My analysis of *Dobrotoliubie* revealed a very similar spirit/flesh dualism (see Chapter 4).

Khrapovitskii analyzed *The Kingdom of God is within you* in an article from 1897, focusing primarily on Tolstoi's nonviolence. The bishop rejected the claim that the Church accepts violence without reservations and reminded his readers that canonical law excludes from the Eucharist for three years any person who has killed anyone, irrespective of the circumstances (rule 13 of Basil the Great) – this pertains also to soldiers acting under orders in war. Priests who have participated in murder are defrocked, even if they have acted in self-defense (Antonii [Khrapovitskii] 1897, 32). Eleven years later, Tolstoi in his pamphlet *On violence and love* referred to the same canonical provision, but interpreted it differently: He used it as evidence that the older Church had a very different view on violence than the Orthodox Church of his own time (Tolstoi PSS 37, 183). In fact, both Khrapovitskii and Tolstoi were in a sense right. None of the decisions and regulations that together make up Orthodox canonical law have ever been rescinded, but many of them are quietly ignored – including Basil the Great's injunction against involuntary killing.

Khrapovitskii could not accept Tolstoi's claim that the principle of nonviolence is pivotal to the entire ethical code. Nonviolence is a secondary, not a primary postulate, he maintained. Before one can instruct people that they must not use violence in order to achieve their goals, they must be taught which goals to strive for. Khrapovitskii saw Tolstoi's ethics as an individualistic doctrine of purity: If the individual manages to fulfill the five commandments of the Sermon on the Mount, he is blameless.

> Let people around him defile children, kill old people and teach the youth to become thieves and swindlers: As long as he has proffered his advice, he may calmly walk past all these horrors and take pleasure in his own contentment. The Christian, on the other hand, says with the apostle: 'Who is weak, and I am not weak?' (2 Cor. 11, 29) (Antonii [Khrapovitskii] 1897, 33)

As against Tolstoi's view, Khrapovitskii claimed that one may indeed sin gravely when committing violent acts – but might sin even worse if one were to avoid resorting to violence when it would have been possible to resist evil.

In *The Kingdom of God*, however, Khrapovitskii found the seeds of another moral doctrine that ran counter to what he regarded as Tolstoi's nonviolence fanaticism. The virtuous life is here presented as a gradual, step-by-step approach toward perfection. With this concept, Tolstoi once again drew close to a Christian understanding of life; one that Khrapovitskii hoped would eventually displace Tolstoi's uncompromising demand for perfection.

On March 15, 1892, Khrapovitskii visited Tolstoi at his home and conversed with him about religious matter. In certain Church circles, the fact that the principal at an Orthodox theological academy entered into dialogue with this "hardened heretic" did not go down well. Rumor had it that, for instance, Lev Tikhomirov – a former socialist revolutionary turned Orthodox reactionary – had been shaken to learn of this meeting, a point that Tolstoi noted with undisguised satisfaction (Tolstoi PSS 66, 191). A major theme during Tolstoi's conversation with Khrapovitskii had apparently been whether it was possible to derive a positive morality from Christian dogma (Antonii [Khrapovitskii] [1897] 1967c, 177). Khrapovitskii had been pondering the relationship between dogma and ethics for a long time and had written several articles on this topic, some of them published in the second volume of his collected works. He sent a copy to Tolstoi, having first highlighted all paragraphs where the moral applicability of the dogmas of the Church was explained (*Biblioteka* 1972, Ia, 45). Also Khrapovitskii's article on Tolstoi's *Examination of Dogmatic Theology* (1897) focused on this topic. Here, the bishop claimed that life itself testifies to the practical usefulness of the Orthodox catechism. Great writers such as Pushkin, Dostoevskii, Turgenev and even Tolstoi himself had clearly demonstrated in their novels that only a person who believes in the living God, in Christ and in the Church, is able to live a truly virtuous life (Antonii [Khrapovitskii] [1897] 1967c, 192).

Like Tolstoi, Khrapovitskii had several reservations against Russian academic theology of the time, which he believed accorded too much weight to Western scholasticism over the Eastern Church Fathers. While Khrapovitskii clearly recognized the considerable distance between his own and Tolstoi's criticisms of Russian dogmatics, he also found several points of connection between Tolstoianism and his own understanding of the Gospels. Already in 1889 he maintained that Tolstoi in many respects "unconsciously repeats the doctrine of the Church" (Antonii [Khrapovitskii] [1889] 1967a, 69). Khrapovitskii also used the same characterization as Sergei Bulgakov would use thirteen years later: The thinker at Iasnaia Poliana was a schoolmaster who leads the children to Christ, without being a Christian himself (Antonii [Khrapovitskii] [1899] 1967a, 69). This perspective Khrapovitskii elaborated in a lecture he held in November 1910 after the death of Tolstoi, "How the Influence of Orthodoxy is expressed in Count L. N. Tolstoi's later works." The title indicates not only that he saw similarities between Tolstoianism and Orthodoxy, but also that these similarities were due to direct influence.

Initially, Khrapovitskii accepted the view that Tolstoi's metaphysics had been lifted from the works of Schopenhauer, but he added, "into this doctrine Tolstoi introduced significant changes which brought him close to ... Orthodox Russian views" (Antonii [Khrapovitskii] [1910] 1967e, 248). He saw Tolstoi as "an inner schismatic," a *raskolnik* – using a term normally reserved for the Old Believers – Russian religious dissidents of clearly Orthodox origin. According to Khrapovitskii, the relationship between Tolstoianism and Russian Orthodoxy went deeper than Tolstoi himself had realized. Despite his cosmopolitanism, Tolstoi had remained a distinctly national Russian thinker.

The individual's spiritual perfection and his close connection with the deity are crucial to both Tolstoi and the Orthodox Church, Khrapovitskii maintained. Further, Tolstoi's view that man must be reborn was an Orthodox concept that any Russian reader would immediately recognize as such. Indeed, Khrapovitskii felt that much of Tolstoi's considerable success in Russia was due to his continuing in the footsteps of traditional Russian thought (Antonii [Khrapovitskii] [1910] 1967e, 248, 252, 257–58).

The most significant similarities between the teachings of the Church and those of Tolstoi Khrapovitskii were found in their views on asceticism:

> As is well known, [Tolstoi] advocated the three rules of asceticism – abstinence from meat, chastity, and poverty –, and he himself also practised them more or less strictly. Here he comes close to the demands of the monastic life. The monks teach that precisely by renouncing pleasures one kills the principle of self-love and elevates the sacred love of God and of our neighbour. (Antonii [Khrapovitskii] [1910] 1967e, 256)

In Tolstoi's fictional writings, the ideal of chastity features first and foremost in *The Kreutzer Sonata*. Khrapovitskii thought it was not clear whether Tolstoi in this novella condemned marriage *tout court*. However, a reasonable interpretation, he believed, was that marriage is a lesser evil, a possibility open to the average man who is unable to live a life of absolute chastity. Marriage offers the opportunity to weaken the passions: When they are linked to childbirth and spousal love, they will lose their animal character and gradually fade away. Based on this interpretation of *The Kreutzer Sonata*, Khrapovitskii felt that Tolstoi had "approached the principles that our simple people live by, something which he himself openly declared" (Antonii [Khrapovitskii] [1910] 1967e, 257).

A significant common feature in the thinking of both Tolstoi and Khrapovitskii was their accentuation of the moral aspect of the Christian doctrine. Khrapovitskii shared Tolstoi's view that the credibility of religion hinges largely upon its ability to spur the believers toward a truly ethical life. "The tree is known by his fruit" (Matt. 12, 33). This attitude led the bishop to direct sharp criticism against the religious practices of the Orthodox themselves: "We like to reproach [Tolstoi] for distorting Orthodoxy, but have we shown him the truth of Orthodoxy in our daily life?" Many Russians, also believers, actually led the lives of heathens – thereby providing a breeding ground for heretics like Tolstoi. His teachings could be picked apart on the theoretical level, but they would continue to exert a strong attraction as long as Orthodoxy was practised only by peasants and a few monks, the bishop declared (Antonii [Khrapovitskii] 1891, 47).

Tolstoi Demonized

The self-critical approach toward Tolstoi and Tolstoianism that permeates the writings presented above was only one of several currents within the Russian Church, and not the most influential one either. A more common reaction was simply to denounce Tolstoi and his teaching completely – with no caveats, qualifications or nuances. Tolstoi was a deceiver, an apostate and a blasphemer. Did he give spiritual guidance such as the famous Orthodox elders at the Optina Pustyn' monastery did? If so, then he was an "impious elder" (*nechestivyi starets*) (Aivazov 1908, 1624). Did he want to be a prophet? In that case, he was a prophet of Baal (Vostorgov 1909, 1).

Many irate Orthodox writers who wanted to drag Tolstoi through the mud sought suitable epithets in the Scriptures. Some of the most obvious biblical metaphors were those involving the word *lion* since they could be linked directly to Tolstoi's given name, Lev (Leo)[6] (Sergiev 1907, 26; see also Griniakin 1904, 502 and 565). Tolstoi was "a roaring lion, seeking someone to devour" – a clear allusion to the devil (see 1 Peter 5, 8) (Sergiev 1960, 15).

Another drastic metaphor applied remarkably often to Tolstoi was "the Antichrist." Some authors seem to have used it simply as a term of censure, as the strongest invective imaginable (Kraniev 1913a, 15 and 20; Bronzov 1912, 463–82). In the New Testament, "Antichrist" is used both as a proper name and as a common noun, and in some modern European languages, including Russian, it has retained this ambiguity.[7] Several Orthodox writers made full use of this, for instance Mikhail Sopots'ko, a former Tolstoian-turned-Orthodox lay preacher. Sopots'ko warned his readers about his former mentor, whom he now described as an "undisguised Antichrist." Even this, Sopots'ko insisted, was "too mild" (Sopots'ko 1908, 29). For Sopots'ko, the term *Antichrist* seems to have lost its eschatological dimension. However, the vast majority of those who described Tolstoi as an Antichrist, or *the* Antichrist, clearly wanted to capitalize on the apocalyptical connotations.

Aylmer Maude and Ernest Simmons both relate that when Tolstoi established soup kitchens for peasants during the great famine of 1890–92, many did not dare to accept support from him, as they had been told that he was Antichrist. Both these Western authors believed that this was not a result of a spontaneous mythologization, but of deliberate propaganda from the side of the clergy. "Under the impetus of the priests,

[6] See Rev. 13, 2.

[7] Also in German, *der Antichrist* may refer to both the eschatological persona and to each and every opponent of Christianity. Friedrich Nietzsche plays upon this duality in the title of his book *der Antichrist*.

home folklore grew up in the region [of Begichevka], about Tolstoy as Antichrist" (Simmons 1947, 532; see also Maude [1908–10] 1987, 308).

One devotional journal, *Dushepoleznoe chtenie,* repeatedly presented Tolstoi as Antichrist or a precursor of Antichrist (see, for instance, Muretov 1893, 384–85). For instance, in 1899 the journal printed an anonymous letter from a reader who claimed to have incontrovertible mathematical proof that Tolstoi was Antichrist. All characters in the Church Slavonic alphabet are assigned a numerical value, and by replacing the letters in Tolstoi's name with their numerical equivalents, this reader achieved some startling results.[8]

L = 30	T = 300
E = 5	O = 70
V = 2	L = 30
	S = 200
N = 50	T = 300
I = 8	O = 70
K = 20	I = 10
O = 70	= 980
L = 30	
A = 1	
I = 8	
Ch = 90	
= 314	

Dushepoleznoe Chtenie
1899, no. 5, 142–48.

The anonymous mathematician-cum-mystic first added the values of all the characters in Tolstoi's first name and patronymic; next, he went through the same procedure separately with the characters in Tolstoi's last name. Finally, the former sum was subtracted from the latter. The reason for this final calculation, it was explained, was Tolstoi's apostasy: Because he had left the Church, one had to take away from him the names he had been given by the Church. The final result was 666 – the number of the Beast in the Apocalypse.[9]

8 Such numerology had a long pedigree in Russian apocalyptic speculations (see, e.g., Ryan 1997, 48).

9 The anonymous calculator had to take a few liberties in order to arrive at the desired result. It is not obvious why also the patronymic had to be subtracted from Tolstoi's surname: After all, it is derived from the person's carnal parentage, not the Church sacrament. Also, the patronymic was rendered

The editors of *Dushepoleznoe chtenie* indignantly rejected claims presented in the secular Russian press that they had identified Tolstoi with the Antichrist. An editorial note explained that if simple-minded Russians did so, Tolstoi's followers were themselves to blame. The Tolstoians allegedly hailed their ringleader as "a perfected Christ," and this blasphemous epithet had prompted some Orthodox believers to see Tolstoi as a harbinger of the End of Times, the journal asserted (*Dushepoleznoe chtenie* 1899, no. 5, 142; *Dushepoleznoe chtenie* 1901, no. 9, 143). While denying any authorship of the Antichrist legend, the editors of *Dushepoleznoe chtenie* nevertheless kept up interest in it by reprinting the number-juggling with Tolstoi's name two years later (*Dushepoleznoe chtenie* 1901, no. 9, 143–44).[10] The journal continued to inform its readers about new religious tracts that presented Tolstoi as Antichrist or as a person in Antichrist's entourage. In particular, they showed great interest in the apocalyptic and anti-Tolstoian writings of St. John of Kronstadt (see, e.g., *Dushepoleznoe chtenie* 1901, no. 7, 488).

John (Ioann) Sergiev (1829–1908), canonized as St. John of Kronstadt, was one of the most remarkable Russian Church figures in the last decades of the Tsarist empire. For most of his adult life he served as a parish priest of Kronstadt, on Kotlin Island in the Gulf of Finland. He traveled all over Russia, attracting large throngs of the faithful to his outdoor services wherever he went. Father John allegedly also possessed healing powers. Politically he was an ardent supporter of tsardom, and after 1905 he became an honorary member of several Black Hundred organizations (Kizenko 2000, 244). Whereas Father John was worshipped by his followers, he was a hate figure for the radical Russian intelligentsia.

The anti-Tolstoian writings of John of Kronstadt are not noted for their profundity. However, in the history of ideas they occupy an important place because they reached a wider audience than similar Orthodox writings. Some anti-Tolstoian pamphlets had print-runs of no more than a few hundred copies, but the writings of John of Kronstadt were printed

in the abridged, colloquial form "Nikolaich," not the full version "Nikolaevich." "Nikolaich" is quite common in oral speech, but not in writing.

10 The calculation was also reprinted in other Orthodox, anti-Tolstoian publications, such as *The Complete Unmasking of the Heretic of Iasnaia Poliana* (Golubtsev & Alekseev 1909). In this version, the calculation was assigned "peasant A. Golubtsev," who may have been identical with the anonymous author in *Dushepoleznoe chtenie.* Unless Golubtsev was hiding behind a false professional title, this shows that priests were not the only contributors to the myth of Tolstoi as Antichrist.

and reprinted by various publishers, with up to 40,000 copies in each printing.

In his diverse writings, Father John repeatedly mounted scathing attacks on Tolstoi and his teachings. The scattered anti-Tolstoian passages in his books and pamphlets were collected and issued separately by his devotees (Sergiev 1907; Sergiev 1960). In one of these brochures, Tolstoi's teachings were declared to be systematic and consistent lies. On one and the same page, the words *lie, lying* and *mendacious* appeared no less than fifteen times, until the reader gradually realizes that it is not any ordinary "lie" John is referring to, but the great Lie at the End of Time (see 2 Thessalonians 2) (Sergiev 1907, 47). With reference to 1 John 2, 22, Father John exclaimed: "Look at these modern, impudent apostates, Tolstoi and his followers: They are the true Antichrists. They are liars, as John the Apostle says: Who is the liar, but he who denies that Jesus is the Christ?" (Quoted in *Dushepoleznoe chtenie* 1901, no. 7, 488). The argument was intriguingly simple: A: Those who deny that Jesus is the Christ are liars and Antichrists. B: Tolstoi denies that Jesus is the Christ. C: Tolstoi is (an) Antichrist.

In another passage, Father John identified Tolstoi as the dragon mentioned in Revelation 12, 4 (Sergiev 1907, 6). Raising the stakes still further, John insisted that the blasphemy committed by Tolstoi was worse than that of the Devil – the Devil, however evil, believes in and fears God (see James 2, 19). Tolstoi, however, did not believe in the Son of God and ridiculed the truth of the Gospel. "Thus you shall know the godless one by his fruits. When he abuses the entire Christian congregation, you will know who he is. This is antichrist – this is the beast with ten horns that ascends from the bottomless pit" (Sergiev 1907, 34; see Revelation 11, 7; Revelation 13, 1).

Father John continued to exert a strong influence on perceptions of Tolstoi among Russian Orthodox believers after his death, in particular among the members of the Russian Orthodox Church Outside Russia (ROCOR). As noted, Metropolitan Antonii Khrapovitskii ended his career as head of this church, so one might perhaps expect Antonii's balanced assessment of Tolstoianism to dominate the attitudes of this church. ROCOR has dutifully republished all of Antonii's writings, including his articles on Tolstoi, but in their own writings its members tend to follow Father John of Kronstadt and not their own first leader.[11] On the occasion of the fiftieth anniversary of

[11] ROCOR was also the first church to canonize him, in 1964, 26 years before the Moscow patriarchate did, in 1990.

Tolstoi's death in 1960, a ROCOR priest, Archimandrite Konstantin (Zaitsev), pointed out that Father John had regarded Tolstoi as worse than Satan. Normally, such an assertion would have been dismissed as absurd, Konstantin admitted, but as it had come from no less an authority than John of Kronstadt, there must be a deeper meaning: "Perhaps this reveals the mystery of Antichrist as a human being, as satanic Evil incarnated with greater power?" (Konstantin [Zaitsev] 1960, 16).

During perestroika, apocalyptic writings enjoyed a massive resurgence in Russia, and speculations about the Antichrist flourished. Among right-wing Russian Orthodox polemicists, Tolstoi was still regarded as a highly odious figure. The artist Il'ia Glazunov, for instance, in his famed painting "Eternal Russia" depicted him on the left, gloomy side of the canvas as one of the leaders of the forces of darkness, together with Lenin, Stalin and Trotsky (Novikov 1994, 58–59).[12]

The Solov'evian Synthesis: Antichrist as a Double

The majority of those who regarded Tolstoi in an eschatological perspective were priests or unlearned Orthodox believers. However, one of the most original and profound Russian philosophers, Vladimir Solov'ev (1853–1900), saw the appearance of Tolstoianism as a sign that the world as we know it was coming to an end. He presented this view in his final major work, *Three Conversations about War, Progress and the End of History,* to which *A Short Story of Antichrist* was appended. Published in the year Solov'ev died, this work has been hailed by many Russian writers as one of the most brilliant refutations of Tolstoianism ever written. (See, e.g., Trubetskoi 1900, 62; A. Nikol'skii 1910, 110; Billington 1970, 469, 492; Kornblatt 1996, 68–87).

Solov'ev had known Tolstoi personally and corresponded with him. Their relationship was always complicated, and quarrels alternated with reconciliations. In most respects, Solov'ev's spirituality was far removed from that of Tolstoi. While Tolstoi was attracted to all that was simple and ethically practicable, Solov'ev was drawn toward speculation and mysticism. Throughout his adult life, Solov'ev regarded himself as an Orthodox believer, but his scepticism toward the Russian Church gradually increased. The paramount mission of the Christian Church, as he saw it,

[12] To drive home the eschatological point, Trotskii and Stalin are riding in a sleigh drawn by three of the horses of the Apocalypse. Of course, the horses of the Apocalypse are four in number, but Glazunov apparently wanted to make this look more "Russian" by reducing it to a troika.

was to infuse the world with the principles of love and freedom. Solov'ev elaborated a theory of what he called "the free theocracy," according to which the State must merge with the Church in a higher synthesis, under the leadership of the latter. However, Orthodoxy had withdrawn from the world, passively accepting a subservient position vis-à-vis the worldly powers. The Eastern Churches had renounced any ambition of influencing society and were thus incapable of filling their soteriological mission. Instead, Solov'ev held, free theocracy could be implemented if the active and extrovert Catholic Church were to join forces with the powerful Russian tsardom. He presented this utopia in his *Russia and the Universal Church,* published in Paris in 1889 (V. Solov'ev [1889] 1967).

Toward the end of his life, however, Solov'ev completely lost faith in his idea of a free theocracy, and it is against this backdrop that his last major work, *Three Conversations*, must be understood. Here Solov'ev pronounced a harsh verdict on his own socio-religious vision, but also on Tolstoi.

Modeled on Plato's dialogues, *Three Conversations* is structured as a discussion among five Russians on holiday somewhere in the Mediterranean. *The General* is an old-fashioned man of honor and dignity, *The Politician* represents modern, Western ideas, while *Z* is a Christian mystic. In the course of the conversation all three set out thoughts that Solov'ev himself could have subscribed to, but only the latter is his alter ego in a stricter sense. The sole female member of the group is *The Lady*, whose philosophical position is somewhat hazy. The final participant, *The Prince*, professes religious anarchism and is the constant target of sardonic attacks from the others. *The Prince* never explicitly associates himself with any particular school of philosophy, but contemporary as well as modern commentators have unfailingly identified him as a Tolstoian. Not only his message but also his style is closely modeled on Tolstoi's didactic pamphlets.

Already in the first paragraph of the preface to *Three Conversations* Solov'ev succinctly formulates the theme to be discussed: "Is *evil* only a natural defect, an imperfection disappearing of itself with the growth of good, or is it a real power, possessing our world by means of temptations?" (V. Solov'ev 1903, 453; emphasis in the original).[13] Earlier in his life Solov'ev had been inclined to agree with St. Augustine: Evil has no substance. It is nothing but an absence of good, a *privatio boni*

[13] Here and in other quotations below I follow Alexander Bakshy's translation in *War, Progress and the End of History* (London, 1915).

(Mochul'skii 1951, 250). By the time he wrote *Three Conversations*, however, his opinion had changed radically: Evil had become a real force. *General* had fought in the Russo–Turkish War of 1877–78 and in his mind there is no doubt that evil, as manifested in the atrocities perpetrated by the Turks, has to be resisted by force of arms. In response, *Prince*, as a consistent pacifist, argues that to take the life of another human being is unmitigated evil. Any person who commits manslaughter stoops to the level of the beasts. To be killed, on the other hand, can hardly be regarded as an evil at all: It is no worse than dying of cholera or pneumonia. *Z* immediately points out the inconsistency here: According to *Prince*'s logic, it is an unmitigated evil to commit an act that represents no evil to the victim (V. Solov'ev 1903, 469–70). Solov'ev's most basic objection to Tolstoi's teaching is then presented: Tolstoi does not accept the reality of evil. That is why Tolstoi believes in the possibility of establishing the Kingdom of God on earth. This objection, however, was devastating not only for Tolstoianism but also for Solov'ev's own earlier idea of a free theocracy, as Solov'ev fully realizes. He therefore concludes that all dreams of an earthly Kingdom of God are equally objectionable: In essence, they are not only utopian but anti-Christian.

In *Three Conversations*, the discussion now turns to the issues of war and progress. In *Politician*'s view, war is not an Absolute Evil. As mankind progresses toward an ever more perfect society, war will wither away like an atrophied organ. Instead of God and war, there will be culture and peace. *Z* does not disagree with this prognosis but adds that he regards such progress as a symptom – a symptom of *the end*.

POLITICIAN: ... The end of *what*, I ask you?
MR Z.: Naturally, the end of what we have been talking about. As you remember, we have been discussing the history of mankind, and that historical 'process' which has doubtless been going on at an ever-increasing rate, and which I am certain is nearing its end.
LADY: *C'est la fin du monde, n'est-ce pas?* The argument is becoming a most extraordinary one!
GENERAL: At last we have got to the most interesting subject.
PRINCE: You will not, of course, forget Anti-Christ either.
MR. Z: Certainly not. He takes the most prominent place in what I have to say. (V. Solov'ev 1903, 524–25)

Prince suddenly excuses himself and leaves. The others comment on his hasty departure: *Lady* suggests that he may have taken *Z*'s remarks as a personal attack and asks whether one ought to consider him as the Antichrist incarnate. *General* answers somewhat indeterminately.

> Well, not personally, not he personally; it will be a long time before he gets as far as that. But he is on that track, all the same. As it is said in the Gospel of St. John: "You have heard, my little ones, that Anti-Christ is coming, and there are many Anti-Christs now." So one of these "many." (V. Solov'ev 1903, 526)

The book has suddenly taken a surprising turn: While *Prince* was initially accused of *denying* the reality of evil, he is now presented as a *servant* of the Evil One. When *Prince* rejoins the company after a short while, he is given a rough ride by Z. The "lord" that *Prince* wants to serve insists that men shall do good, but he does not manifest his own goodness in any acts of love himself. Until the opposite has been proven, *Z* will therefore assume that *Prince*'s "lord" is not identical with the Christian God, but with *the lord of this world* – the Devil (V. Solov'ev 1903, 552).

What prompted Solov'ev – alias *Z* – to pass such a drastic verdict on *Prince*, and by implication on Tolstoi? It was not the clearly and unambiguously anti-Orthodox aspects of Tolstoi's teaching that led him to this conclusion. Open enmity toward the Christian faith is nothing to be afraid of, Solov'ev believed. An honest opponent of the Truth may at any time become a new St. Paul. Zealots like *Prince*, however, were an entirely different matter. Their stance reminded *Z* of Judas the Betrayer (V. Solov'ev 1903, 554). Their teaching is not merely false religion: It is *deception*.

To *Z*, it is those aspects of Tolstoianism that too closely model true religion that make it particularly sinister. *Z* admits that it took him a long while to recognize this, and to identify its anti-Christian essence. Moreover, he does not doubt that *Prince* is convinced that he is serving God when he is actually doing the devil's work. But we should not forget that the lord of this world is a wily gentleman who hides himself behind *a mask of goodness* (V. Solov'ev 1903, 553).

In *A Short Story of the Anti-Christ*, which completes *Three Conversations*, Solov'ev developed these ideas further. Antichrist is presented as a remarkable figure who emerges in the twenty-first century. At the age of 33, he is already hailed as a great thinker, writer and social reformer. He is loved and respected, unselfish and constantly active as a philanthropist. He lives the life of an ascetic, swayed neither by base passions nor by the sweet lure of power. In contrast to most people of the time, this person is a convinced idealist. He believes in both Goodness and God. This is what he *believes* in – but he *loves* only himself. Initially, he recognizes the messianic dignity and significance of Christ, but gradually turns against Him, wanting to be God's only chosen representative on earth. In a fit of rage he yells, foaming at the mouth: "He has not risen!" (V. Solov'ev 1903, 562). Now he tumbles like a ripe fruit into the net of the devil, who chooses him as *his* only-begotten son, the Antichrist. The Antichrist's first act after his initiation is to write a book, *The Open Way to Universal Peace and Well-Being*. This brings him world fame, and he is elected President of the United States of Europe. In the end, the last Pope suddenly realizes the Antichrist's true identity and excommunicates him. The Antichrist is killed in a battle against the Jews, and Christ returns to rule on Earth for a thousand years.

This Antichrist is not identical to Tolstoi or to *Prince*, as explicitly pointed out in the book itself (V. Solov'ev 1903, 554). Nevertheless, the three are closely related. On several specific points Tolstoi has clearly served as a model for the devil's latter-day representative in Solov'ev's conception (Mochul'skii 1951, 259). Like the Antichrist, Tolstoi won his fame as a great thinker, writer and social reformer. He was a religious idealist and a believer in God and Goodness. The Antichrist's immunity to the temptations of the flesh and worldly power may be read as alluding to Tolstoi's asceticism and anarchism. Finally, and most importantly, they both, as Solov'ev saw it, alter the message of Christ into its exact opposite in such a subtle way that even experienced observers might be deceived. As pointed out by the noted scholar of Russian Orthodoxy, Paul Valliere, in the story of the Antichrist Solov'ev shows how "the father of lies can subvert any ideal, even the most sublime. This is a crucial point in the polemic against Tolstoyanism" (Valliere 2000, 221).

Most of Solov'ev's books were heavy academic reading inaccessible to the masses, but the vivid fictional style of *Three Conversions* was different. This work became widely known, and found resonance among the Russian Orthodox radical right, as with Sergei Il'menskii's pamphlet *More Clearly Than Most, Count L. Tolstoi Expressed the Spirit of the Impending Antichrist*, published in Saratov in 1911. Il'menskii claimed that it was becoming increasingly difficult for Christians to distinguish between true and false preachers since even the worst enemies of God now hid behind purity and invoked the name of Christ. This, in Il'menskii's opinion, was a true sign of the End. There existed a widespread but nevertheless quite erroneous notion of the Antichrist as some kind of terrible beast with flaming eyes. Such ideas were simply ludicrous. Il'menskii pointed out that in *Three Conversations* Solov'ev had disclosed the true nature of Christ's ultimate opponent: He would march forth under the banner of philanthropy. Moreover, Solov'ev had also shown who was carrying the banner: "Of all the precursors of the imminent antichrist, Count Tolstoi, in our view, is the most horrible and seductive. Under the cover of personal goodness he manages to draw even the chosen ones, at the end of the world, into the gaping abyss of evil" (Il'menskii 1911, 1).

Tolstoi had preached individual moral perfection, chastity, spiritual heroism, and service to society. He stood forth as a preacher of goodness, bolstering his message with references to the Gospels. In fact, however, according to Il'menskii, Tolstoi's relationship to Christian truth was purely external, as he did not recognize the divinity of Christ. Tolstoi's aspirations to establish a new, rationalist religion clearly demonstrated his anti-Christian arrogance.

> All of this reminds us of the last antichrist, who, as the word of God and the church tradition tell us, will insist on being treated with godly honours. He will proclaim himself the benefactor of all mankind and speak lofty and exalted words about some universal, unifying religion based on earthly reason. He will throw a shining cloak of goodness and truth over the mystery of extreme lawlessness. (Il'menskii 1911, 3)

To Il'menskii it was precisely this "shining cloak" of goodness and truth that set Tolstoi apart from the myriad of ordinary blasphemers and gave him Anti-Christian dimensions.

Similar reflections can be found in the diary of Archimandrite Arsenii (Zhadanovskii). According to this monastic, Tolstoi had been godless in the full and true meaning of the word. But how then to explain that he had constantly been talking about God, the Gospels, love and other Christian principles? The key to this mystery could be found in the Scriptures: Christ himself had said that the deceivers would not be clad in their own garments, but would hide their iniquity behind the Truth: "Many will come in my name, saying 'I am the Christ,' and they will lead many astray" (Matt. 24, 5). This, Arsenii held, accurately foretold the coming of Tolstoi.

> Did not Tolstoi come in the name of Christ, call himself a Christian, expound the Gospel and allegedly preach about Christ? Did he not seduce many? The Antichrist himself, according to the faith of the Church, will make use of exactly this method of enticement. Initially, he will captivate people by means of Christian principles, later he will openly rise up against Christ. (Arsenii 1912, 73)

The Orthodox literature on Tolstoi is vast and varied. Many Russian theologians and laypeople have concentrated on one specific aspect of Tolstoianism or one of Tolstoi's many tracts and articles, scrupulously refuting them point by point, showing how and where his teaching deviated from Orthodoxy as they defined it. Some of these were quite solid and erudite works, but their dry style attracted few readers. Other anti-Tolstoian authors, however, treated Tolstoianism in broad and sweeping terms. These polemicists were less concerned with nuances and distinctions and tended toward extreme, eye-catching characterizations such as "Tolstoi the Antichrist."

Of course, identifying Tolstoi as the Antichrist or as a being with anti-Christian powers reflects the deep conviction that Tolstoi was an irreconcilable adversary of Christ. In itself, however, that view, however strongly held, would hardly suffice to cast him in this most sinister of roles. Russia at the turn of the nineteenth and twentieth century was teeming with militant atheists and blasphemers whom no one would dream of associating with this most hideous persona of the Apocalypse. But Tolstoi differed crucially from these other enemies of the Church on one decisive point, it was believed: He concealed his rebellion against God behind a *mask* of goodness and godliness, as Solov'ev expressed it. The heretic of Iasnaia Poliana was seen as presenting a counterfeit version of the true religion, a version that bore a disturbing resemblance to the real thing. That helps to explain why the Church leadership came to invest so much energy in attempting to roll back his dangerous influence.

CHAPTER 12

The "Excommunication" and Its Aftermath

On February 24, 1901, a formal statement was printed in the official organ of the Synod, *Tserkovnye vedomosti,* titled "Decree (*Opredelenie*) of the Holy Synod of February 20–22, 1901, No. 557, on Count Lev Tolstoi, with a Circular Letter (*poslanie*) to the Faithful Children of the Orthodox Greek-Russian Church" (hereafter: the *Circular Letter*). The next day, it was read aloud in the Uspenskii Cathedral and later in all Cathedral churches throughout Russia. This is the most famous of all documents dealing with Tolstoi's relationship with Orthodoxy, and deserves to be reproduced in its entirety:

> In caring for the children of the Orthodox Church, to preserve them from pernicious temptation and to save those who have gone astray, the Most Holy Synod has found it timely to publish the following message (*poslanie*) with a statement about Count Lev Tolstoi and his anti-Christian and anti-religious teaching. By printing it in *Tserkovnye vedomosti* the Synod intends to prevent the peace of the Church from being broken:
>
> By the mercy of God,
>
> From the Most Holy All-Russian Synod to the Believing Children of the Orthodox, Greek-Catholic Russian Church: Rejoice in the Lord . . .
>
> 'Now we [sic] beseech you, brethren, mark them which cause divisions and offences contrary to the doctrine which ye have learned; and avoid them'. (Romans 16, 17)
>
> From the beginning, the Church of Christ has endured mockery and attack from numerous heretics and false teachers who have attempted to overthrow her and shake her very foundation, the belief in Christ, the Son of the Living God. But, according to the Lord's promise, all the powers of hell shall not prevail against the Holy Church, which shall remain forever unconquered. Also in our days, God has allowed yet another false teacher, Count Lev Tolstoi, to appear. Count Tolstoi, a world-renowned writer, is

Russian-born and Orthodox by baptism and upbringing. Lured by his proud reason, he has brazenly rebelled against the Lord and His Anointed One and His holy property. For all to see, he has openly renounced his Mother, the Orthodox Church, which has nourished and nurtured him, and devoted his literary activity and his God-given talent to spreading among the people doctrines contrary to Christ and the Church. He seeks to eradicate from the minds and hearts of men the faith of their fathers, the Orthodox faith which upholds the universe, the faith by which our ancestors lived and died and which holy Russia has been kept by and has taken her strength from to this day. His works and letters have been spread by him and by his disciples in large quantities throughout the world, in particular within the borders of our beloved Fatherland. In these, he tries with the zeal of a fanatic to overthrow all dogmas of the Orthodox Church and the innermost essence of Christian belief:

He rejects the personal, living God that is glorified in the Holy Trinity, the Creator and Sustainer of the universe. He rejects the Lord Jesus Christ, God-Man, Redeemer and Savior of the world, who suffered for humankind, and for the sake of our salvation and who arose from the dead. He rejects that Christ the Lord was conceived into the human race without semen and that the purest Mother of God and Eternal Virgin Mary was virgin before and after His birth. He does not recognize life after death and eternal retribution, denies all the Sacraments of the Church and the grace-giving work of the Holy Spirit through them. He blasphemes against the most sacred religious objects of the Orthodox people, and has not refrained from mocking the greatest of all Sacraments, the Holy Eucharist. All this Count Lev Tolstoi propagates incessantly, in speech and writing, to the temptation and horror of the entire Orthodox world. He has not acted in secret, but openly among everyone. Deliberately and intentionally, he has torn himself away from any community with the Orthodox Church. In vain have attempts been made to admonish him. Therefore, the Church no longer counts him among her members and cannot do so until he repents and restores his fellowship with her. This we hereby testify before the entire Church to support those who stand steadfast and to reason with those who have gone astray, and in particular, to reason one more time with Count Tolstoi himself. Many of his loved ones who have kept the faith think with sadness that when his days are counted he will stand without faith in God and in our Lord the Savior. Then he will have spurned the Church's blessings and prayers and any fellowship with her.

Therefore, as we testify that he has fallen from the Church, we at the same time also pray that the Lord give him repentance so that he knows the truth (2 Tim. 2, 25). We beseech You, merciful Lord, who desires not the death of any sinner: Hear us and have mercy, and bring Him back to Your Holy Church. Amen.

Original signatures:
Antonii, humble Metropolitan of St. Petersburg and Ladoga.
Feognost, humble Metropolitan of Kiev and Galitsiia.
Vladimir, humble Metropolitan of Moscow and Kolomna.
Ieronim, humble Archbishop of Kholm and Warsaw.
Iakov, humble Bishop of Kishinev and Khotin
Markell, humble Bishop.
Boris, humble Bishop

(Opredelenie 1901)

Who Were the Authors of the Circular Letter and What Were their Motives?

Public statements with strong condemnation of named persons have not often been issued in the Russian Church. The promulgation of the Circular Letter on Tolstoi is not only a key chapter in Tolstoi's biography but also one of the most important events in the history of the Russian Church during the reign of Nicholas II. Much has been written about this, but many circumstances were for a long time shrouded in semidarkness due to several factors. The actual text of the Circular Letter was marked by considerable ambiguity and allowed for many different interpretations (Weisbein 1960, 374). Moreover, in the Soviet period, those who had the best access to the relevant sources in the archives, Soviet researchers, chose to publish only parts of what they knew. By putting these parts together in certain ways, they managed to create a distorted impression of who were the persons behind the Circular Letter, and their motives. Western scholars had little opportunity to check on their Soviet colleagues, and often passed on the Soviet version uncritically. Then, when Russian archives were opened under perestroika, it became possible to correct their conclusions.

Although the Circular Letter was signed by Synod's seven ecclesiastical members, it was not altogether clear that they were the persons who had taken the initiative to it. The Church had a long tradition of subordination to the State, and the members of the Synod usually signed all documents submitted to them without major objections. This tendency was strengthened rather than weakened in the years before the 1917 Revolution (Curtiss 1940).

The question of the authorship of the Circular Letter is important for assessing the intentions behind its publication. Various motives were stated in the Circular Letter itself: To maintain the peace of the Church; to support the faithful; and to administer an admonition to all who had gone astray, and to Tolstoi in particular. If the hierarchs themselves were behind the Circular Letter, we must assume that these concerns, or some of them, were decisive. If, however, if the Synod was acting on behalf of the tsarist state, there are reasons to believe that publication of the Letter was more politically motivated.

The person who possessed most political power in the Russian Church at the time was Chief Procurator Konstantin Pobedonostsev. He fulfilled in many respects a dual function: He represented the interests of the Tsarist power vis-à-vis the Church and the interests of the Church vis-à-vis the Tsar. If the origin of the Circular Letter can be traced back to him, it would be difficult to determine on behalf of which of these two institutions he was acting in this specific case. However, it has also been claimed that he was acting for his own sake, driven by personal revenge motives. In 1900, Tolstoi had published the novel *Resurrection* where he had created the character Toporov (Chapter XXVII), a highly unsympathetic Church politician obviously modeled on Pobedonostsev, whom he loathed.[1] Therefore, many Russians believed that they could glimpse Pobedonostsev's claw between the lines when they read the Circular Letter (G.I. Petrov 1978, 49). Also, many modern authors have pointed the finger at Pobedonostsev, viewing the publication of *Resurrection* as the single most important impetus behind the Circular Letter (e.g., Kurov 1979, 266; Troyat 1980, 775; Wilson 1989, 457–59; Nickell 2006, 35; Orekhanov 2016, 446).

One of the first persons who publicly raised question of the authorship of the Circular Letter was Dmitrii Merezhkovskii (1865–1941). A leading figure in the "new religious consciousness" movement, he worked tirelessly to put religious and other spiritual topics on the agenda of the intelligentsia. His ideal was a future-oriented Christianity with strong expectations of a new, liberal age in the sign of the Holy Spirit. Unlike Tolstoi, he did not want to remove the dogmas from the faith; on the contrary, he looked forward to new revelations (Scherrer 1973, 23). At the same time, Merezhkovskii wanted to reestablish contact with historical Christianity, and invited representatives of the official Russian Church to dialogue. This

[1] In December 1900, Tolstoi in a letter to Nicholas II had referred to Pobedonostsev as "your repulsive, heartless and unscrupulous advisor in religious affairs, a scoundrel whose name will go down in history as the prototype of a scoundrel" (Tolstoi PSS 72, 516). Pobedonostsev may well have been aware of the content of this letter.

resulted in the "Petersburg Religious-Philosophical Society," which became an important forum for Russian cultural debate around the turn of the nineteenth and twentieth centuries.

At the third meeting of the society, in spring 1902, Merezhkovskii presented the evening's lecture himself, on the topic of "Lev Tolstoi and the Church," and touched upon the Circular Letter. Merezhkovskii reminded his audience that, according to Fedor Dostoevskii, the Russian Church had become "paralyzed" when Peter the Great abolished the patriarchate. It was therefore remarkable that the Church had now mustered the courage to publish such a hard-hitting document. Either this meant that the Church had risen from its sickbed and made an independent act in its own defense, "or it is still paralyzed, and someone else is standing over it, raising the withered hand of the emaciated patient to hit out against its own enemy" (*Zapiski* 1906, 73–74). If the latter were the case, this "other" could only be the Tsar, Merezhkovskii believed. He did not, however, have any information that enabled him draw firm conclusions.

Several Soviet scholars maintained that they could indeed answer this question unambiguously. B. Meilakh claimed in 1960 that "the excommunication, we now know (*teper' izvestno*), was not at all an independent act by the Synod, but coordinated with Nicholas II" (Meilakh [1960] 1979, 144). Meilakh also believed that he knew the motive behind the Circular Letter: "The purpose of this act was primarily to arouse all the dark forces against Tolstoi" (ibid.; cited also by Pozoiskii 1963, 25; G. I. Petrov 1978, 34), but Meilakh did not explain how we could know this. Another Soviet Tolstoi expert, Lidiia Opul'skaia, gave the following explanation as to why the tsarist regime should react in this manner: "Russia and the Russian people were moving with rapid steps towards their first revolution. Fear of the revolution compelled the Tsarist government to throw itself into one senseless act after the other: banning Tolstoi from the Church, starting a meaningless war in the Far East, and so on" (Opul'skaia 1978, 6). Almost identical opinions were put forward by other Soviet scholars (Pozoiskii 1963, 24–25; Lomunov 1979, 3–4). But if the Tsar really hoped to stem the revolution by attacking Tolstoi, he had very shortsighted advisors indeed. Such an act would give the rabble-rousers a new symbol to rally around, while Tolstoi would have been able to continue his subversive activity undisturbed. Moreover, Tolstoi was the only main ideological opponents of the regime who consistently advocated nonviolence in the struggle against the state. If the tsarist regime were concerned about the increasing revolutionary violence, it therefore ought to have promoted Tolstoian pacifism as a possible counterweight rather than combating it. In an article in *Moskovskie vedomosti* in 1897, the reactionary thinker and former revolutionary Lev Tikhomirov, who had excellent contacts in the government and at the court, confirmed that this was a widespread opinion in these circles: "Regarding the intelligentsia, one can often and also today hear the argument that it would be better if it made a fool of itself in Tolstoian colonies rather than engage in political conspiracies" (Tikhomirov 1897, 51). However, Tikhomirov did not share this opinion himself; on the contrary, he saw Tolstoi as a highly dangerous deceiver of the people.

Moreover, Opul'skaia's assertion also contradicts very much of the material presented by the Soviet researcher G. I. Petrov in his monograph on the excommunication of Tolstoi – a book that Opul'skaia wrote the preface to. Petrov tells us that already in 1892 concrete plans had been made to excommunicate Tolstoi:

> It seems that the synod had made everything ready, also chief procurator K. P. Pobedonostsev leaned in the direction of the synod's majority. But all the plans came to naught, crushed against Alexander III's unbending resistance. He remained faithful to his promise 'not to add a crown of a martyrdom to Tolstoi's fame' . . . . The synod had to retreat and wait for a more convenient moment before it could settle accounts (*rasprava*) with Tolstoi. (G. I. Petrov 1978, 23)

The issue of excommunicating Tolstoi could not be raised again as long as Tsar Alexander III remained alive (Orekhanov 2016, 456). By the time Tolstoi was actually excommunicated in 1901, however, Alexander III had been succeeded on the throne by his son, Nicholas II. The young Tsar was far less pragmatic than his father, and might conceivably have brushed aside Alexander III's caution. However, we do not have any indications of this, rather the contrary.

There exists a testimony of how the Circular Letter in 1901 came about from a person who contributed actively to drafting it. In 1915, privy councillors Vasilii Skvortsov wrote an article in his newspaper *Kolokol* on "The History of the Excommunication of L. N. Tolstoi." Skvortsov here explained that there had been growing concern in the Church leadership about the influence of Tolstoi among the younger clergy. Hectographed versions of Tolstoi's anti-Orthodox works were circulating in Moscow. So, in mid-February 1901 Skvortsov was summoned to Deputy Chief Procurator V. K. Sabler, who commissioned him to prepare a report with an accurate account of Tolstoi's teachings. This Skvortsov did the same evening, and the next day the report ended up on Pobedonostsev's desk.

On the basis of this document, the Chief Procurator wrote a first draft of the Circular Letter, which was discussed at two meetings in the Synod. Here the prelates made some amendments that were incorporated into the text. When the document had already been printed in the Synod's official organ *Tserkovnye vedomosti*, a copy of this journal was brought up "to the higher levels." "Only now were they informed about this historic step, which the supreme Church authority had undertaken on its own initiative," Skvortsov wrote (quoted in G.I. Petrov 1978, 32–33; Orekhanov 2010, 510).

G. I. Petrov claimed that Skvortsov was deliberately lying: He wanted to remove the onus of responsibility for the Circular Letter from the Tsar and shift it onto the prelates. Five of them had already passed away when Skvortsov's article was printed, and it was convenient to blame them for this disgraceful act (G.I. Petrov 1978, 32). This reasoning, however, is based on a faulty premise: That, in Skvortsov's opinion, the Circular Letter was something to be ashamed of. Everything else which Skvortsov wrote and said testified to the opposite. At the meeting in the Petersburg Religious-Philosophical Society in 1902 where Tolstoi and the Church were discussed, Skvortsov had taken the floor and defended the Circular Letter in all its aspects. If the Synod were to be reproached for anything, he indicated, it was for having waited too long before taking action (*Zapiski* 1906, 86–88). In 1904, Skvortsov also published a voluminous edited volume (more than 500 pages) with articles from his journal *Missionerskoe obozrenie*, which discussed the excommunication of Tolstoi from every imaginable angle. This book was printed in no less than four editions; in the last one, the page total had increased to almost 700, with forty different contributors. Skvortsov thus did his utmost to ensure that the veil of oblivion should not be allowed to descend on the Circular Letter. Moreover, no information has come to light since 1915 that gives grounds for rejecting Skvortsov's main claim: Even if it might be true that the Russian prelates were often spineless puppets of the state power, in this case, they had acted on their own behalf, exhibiting an unusually high degree of energy and determination.

Not much is known about what Nicholas II thought about the matter.[2] There exist two letters from Pobedonostsev to the Tsar that show that the

[2] Skvortsov's biographer Vladislav Maevskii claimed that the Tsar was very upset when he heard about the Circular Letter. Nicholas II allegedly held Tolstoi in high esteem – not just as a writer of fiction, but also as a religious thinker. On reading the Circular Letter, the Tsar (according to Maevskii) wrote three letters to Pobedonostsev. In particular the first one was very sharply worded, and stated that "in the future such decisions shall not be taken without his [= the tsar's: P.K.] knowledge" (Maevskii

Emperor had been informed orally that a public text was being the prepared against Tolstoi, before it was published. Apparently, he had accepted this, and did not react until he saw the actual text of the document, which he regarded as too harsh (Orekhanov 2016, 499–500).[3]

Skvortsov's account in *Kolokol* in 1915 is not free of inconsistencies. In his article he confused the meeting in the St. Petersburg Religious-Philosophical Society in February 1902 with another meeting, this time in the St. Petersburg Philosophical Society, the year before. Moreover, while maintaining that the first draft of the Circular Letter was penned by Pobedonostsev, he also insisted that the initiative had come from the Metropolitan Antonii (Vadkovskii) (1846–1912), who shortly before had taken over as *primus inter pares* in the Synod (G.I. Petrov 1978, 28). Furthermore, Skvortsov claimed that Antonii was completely devoid of initiative and fighting spirit: Pobedonostsev allegedly used to compare him with a broom that anyone could take in his hands and sweep with. Even so, it was precisely Antonii who, "quite suddenly and with persistent great energy," demanded that the Church should resolutely settle accounts with Tolstoi (V. Skvortsov1915; quoted in G. I. Petrov 1978, 32).

However, the discrepancies in Skvortsov's version most likely had other and more prosaic explanations than a deliberate attempt to mystify his readers. It may well be that his memory failed him on certain points, fourteen years after the event. He did not have access to all relevant documents and information when he wrote his article, but tried to put together a puzzle where some pieces were missing. For instance, he mentioned several important documents that he believed must lie in the Synod's archives, but which he himself had not seen. He assumed that there existed an early version of the Circular Letter written by Pobedonostsev, with the prelates' amendments. These corrections, he believed, all served to soften the tone of the final document (see G. I. Petrov 1978, 32). And indeed, in the Central State Historical Archive in St. Petersburg, there is a typed copy of a draft of the Circular Letter with five handwritten glosses. Contrary to what Skvortsov assumed, however, all of these *sharpened* the tone of the Letter and seem aimed at increasing Tolstoi's burden of sin. While the first draft had accused Tolstoi of wanting to "overthrow all dogmas of the Orthodox Church," it was now

1952, 194). Maevskii's source of this information was a certain General Mosolov, who had allegedly heard the story from the Tsar's adjutant, Baron Frederiks.

3 The Soviet researcher M. N. Kurov provides another reading of this correspondence: In his view, it proves that the Tsar had read the actual text of the Circular letter before it was published, and later tried to extricate himself from the responsibility (Kurov 1979).

added "and the essence of the Christian faith." The statement that Tolstoi did not recognize life after death and eternal retribution was also inserted in this new redaction.[4] One harsh word, "mockery" (*glumlenie*), had been deleted and then reinserted in the final version, which testifies to the complicated process of preparing the document and possible disagreements among the various individuals involved. It is not clear from the document itself who had made the first draft and who added the changes, but an anonymous copyist had provided the document with a piece of information according to which the three most substantial additions came from Pobedonostsev's hand (TsGIAL, f.796, op.182, Ep.khr. 2133, l.4).

It is quite possible that multiple versions of the Circular Letter went back and forth between the offices of the Synod with annotations from various contributors. In any case, the extant material seems to indicate that Pobedonostsev himself did not take the initiative to the Circular Letter or write the first draft (Orekhanov 2010, 472–496).[5] This interpretation is supported by another important document in the Central State Historical Archives in St. Petersburg: A letter from Metropolitan Antonii to Pobedonostsev, dated February 11, 1901 (TsGIAL, g. 1574, op. 2, ep. khr. 133, l. 1). Here Antonii told the Chief Procurator that "everyone in the Synod has now come to the conclusion that a statement on Tolstoi must be published in *Tserkovnye vedomosti*. And it must happen quickly."[6] This is the oldest document we know that advocates the promulgation of a separate Circular Letter against Tolstoi after similar plans had been shelved in 1892 and 1899. Thus, Metropolitan Antonii's central role as initiator of the Circular Letter seems to be beyond doubt.

The above quotation was later reproduced by several Soviet researchers (Pozoiskii 1963, 23; G. I. Petrov 1978, 28). However, Antonii's letter to Pobedonostsev also contains considerable other important information that the Soviet researchers failed to point out. Immediately before the Metropolitan insisted on the necessity of issuing a statement on Tolstoi, he wrote that he had had a conversation with a Petersburg priest, Grigorii Spirodonovich Petrov (1867–1925) the day before. It might seem as if the

[4] The entire text of this draft document, together with the handwritten corrections, is reproduced in Orekhanov (Orekhanov 2016, 481).

[5] Orekhanov goes as far as to claim that Pobedonostsev "while not opposed to state measures against Tolstoi in principle, was nevertheless against the excommunication in 1901. He was extremely skeptical about the possible results of this act, regarding it as untimely and something which, if anything, would only provoke enormous irritation in Russian society" (Orekhanov 2010, 529; see also Orekhanov 2016, 471).

[6] The entire text of this letter is reproduced in Orekhanov 2016, 467–68.

metropolitan here suddenly raised a quite different matter but in fact these two issues were intimately connected, and this provides a crucial key to understanding the motives of the Church leadership behind the Circular Letter.

Father Grigorii was a well-known figure in radical circles of the capital and had authored several books and brochures in which he, in a simple and captivating manner, preached greater social justice and the need to follow the example of Christ in everyday life (Hedda 2008, 106–25, 179–83). In the working-class areas of Petersburg, Petrov enjoyed a popularity comparable only to that of Father Gapon. He was somewhat of an *enfant terrible* in the Church, and often got into trouble with his superiors. Petrov had known Metropolitan Antonii since 1887 when he enrolled at the St. Petersburg Theological Academy where Antonii was rector at the time (Hedda 2008, 108). Jennifer Hedda maintains that the Metropolitan was among Petrov's "many supporters in the church" (Hedda 2008, 118), but if that was the case, it did not keep Antonii from contacting the Chief Procurator to express his deep concern over the priest's behavior.

To Pobedonostsev, Antonii wrote that he had received several complaints about Petrov from other clergy. The Metropolitan claimed that he had been asked to start a regular persecution of Petrov, including a "crusade" in the press. People complained that this priest skipped certain words in the liturgy when he celebrated the Mass if they did not fit into his worldview. Antonii, however, had for a long time held his hand over the radical priest and believed that it should be possible to reason with him.

When the Metropolitan chose to summon Petrov for a longer conversation precisely on February 10, 1901, it was for another reason: Four days earlier the priest had participated at a meeting in the Petersburg Philosophical Society, on February 6, 1901. Here Dmitrii Merezhkovskii delivered a talk on Tolstoi and religion in which it was claimed that "what Tolstoi has written about Orthodoxy are the most shameful pages in Russian literature. Not even the most greenhorn followers of materialism stoop to such a level of blasphemy" (quoted in Orekhanov 2016, 469). After this lecture, however, Petrov as an official opponent had presented a very different view: He accused the lecturer of one-sidedness and excessive strictness (Orekhanov 2016, 470–71). For his part, he wanted to draw a parallel between Tolstoi and the virtuous pagan Virgil who guided Dante, the Christian seeker of truth, through Hell and Purgatory and all the way to the gates of Heaven. By drawing this analogy, the priest was in effect saying that Tolstoi was perhaps not a Christian himself, but his teaching did not harm the Christian faith in any way. On the contrary, in Petrov's view, Tolstoi was, perhaps in spite of himself, doing the work of God. He could lead the people through the "purgatory of life" to the Gospel, even though he himself lacked the full divine enlightenment. Therefore, Tolstoi played "a tremendously important role" for the Church (V. Skvortsov 1901c, 243).[7] Metropolitan Antonii was immediately informed about this by Vasilii Skvortsov, who had also been present at the meeting. Appalled that such flattering descriptions of one of the most vehement detractors of Orthodoxy could be made by a man of the Church, Antonii summoned Petrov to his office. Already the next morning after the meeting Antonii wrote his letter to Chief Procurator Pobedonostsev, telling him that "everyone in the Synod has reached the conclusion that it is necessary to publish a statement on Tolstoi in *Tserkovnye vedomosti*" (TsGIA, g. 1574, op. 2, ed.khr. 133, l. 1).

For the Church leadership, the debate in the Petersburg Philosophical Society must have appeared rather paradoxical. While Merezhkovskii, a representative of the "secular" albeit religiously interested intelligentsia, adopted what they would regard as a sensible attitude toward the preacher of Iasnaia Poliana, one of the Church's own representatives stood up in defense of him (Orekhanov 2010, 511). This must have been the straw that broke the camel's back for Antonii. The letter he wrote to Pobedonostsev five days later opened with the following sentences:

> Yesterday morning I talked to Father Grigorii Petrov for a long time. I summoned him for a conversation about the stupidity he had presented at the Philosophical Society during the discussion on Lev Tolstoi and also about his other stupidities. (TsGAIL, g.1574, op.2, ed.chr. 133, l.1)

With regard to his willful rewriting of the liturgy, Petrov promised to mend his ways, but when it came to his views on Tolstoi he was less amenable. The priest denied that he was a Tolstoian and also

[7] The religious philosopher Vasilii Rozanov (1859–1919), also present at the meeting, gave a slightly different account: According to him, Petrov had said that Tolstoi reminded him of the younger of the two sons who in the parable (Matt. 21, 28–32) were asked by their father to go and work in the vineyard. The older one said yes but did not go, whereas the younger son did the opposite: In Petrov's view Tolstoi could be compared with the latter:

> He stands outside the Church and even goes against the Church, just like the younger son of the vineyard owner. However, is it not precisely [Tolstoi] who preaches modesty in life, purity in our carnal life, diligence, charity, and abstinence even from certain kinds of food (vegetarianism)? These are precisely the tasks and aims that constitute the immediate field of activity and concern for Christianity, the Church, Orthodoxy and the clergy. (Rozanov 1901)

Petrov may well have used both the Virgil metaphor and the New Testament parable.

acknowledged that Tolstoi was not an Orthodox. He nevertheless maintained that he was full of admiration for Tolstoi as a writer of fiction. Concerning his intervention in the Philosophical Society, Petrov claimed that he had been misquoted, and also that what he had expressed were his private opinions only. Had he known that they would be reproduced in the press, he would have kept silent. The Metropolitan, however, was not satisfied.

> If Father Grigorii continues to walk down the path he has entered onto ... he will bring down upon himself the ire of the Orthodox. His bishop will also have to condemn him. This circumstance ... I made him aware of. (ibid.)

Immediately after this sentence, Antonii goes on to say: "everyone in the Synod has now come to the conclusion that a statement on Tolstoi must be published in *Tserkovnye vedomosti.*"

For Antonii, it was essential to make it abundantly clear that in the Church there was no room for Petrov's interpretation of Tolstoi. This would have to be communicated not only to Petrov, but to the entire Church, in the form of a Circular Letter to all believers. At the same time, it was important that attention should be drawn not to Petrov, but to Tolstoi himself. Oddly enough, in the accounts of the meeting of the Philosophical Society written by Orthodox believers, Petrov is not mentioned anywhere by name (Terletskii 1901, 7–8; V. Skvortsov 1901c, 243). They only reported his views, claiming that they showed how widespread sympathy for Tolstoi's teaching was in "worldly" circles.

While the person of Petrov should not be in focus, the Church leadership nevertheless wanted to signal that the debate at the meeting of the Philosophical Society was the immediate trigger behind the publication of the Circular Letter. This was achieved by reprinting in *Tserkovnye vedomosti* an article on Tolstoi which had first appeared in the provincial journal *Poltavskie eparkhial'nye vedomosti*, written by a certain V. Terletskii. Terletskii referred to the meeting of the Philosophical Society with Skvortsov as source and linked the Circular Letter directly to the debate after Merezhkovskii's lecture. Pobedonostsev himself took the initiative to have Terletskii's article reprinted in the Church's most official organ (*Pis'ma K. P. Pobedonostseva* 1938, 209). In the reprinted version, the name of the author was not stated (*Po povodu poslaniia* 1901). In that way, the article could be read as reflecting the opinion not merely of one individual, but also of the Church leadership.

There are many indications that the Soviet scholars intentionally failed to point out the importance of "the Petrov case" behind the decision to publish an official circular letter against Tolstoi. The reason seems obvious: If we accept that this episode was the decisive impetus, we must also admit that the Church's motives were largely of a defensive nature. The prelates were primarily concerned with limiting Tolstoi's influence among Orthodox believers. The motives given in the Circular Letter itself as the most important – concern for the children of the Orthodox Church and to "support those who stand steadfast and to reason with those who have gone astray" – must be accorded decisive weight. The motives that Soviet scholars chose to emphasize, such as personal vengeance from Pobedonostsev's side, attempts to "forestall a pending social revolution" and "incite all dark forces against Tolstoi," must be dismissed or considered far less important.

Anathema?

Although we with a high degree of certainty can trace the initiative to the Circular Letter against Tolstoi to the priestly members of the Synod's, many unanswered questions still remain. An unclear point is which status the prelates gave this document: Did it amount to an excommunication or not? On the one hand, the Circular Letter was promulgated under the neutral heading "A decision (*opredelenie*) from The Most Holy Synod," and as such it entered into the series of other administrative decisions, as No. 557. At the same time, it is constructed according to the pattern of the epistles of St. Paul. The synod wanted to speak with apostolic authority, as shown not least by the introductory words. According to its wording, the Letter simply ascertained, passively and *post factum*, that Tolstoi himself had chosen to leave the community of the Church. By contemporaries, however, also among Orthodox believers, it was immediately perceived as an excommunication (*otluchenie*): An active exclusion (e.g., Romashkov 1902, 46–49). Also in Western literature, the Church's reaction to Tolstoi is almost always referred to as an excommunication.

There are mainly two explanations for the ambiguities surrounding the status of the Circular Letter. First, it seems likely that the Church leaders, for various reasons, tried to frame their reaction in a way that at the same time was and was not an excommunication. Secondly, there was considerable ignorance in Russian society about what an excommunication really meant according to ecclesiastical law: Whom was it used against, how was it justified, and which consequences did this act have in the thinking of the Church for the person affected by it, here on earth and in the afterlife? This ignorance and uncertainty provided an impetus for Orthodox theologians to clarify the Church's excommunication practice, historically, legally and theologically.

The right of the Orthodox Church to expel and curse its enemies is based on both Old Testament and New Testament models. In the Old Testament, God cursed Cain as a punishment for the murder of his brother (Gen. 4, 11; quoted by D. Matveev 1901, 5). For the Church, the epistles of St. Paul, however, were considerably more important. In I Corinthians 5, the Apostle castigates a member of the Corinthian congregation who had committed fornication with his father's wife. Paul instructed the Christians in the city to come together and surrender this man to Satan (1 Cor. 5, 1–5). While excommunication here is used to punish moral transgressions, in his epistle to the Galatians, the "anathema" weapon is wielded in a dogmatic struggle that Paul was engaged in. Here, he twice declared that if anyone preached another gospel than he, Paul, did, he should be "anathema" even if he were an angel from heaven (Gal. 1, 8).).

The Eastern Church usually takes care not to claim that any excommunications it performs on earth have consequences for eternity. Orthodox theologians often emphasize that God is sovereign, and vengeance belongs to Him alone (cf. Rom. 12, 19; quoted, e.g., by Sergii [Stragorodskii] 1905, 97). However, while the Eastern churches do not adhere to the Roman Catholic Counter-Reformation dictum of *extra ecclesiam salus nulla* ("no salvation outside the Church"), they nevertheless taught and still teach that "to be in the bosom of the Church is the most important condition for attaining salvation" (Aggeev 1901, 16). In 1905, an anti-Tolstoian article claimed that "outside the Church, outside obedience to the Church shepherds and without community with Christ, there is also no salvation" (Pravoslavnyi 1905, 78).

In the Russian Church, a solemn curse of its enemies was included in the standard ritual for one of the weeks of the year, the "Feast of Orthodoxy,"' which begins on the second Sunday in the Great Lent. This feast was instituted at the Church Council in Constantinople in 842 to commemorate the victory over the iconoclasts. Gradually, it gained an extended meaning as a celebration of the victory over all heretics and rebels against the Church throughout the ages. New names were added to the list of earlier heretics, such as Stenka Razin in the seventeenth century and Emel'ian Pugachev in the eighteenth century. Neither of them is known to have uttered any theological views, but they were enemies of the state and *eo ipso* also foes of the Church. At the same time, obscure heretics whom no one remembered were deleted from the litany.

In 1869, the Church stopped naming individual heretics in the Feast of Orthodoxy service. Instead, it collectively cursed all those who denied God's existence, who denied God as Creator, the Trinity and so on – each part of the creed. An archdeacon read aloud the various heretical teachings, and then the celebrant priests proclaimed a threefold "Anathema." The curses were also accompanied by prayers that the deluded ones might return to the right path. The "Anathema" service was held only in the cathedrals, the bishops' residence churches, and the bishop himself had to be in attendance.

In Tolstoi's time, the anathema ritual was still in principle valid and normative, although not all parts of it were practised. *The Spiritual Regulation*, the legal regulatory document instituted by Peter I for the Russian Church in 1720, outlined the procedures of the excommunication ritual rather thoroughly. According to Part II, paragraph 16, the bishop has the right to excommunicate and ban, but he shall exercise this right with indulgence and wisdom. Not every sinner shall be cast out from the Church, but

> If someone manifestly blasphemes God's name, or Holy Scripture, or the Church, or is clearly a sinner who is unashamed of his acts and, even more, boasts of them, or does not go to confession and does not receive the Holy Eucharist for more than a year without good reason, or does anything else with clear vilification and mockery of God's law, such a one, who remains stubborn and haughty after repeated punishment, shall be adjudged as deserving that great penalty. Not merely for the sin is he subject to anathema, but for the clear and haughty contempt of God's judgment and of Church authority, with great tempting of weak brethren, and because he exudes from the himself the stench of godlessness. (*Spiritual Regulation* [1720] 1972, 22–23)

It is further stated that the bishop must not himself undertake the act of excommunication, but refer the case to the Spiritual College (the forerunner of the Holy Synod), which will exclude the unrepentant sinner from the Church and "like a useless organ, excise[s] him from the body of Christ's Church" (*Spiritual Regulation* [1720] 1972, 24). If the sinner should later come to reason, he can be reinstated in the fellowship of the believers by standing forth publicly in the Church and humbly praying for forgiveness.

The idea of using the excommunication weapon against Tolstoi appeared in ecclesiastical circles relatively early. In 1888, the Archbishop of Kherson, Nikanor, in a private letter to Nikolai Grot wrote that there were concrete plans to declare several people "anathema," including

Tolstoi (Orekhanov 2016, 461). It remains unknown whether these plans materialized in a written document: In any case, they came to naught. Instead, some zealous priests banned Tolstoi on their own initiative. In 1888, the prior of the Sergiev Pustyn' monastery, Archbishop Ignatii, published a small brochure on Tolstoi, which he concluded by citing Gal. 1, 8. The brochure therefore ended with the words "let him be accursed" ("anathema": Ignatii 1888, 10). The same technique and the same words were used by the priest T. Butkevich in a sermon he held in May 1891 (Butkevich 1891, 283). A year later, Sof'ia Andreevna could tell her husband that the Metropolitan of Moscow, Leontii (Lebedinskii) wanted to have him solemnly expelled from the Church (S. A. Tolstaia 1936, 522). This piece of information, however, cannot be confirmed by other sources.

A new initiative to a Circular Letter against Tolstoi was taken in 1899, when Bishop Amvrosii (Kliucharev) composed a detailed draft. In this document, condemnation of Tolstoi was directly linked to the great Anathema on the Feast of Orthodoxy:

> The Most Holy Synod considers it its duty to declare to all the people that Count Lev Tolstoi is an enemy of the Orthodox Church. At the same time, the Holy Synod reminds all of its Orthodox fellow compatriots about the danger they are facing if they are carried away by Tolstoi's writings and share his blasphemous ideas. This danger is excommunication from the Church. The Church publicly condemns heretics such as Tolstoi on the Feast of Orthodoxy. (*Bibliografiia* 1903a, 166–67)

Here, the excommunication card was flashed not only against Tolstoi, but also against anyone who might sympathize with him. Amvrosii's draft letter was far more belligerent in tone than the version that was adopted and published two years later (Orekhanov 2010, 506). That is probably an important reason why the draft was rejected by the Synod.

In the Circular Letter dated February 20–22, 1901, there are no references to the great Anathema on the Feast of Orthodoxy anywhere in the text. According to the Russian-Orthodox researcher Orekhanov (2010, 514; 2016, 485), the original document had stated that Tolstoi had "excommunicated (*otluchil*) himself," but in the final redaction that was changed to "torn himself away from (*ottorgnul*)." Nevertheless, this annual ritual curse was instantly perceived as the immediate backdrop behind the prelates' decision. There was every reason to do so, as in 1901 this feast day fell on February 18, only one week before Circular Letter was read in the country's cathedral churches, February 24. It is reasonable to assume that the original plan had been to make the announcement on that date, and that bureaucratic inertia or other purely practical reasons had caused the delay. When the Synod's archives were opened during perestroika, this assumption could be confirmed. In the letter that Metropolitan Antonii wrote to Pobedonostsev on February 11, he stated that the Circular Letter ought to be published "next Saturday, on February 17, the day before the Feast of Orthodoxy" (TsGIAL, f.1574, op.2, ep. 133, 1.2). Lidiia Opul'skaia believes that the prelates back-pedaled and deliberately postponed the proclamation of the Circular Letter by one week (Opul'skaia 1978, 8). It seems more likely, as Georgii Orekhanov writes, that the excommunication initiative had encountered resistance from certain members of the Synod, and persuading them took time (Orekhanov 2010, 515). This resistance may explain why the action against Tolstoi was discussed at no less than two meetings in the Synod. However, even if the Synodal machinery had worked at top speed, six days would probably have been too short a time to complete the procedures.

Although Antonii explicitly wished the Circular Letter to be read out during the Anathema service at the Feast of Orthodoxy, the Church dignitaries nevertheless, paradoxically, tried to prevent its being perceived as a bull of excommunication. According to Vasilii Skvortsov, they wished that the Circular Letter "should not have the character of an excommunication, but be a testimony that Lev Tolstoi had renounced Orthodoxy and broken with the Church, and also be an appeal to repentance" (quoted by G. I. Petrov 1978, 32). The expressions used in the Circular Letter were relatively weak: "The Church no longer counts him among her members" and "we testify that he has fallen from the Church." The prelates, however, were not consistent in their editing, and it is possible to find traces in the final version of the Circular Letter indicating the formal anathema ritual. For instance, its opening lines, quoting Rom. 16, 17, is a part of the liturgy of the Feast of Orthodoxy.

Thus, the Circular Letter was from the beginning characterized by an ambiguity that confused many believers. Several Orthodox theologians therefore saw a need to provide clarifying comments. Already on March 1, the liberal priest Konstantin Aggeev published a brochure with the lengthy title *On the discussion which the Circular Letter of the Holy Synod on Count L. Tolstoi has provoked in contemporary, enlightened society*. Aggeev disagreed that the Circular Letter should be perceived as a threat. On the contrary, he would compare it to a letter that a loving mother writes to her son when she learns that a danger awaits him. It was therefore not the letter, but the impending danger that was threatening (Aggeev 1901, 20).

> It was hardly possible [for the Synod] to express its thought with more overflowing love. Any unbiased gaze clearly sees that this is not revenge, not

> even a punishment, but a sad testimony to a fact that had already occurred, independent of the Most Holy Synod. (Aggeev 1901, 37)

In the Petersburg magazine, *Vera i Tserkov'* the editor, the priest Ioann Solov'ev, wrote a long article in the April issue of 1901 titled "The Most Holy Synod's Circular Letter on Count Lev Tolstoi (an attempt to uncover its meaning and significance)." Solov'ev gave a thorough introduction to the Orthodox doctrine on Church discipline and the Anathema ritual, which he contrasted with a bull of excommunication that Pope Leo XIII had issued the year before. The papal ban had cursed the excommunicated person limb by limb, and diseases were invoked over his body "from the crown of his head to the sole of his foot." In contrast to this "medieval" language, the Orthodox anathema was intended as a prayer to God that the sinner should repent, Solov'ev argued (I. Solov'ev 1901, 553–54).

In addition, Metropolitan Antonii himself came forward publicly with some "thoughts" about Tolstoi's apostasy. As one of the main architects behind the Circular Letter, he should be better able than most people to explain how this document ought to be understood. Antonii told that Tolstoi's "mad blasphemy" had hurt him deeply. It was an open declaration of war against Christ, the Son of the living God.

> I had always had difficulty understanding the threatening words of the Apostle Paul: 'If any man love not the Lord Jesus Christ, let him be Anathema Maranatha'(1 Cor. 16, 22). Now the meaning was suddenly clear to me. (Antonii [Vadkovskii] 1905b, 94)

Here it seems that Antonii unambiguously placed Tolstoi among those whom the Church must actively expel. However, a few lines further down, the Metropolitan explained that in Tolstoi's case it was a case of "self-excommunication" (*samoanafemstvovanie*) (ibid.). Antonii's "thoughts," then, do not bring us any closer to clarifying the relationship between the active and passive elements in the Circular Letter. On the contrary, they confirm the impression of intentional ambiguity.[8]

Today, many Russian Orthodox believers deny that Tolstoi was ever excommunicated. For instance, in an article published on a website affiliated with the Moscow Patriarchate, it is claimed that whoever reads the text of the Circular Letter carefully will easily see that it contains "not even a hint of a damnation (*prokliatie*). The Russian Orthodox Church

[8] The modern German theologian Martin George concludes that while the Circular letter did not fulfill the formal criteria of excommunication it nevertheless amounted to a "de facto excommunication" (George 2015, 218).

simply with bitterness noted a fact: the great Russian author, Lev Nikolaevich Tolstoi, had stopped being a member of the Orthodox Church" (Tkachenko 2006). However, in order to reach such a straightforward and unambiguous conclusion it is necessary to ignore much of the prehistory and context of this document.

Reactions to the Circular Letter

The Russian authorities were obviously unsure of how the educated part of the population would react to the Circular Letter against Tolstoi. Minister of Interior Dmitrii Sipiagin feared the worst, and issued a general ban on discussing this document in the secular press. The ban was largely complied with. In virtually all Russian newspapers, the Circular Letter was printed *in extenso* or in long excerpts, but without any commentary. However, Konstantin Pobedonostsev felt that Sipiagin had overreacted. With this censorship, the secular authorities had signaled that they regarded the proclamation of the Circular Letter as a shady act that could not be exposed to a free exchange of opinions. The Chief Procurator was convinced that many newspapers would have supported the Synod's action if they had had the opportunity to express their attitude (*Pis'ma K. P. Pobedonostseva* 1938, 209).

The intervention of the censorship authorities makes it difficult to get a clear overview of how Russians responded to the Synod's statement on Tolstoi. However, there is much evidence to indicate that reactions were strong and in very many cases negative. Large parts of the secularized upper classes regarded the Circular Letter as yet another folly committed by the Church leadership. Indeed, some left the Church in solidarity with the expellee (G. I. Petrov 1978, 46–49).

To Tolstoi's mailbox a stream of sympathy declarations were sent with a total of thousands of signatures. In many cities, students and others organized solidarity demonstrations. In St. Petersburg, a group of people gathered around Repin's portrait of Tolstoi exhibited in one of the city's art galleries. The picture was wreathed by flower bouquets while the persons present shouted "hurray." After this incident, the picture was removed from the exhibition (S. A. Tolstaia 1978, II, 18).

The Russian police conducted a kind of "poll" by opening the letters of some prominent individuals in Russian society after the publication of the Circular Letter. As expected, many contained reactions to the Synod's decision. While virtually none of the letter writers were adherents of Tolstoi's teaching, the vast majority expressed strong disapproval of the

Church's conduct. The famous Panslavist and diplomat Nikolai Ignat'ev wrote that the excommunication "will probably enhance Tolstoi's reputation and make people even more hostile towards the Orthodox Church order." In another letter, it was claimed that "Russia has brought shame on herself throughout the world. So tactless it is to try to settle personal scores by politics. This is Pobedonostsev's personal revenge to Tolstoi for making him a laughingstock in *Resurrection*." "The upper classes laugh boisterously, while the lower classes do not understand a thing and do not care," another asserted. According to one report from the countryside, "The muzhiks explain the excommunication like this: It is all because of us. Tolstoi defended us, so the priests are mad at him" (all quotes from G. I. Petrov 1978, 48–49).

The prohibition against public discussions of the Circular Letter did not extend to the ecclesiastical press, and several articles were printed. While many of them gave diverging interpretations of the document, virtually every public Orthodox response nevertheless expressed support for the Church's handling of this delicate matter. To the extent that critical opinions were voiced, they usually indicated that the prelates had not reacted resolutely or early enough. For example, one believer, writing under the pseudonym "Orthodox Christian," held that the Synod's actions were so Christian and humane as to be perceived as a sign of weakness. He hoped that far stronger reactions would stop Tolstoi's activity (*Pravoslavnyi mirianin* 1901b, 4).

Perusal of the Russian Orthodox press from 1901, then, can easily give the impression that the Church authorities enjoyed almost full backing among their own in this matter. However, there are indications that the reactions of village priests and lay believers were highly mixed. Several Orthodox writers who themselves supported the Synod's actions also noted that the Circular Letter had caused consternation among many sincere believers (Aggeev 1901, 7; I. Solov'ev 1901, 526; Ol'shevskii 1901, 391). In *Missionerskoe obozrenie*a certain Aleksandr Mironenko wrote that the Circular Letter against Tolstoi had hit him and other believers like "snow falling on our heads."

> It could not but bewilder us. We, who admired his talent, saw in him not only a great writer but also a serious thinker and a positive person, and certainly not someone who would frivolously shake the foundations of Christianity... . It was a great temptation to us, sinners as we are. Involuntarily, strange thoughts crept into our hearts: Suppose Count Lev Nikolaevich is actually right? (Mironenko 1905, 221–22)

Mironenko himself, after a thorough study, had reached the conclusion that the Synod had been justified in its action, but not everyone took the trouble to examine the case as thoroughly as he had. Some Orthodox priests wrote to Tolstoi to express their sympathy with him and their contempt for the Church leadership (see, for instance, Pozoiskii 1979, 101–3). There was also what we may call "loyal" criticism of the Circular Letter from Orthodox quarters. The loyal critics wished the Church well, and for that very reason wanted to express their concern over the Synod's action. These attitudes were difficult to express in the ecclesiastical press, so such evidence is to be found primarily in private correspondence.

The "loyal" believers rarely wrote to Tolstoi: It was more natural for them to approach their spiritual shepherds. The manuscript department of the Public library in St. Petersburg contains letters from private individuals that Metropolitan Antonii received after the publication of the Circular Letter (PB. Otdel rukopisei St. Petersburg Dukhovnaia akademiia, 1/289).[9] The views expressed range from scathing condemnation to the most unreserved endorsement.

A dozen or so letter-writers let it shine through that they themselves were not believers and had only disdain for the Church. Virtually all of these letters were anonymous. One wrote that he was horrified and deeply indignant at the misdeeds committed by "the lousy (*parshivyi*) synod." "It consists of parasites such as you." The letter-writer wanted to make Antonii aware that no one had such low esteem in society as did the clergy. "Even those who kiss the hands of the popes call them devils. And indeed devils you are"(No. 58). One can only marvel at the collector's instinct that made Antonii keep such letters for posterity.

A few letter-writers claimed that they were speaking on behalf of Orthodox believers, but filled their missives with so many invectives that their criticism could hardly be called "loyal" (for instance No. 6). However, a dozen of faithful Orthodox also expressed concern and confusion rather than blatant criticism. Some anonymous letter-writers were primarily concerned with the legal and canonical aspects of the Synod's action. One reminded Antonii that, according to Russian law, the tsar was the head of the Church. "The Synod does not have any power independent of the autocratic tsar. He is the one, common, shining center that penetrates everything, like the sun" (No. 22). Therefore, according to the author of this letter, such an important document as the Circular Letter

[9] Many of these letters have been published by G. Orekhanov (2005).

should have been issued not only in the name of the Synod, but also in the name of the autocrat.

Also a believer from Khar'kov expressed concern at the formal aspects of the Circular Letter. Firstly, he regretted the bureaucratic tone of the document. This could have been avoided if the prelates had supplied clear references to which provisions in canonical law they based their decision on, he believed. Secondly, he noted that many Russians, believers as well as nonbelievers, perceived the excommunication as unreasonable, simply because they had poor knowledge about Tolstoi's teaching. Those of Tolstoi's works that had been published in Russia had been so groomed by the censorship that they no longer contained any anti-religious, anti-Orthodox assaults, at least not anything that could be spotted by an untrained eye. "The result is that the clergy have split into two camps, one in favor of the Synod and one in favor of Tolstoi. In secular society, almost everybody supports Tolstoi" (No. 12).

In case the Metropolitan doubted that the censorship could have such unfortunate consequences, some of the other letters he received should have convinced him. For example, a certain Aleksandra Konetanskaia confided to him that when she had read the Circular Letter she was at a complete loss: She had just finished reading *Resurrection* and had not found a single sarcastic remark about the Church or the Christian faith in this book. Admittedly, an erudite professor of theology had explained to her that this novel had also been published abroad in an uncensored form and contained gross mockery of religion and the priests. Apparently, Konetanskaia did not know whether she could fully trust this professor, and therefore asked Antonii to point out which blasphemous words and expressions Tolstoi was guilty of, and in which works (No. 7). Antonii also received other letters with an almost identical message (e.g., No. 47). It is not known whether he replied to any of them.

Tolstoi's "Reply to the Synod" and Orthodox Responses

If the Circular Letter against Tolstoi was a tactical blunder, there can be no doubt that the factual basis for it was undeniable. While Tolstoi's teachings – as I argue in this book – on several points were inspired by an Orthodox way of thinking, not only the Russian state Church, but all the main Christian denominations would necessarily find it heretical. Clear confirmation of this can be found in *Reply to the Synod*, which Tolstoi wrote two months later. Here he fiercely attacked the Circular Letter, which, he claimed, had distorted his message. It gave people the impression that he denied truths that were vital to him, such as faith in God. Tolstoi also resolutely rejected the charge of blasphemy. He had just called things by their proper names: The iconostasis was a partition wall and the chalice was a cup. However, he also confirmed that he did consider the Trinity to be a "fable," found the doctrine of the virgin birth to be "blasphemous" and the sacraments "vile." The institution of the confession was a harmful fraud that stimulated immoral life. In Tolstoi's view, the doctrine of the Church was "theoretically a crafty and harmful lie, and in practice a collection of the most crude and superstitious sorcery" (Tolstoi PSS 34, 247).

In his *Reply to the Synod*, then, Tolstoi drew the demarcation line toward the Orthodox Church more sharply than ever before. The notion that Orthodoxy consisted of "lies interwoven with truth," as expressed in *A Confession*, had disappeared. Like the authors of the Circular Letter, he only emphasized that which divided, nothing of what united them. Thus, he paradoxically provided solid validation for the Church's action against him. The prelates could now, with renewed strength, claim that their reaction had been justified. As Metropolitan Antonii noted, "[T]he Count, in fact, fully confirms the correctness of the Synod's statement about him" (Antonii [Vadkovskii] 1905b, 92).

One Church leader who early on realized the potential of Tolstoi's *Reply* for the Church's counterpropaganda was privy councillor Vasilii Skvortsov. He believed that this document "could serve as the most convincing apology for the Holy Synod's conduct and show how correct and expedient it was" (V. Skvortsov 1905, x; see also V. Skvortsov 1901b). Just to make sure, Skvortsov first wrote to Iasnaia Poliana, asking Tolstoi to confirm that he was indeed the author of *Reply to the Synod* (Tolstoi PSS 54, 570); next, he asked permission from the censorship authorities to print this document in *Missionerskoe obozrenie*. The privy councillor had to accept that approximately 100 lines that were perceived as particularly pernicious were deleted from the text: This lacuna was carefully marked with multi-points. *Reply to the Synod* could then be read in the July 1901 issue of Skvortsov's journal, which was immediately bought up by curious readers. Some bookstores put in ads in the newspapers to announce that they had it for sale (*Obozrenie* 1901, 520). Later, *Reply to the Synod* was also printed in other ecclesiastical journals, such as the September 1901 issue of *Dushepoleznoe chtenie*.

In *Reply to the Synod*, Tolstoi directed a series of specific accusations against the Church leadership with regard to the content of the Circular Letter as well as the circumstances surrounding its publication. These accusations can be arranged in five points, all of which gave rise to lively discussion in the ecclesiastical press.

1. If the Circular Letter was to be perceived as an excommunication, it was illegal, Tolstoi maintained, because it did not meet the requirements of canonical law for such an action. If, on the other hand, the Letter was not meant as an excommunication, then it was intentionally ambiguous, since it could easily be perceived as just that. We have already found that there was basis for this accusation.

In 1908, when the Russian public was making plans to celebrate Tolstoi's eightieth birthday (see below), Vasilii Skvortsov's fourth missionary congress, as a counterinitiative, called for anathema rituals to be arranged, which should begin with a reading of the Synod's Circular Letter (*Publikatsii* 1960, 366). If this proposal had been acted upon, the ambiguity of the Circular Letter would have been removed and the excommunication would have acquired more binding legal forms. However, such rites were never performed.

2. According to Tolstoi, the Circular Letter was arbitrary because it was aimed only at him, whereas almost all educated persons in Russia had left the faith of the Church. Several Church apologists took up the gauntlet. Bishop[10] Sergii (Stragorodskii) claimed that the Church always tried as long as possible to bear over with human ignorance. It therefore proclaimed anathema only in "extreme cases, only when the offense was exceptionally great and there was no hope of influencing this person by other means" (Sergii [Stragorodskii] 1905, 96). If Tolstoi had simply advocated atheism without making any attempts to undermine the precious truths of the Faith, the Church could have ignored him, the bishop opined. Vasilii Skvortsov noted that it had always been Church practice to ban only the originators of new heretical movements, the heresiarchs (V. Skvortsov 1901b, 71).

Ten years later a very prosaic, but probably just as adequate, explanation of why the Circular Letter targeted only Tolstoi was given by the priest N. Drozdov:

> We believe that Tolstoi's well-deserved world fame provoked the Synod to expel him from the Church. In order to warn against the great temptation that the heresy of this great writer represents, it was necessary to do it with some noise. There is no need for solemn excommunication of writers

[10] The future patriarch (1943–44).

> whom very few, if any, read. In order to dispel their delusions, a confessional suffices. One does not kill a fly with a hammer axe, but [to kill] a lion [*lev*, Leo], a hammer axe is definitely required. (Drozdov 1911, 783)

3. However, Tolstoi did not agree that he was a successful preacher:

> I know perfectly well that only some hundred people share my views, and thanks to the censorship, the dissemination of my writings on religion is so insignificant that most of those who read the Synod's statement do not have the slightest idea of what I have written about religion. (Tolstoi PSS 34, 246)

Tolstoi asserted that he had never made any attempts to propagate his teachings. True, he had never tried to keep his texts hidden from people, but on the other hand, he had never done anything to get them printed. "I have spoken to people about how I understand Christ's teachings only when someone has asked me about it." However, the Church apologists perceived these arguments as a mixture of unbecoming false modesty and pure sophistry (V. Skvortsov 1901a, 73). Tolstoi's books and articles had reached and influenced hundreds of thousands, many more than those who stood forth as professing Tolstoians. Bishop Sergii thought it was rather immaterial who had physically brought Tolstoi's books to the printer's shop. "Whoever gives poison to another man is of course guilty, but even greater guilt bears the person who made this poison, knowing what it would be used for" (Sergii [Stragorodskii] 1905, 98).

The correspondence between Tolstoi and his closest collaborators clearly shows that Tolstoi took a keen interest in whether and how his works were published. For instance, when a Tolstoian was taken to court in 1909 for having distributed forbidden Tolstoi texts, Tolstoi wrote to the police investigator and stated that the indictment had to include him, the author of those writings, as well. "I have already stated several times and do so again, that my conscience commands me to spread these texts and as well as other things I have written" (Tolstoi PSS 79, 93–94). Thus, Tolstoi's claim in the *Reply* that he did not do anything to spread his teaching seems rather disingenuous.

4. Tolstoi further claimed that the Circular Letter had incited unenlightened people to express hatred and malice toward him. On the street, strangers had hurled accusations such as "devil in human shape" at him. In some of the letters he had received there were undisguised murder threats. One person wrote, "I have my methods to annihilate a scoundrel like you" (Tolstoi PSS 34, 246). Tolstoi claimed that the Synod should have anticipated such reactions, and was therefore

responsible for them. Soviet scholars took this accusation one step further, claiming that this effect had been created intentionally by the Synod, and was one of the main causes behind the publication of the Circular Letter (for instance, Meilakh [1960] 1979, 144). However, such a claim, while virtually impossible to verify or falsify, is not very likely.

5. Finally, Tolstoi claimed that the Circular Letter contained direct falsehoods. While the prelates stated that the Church had in vain tried to reason with Tolstoi and attempted to bring him back on the right path, Tolstoi insisted that no such attempts had been made. This was one of the points in Tolstoi's *Reply to the Synod* that was most extensively commented upon in the ecclesiastical press. If Tolstoi had not received any official warning or admonishment before the Circular Letter was promulgated, this document, according to canonical law, could not be considered a legitimate excommunication. Canonical regulations explicitly stipulate that no one shall be expelled from the community of believers until he has been admonished and given a chance to mend his ways (2 Thess. 3, 15). In Tit. 3, 10, it is required that such an admonition (*vrazumlenie*) be made at least twice, and Matt. 18, 16 specifies that the second time the conversation must be held in the presence of one or two witnesses (V. Skvortsov 1901, 66–67).

Vasilii Skvortsov felt he was on very safe grounds when he hit back at Tolstoi on this point: Not once, but repeatedly, various men of the Church had attempted to admonish Tolstoi. Both Bishop Nikandr and the priest A. Ivanov in Tula had had talks with Tolstoi about religious questions in 1879. Later, the principal at the Tula Theological Seminary, Romanov, visited Iasnaia Poliana on behalf of his bishop. When Tolstoi fell seriously ill in 1900, Metropolitan Vladimir of Moscow had sent Tolstoi's former religious teacher, Father Solov'ev, to Iasnaia Poliana. Three times the priest had announced his arrival, but as many times he had been turned back (V. Skvortsov 1905c). The prison priest in the nearby Tula prison, Dmitrii Egorovich Troitskii, had been more fortunate: He had not only had several meetings with the famed author, but had also conducted an extensive correspondence with him.

Not all of the items on Skvortsov's list were equally convincing as documentation. Tolstoi's talks with Nikandr and Ivanov had come about at his own initiative and had taken place before he had stood forth as an anti-Orthodox preacher. Romanov and Solov'ev's admonitory attempts are not confirmed by independent sources. Thus, the controversy over admonitions concentrated on the attempts made by the prison priest Troitskii (Antonii [Vadkovskii] 1905b, 94; E. Ia 1905, 683; see also Orekhanov 2016, 539).

In 1913, Dmitrii Troitskii published his correspondence and an account of his conversations with Tolstoi in a booklet that he titled *An Orthodox-pastoral admonition (*uveshchanie*) of Count L. N. Tolstoi.* As the title indicates, he clearly regarded his visits to Iasnaia Poliana as a spiritual admonition. The Soviet scholar Boris Meilakh claims that in this brochure Troitskii admitted that he had visited Tolstoi in the capacity of a spy (Meilakh [1960] 1979, 138) – but in fact, the prison priest never acknowledged any such thing. On the contrary, he emphasized that he had come on his personal initiative and solely in a spiritual errand.

In the introduction, Troitskii explains that he regarded Tolstoi as the leading detractor of the Church in Russia's modern history. The last four decades, in his opinion, could well be called "the period of Tolstoian aberrations." At the same time, Tolstoi was a richly equipped soul with strong spiritual yearnings. He therefore ought to be particularly receptive to Orthodox guidance. However, if one should have any hopes of reaching him with the grace of God, one would have to seek him out personally. Troitskii therefore sent a letter to Tolstoi in 1897:

> It seems to me that you are striving for true faith, true love and true fear of God . . . . I like to discuss questions of faith, and people usually do not shun me. Therefore, please let me have a conversation with you if it should so please you . . . . Rest assured that I have no other intentions or motives than those that I have mentioned. (D. Troitskii1913, 13)

The joy was great when Tolstoi accepted the offer and invited Troitskii to Iasnaia Poliana. Here, the prison priest was promptly asked who had sent him, and Troitskii replied that he came on his own initiative, but with the approval and blessing of his bishop. Troitskii writes that he avoided as far as possible broaching any religious topics during their conversations, as this only provoked Tolstoi's irritation and mockery. Instead, the priest sought to work through his mere presence, his love and humility. He would be "wise as a serpent, and harmless as a dove" (cf. Matt. 10, 16).

The Synod's Circular Letter of 1901 came at a very inconvenient time for Troitskii, who after several meetings felt that he was in the process of achieving a good ambience. "[Tolstoi] began to look upon his former friend and interlocutor as an envoy from the institution he was so hostile to." After the Letter was issued, the visits continued but the unrestrained atmosphere Troitskii had meticulously built up was irretrievably broken. The last contact between them was by letter, only weeks before Tolstoi's death. Troitskii apparently felt that time was running out and resorted to direct calls for repentance: "I plead with you: Come, let us fall down at the feet of Christ." Tolstoi found Troitskii's new language "strange" (Tolstoi PSS 82, 185).

As far as we can judge, Troitskii was one of very few, if not the only, official representative of the Russian Orthodox Church who achieved any degree of close contact with Tolstoi after 1880. His credible and often highly self-revealing report testifies that this rapprochement was achieved at the price of a considerable measure of pretense. It is evident that for Troitskii it was far more important to succeed in his missionary work than to be able to report back to his superiors that a formally correct ecclesiastical admonition had been carried out. In the dispute between Tolstoi and the Synod as to whether there had been any official ecclesiastical admonition, we must assume that both parties made their claims in good faith.

Church Strategies after the Circular Letter

The Church leaders' management of the Tolstoian heresy was characterized by an odd duality – firmness and softness, boldness and caution at the same time. Several circumstances may explain this ambiguity. It might be because the prelates, when the chips were down, stopped short of excommunicating Tolstoi outright because they did not know how the public would react to such an act. Moreover, since no new named heretics had been expelled for more than a century, there were no clear procedures for how this should be carried out. Another important reason behind the ambiguity, in my opinion, is that the Circular Letter was intended to perform two tasks simultaneously. On the one hand, it was directed toward the faithful members of the Church: To make them aware of the danger that Tolstoianism represented and deter them from giving in to it. A clear expression of this line of thought can be found in the journal *Missionerskii sbornik* in 1911, in a commentary to the Circular Letter:

> If a sinner remains stubbornly unrepentant, if all measures taken turn out to be in vain, then one should take resort to the last, decisive measures and be concerned not about saving the sinner who is going to perish, but to save the other members of the Church. (Zaraiskii 1911, 124)

When a limb is diseased and cannot be healed, it must be cut off: It is better "that one of thy members should perish, and not that thy whole body should be cast into hell," the author of this article wrote (cf. Matt. 5, 29).

On the other hand, the *Circular Letter* was addressed also to Tolstoi himself in the hope that he would repent and return to the Church fold. That would require a miracle – but in the Church there was room for faith in miracles. Several Orthodox authors noted how, by divine intervention, the most vehement adversary of Jesus, Saul, had been made His most impassioned disciple (*Po povodu poslaniia* 1901, 576; Romashkov 1902, 50; Amicus 1899). The priest Ioann Solov'ev expressed this hope very clearly:

> Who knows, perhaps, thanks to the Church's prayers . . . the day will come when Lev, as once Saul, will be overwhelmed by the Light of Christ through the Holy Spirit, and be stricken by a sign like that on the road to Damascus. Then he will bow in the dust with his proud, pagan wisdom, kneel down before the Crucified, and together with the Roman centurion proclaim, 'Truly, he was the Son of God!' (Matt. 27, 54). Oh, how much rejoicing will there be in heaven and on earth! (I. Solov'ev 1901, 557)

Father Ioann dispatched a copy of his brochure with these closing words to Iasnaia Poliana (*Biblioteka* 1972, Ib, 252).

Moreover, the belief that Tolstoi might find his way back to the Church was based not only pious hopes for a miracle: There were certain aspects of the Tolstoi phenomenon that could nourish these expectations. Firstly, the Orthodox noted that Tolstoianism was not a petrified dogmatic system of thought; on the contrary, Tolstoi's ideas were constantly in flux, in a perennial, restless search for truth. Sometimes in the past, the ideas of the thinker at Iasnaia Poliana had turned around 180 degrees on certain questions, as for instance on whether a woman ought to give birth to many children. Orthodoxy was a station at which Tolstoi had stopped once already. Who could know whether his intellectual wanderings might once again lead him there? Another scriptural passage that some Orthodox believed might fit Tolstoi, in addition to the Saul/Paul parallel, was the parable of the prodigal son who returned to his father's house (Belkin 1909; N. Ostroumov 1909, 61).

Some people in the Church noted that the Tolstoian system of beliefs already contained certain Orthodox elements, as I have also indicated in this book. The best strategy against Tolstoianism, they thought, would be to make Tolstoi aware of the extent to which he was in fact thinking along Orthodox lines and to prod him to further develop those aspects of his teaching.

In 1902, the priest D. I. Romashkov published a brochure titled *On Tolstoi's Spiritual Death and Spiritual Resurrection*. Romashkov believed that Tolstoi was now spiritually dead indeed, but immediately went on to say that the novel *Resurrection* gave grounds for hopes that its author, like the main character, could experience a resurrection. For instance, the account of Nekhliudov's spiritual development showed that those who indulge in carnal pursuits are led into perdition. "On this point, Tolstoi's views fully coincide with the teaching of the Orthodox Church," Romashkov declared (Romashkov 1902, 18–20). Even though Tolstoi was excommunicated, there was therefore definitely a chance for him to return to Church and be saved:

> What a bright day of joy that would be for our country! For Tolstoi is the one who gives direction to, and, one might say, leads the intelligentsia in our time. In droves, the youth look up to him and follow him whom they call their teacher and guide. (Romashkov 1902, 54–55)

Clearly, Romashkov was aiming higher than to save just one lost soul: He hoped that, if and when Tolstoi returned to the Church, he would bring along with him large swaths of the intelligentsia. Not unexpectedly, Romashkov sent his brochure to Iasnaia Poliana (*Biblioteka* 1972, Ib, 172). He addressed it to Sof'ia Andreevna; apparently, he thought he might count on her as a potential ally in his endeavors to influence Tolstoi.

As long as the ecclesiastical initiatives in the "Tolstoi affair" were dictated by a need to shield the faithful from the dangerous influences of Tolstoianism, this heresy needed to be strongly condemned without beating about the bush. But since the apostate should also be lured back into the fold, the door had to be kept ajar for him to reenter. Therefore, active conversion attempts towards Tolstoi and dire warnings against having anything to do with him could be communicated side by side in the same publications. In his large collection of articles on the excommunication, privy councillor Vasilii Skvortsov published an open letter to Tolstoi "from a reader and theologian who loves you," which was one long, high-pitched entreaty to Tolstoi to be reconciled with the Church: "My brother! I cry for you and suffer. My soul longs for you to bring you to Christ and the Church. Turn around, my beloved!" (T., P.P. 1905, 173). However, just four pages further down in the same volume, diocese missionary N. Bulgakov quoted John 8, 44: "Ye are of your father the devil, and the lusts of your father ye will do." As the title of his article, the missionary had taken another Biblical verse: "He that reproveth a scorner getteth to himself shame (Proverbs 9, 7) (N. Bulgakov 1905, 178). It is difficult not to read this as a disavowal of the conversion attempts made toward Tolstoi.

This vacillation between ingratiation and condemnation marked the Church's handling of the Tolstoi case all the way from the proclamation of the Circular Letter in 1901 until his death nine years later. Now the first, now the second consideration was paramount. In connection with the preparations for a grand celebration of Tolstoi's eightieth birthday in November 1908, the confrontation line was dominant.

In 1908, it was rumored that the authorities – the secular and/or the ecclesiastical – might be readjusting their views on how to relate to Tolstoi. Some people feared – while others hoped – that the Synod would use the occasion of the eightieth anniversary to "correct the error" from 1901 and repeal the Circular Letter, or at least give it a watered-down interpretation (Pozoiskii 1979, 115). An official at the Chancery of the Synod, S. P. Grigorovskii, felt compelled to deny these rumored to journalists in the capital. He reiterated that "the excommunication can only be lifted by personal desire from Tolstoi's side. A few words from him will suffice" (same place).

One might perhaps think that with its Circular Letter the Church had made it abundantly clear what it meant about Tolstoi's teachings, yet the Synod found it necessary to publish an article by Bishop Sergii (Stragorodskii) in the official organ *Tserkovnye vedomosti* under the heading "How should an Orthodox Christian relate to the forthcoming celebrations of Count Tolstoi?" The fact that Sergii regarded it as necessary to ask this question indicated that for many Russian Orthodox believers the answer was not obvious. The Bishop concluded that the faithful should not take part in the festivities nor allow their children to do so. Instead, they should reinforce their prayers to God that He should humble this deluded sinner's spiritual pride and lead him onto the path of repentance (Sergii [Stragorodskii] 1908, 1622).

In the same issue of *Tserkovnye vedomosti*, diocese missionary I. Aivazov wrote another article that repeated the charges set forth against Tolstoi in the 1901 Circular Letter, but in a considerably more acerbic tone. Aivazov argued that Tolstoi "with the dirty hand of an old man and with blasphemous language has insolently trampled on all the innermost holy objects of Christians." In blasphemy, Tolstoi exceeded even "the father of lies" (Aivazov 1908, 1623–24). Aivazov's outpourings were later published as a separate brochure and distributed across the country in no less than 30,000 copies. One month later, however, the brochure was withdrawn by the censorship: In order to document Tolstoi's wickedness, Aivazov had quoted some coarse expressions from the "blasphemer's" forbidden books. (Makovitskii 1979, III, 209–10). It is remarkable that an article that had first been printed in Synod's official organ should later be confiscated. This indicates that the ecclesiastical campaign against the celebrations prepared for Tolstoi's eightieth birthday was poorly planned and poorly executed.

The Orthodox anti-celebration campaign was followed up in the provinces (Gorain 1908, 537–38). In Saratov, the reactionary bishop Germogen published a vigorous attack on "the anathemized (*anafemstvovannyi*) atheist and anarchist revolutionary Lev Tolstoi" (quoted in Meilakh [1960] 1979, 149). This shows that at this time many in the Church had begun to regard the Circular Letter as proclaiming an unqualified "anathema."

On July 25, 1908 Vasilii Skvortsov's fourth missionary congress had adopted a resolution requesting the Holy Synod to publish a new *Circular Letter* stating clearly that "the Orthodox cannot take part in the celebration of Count L. N. Tolstoi as he has been expelled from the Church" (*Publikatsii* 1960, 366). This recommendation was followed up on. In an official Decision of the Most Holy Synod on August 20 the same year, it was declared that those who participate in the anniversary celebration "will become accomplices in [Tolstoi's] activities and invoke upon their heads the same heavy burden of responsibility for God" (*Opredelenie* 1908, 272). Here, participation in the celebrations was presented as nothing less than a matter of salvation or perdition. By stating the matter so sharply, the Church leadership only managed to highlight how little authority it wielded even over supporters of the regime. The pro-Tsarist newspaper *Novoe Vremia*, the country's largest, insisted that it ought to be possible to celebrate the great writer of fiction without this being perceived as an endorsement of his theological or political views. An unsigned commentary in that paper claimed: "all Russians can wholeheartedly take part in this great celebration of Russian literature . . . and still remain Orthodox, fervently Orthodox" (*Nepostizimoe vmeshatel'stvo* 1908).

The organizing committee for the anniversary celebrations, however, had forgotten to ask Tolstoi what he thought about their initiative. As it turned out, he took the side of the Orthodox and the anti-Tolstoians. In February 1907, he received a letter from an elderly countess, Mariia Dondukova-Korsakova, who declared that the planned celebrations were an insult to all Orthodox believers (N. Gusev 1973, 113). To this, Tolstoi replied, expressing complete agreement:

> I am trying to get out of this bad business, out of participating in it. I do not want to offend people like you, who are incomparably closer to me than the

> non-believers who, for God knows what reason, want to eulogize me with some banal, useless speeches. (Tolstoi PSS 78, 70)

The correspondence between the count and the countess became known in the press, causing considerable annoyance in liberal society: It was perceived as if certain church circles had been putting crude pressure on Tolstoi (N. Gusev 1973, 393). Nevertheless, the organizing committee chose to comply with his wishes. However, the message that the celebrations had been called off was sent out too late to prevent anniversary manifestations from occurring in several cities (Troyat 1980, 848).

Two instruments available to the Church in its attempts to win Tolstoi back were intercession and personal contact with the man. Already in the excommunication document, Church leaders had stressed the importance of praying for Tolstoi. However, such intercession was left entirely to the individual believer. Nowhere were any special prayer services conducted for Tolstoi, nor was his name mentioned in the prayers during regular services. However, some voices in the Church suggested that such special prayer services should be held. In *Missionerskoe obozrenie*, Liubov' Prebsting wrote of "the necessity of public church prayers for Count Tolstoi and other apostates." Some Orthodox believers with whom she had spoken had insisted that prayer for such sinners as Tolstoi would be an insult against God. In Matthew 18, 17 Jesus had indeed said that we shall treat such people as if they were "publicans and sinners." But Prebsting pointed to what Jesus himself had practised: He had sought out precisely such people. Perhaps even more important were His words on the Cross where He prayed for those who had brought about His death (Prebsting 1905, 201).

In lieu of public intercessions, the Church leaders attempted "silent diplomacy." One year after the excommunication, Tolstoi fell seriously ill during a stay in Gaspra in Crimea. Metropolitan Antonii wrote to Sof'ia Andreevna and pleaded with her to help her husband to be reunited with the Church:

> Perhaps the Lord has already ordered the Angel of Death to recall him from among the living within a few days .... Will you then really allow this to happen without his reconciliation with the Church, without the accompaniment of the Sacrament of the Body and Blood of Christ? O, dear Countess, implore the Count to fulfill this request, convince him, appeal to him! His reconciliation with the Church will be a bright feast day for the Russian Orthodox people, it will bring joy to heaven and earth. (Quoted in M., B. 1915, 214–15; Orekhanov 2016, 527, both of which render the text of the letter in full.)

The Metropolitan could hardly have expressed more directly how much it would mean for the Church to have Tolstoi return to its fold. The Countess showed the letter to her husband, who stated flatly: "There can be no reconciliation with the Church. I will die without any enmity or malice, but what is the Church? How should it be possible to be reconciled with it? With such an indefinite entity?" (Tolstaia 1978, II, 54). Antonii received a reply from Tolstoi's son Sergei, requesting the Metropolitan to leave both his parents in peace (Tolstaia 1978, II, 487).

But Sof'ia Andreevna apparently followed up on Antonii's initiative in her own way. In the archives of the Synod, the Soviet researcher Semon Pozoiskii found a letter from her to the Metropolitan. Here she indicated that if Tolstoi died, she would summon a priest; supposedly her terminally ill husband had expressed a wish for this himself. When the man of the Church came, she would express regret that he had arrived too late. This story should then supposedly be used as a basis for asking the Church leadership to grant a Christian burial. Having explained Sof'ia Andreevna's plans to the Chief Procurator, Bishop Antonii added: "On the one hand, this could be a good thing and could paralyze the attraction of the Tolstoians – but on the other hand, this would be dishonest, and also dangerous, because the Tolstoians might later be able to disclose the fraud (quoted in Pozoiskii 1979, 112). So Sof'ia Andreevna's initiative was not followed up on.

In 1909, yet another attempt was made to sway Tolstoi. On January 20, Bishop Parfenii of Tula arrived at Iasnaia Poliana together with a large entourage. Sof'ia Andreevna wrote in her diary: "Everyone liked the bishop, who was wise, plainspoken and gracious." Tolstoi was apparently touched and thanked the bishop for having had the courage to seek out a person who had been expelled from the Church (S. A. Tolstaia 1978, II, 278). To the journalist Sergei Spiro from *Russkoe Slovo*, Tolstoi said that the bishop had given him some useful information about the monastic life. "In general, the bishop made a pleasant impression, as a wise and good person" (Spiro 1909).

Bishop Parfenii had apparently also benefited from his conversations with the count. When Tolstoi the year after left his home and set off on his final journey (see Chapter 6), the bishop in a newspaper interview on November 3, 1910, said this about his talks with Tolstoi:

> I was at Iasnaia Poliana and talked for a long time with Lev Nikolaevich. The elder (*starets)* asked me not to tell anyone about [the content of] our conversation. 'I speak to you', Tolstoi said to me, 'as every Christian speaks to a pastor of the Church during confession'. (*Preosviashchennyi Parfenii* 1910)

Parfenii intimated that he had reason to believe that Tolstoi's departure from home marked a desire to return to the Church. After his meeting with Tolstoi in 1909, the bishop had written a confidential report to Chief Procurator Petr Izvol'skii. It concluded with the claim that Tolstoi at present found himself in a religious crisis (*perelom*), and, in his [Bishop Parfenii's] view was drawing closer to Orthodoxy (*Poslednie dni* 1910, 96). The Synod leadership apparently attached great importance to Parfenii's report when they the next year deliberated over how to respond to Tolstoi's leaving home and subsequent illness.[11]

Unfortunately for Parfenii, however, Tolstoi had made a record of the conversation they had had in 1909. His diary notes from that meeting pulled the rug from under the bishop's hypothesis. Tolstoi wrote that he had spoken "candidly" with the bishop. Afterwards, however, Parfenii had asked Sof'ia Andreevna to send word when Tolstoi was dying, and Tolstoi took this as a sign that people in the Church would try to make it look as if he had recanted on his deathbed.

> Therefore, I declare, or rather repeat, that it is just as impossible for me to return to the Church or take Communion before I die as it would be to utter obscene words or look at smutty pictures. Everything they might say about me having repented or accepted Communion on the deathbed will be a lie. (Tolstoi PSS 57, 16)

Conclusions

The contemporary Russian Orthodox researcher Orekhanov (2016, 478, 585) maintains that the excommunication act "was the only serious independent act taken by the Synod during its almost 200 years of existence." Further, he holds that the Synod's Circular Letter was "a courageous and well-considered step taken by the Church, practically an act of Church testimony (*ispovednichestvo*) . . . canonically as well as historically unavoidable."

I agree with first but not the second of these claims. With regard to its legal, canonical status, the prelates strenuously tried to present and not present the document as a genuine excommunication. Whether it was well considered is also open to debate. Subsequent events, as we shall see in

[11] Parfenii's report was first kept secret, allegedly because some prelates, in particular the arch-reactionary Bishop Nikon, strongly objected to any association with heretics. The report, however, was read by the Tsar, who also was informed of why it could not be shown to the entire Synod. His (alleged) comment was that the Savior himself had visited publicans and sinners (Orekhanov 2016, 531).

the next chapter, show that the Church leadership had painted itself into a corner from which it made several unsuccessful attempts to extricate itself. William Nickell is no doubt right when he maintains that "Tolstoy's popularity and authority only grew as a result of the excommunication" (Nickell 2006, 35).

Peter I's Spiritual Regulation of 1720 required the members of the Spiritual College – the forerunner of the Synod – to take an oath in which they solemnly swore that "the final judge of this Spiritual College is the Monarch of All Russia himself, Our Most Gracious Sovereign" (*Spiritual Regulation* [1720] 1972, 6). This oath flagrantly contradicted canonical law and has often been regarded as the epitome of the abjectly submissive role of the Church in the synodal period. It remained in force for more than 180 years, but on February 23, 1901, it was finally abolished – at the request of the Synod (Kartashev 1959, II, 353; Szeftel 1978, 131). Only *one day later*, the Synod issued its public pronouncement on Tolstoi's teaching – a remarkable coincidence that seems to have passed unnoticed in the literature. In this perspective, we may see the Circular Letter as the first, spectacularly unsuccessful, attempt of the Russian Church to test its ability to act independently and in its own interests.

***

An abortive attempt to repeal the excommunication was taken in 1922 by a group of radical Russian Orthodox priests who belonged to the "Renewal movement" (Bonch-Bruevich 1929, 56; Stepanov 1922, 14). The "renovationists" sought accommodation and collaboration with the officially atheist Soviet power and had broken with patriarch Tikhon, who at the time was in house arrest (Roslof 2002). The vast majority of Russian Orthodox faithful, however, remained loyal to the Patriarch, and when he regained his freedom two years later, the renovationist movement collapsed – and the idea that Tolstoi ought to be posthumously reinstated in the Church was thoroughly and lastingly discredited. When Vladimir Tolstoi, the director of the Tolstoi Museum at Iasnaia Poliana and great grandson of the famed author, at the occasion of the centenary of Tolstoi's death appealed to Patriarch Aleksii II to reconsider the excommunication, the plea was turned down (see, George 2015, 201, fn 16). There is reason to believe that the association with the renovationists that this initiative gives Orthodox believers is part of the explanation why the Russian church will not reopen the excommunication process.

CHAPTER 13

A Requiem for a Heretic? The Controversy over Lev Tolstoi's Burial

As we saw in Chapter 12, the Church's public statement on Tolstoi in 1901 ended with the following statement:

> [T]he Church no longer counts him among her members and cannot do so until he repents and restores his fellowship with her. This we hereby testify before the entire Church to support those who stand steadfast and to reason with those who have gone astray, and in particular, to reason one more time with Count Tolstoi himself. Many of his loved ones who have kept the faith think with sadness that when his days are counted he will stand without faith in God and in our Lord the Savior. Then he will have spurned the Church's blessings and prayers and any fellowship with her. (*Opredelenie* 1901)

Most Western authors who have commented upon this document have seen its main message in the first words of this quote: "The Church no longer counts him among her members." However, if issuing this proclamation had been the impetus behind the Circular Letter, it would have been a superfluous, indeed meaningless, statement, as Tolstoi's apostasy was already obvious to any Russian with even a minimum of interest in contemporary affairs. On numerous occasions, he had clearly renounced, indeed denounced, the Church and all it stood for. Therefore, we should seek the main message of the Circular Letter in the final sentence: If he died unreconciled, he would "have spurned the Church's blessings and prayers and any fellowship with her." The crux of the matter was the requiem ban.[1] This is also Pavel Basinskii's interpretation (Basinskii 2019, 505). He points out that Tolstoi had been severely ill the year before the Circular letter was promulgated, and the question of whether or not to grant the great author an Orthodox burial had become acute. For that

[1] Although the term "requiem" admittedly has a Catholic ring, I use this word since all possible substitutes, such as "prayer for the departed" or "commemorative service," are either long and cumbersome and/or have a Protestant ring, which would be even more misleading.

reason, he believes that the main addressee of the Circular letter was the Orthodox clergy, who were the ones who could perform such rites, rather than the laity.

While Tolstoi himself clearly did not want any priest to officiate at his funeral, this circumstance by itself was not sufficient to put the issue to rest. As soon as he died, it would be up to the bereaved to decide what should be done with his body. Both his wife and at least one of his sons were known to be Orthodox believers and were expected to press for a burial on consecrated ground. If they did, it would be up to the Church to decide whether a requiem could be performed. While the message of the Circular Letter was formulated in verbose and roundabout language, the practical conclusion was nevertheless clear enough to those whom it concerned: No last rites or memorial prayers – whether *otpevanie, panikhida*, or *pominovenie* – could be performed after Tolstoi's death unless he repented.

An *otpevanie* is a Christian (Orthodox) burial. *Pominovenie* is a short prayer of intercession for one or more deceased persons, read as a part of a regular service, whereas a *panikhida* is a separate memorial service. Strictly speaking, a *panikhida* is not a requiem, as there is no celebration of the Eucharist or other sacraments. *Otpevanie, panikhida*, and *pominovenie* are three distinct services, but they were often confused in the requiem debate that followed Tolstoi's death. It is also quite clear that if one of them were to be permitted, there would no longer be any reason to deny the performance of the other two.

The Orthodox Church does not have any clear teaching on Purgatory, but nevertheless prays for the dead. *Panikhida* is usually read on the third, ninth and fortieth day after the bereavement, and then once every year on the day of the departure of the soul. In addition, a worshipper may always come to a church, at any time and any place, and ask for a *panikhida* to be performed. Whether the supplicant is related to the deceased is irrelevant.

The requiem ban pronounced by the Holy Synod over Tolstoi unleashed a protracted and at times clamorous debate that agitated the Russian public for an entire decade before his death and continued a good three years afterward as well. The debate vividly illustrates the massive difficulties the Church experienced in communicating its message in the contemporary world. Since the decision on the requiem had been taken without consultation with the state authorities, it also sheds light on Church–State relations in late Tsarist Russia.

The requiem debate has been largely ignored by Tolstoi scholars in Russia, the Soviet Union and in the West (conspicuously absent in, e.g., Meilakh [1960] 1972; Nickell 2010; virtually all biographies). While most aspects of the circumstances surrounding Tolstoi's death and burial have been minutely chronicled, the involvement of the Church has been overlooked or mentioned in a few passing sentences only. The predicament in which the Church found itself during Tolstoi's agony at the Astapovo railway station has been poorly understood. Thus, for instance, Tolstoi's otherwise eminent biographer A. N. Wilson, as we shall see, got it all wrong when he claimed that "in spite of the fact that Andrei Tolstoi had pleaded with the Bishop of Tula to allow them a full Orthodox funeral, permission for this was forbidden by the Church authorities" (Wilson 1989, 517). Similarly, William Nickell, who has written an entire monograph devoted to Tolstoi's death at the Astapovo rail station, castigates the Russian Church for "[refusing] to perform services for its great enemy" (Nickell 2010, 70; see also Nickell 2006, 38) – but this is a most peculiar accusation, repeating hackneyed Soviet anti-Church propaganda. As this chapter will make clear, the Church went to extreme lengths to try to find a way to allow a requiem mass to be said for Tolstoi. If the prelates ought to be reproached for anything, it would probably be for the converse: For having thrust themselves on him for too long, too fiercely, against his express will.

The Requiem Debate: Ante Mortem

The requiem issue came to the fore in 1900, the year before the Circular Letter was promulgated, in a confidential circular to all the dioceses from the Synod's *primus inter pares*, Metropolitan Ioannikii (Rudnev).[2] Tolstoi had fallen seriously ill, and it was feared that he might die soon. As he was still formally a member of the Russian Church, it was conceivable that some of his close relatives might request permission for him to be buried according to the Orthodox ritual. The confidential circular stated that such a request should be granted only if he had repented and reconciled himself with the Church before he died; otherwise this might lead to temptation (*soblazn*) among the believers. Ioannikii pointed out that Tolstoi in several of his works had stood forth as an enemy of the Church, and added that "at the Feast of Orthodoxy, the Orthodox Church, in the presence of its faithful children, declares that such people stand outside the community of

[2] Georgii Orekhanov, who has researched this in Russian archives, has found that Ioannikii himself wanted to make this circular letter public, but this idea was rejected by the other members of the Synod (Orekhanov 2016, 465).

the Church" (TsGIAL, f.796, op. 182, ep.ch. 2433, reprinted in Kovalev 1960, 350). Ioannikii assumed that a separate excommunication ceremony was not required, since the viewpoints Tolstoi advocated clearly belonged to those condemned as heretical at the Feast of Orthodoxy. While the text of this secret circular did not use the words "excommunication" or "anathema," it was in form and content more similar to Archbishop's Amvrosii's draft text from the year before than to the final document published one year later (Orekhanov 2016, 466).

Ioannikii's confidential circular soon became publicly known, and aroused strong indignation. In many quarters, people reacted both against the actual requiem ban and the secrecy surrounding it. This circular was widely perceived as a form of excommunication, albeit a most irregular one. A polemical pamphlet against it was issued by a Russian publisher in Switzerland under the title *The Synod Revenges itself on Tolstoi with an Anathema. On the Occasion of the Excommunication (otluchenie)* of L. N. Tolstoi (*Sinod mstit* 1900).

The hierarchs realized that they would have to issue a public justification of their refusal to give Tolstoi an *otpevanie* (Weisbein 1960, 371). The Circular Letter that was promulgated the next year was such a justification. In his letter to Konstantin Pobedonostsev on February 11, Metropolitan Antonii, who by that time had taken over as presiding member of the Synod after Ioannikii, explained that a public Circular Letter "will not be a judgment of a deceased person, as the confidential circular is being depicted, nor a censure against which the accused is unable to defend himself. Instead, it will be a 'warning' to a living person."[3] Indeed, in an early draft of the *Circular Letter* that was discussed by members of the Synod, the connection between the two documents was made quite explicit already in the title. In this version, the address was called "A circular letter to the children of the Orthodox Church, [to notify them] that no *pominovenie* must be held over count Lev Tolstoi after his death."[4] For reasons unknown, the direct reference to the requiem ban was later dropped from the title of the Circular Letter.

The day after the publication of the Circular Letter, Sof'ia Andreevna wrote four identical letters, which she addressed to Konstantin Pobedonostsev and to the three metropolitan members of the Synod. She told them that the Circular Letter had filled her with boundless sorrow and indignation. The Church, to which she still belonged, had in her opinion been established by Christ the Lord in order to sanctify all

[3] RGIA, f.1574, op. 2, d. 133, l. 2. [4] RGIA, f.796, op. 182, d. 2433, l. 4.

significant moments in the life of man – birth, matrimony and death, all sorrows and joys. But now the Church had declared that it would withhold its blessings from her husband when he died, even though Christ has taught us that we shall love our enemies.

> Whom do you want to punish? The departed one, who can no longer feel any pain, or his closest relatives, believers who stand around him? Is this meant as a threat, and if so, against whom or what?
>
> Would it really be impossible for me to find a decent priest who will perform a *panikhida* over my husband and pray for him in the church, one who fears men less than he fears the real God of love, or perhaps to find a 'not so' decent priest, whom I could bribe handsomely to officiate? (S. A. Tolstaia 1905)[5]

Sof'ia Andreevna nevertheless concluded that she could do very well without such a service. In no way did the eternal fate of Tolstoi depend on the decisions of men: It would be decided by the will of God alone.

Initially, Metropolitan Antonii apparently intended to pass over the Countess's letter in silence. However, it was soon printed in several foreign newspapers and copies of it circulated in Russia as well. The reticence of the prelate was widely interpreted as showing that he could not come up with an answer. One of many anonymous letters sent to him during those days claimed that "thousands of thinking people in Russia are expecting an answer from you in the press. If no reply is forthcoming, your silence will be regarded as additional confirmation of your feebleness and mendacity vis-à-vis God and society."[6]

On March 16, Antonii sat down to write. His reply to Sof'ia Andreevna was published in *Tserkovnyi vestnik*, together with the Countess's letter (Antonii [Vadkovskii] 1905, 69–71). It was most unusual for a high Church dignitary to involve himself in a public dispute concerning a decision made by himself and his colleagues. This is an indication of the considerable communication problems that the Church experienced in its relations with the Russian public.

Antonii denied that the requiem ban should be seen as a threat of any kind. Furthermore, he agreed with the Countess that it was one of the

[5] Indeed, a certain village priest in Vitebsk diocese, Pavel Pravdin, wrote to Antonii and confirmed the Countess' assumption: "Your Highness, do not believe that there will be difficulty finding a priest who will pray for Lev Tolstoi after his death – even if he does not recant. Enough hypocrisy. Such priests, happily, are abundant." (quoted in Orekhanov 2016, 535).

[6] Publichnaia biblioteka imeni Saltykova-Shchedrina (PBSS), manuscript department, St. Petersburg Dukhovnaia akademiia, A I no. 289, letters to Metropolitan Antonii (Vadkovskii), letter no. 39.

main tasks of the Church to sanctify all solemn moments in the life of men – but he added that the Church had never done so with regard to nonbelievers, heathens or blasphemers. While it is true that the love of God is limitless, this love does not forgive everything and everyone. Antonii cited Matthew 12, 32 as biblical evidence that sin against the Holy Ghost will not be forgiven, not in this life, nor in the next. Thus, if an Orthodox priest were to be bribed into officiating at a requiem mass for Tolstoi, that would be tantamount to a "criminal profanation of the holy ritual," the Metropolitan asserted. Moreover, it would be an offense against the deceased, as Tolstoi had on numerous occasions explicitly asked not to be given a Christian burial (Antonii [Vadkovskii] 1905, 69).

If the Metropolitan had hoped that his reply would put an end to this delicate matter, he miscalculated badly. His letter poured additional fuel to the flames of the debate. While no articles were printed in the secular press about the correspondence between Antonii and the Countess due to minister Sipiagin's publication ban (see Chapter 12), it was discussed in drawing rooms and at street corners all over Russia. Since the publication ban did not extend to the organs of the Church, the ecclesiastical journals and papers could dominate the printed requiem debate unchallenged.

Unsurprisingly, all who expressed their opinion in the religious press supported the Metropolitan. Some of the articles, however, were so aggressively anti-Tolstoian that Antonii may well have been more embarrassed than comforted by them. Whereas his own letter to the Countess, some harsh words notwithstanding, had clearly been an attempt to calm the waters, some of his supporters, deliberately or inadvertently, raised the temperature to new heights. Many of them were anonymous.

A doctor from Moscow reminded the Countess of Job's wife in the Old Testament: She had advised her husband to curse God and die (Job 2, 9) (N. F. 1905, 81). An "Orthodox believer" insisted, in direct disagreement with the Metropolitan, that the requiem ban should indeed be regarded as a threat: Did not Sof'ia Andreevna know that the God of love is also the God of revenge? Tolstoi, this writer asserted, belonged to those whom Jesus condemned in Matt 25, 41: "Depart from me, ye cursed, into everlasting fire, prepared for the devil and his angels" (Pravoslavnyi 1905, 76–77).

However, Antonii had no reason to believe that such outpourings were typical reactions among the Russian public. He received clear indications that the private debate, which stirred emotions all over the country, was dominated by quite other viewpoints. As it was not possible to express these viewpoints in public, several persons decided that they would convey their opprobrium of the Metropolitan's action to him directly by mail.

Among the letters to Antonii that are kept in the Saltykov-Shchedrin library in St. Petersburg, several touch on the requiem question (Kolstø 2000, 84). The irreligious and anti-clericals upbraided him, while most professing believers supported him. That was quite predictable. More disconcerting, from the bishop's point of view, was probably the fact that also some who shared the faith of the Church took the side of the Countess in this matter.

One author, who preferred to remain anonymous, reminded the Metropolitan about the thief on Golgotha who repented in the very last moment: No one could tell what went on in Tolstoi's soul in the moment of death, he argued. Tolstoi's peace of mind, however, was not his main concern. He was far more worried about the possible consequences of the requiem ban for public order. As he saw it, many who sympathized with Tolstoi were actually quite irreligious but carried the famed author in front of them as a banner in an assault on the establishment. For them, a secular burial of Tolstoi could provide a golden opportunity to mobilize opposition against the regime. The only measure that could prevent such a development would be for the Synod to issue a declaration stating that the Circular Letter should not be interpreted as an excommunication of Tolstoi, and that whoever wished to pray for his salvation was free to do so. In that case, it was certain that people would come rushing to the Church, and any attempt at revolutionary turmoil would fall flat to the earth, he believed.[7]

Perhaps the most interesting letter in this category was written by a retired naval officer, Ivan Pavlovich Iuvachev. He was a man of letters who had, over the years, contributed several articles and travelogues to Orthodox journals. He was well read and apparently also versed in Greek. As a sincere Orthodox believer, Iuvachev wrote, he rejected Tolstoi's ideas on the Church, on the sacraments, etc. On the other hand, he could not but respect and love a man who obviously "hungers and thirsts for righteousness." This, however, was not the reason why he had come to the conclusion that a requiem mass over the great author ought to be allowed. Rather, he based his argument on a theological understanding of the Christian Church. "As is known, our Orthodox Church, in contrast to many other denominations, prays for the deceased, not asking whether or not they deserve to be accepted into the Heavenly Kingdom. This is one of the reasons why we love this Church so much."

[7] PBSS, A I, no. 289, letter no. 64.

Iuvachev pointed to Jesus' healing of the lame in Matt. 9 (with synoptic parallels in Luke 5 and Mark 2): "Jesus, seeing their faith, said unto the sick of the palsy: Son, be of good cheer; thy sins be forgiven thee." As Iuvachev pointed out, the Gospel is here talking not about "his" faith (*avtou*), but "their" (*avton*; all three versions of the miracle agree on this). This must mean that the faith of those who surround a stretcher – or a bier – is sufficient for God to forgive the sins of the person lying on it.[8]

The Metropolitan's Trump Card: Tolstoi's Will

The main reason why the Church did not listen to such voices but stood firm on the requiem ban was probably the one given by Metropolitan Antonii in his letter to Countess Tolstaia: Tolstoi himself had in no uncertain terms let it be known that he would very much resent the presence of any ecclesiastics at his funeral. Thus, starting from diametrically opposite positions, the Church leadership and Tolstoi ended up with identical conclusions.

Tolstoi had discussed his funeral in his diary as early as in 1895, in a passage to which he would later refer as his "will."

> Bury me where I die. If it is in a city, let it be in the very cheapest graveyard and in the very cheapest coffin, such as beggars are buried in. Neither flowers nor wreaths should be placed upon it, and no speeches shall be said. If possible, let it also take place without any priest and *otpevanie*. However, if this is distressing for those who shall bury me, let it be done by the usual ritual, but as cheaply and simply as possible. (Tolstoi PSS 53, 14–15)

Both Sof'ia Andreevna and the metropolitan could in fact turn these lines to their account. However, in his *Reply to the Synod* Tolstoi gave a closer interpretation and sterner expression of his will:

> In my will to my dear ones I have written that they shall not allow any representative of the Church to be present when I die, and my dead body shall be removed as quickly as possible, without any adjurations or prayers, and as any other unpleasant and useless matter it shall be removed so that it does not interfere with the lives of those who live on. (Tolstoi PSS 34, 248)

These lines, an ecclesiastical author claimed, made it sound as if the priests would come running as soon as it was rumored that a person was in the throes of death and besiege the deathbed (*O vneshnykh obriadakh* 1905,

[8] PBSS, A I, no. 289, letter no. 18.

55–57). Whereas Russian priests probably did not regularly evince such zeal, they certainly did when Tolstoi was dying in 1910.

***

The news that Lev Tolstoi was nearing his end at a railway station in the provincial town of Astapovo in Kaluga *guberniia* in November 1910 triggered a hectic round of meetings in the Holy Synod. Its members convened for more or less continuous sessions and informal consultations from November 3 through 7, sometimes both morning and evening. To some extent, this frantic activity was no doubt prompted by pressure from the secular Russian authorities. If the newspaper *Russkoe slovo* is to be believed, Prime Minister Petr Arkad'evich Stolypin approached the Synod leadership, inquiring what the Church intended to do in the event of the drama in Astapovo terminated in death. This inquiry led to a hastily convened extraordinary meeting of the Synod where Tolstoi's bishop, Parfenii of Tula, happened to be in attendance.[9] At this meeting the Chief Procurator of the Synod, Sergei Luk'ianov, raised the issue of giving Tolstoi a Christian burial. The bishops pointed to their *Circular Letter* from 1901, adding that Tolstoi had shown no signs of repentance since that document had been issued (*Zasedanie Sinoda* 1910).

Even so, they agreed, so many questions remained unanswered that the matter would have to be investigated further. It was therefore decided to send Bishop Parfenii to Astapovo as an observer on behalf of the Synod. In addition, a telegram was dispatched to the bishop of Kaluga, in whose diocese Tolstoi now lay, instructing him to make a final attempt to elicit a change of heart from the great writer. This mission the bishop of Kaluga passed on to the elders of the nearby Optina Pustyn' monastery (*Zasedanie Sinoda* 1910). As we saw in Chapter 6, Tolstoi's first stop on his "flight" from his family that ended in Astapovo, had been at Optina. He had not taken contact with any of the elders while he was there, but it was rumored in the press that he had wanted to do so. What had kept him back was the knowledge that he was under interdict (*Sredi gazet i zhurnalov* 1910).[10] Acting upon this information, the abbot of Optina, Varsonofii (Plikhankov), in the company of a deacon named Panteleimon, took it

9 William Nickell (Nickell 2006, 38) erroneously claims that Parfenii was a member of the Holy Synod. Parfenii happened to be in St. Petersburg at the time and was summoned to the Synod meeting in his capacity as bishop in Tolstoi's diocese.

10 These rumors were later confirmed by Dushan Makovitskii, Tolstoi's doctor, who accompanied him on his last journey. See Makovitskii 1979, IV, 407–08.

upon himself to travel to Astapovo in person to inquire into the causes of Tolstoi's abortive visit to the monastery. The abbot arrived in the evening of November 5, but Tolstoi's daughter Aleksandra, who was keeping vigil over the sick man, denied him entrance (*Iz materialov* 1923, 338–64; Tolstaia 1923, 181–82). According to the local chief of police, if only Tolstoi would utter the two syllables "I regret" (*kaius*), the abbot had the authority to regard this as indicating that Tolstoi had retracted his heresy. Varsonofii also brought with him the sacraments for this cause. He wrote two letters to Tolstoi's daughter Aleksandra and asked for a meeting with Tolstoi. The abbot wanted to bless him, and promised not to engage in any conversations about religion that could disturb the patient (*Iz materialov* 1923, 351). In the second letter, he wrote:

> You, Countess, know that to his sister, who is also your aunt, mother Mariia, the Count expressed a desire to meet with us and talk to us to get peace in his soul. He was also very sorry that he had not acted upon this wish. In light of this, I pray that you should not refuse to tell the Count that I have arrived in Astapovo. If he wants to see me for as little as two or three minutes, I will immediately come to him. But in case the Count should not want such a meeting, I will return to Optina Pustyn' and leave the matter to the will of God. (A. L. Tolstaia 1923, 181–82)

This inquiry did not elicit any response.

Bishop Parfenii, having a longer way to travel, arrived only after Tolstoi had died, on November 7, at six o'clock in the morning. To the press he denied that he had been sent from the Synod (*Ep. Parfenii* 1910), but to police chief Savitskii he gave a different version: The Tsar had personally wanted him to inquire whether any information had come to light during Tolstoi's stay in Astapovo to indicate that he had repented his delusions (*Iz materialov* 1923, 352). However, no one could provide such information, and the bishop took off again within less than an hour, without having left the train carriage.

In the meantime, Metropolitan Antonii had sent a personal telegram to the patient, beseeching him to return to the Church:

> From the very moment when you broke with the Church, I have incessantly prayed that the Lord may lead you back to it. Perhaps He will soon summon you to His court, and I implore you now on your sickbed: be reconciled with the Church and with the Orthodox Russian people. May the Lord bless and keep you. Metropolitan Antonii. (*Smert' Tolstogo* 1929, 70)

The Metropolitan no doubt realized that he was investing very much of the prestige and authority of the Church in this endeavor. His telegram might well be presented in the secular press as an importunate obtrusion; moreover, such desperate entreaties to a man who had heaped merciless scorn on him and his Church for decades might easily turn the Metropolitan into a pitiable laughing stock. The strong pressure coming from the secular authorities is probably not sufficient to explain why Metropolitan Antonii nevertheless persisted. Most probably the Church leaders actually hoped, to the very end – like Abraham "against all hope" (Rom. 4, 18) – that a miracle might occur and their prayers would somehow be answered.

Several Russian Orthodox writers have insisted that it was the circle of Tolstoians around Tolstoi's deathbed who prevented a reconciliation between him and the Church (D. Skvortsov 1911, 14–15; *Poslednie izvestiia* 1910, 734; Gladkov 1914, 59). Also the writer Ivan Bunin, who later received the Nobel Prize in literature, assumed that if Varsonofii had been admitted to the sickbed, the dying man might have been reconciled with the Church. Bunin supposed that Aleksandra Tolstaia nourished the same thought and that that was why she would not let any Orthodox approach him (Bunin 1967, 9, 28). When even a freethinker like Ivan Bunin could reason along these lines, it may appear less surprising that, until the very end, the Church clung to the hope that a reconciliation could be effected.

It is possible that pressure on the Church to achieve reconciliation with Tolstoi emanated not only from the government and the Prime minister, but also from Tsar Nikolai II himself. The newspaper *Russkoe slovo* asserted that there was deep concern "at the highest levels" over the embarrassing situation that the Circular Letter had created. "According to certain rumors the Synod was informed that a positive solution – *no matter how* – on the question of revoking Tolstoi's excommunication was highly desired" (*Zasedanie sinoda* 1910, emphasis in the original). This information is corroborated by Lev Tikhomirov, who had good connections in inner court circles as well as among the Church leadership. On November 8, Tikhomirov commented in his diary upon a conversation he had had the day before with Bishop Parfenii. The bishop had confided that the Tsar himself had expressed a deep desire to have Tolstoi reinstated in the fellowship of the Church on his deathbed. Parfenii also claimed that the members of the Synod had pledged to do their utmost to accede to the wish of His majesty in this matter.[11]

[11] However, as we have seen in this and the previous chapter, Bishop Parfenii was not above bending the truth on occasion, so his information here should possibly be taken with a pinch of salt.

In Tikhomirov's personal opinion, the Synod would "be spitting itself in the face" if it gave in to this pressure. Indeed, it would reveal such fatal weaknesses in the Church leadership that it might lead to a schism, he believed (Tikhomirov 1936, 180). This prediction, while probably exaggerated, is nevertheless an indication of the strong emotions that the burial controversy stirred up.

The pressure to give Tolstoi an Orthodox funeral, however, stemmed not only from without, but also from within the Church itself. Influential clergymen were willing to officiate if given permission so to do. According to Bishop, later Metropolitan, Antonii (Khrapovitskii), during these fateful November days a group of priests approached the Synod and suggested that they could perform a burial service at Tolstoi's funeral using another ritual than the one ordinarily used (Antonii [Khrapovitskii] [1910] 1978, 14, 268).[12] The ritual they had in mind was *Sviatyi Bozhe*, which was used when a member of a non-Orthodox (Western) denomination was buried in a Russian Orthodox graveyard. This ritual had been instituted in 1797 to provide for the non-Russian Christian officers who served in the Tsarist army and died on Russian soil. These were persons who, while not followers of the true faith, nevertheless "adhered to the teachings of the Gospel, and put their trust in Christ the Lord, the Savior of Mankind" (Kuznetsov 1913, 891). The *Sviatyi Bozhe* ritual was still in use at the time of Tolstoi's death – indeed, it had been reconfirmed and reformed as late as in 1904, and found ever-wider application.

The group of clergymen apparently reasoned that by using the rites of *Sviatyi Bozhe*, the famed writer could be given a Christian burial while conveniently bypassing the thorny issue of his relationship to the Orthodox Church. This suggestion, however, was at best questionable, and the political benefits to be drawn from it highly uncertain. Theologically, it might leave the impression that the Russian Church put Tolstoianism on a par with Catholicism and Lutheranism (Kuznetsov 1913, 892–93). In addition, even if, by choosing this solution, the Church could no longer be accused of "punishing" the deceased heretic, it would immediately face another accusation from the opposite side: That of trying to make political capital out of him. It seems that whatever the Russian Church leadership did or failed to do, it would be pilloried all over the globe as an assembly of callous, self-righteous bigots: A clear no-win situation.

[12] In all likelihood, Antonii himself was among the priests in this group (see, Kuznetsov 1913, 891).

While the available evidence is inconclusive, it appears that the Synod seriously debated the *Sviatyi Bozhe* ritual, seeing it as a straw to cling to. The commemorative book, *The Last Days of Tolstoi,* published shortly after the writer's death, claims that a decision was indeed made in the morning session of November 7 to settle for this compromise solution. Why, then, was it not implemented? Probably because Stolypin at three o'clock that afternoon had received a telegram from the governor of Riazan', Prince Obolenskii, stating that Tolstoi's family had decided to perform the funeral in accordance with the dead man's own instructions. In other words, the close relatives were requesting that no religious observances be made over the coffin (*Poslednie dni* 1910, 98).

The editors of *The Last Days of Tolstoi* do not say how they had acquired this piece of information. The preface only states that the material printed in the book had been culled from various newspapers and journals, and had been verified as much as feasible (*Poslednie dni* 1910, iv). As far as I can see, this information has neither been referred to nor commented upon in any later accounts of Tolstoi's death, in Russia or in the West. But the episode merits some attention. The *Sviatyi Bozhe* debate is an indication that there was far greater confusion and vacillation within the Church leadership than usually assumed. Outwardly, it might seem as if the Synod retained a consistent and unwavering attitude on the question of Tolstoi's burial, never deviating from its 1901 statement – but this appearance may well be deceptive.

The fact that detailed reports from the confidential deliberations of the Synod could be printed in *The Last Days of Tolstoi* was in itself not very sensational. Leakages from the highest organs of the Church were common: Indiscretions frequently resulted in news stories in the Russian press. Even though the *Sviatyi Bozhe* decision has not been directly confirmed by independent sources, it is nevertheless given some credence by the testimonies of Lev Tikhomirov and Antonii Khrapovitskii. Bishop Antonii explained that the proposal of the clerical group was turned down "as it in all likelihood would not have been accepted by the relatives" (Antonii [Khrapovitskii] [1910] 1978, 269).

The attitudes of the Tolstoi family on the requiem issue had long been uncertain. Rumor held that certain relatives had asked permission of the Synod to have an Orthodox ritual performed at the grave (*Smert' Tolstogo* 1929, 280). Highly placed persons of authority believed in these rumors. A Ministry of the Interior official, N. P. Kharlamov, sent a telegram from Astapovo to his superiors in Moscow at 12.30 p.m. on the day of Tolstoi's death, informing them that "the family desires a church burial (*tserkovnoe pogrebenie*)." On the basis of this telegram, his superior, P. G. Kurlov, sent a message to the governor of Riazan', instructing him that the police authorities should not interfere in the event of a priest wanting to perform *panikhida* over Tolstoi. If such an eventuality did arise, however, the priest would have to notify the police authorities in advance about his intentions, "lest the *panikhida* turn out to be a disguised attempt to organize an anti-government demonstration" (*Smert' Tolstogo* 1929, 11–12).

The fear that radicals would seek to exploit Tolstoi's demise for their own purposes was a real one. Funerals had been turned into political manifestations before, and the Soviet scholar Boris Meilakh has documented that numerous strikes, mass meetings and street demonstrations were indeed held in connection with Tolstoi's death. "Not only in Petersburg and Moscow, but also in other cities this movement took on such dimensions that the reactionary press began to talk about a repetition of the events leading up to 1905" (Meilakh [1960] 1979, 316). Tolstoi's funeral, however, proceeded in an orderly way.

Among Tolstoi's children only Andrei strongly favored an Orthodox funeral for his father, but in order to preserve peace with his siblings he did not press the issue (*Iz materialov* 1923, 353). Andrei had a long conversation with Bishop Parfenii at Astapovo during which he told the prelate about his decision. Based on this and other conversations he had at Astapovo, Parfenii wrote a comprehensive report to the Synod leadership. Already on the evening of November 7, a circular telegram was sent to all Russian dioceses confirming the requiem ban (Tal'berg 1956, 5–7). If any priest anywhere were approached by someone asking for a *panikhida* over "God's servant Lev," the priest should, contrary to regular custom, inquire about the surname of the deceased before granting the request. If the surname were "Tolstoi," no such prayers should be read (G. P. Petrov 1978, 100).

Postmortem

Tolstoi's death caused widespread mourning throughout Russia, and indeed all over the world. With an escort of 7,000–8,000 mourners, his coffin was brought home to Iasnaia Poliana, where he was laid to rest in the park under several large oak trees (*L. N. Tolstoi: iz nashego* 1910).[13] Tolstoi's will was respected. There were no priests present, neither at his deathbed nor at the funeral; there were no wax candles, crosses or icons.

[13] Other sources give much lower estimate of the number of mourners, down to 3000.

The mourners sang *Vechnaia pamiat'* (Eternal Memory), which is chanted as part of the Orthodox funeral ritual but was nevertheless regarded as a neutral way to part with the great writer. Tolstoi was the first public figure in modern Russian history to be buried without an officiating priest (Wilson 1989, 517). Several Orthodox writers interpreted this as a fulfillment of Jeremiah's prophesy in Jer 22, 19: "He shall be buried with the burial of an ass" (Varzhanskii 1913, 672; Bronzov 1912, 482; Katanskii n.d.)

Tolstoi's burial place immediately became a popular destination for modern pilgrims.[14] On the occasion of his birthday the next year, August 28, more than 300 persons congregated at his grave (S. A. Tolstaia 1978, 355). Shortly thereafter, a small paragraph appeared in several Orthodox journals with the heading "A serpent on Tolstoi's grave." The anonymous writer claimed that during the commemoration on August 28, a boy had been bitten by a serpent that suddenly had appeared at the grave site. The poison had been transmitted to the chest and it was not known whether the boy had survived. The boy was the son of Tolstoi's biographer, the famous Tolstoian Pavel Biriukov, it was asserted (*Zmeia na mogile* 1911, 767–69).

The magazine *Troitskoe slovo*, whose editor was known to have close connections to the Black Hundreds, explained the incident as a divine intervention.

> Not a hair of your head will perish but for the will of God. This is the word of Christ the Savior himself. Could the evil reptile bite the innocent boy without God's permission? . . . If the boy has died, it means that God had taken him to Himself so that he shall not be infected by the same poison as his parents. And for us all this shall be a lesson: Let us protect ourselves and our children from the pernicious teaching of the excommunicated heretic. (Ibid.)

One and a half years later, an Orthodox writer insisted that, as a result of this incident (and, we might perhaps add, as a result of the interpretation it had been given in the Orthodox press), the number of visitors at Tolstoi's grave had decreased (Varzhanskii 1913, 4, 672).

"Mr. X in a Cassock" Officiates

In 1912, the requiem mass debate entered a new phase. On September 3, a professor at the Moscow Theological Academy, S. Glagolev, opined that

14 Contemporary pictures reproduced in Nickell (2010, 71) carry the caption "Pilgrims (*palomniki*) at the grave of the great writer."

while it had been a correct decision not to give Tolstoi a Christian burial when he died, the situation had changed since then. Perhaps the time was now ripe for having a *panikhida* said over him (Glagolev 1912, 277). Apparently unconnected to this suggestion, a man turned up in Iasnaia Poliana three months later, spurred by "God's inspiration," he claimed. The person presented himself as a priest of the Russian Church and asked permission to celebrate a requiem mass over Tolstoi. The knowledge that such a "beautiful soul and good man as Tolstoi, who believed in both Christ and God," should lay buried in the ground without the blessing of the Church, filled him with deep anxiety (S. A. Tolstaia 1912).

The priest's request was granted. First, he performed *otpevanie* by the grave site, then *panikhida* in Tolstoi's bed chamber. Only Sof'ia Andreevna, Tolstoi's last secretary Valentin Bulgakov, and four more persons were present. That same evening, the priest moved on. Sof'ia Andreevna described him as "an energetic and wise priest, twenty-seven years of age" (S. A. Tolstaia 1978, 2, 383). To Bulgakov he had presented himself as Grigorii Lavrentevich Kalinovskii (V. Bulgakov 1926, 3, 120). It was later revealed that he came from the village of Ivan'kovo in the Pereiaslavl *uezd* (Chisnikov 2008, 222).

Sof'ia Andreevna had hoped that the incident could be kept secret, but the press soon got wind of the story. On December 21, the journalist Aleksandr Savvich Pankratov wrote a short sardonic article in *Russkoe slovo.* He doubted whether "Mr. X in the cassock" really was an ordained priest – he could just as easily have been a dressed-up lackey or barber. In any case, his action revealed deep ignorance of canonical law as well as contempt for the Holy Synod. According to Pankratov it was "utterly absurd" to perform *otpevanie* two years after a funeral, over a person who had been expelled from the Church and who, to cap it all, had explicitly requested burial without Orthodox ritual. Pankratov found it quite natural that this person had not revealed his identity: No criminal leaves his calling card on the site of his crime (Pankratov 1912).

One week later, Sof'ia Andreevna defended the incident in a letter to the editors in the same newspaper. She referred to Tolstoi's words in his diary of 1895 where he wrote that if it would mean a lot to his family, they might give him an Orthodox funeral. His far harsher words in his *Reply to the Synod* she passed over in silence. Sof'ia Andreevna explained that she had had no religious scruples about the priest's proposal, quite the contrary:

> How could I, a believer in the grace of the Church, feel anything but joy and gratitude toward a priest who understood that a sincere, fervent prayer

> for a dead man is an expression of love and Christian forgiveness and nothing else? (S. A. Tolstaia 1912)

It was true that the two rites had to be held in privacy – but also the first generation of Christian believers were obliged to hide from their enemies. After the services, the priest, in the words of the Countess, had jubilantly exclaimed: "Now Lev Nikolaevich is no longer a heretic, I have forgiven him his sins."

The news about the clandestine last rites created considerable commotion and indignation among Russian Orthodox believers. Archpriest N. Drozdov was surprised that the anonymous priest did not know that whereas most sins can be forgiven, mortal sins against the Holy Spirit cannot. Tolstoi's rebellion against the Church belonged to the latter category, he insisted. The bishops Nikanor of Kherson and Nikolai of Warsaw opined that the perpetrator should be defrocked and Sof'ia Tolstaia excommunicated (Kraniev 1913a, 8; Chisnikov 2008, 220). Others went even further and demanded that the disobedient priest should be locked up in a monastery (Chisnikov 2008, 220).

The Synod rose to action, and, as on earlier occasions, commissioned Bishop Parfenii of Tula to look into the matter. On January 3, 1913, Parfenii presented his report: He had not managed to establish the identity of the anonymous priest, and therefore assumed that the two rites had been a veritable "mystification": Sof'ia Andreevna had been hoodwinked by an impostor. However, the Synod held on to the hypothesis that the services had been performed by a real priest (Kraniev 1913a, 7) – as indeed proved to be the case. He was tracked down by the local gendarmerie in his home region, and in the secret police report it was claimed that he was already under investigation for killing a peasant while intoxicated. Allegedly he was "an inveterate drunkard and capable of all kinds of dirty business" (quoted in Chisnikov 2008, 222). However, the police report was never made public and had no consequences for Kalinovskii.

In February 1913, Kalinovskii, still anonymous, justified his action in a letter to the editors of *Russkoe slovo*. In his view, an *otpevanie* may be conducted after the funeral just as well as during it. This was commonly done in several places in Siberia and in other remote regions where there are no priests. In any case, an *otpevanie* is not a travel document that the soul must present to the border guards when he crosses over from earth to heaven. It is a *prayer* – and it is never too late to pray. The Church ought always and under all circumstances to pray for all sinners, even for the condemned. The early Christians had prayed for their executioners. The anonymous priest averred that he did not share Tolstoi's religious convictions, and had been motivated by no other reasons than that he, a sinner, wished to pray for another sinner (Chisnikov 2008, 220–21; Varzhanskii 1913, 672, where the priest's letter is reprinted in full).[15]

The priest did not confirm Sof'ia Andreevna's startling assertion that he had erased Tolstoi's heresy. Most Orthodox writers who condemned him in writing nevertheless assumed that it had indeed been his intention to do just that. The signature "B." in *Tserkovno-obshchestvennyi Vestnik* believed that the priest had tried to turn the prayers of the Church into a magical formula that would work mechanically, independent of the will of man. The grace of God, however, cannot save by force. Intercession for the dead, therefore, makes sense only if those who live on can be sure that the deceased would have joined them in prayer if he had been still alive (B., 1913, 11–13). "B" had no doubt in his mind that the *otpevanie* had been an illegal act and that the priest would be severely punished if he were to be exposed.

Anton Vladimirovich Kartashev (1875–1960), professor of church history at St. Petersburg Theological Academy and four years later appointed Minister of Religious Affairs in the Provisional Russian government, commented upon the requiem mass for Tolstoi in *Russkoe slovo* in January 1913. Kartashev pointed out that the priestly ministry is not a personal spiritual power invested in the individual person but is an organ of the Church. Religious rituals performed by a priest, therefore, make sense only when they are performed *on behalf of* the Church. When a priest officiated by Tolstoi's grave without the blessing of his bishop, therefore, he could only act in the capacity of private person, with no ecclesiastical authority (Kartashev 1913).

However, Kartashev also reminded his readers that Christ had given the Church "an heroic, superhuman commandment": Pray for your enemies. In the opinion of the professor, therefore, a special ritual ought to be instituted for that purpose. "That would provide us with a remedy against the feeling of religious impotence which the men of the Church experience in the extraordinary situation brought about by Tolstoi's death."

In the journal *Otdykh Khristianina*, the liberal Orthodox author N. Kuznetsov gave an erudite theological and canonical analysis of the

[15] While Kalinovskii did not charge any fee for the requiem mass, he later sent several letters to Sof'ia Tolstaia asking for money, first in order to go to Switzerland for a cure for his tuberculosis, and when he did not receive any reply to that request, he in several new letters explained that he had been defrocked after killing a peasant, and had no means to sustain his family. Also these letters remained unanswered (Chisnikov 2008, 223–25).

practice of prayer for heretics throughout the history of the Church, and tried to answer two related questions.

> 1: Was the action of the anonymous priest at Iasnaia Poliana a breach of church discipline? To this his answer was an unequivocal "yes." The ecumenical councils had adopted clear restrictions against priests acting on their own without the consent of their bishop, and Slavic canonical law (*Slavianskaia Kormchaia*) confirmed this prohibition.
>
> 2: Had the prayer at Tolstoi's grave been a sacramental action? Kuznetsov emphasized that the Bible clearly invites us to pray for all people (1 Tim 2, 1), including our enemies (Matt 5, 44; Acts 7, 60). Such prayers can also be found in Orthodox prayer books, he pointed out. However, it is always tacitly understood, and sometimes explicitly stated, that one shall pray for *living* people who have a chance to repent and make amends. Even so, in the history of the Church there had been certain exceptions from this principle. In the eighth century St. Theodorios the Studite gave permission to pray for diseased iconoclasts on one condition: such prayers must be said privately, not in the Church. By applying this rule to the *otpevanie* at Tolstoi's grave, Kuznetsov concluded that it could be perceived as a private act of commemoration and prayer. However, there had been no liturgical ceremony or sacrament as this is understood and practiced by the Church. (Kuznetsov 1913, 919–22)

For many Orthodox Russians, private prayer provided the solution to how they should relate to Tolstoi's departed soul. In his memoirs, his son Il'ia wrote that his aunt, the nun Mariia Tolstaia, had asked permission from her confessor, elder Iosif at Optina Pustyn', to pray for her deceased brother. Initially, this had been denied, with reference to the excommunication. However, when this answer failed to give her peace of mind, she approached another priest, hoping to meet greater understanding for her agony. Again, the reply was negative. According to Il'ia Tolstoi, this affected her so badly that it threatened her mental stability. Luckily, her confessor finally realized the gravity of the situation and allowed her to pray for Lev, on the condition that she did so alone, in her cell, lest others be led into temptation (I. Tolstoi 1969, 250).

***

In the requiem debate much was at stake for the Church: Its general reputation and theological trustworthiness as well as its relationship to the state authorities, to the general public, and to the faithful. The vacillating positions of the Church leadership reflected these concerns and pressures from all these quarters. As always regarding Tolstoi and Tolstoianism, the

Church tried to pursue containment and damage limitation, on the one hand, and bring about Tolstoi's conversion, on the other hand.

The requiem ban was apparently intended not so much as a punishment as an element in the Church's strategy to bring Tolstoi back into the fold. Experienced confessors as they were, the bishops knew that people who feel that the end is approaching often seek the sacraments and the comfort of the Church even if they have not done so before. The many attempts that were made to approach Tolstoi with admonitions and pleas, right up to the moment of his death, indicate that the Church leaders never relinquished this hope.

But how should the Church react if the requiem ban failed to produce the desired result? The prelates had no alternative strategy to fall back on. The ban functioned as a self-imposed limitation on the Church's future actions, a limitation that could not be ignored without "spitting itself in the face," as Lev Tikhomirov expressed it. To use another metaphor: Tying oneself to the mast may sometimes be a rational strategy, but only when both sides want something that the other side can provide. The problem for the Russian Church leaders was that, while they desperately craved something from Tolstoi (his conversion), there was nothing the Church could offer in which he was genuinely interested.

In promulgating the requiem ban, the Church painted itself into a corner. It linked its future actions to what Tolstoi did, thereby leaving the initiative to the adversary. Having made itself hostage to Tolstoi's spiritual development, the Church could not change its decision unless he pronounced those two fateful syllables "*kaius*": *I repent.* And Tolstoi did not.

CHAPTER 14

Summary and Conclusions

I am not the first scholar to point out the strong residual elements of Orthodox ideas and thought patterns in Tolstoi's religious worldview. For instance, Robert Donahoo has noted that in Tolstoi's theology "there is a strange mixture of Orthodox Christianity, nineteenth-century European humanism, and Tolstoi's personal idiosyncrasies" (Donahoo 1991, l). And in his Tolstoi biography, A. N. Wilson maintained that, just as Ernest Renan's religious criticism must be understood against the backdrop of French Catholicism and David Friedrich Strauss as a product of German Protestantism, 'Tolstoi is in some ways oddly a Russian Orthodox' (Wilson 1989, 321). These statements, in my view, express an important insight to which earlier Tolstoi research failed to pay attention. For a long time, scholars rather uncritically assumed that Tolstoi was influenced by those whom he himself mentioned as his most important inspirations, and no one else. The closer we get to Tolstoi's own time, the stronger does this tendency become. A clear example of this approach is the German scholar Felix Haase. In his study of the *Quellen der Weltanschauung L. N. Tolstoi* from 1928, he magnanimously concluded that Tolstoi "received impulses and essential contributions to his worldview from all ages and peoples" (Haase 1928, 199). Haase mentioned virtually every possible source – with the conspicuous exception of Orthodoxy.

Under the influence of semiotics, the sociology of knowledge, and hermeneutics, however, there has come a growing understanding of the interplay between text and context, between ruptures and continuity in historical development of ideas. Today, we no longer regard it as highly likely that a thinker can be significantly influenced by *all* national cultures and *all* epochs. The culture one has grown up in and which forms the framework for what Berger and Luckmann call "primary socialization" in important respects enjoys cognitive primacy, also for those who rebel against it.

Tolstoi's relation to the Orthodox faith was not of key interest for either A. N. Wilson or Robert Donahoo, and their passsing references to Tolstoi's Orthodox background have not been followed up elsewhere in their works. Only two modern researchers, Richard F. Gustafson and Georgii Orekhanov, have set out to discuss Tolstoi's thinking and writing against an Orthodox background in any detail. By profession, Gustafson is a literary historian, not a theologian or historian of ideas, but extensive reading of Orthodox theology enabled him to conclude that several ideas and positions that characterize this particular variant of Christianity can be found in Tolstoi's writings. On this basis, he postulated that Tolstoi must be understood as "an eastern Christian artist and theologian of the Russian Orthodox culture" (Gustafson 1986, 457). Gustafson's theory is intriguing, but he often jumps to conclusions and fails to document precisely which sources of Orthodox theology and spirituality Tolstoi was actually familiar with. A critic well versed in Orthodox theology, Charles Lock goes so far as to claim that Gustafson "does not fulfill [his] polemical aim of placing Tolstoy within the culture of Russian Orthodoxy" (Lock 1987, 181). Therefore, it might seem as if Gustafson came close to "proving" precisely the opposite of what he wanted: There are few, if any, significant connections between Tolstoi's thinking and Orthodox Christianity. The Orthodoxy hypothesis turned out to be a dead end, and we can return to the commonly accepted understanding: For Tolstoi, Orthodoxy was only the negative starting point, a monstrous blend of blasphemous lies that he had to confront in order to find the underlying true Christianity.

The second ambitious attempt to analyze Tolstoi's relationship to Orthodoxy is found in the two large volumes by the Russian Orthodox theologian and historian Georgii Orekhanov. Orekhanov has devoted a lifetime of study to the subject, but his apologetic approach makes it less valuable than it could otherwise have been. Through his research, he wants to demonstrate that Tolstoi was "a prophet without honor" (the title of one of his books) and that the Russian Orthodox Church acted "correctly" in excommunicating him. While Orekhanov's works contain much valuable information, the normative starting point means that his research belongs more to polemical than to academic literature.

Any attempts to show Tolstoianism as emerging from an Orthodox context that are based on purely structural analysis will quickly encounter serious methodological problems. The same conceptual parallels that can be demonstrated between Tolstoianism and Orthodoxy can often be found also between Tolstoi's thinking and other sources. Since "the Orthodoxy interpretation" to a greater extent than rival explanatory models goes against Tolstoi's self-understanding, it will have a hard time competing for attention if based on ideational coincidences alone. To be able to prove its worth, an approach focusing on Orthodoxy must therefore be supported by additional methods. Of these, I have taken recourse to two: Historical-genetic and reception analysis. I have traced the specific sources of Orthodox thinking and spirituality to which Tolstoi was exposed, which books by Orthodox authors he read, and how he reacted to them. I have also examined how Tolstoi and Tolstoianism were perceived by contemporaries, Russian Orthodox believers in particular, and how they assessed the similarities and differences between their own ideas and his.

Although Tolstoi lived in a society where Russian Orthodoxy was the state religion, we cannot without further investigation assume that he was immersed in its theology and beliefs. Many Russians of that time (especially among the upper classes) had no more frequent contact with the Church than what is common in many Western societies today: One is baptized in it, then confirmed, married, and finally buried there. Although their worldview and values in essential respects may be significantly informed by this Christian cultural background, this is not something that most people think about on a daily basis.

For Tolstoi it was different. He had grown up in a home where almost all his primary persons and educators were Orthodox believers who took their faith seriously. Tolstoi's autobiographical novel *Childhood* also documents that he early on came in contact with fiery representatives of popular Russian piety, holy wanderers and "holy fools." In all likelihood, Tolstoi was almost irreligious for a period in his youth, especially during his stay at Kazan' University and in the years immediately thereafter, but when he joined a military unit in the North Caucasus in 1851, religion made a remarkable comeback in his life. This was obviously not the result of any positive influence from the external military environment, with its coarse ideals of soldiery: Indeed, it might have been a reaction against the prevailing atmosphere in the camp.

Tolstoi's religious pondering constantly brought him beyond the limits of the Orthodox faith he was raised in, as he himself was fully aware of. Testimony to this was the idea of founding an entirely new religion, which he noted in his diary in 1855. This has been reproduced in virtually every study of Tolstoi's life and thinking, because it offers an interesting foreshadowing of his ministry and urge to preach in his older days.

Tolstoi's return to the Orthodox fold around 1876-77 was prompted by a deep existential crisis. Also several times earlier, he had begun to doubt whether life (specifically, his own life) had any meaning, but this time the doubts were more all-encompassing. He found a new foothold by placing himself on the same spiritual ground as the Russian peasants. Tolstoi had noted that the peasants had a far less complicated understanding of life than he had himself. Therefore, he concluded, peasant life was more true and genuine. Since the religion that the simple Russian people professed was Orthodoxy, Tolstoi felt he would have to embrace this faith. Previously, rational objections to the main Christian dogmas had kept him at a distance from the Church. Although he still acknowledged the criticism of reason as valid in and of itself, he now decided that he could permit himself to ignore it, since reason was not able to give an enduring meaning to life, as faith did.

However, even in his most intensely "Orthodox period," Tolstoi was repelled by many aspects of the message and practice preached by the Church, as he expressed it in his diaries and personal letters. The new peace of mind he had found was forced and, as it turned out, not lasting. Tolstoi was prepared to offer great sacrifices on the altar of faith, and to forsake material goods, pleasure, honor and fame, if that was required of him. The only sacrifice he in the long run was unable to present was *sacrificium intellectus*, as that would require him to be hypocritical and dissembling.

Thus, Tolstoi was left with three elements to a worldview, all of which for him were axiomatic, but very difficult to reconcile: (1) his firm conviction that life has and must have a deeper meaning; (2) an experience that told him that very many people actually found such meaning and that this was almost always in religion; and (3) his sense of reason, which he still recognized as the main source of cognition, but which, as it turned out, could only be used to tear apart nonrational worldviews, not to put together an alternative.

This Catch-22 situation forced Tolstoi into a new, restless search for coherence and meaning in life. Apparently, he found the answer in what became known as Tolstoianism, his own interpretation of the New Testament message. However, this was as "apparent" as was the reconciliation with the Russian Church in his "Orthodox" period. Many testimonies show that Tolstoi was at least as little "Tolstoian" as Marx was a Marxist. For instance, Maxim Gorkii, in his *Memories of Tolstoi*, revealed astonishingly "un-Tolstoian" sides of the thinker at Iasnaia Poliana (Gorkii 1919). Tolstoi's diaries show that in the years after 1880 he continued his spiritual odyssey, a journey that eventually (unlike that of Odysseus) did not bring him home, but instead led to his departure from home.

Also after 1880, Tolstoi's intellectual biography must be characterized as a story of restless wandering, but in some respects it was like walking in circles. In his novels and stories, publicist writings, letters and diaries, he constantly returned to the same topics and mulled over the same paradoxes. Sometimes he contradicted himself egregiously: Indeed, attempts to reconstruct Tolstoianism as a well-rounded, consistent system of thought (e.g., V. Bulgakov 1917) must be dismissed as unsuccessful. Nevertheless, we can observe that Tolstoi from around 1882 to his death firmly adhered to certain crucial principles. This makes it possible to identify some key clusters of motifs that form a kind of mainstay in his thought structure.

Most of Tolstoi's main ideas were taken from the Christian heritage, but his selection of and creative elaboration on them show that his life's work did not consist in rediscovering Christ's unadulterated doctrine as it had been before the Church perverted it, such as Tolstoi himself claimed. Instead, it was a reinterpretation and alteration of the Christian faith that he had encountered in his own life.

Central evidence for this claim I find in Tolstoi's voluminous, combative text against Orthodox school theology, *Examination of Dogmatic Theology*. In this massive tome, in which Tolstoi the stylist is conspicuously absent, the polemic is so coarse and overplayed that few readers have managed to get through more than a few chapters before giving up. But even if we cannot learn much about Orthodox theology by reading this work, we can gain important information about Tolstoi's own theology by reading *Examination* "against the grain," as it were.

Firstly, in some cases we can infer antithetically, from Tolstoi's criticisms of Orthodoxy, to his own positive standpoints. Secondly, the fact that certain aspects of Orthodoxy, as expressed in the books he read, escaped his scathing sarcasm indicates that, on these points, Tolstoi was more in agreement with Orthodox theologians than he liked to acknowledge, even to himself. Thirdly, the structure of his counterarguments is often built on an Orthodox template. Finally, in a few places Tolstoi openly recognized that he shared the theologians' views and was even indebted to them. This way of reading *Examination*, in conjunction with remarks gleaned from Tolstoi's diaries and some other sources, shows that Tolstoi's theology contained some clearly Orthodox features.

A particularly significant influence from Tolstoi's reading of Orthodox literature can be traced in his *theology* in a narrow sense, that is, in his doctrine about God. Of fundamental importance to any Orthodox understanding of God is the duality between apophatic (negative) and cataphatic (positive) theology. Using these two complementary approaches,

Orthodox Christians believe that it is possible to maintain at the same time that God is completely inaccessible *and* fundamentally accessible to humans. This is very similar to Tolstoi's own understanding of God as, on the one hand, utterly unfathomable, and on the other hand, the fountainhead of love and the giver of meaning in life. In fact, he criticized the leading Russian theologian of the time, Metropolitan Makarii, for distorting "the deep and sincere speech of the Apostles and Church Fathers who prove that God is incomprehensible" (Tolstoi PSS 23, 71). For Tolstoi, Makarii's theology was not apophatic *enough* – one could even say: Not Orthodox enough.

But even though Tolstoi's teaching exhibits clear affinities with mainstream Orthodox theology, he reorganized these common elements to such an extent that the end result was distinctly Tolstoian. Orthodox theology is strictly theocentric and understands man in light of God the Creator, while Tolstoi explicitly went in the opposite direction. For him, man is the given entity (which he knew primarily by means of introspection), whereas God is the unknown x which must be postulated in order to solve the calculation of human life (= give life meaning). This makes Tolstoianism a sort of upside-down Orthodoxy. With his strong anthropocentrism, Tolstoi showed that he was a child not only of Russian Orthodox culture, but also of the secular Russian thinking of his time. The Russian intelligentsia of the nineteenth century were almost exclusively concerned with anthropological – social and moral – questions (Kline 1968, 4).

An important reason why Tolstoi rejected Orthodox dogmatics so fiercely was that he considered a purely theoretical approach to faith, disconnected from the lives of the believers, as useless. He had far greater sympathy for the Orthodox mystic-ascetic devotional literature associated with the Hesychast movement. The major Hesychast writings were collected in *Philokalia* (*Dobrotoliubie*), a basic text of Orthodox spirituality. In his well-thumbed copy, Tolstoi found confirmation of his own strongly negative view of the body and the passions. A fundamental tenet of Orthodox monastic spirituality is that it is not enough to channel the passions in a healthy direction or to keep them in check. The *Philokalia* authors taught that it is both possible and desirable to *extinguish* the passions. Passionlessness, *apatheia*, a concept found also among the Stoics and in Buddhism, should be the aim of the Christian life. This was an ideal that also Tolstoi preached and which informed many of his ideas, such as the importance of physical labor, nonresistance to evil, and abstention from property ownership, drugs, alcohol and even sex.

In Eastern Orthodox traditions, asceticism is not an isolated exercise but forms an integral part of a more comprehensive doctrine about the path to the perfect life. Asceticism, *praxis*, involves approaching God through our bodies, and must be accompanied by a quest for God with our minds, *theoria*. Practice and theory are two parallel pathways, both equally important. The goal for both is divinity, *theosis*. All those who reach this stage will not only have freed themselves from the captivity of the passions, but will also been filled with love. All of these elements in classical Orthodox spirituality we find reproduced – but also remolded – in Tolstoianism.

In countries historically dominated by Orthodox culture, some specific forms of piety have developed to which there are no direct parallels in the West. Three of the most important are the elder (*starets*), the holy wanderer (*strannik*) and the holy fool (*iurodivyi*). Tolstoi was well acquainted with all of these forms of spirituality, through reading as well as personal contact. The major center of elder piety in Russia at Tolstoi's time was the Optina Monastery, located not far from Tolstoi's home at Iasnaia Poliana, and he visited the elders several times. And, as noted, he had been acquainted with holy wanderers and holy fools since his early childhood years.

Tolstoi's statements about these three forms of piety are divergent. He was somewhat skeptical to the activities of the elders, but generally referred to the wanderers and holy fools with greater respect. More important, however, is that Tolstoi himself entered all three of these roles himself, adapting them to his purposes. He apparently never used any of these appellations about himself, and it is also an open question to what extent he actively and consciously chose to enter any of these forms – in a certain sense, they "chose him." These were three of the best-known roles for, respectively, religious guidance, religious quest and nonmonastic religious asceticism in Russia at the time, available to anyone who wanted to convey and practice a religious message. Tolstoi's affiliation with these forms was so conspicuous that he was readily associated with them by several contemporary Russian (but few non-Russian) observers.

Occasionally, Tolstoi openly acknowledged that his views were related to what Orthodox Christians believe. In one diary entry, he expressly distanced himself from pantheism, subscribing instead to the idea of "what the Orthodox call the living God" (Tolstoi PSS 53, 118). However, such explicit statements about spiritual kinship with the Russian Church were not very common. Many times, Tolstoi had probably forgotten that the thoughts he presented as his own had been culled from an Orthodox repertoire.

Russian Orthodox Reactions

In the decades leading up to the events of 1917, the Russian Orthodox Church regarded Tolstoi as significantly more dangerous than all other freethinkers, critics, sectarians and non-Orthodox evangelists. There were several reasons for this. Firstly, Tolstoi was a world-famous author and could therefore attract a much larger audience with his message. Secondly, the Orthodox found it far more difficult to draw a demarcation line regarding his teachings than vis-à-vis professed atheists and adherents of Western-inspired faiths. Although Tolstoi clearly broke with the doctrine of the Church on many essential points, he still maintained so much of it that it was not always easy to see where his heresy began and his valuable (from an Orthodox viewpoint) thoughts ended. This created considerable frustration, insecurity and confusion among Russian Orthodox believers.

Orthodox theologians and laypersons could, and often did, use the same weapon against Tolstoi as he used against them – the pen. The stream of Orthodox articles, pamphlets and books about and against Tolstoi from Russian Orthodox quarters was formidable, albeit largely overlooked by scholarship. Much of this literature was run-of-the-mill or worse, but there was also some highly sophisticated analysis that merits greater attention.

Several of Russia's major theological capacities at the time plunged into the debate on Tolstoianism. None of them conducted "pure," uninterested research in writing on Tolstoi (but that can hardly be said about any of Tolstoi's secular opponents either). Most Russian Orthodox scholars tried to "unmask" the "true" Tolstoi; even so, some of them were remarkably fair and objective, considering the high temperature in the debate. They had solid training not only in theology, but also in philosophy and history – and, unlike many others, they made a thorough study of Tolstoi's teachings before passing judgment on them. One professor of theology, Aleksandr Gusev, wrote his doctoral dissertation on *The essence of L. N. Tolstoi's religious-moral teaching* (A. Gusev 1902, 619 pages) and in addition published three other books plus a series of articles against the thinker on Iasnaia Poliana. In the secular-radical camp, only one person, Liubov' Akselrod-Ortodoks, did anything remotely similar (Akselrod-Ortodoks 1902).

All of Russia's academic theological institutions, all Orthodox journals, and adherents of all political orientations and social milieus within the Church engaged in this endeavor. In more than twenty-five Russian cities, Orthodox anti-Tolstoian literature was published, which suggests that we might do well to reconsider the widespread view that Russian cultural life prior to the Revolution was exclusively concentrated on St. Petersburg and Moscow.

Two factors can explain the extent of Orthodox literature against Tolstoi. First, there was the significant impact of his ideas on Russian opinion. The circle of professed Tolstoians was minuscule, but the number of sympathizers was enormous. Around the turn of the nineteenth and twentieth centuries, it was Tolstoi who, more than anybody else, set the ethical and religious agenda in Russia, to some degree also elsewhere in the world. Others could either relate to the issues he raised or opt out of the general cultural debate altogether. Remarkably, even quite a few Russian Marxists and other socialists who professed materialism and atheism, felt compelled to take part in these polemics (see Oberländer 1965).

Attitudes toward Tolstoi expressed by Russian Orthodox authors in books and articles covered a vast range of positions. Some condemned him as a blasphemer and an enemy of God worse than Judas Iscariot. As the many derogatory epithets used about Tolstoi gradually lost their force through overuse, Orthodox writers resorted to increasingly harsher language. In the end, the thinker at Iasnaia Poliana was associated – partly also identified – with Antichrist. By converting the letters in Tolstoi's name into their numerical values in the Church Slavic alphabet, it was demonstrated – with a little cheating – that he bore the number of the beast, 666, in the Apocalypse. However, sometimes even such coarse polemics, paradoxically, indicated that Tolstoi's Orthodox critics recognized in his teaching many of their own views, albeit in distorted form. An important hallmark of Antichrist, as portrayed in the New Testament, is that he puts himself in Christ's place and with his striking likeness to the Savior leads many sincere Christians astray. It was precisely this aspect of the Antichrist figure that induced the leading Russian philosopher of the time, Vladimir Solov'ev, to interpret Tolstoianism as anti-Christian and Tolstoi as a precursor to Antichrist. However, judgmental characteristics of Tolstoi were countered by others in the Church. Some Orthodox believers, while retaining considerable skepticism toward his teaching, nevertheless recognized in him a trailblazer for a spiritual renewal of Russian society. Some of the most generous interpretations of his teaching tended to ignore the anti-Orthodox (and anti-Christian) elements in it, and were obviously more wishful thinking than analysis.

In its struggle against Tolstoi, the Russian Church, as a state church, could draw on various institutions of the state apparatus, such as censorship, but using that remedy often had just as many negative consequences as positive effects. Only the most offensive of his writings were totally forbidden; many others passed through the screening, either in the original version or with minor alterations. As a consequence, to the reading public in Russia, Tolstoi's anti-Orthodox message appeared as far more blunted and inoffensive than it actually was. Many Russians had great difficulty understanding why the Holy Synod in 1901 found it necessary to publish a special *Circular Letter*, warning against his doctrine. It was widely (but erroneously) held that the initiative to the *Circular Letter* stemmed not from the Synod itself, but from the state authorities – an assumption that now-available archival materials show we can safely put to rest. With its *Circular Letter*, the leadership of the Russian Church exhibited an unusually high degree of initiative and vigor, but also a surprisingly low degree of discernment: It failed to anticipate the reactions to the promulgation of this statement or its repercussions.

Also posterity has found it difficult to understand what the Church wanted to achieve with its spectacular action. The prelates had coached their message in rather tortuous language, unwilling to state plainly that they were excommunicating the great author – obviously fearing a boomerang effect. Despite their cautious and convoluted style, however, virtually everyone at the time (and later) understood the *Circular Letter* as an open excommunication, and denounced it on that basis. Although the state censorship prohibited discussion of the *Circular Letter* in the secular (but not in the ecclesiastical!) press, we have clear testimony, including a series of private letters to the primate of the Russian Church, that dissatisfaction with the Synod's actions extended far into Orthodox milieus.

In the *Circular Letter*, the prelates warned that no Orthodox priest would be allowed to officiate at Tolstoi's funeral unless he repented. When he died unreconciled, that landed the Church leadership in a severe predicament. If the requiem ban was upheld, they would be accused of callousness; in the opposite case, they could be charged with opportunism and/or weakness. Certain evidence, hitherto overlooked, indicates that the Synod, after strong pressure from secular Russian authorities, finally agreed to give Tolstoi a Christian burial according to the ritual used for fallen soldiers in the Tsarist army of Western denominations who were interred in Russian soil. However, this decision was not put into effect, nor published, because of opposition from Tolstoi's family. Tolstoi was buried without the blessings of the Church, the first such secular funeral in Russia in living memory. For many Russians, this was a shocking circumstance; for others, a symptomatic expression of the Church's hard-pressed position in Russian society. An Old-Believer Orthodox writer commented on this situation as follows:

> They got hold of one man, Tolstoi, and excommunicated him, and not even on their own initiative. The result we can see: A grandiose burial for Tolstoi, and virtually everyone, from the lowest to the highest, bow to his memory. This shows the complete spiritual feebleness of the ruling church. It has completely lost its moral authority and influence over people. (V. M-ov 1910, 707)

***

The purpose of this book has certainly not been to enlist Tolstoi posthumously among the members of the Russian Church against his will. His self-understanding as a rebel against and critic of the Orthodox form of Christianity remains. However, I demonstrate that in his encounters with Orthodoxy, important elements of Orthodox thinking rubbed off on him, and in his polemics against the Church he often employed arguments he could, and did, find in texts written by Orthodox authors.

The Russian religious philosopher Vasilii Rozanov once remarked that each Christian church gets the heretics it deserves. By this, he meant that a common trait of sectarians is their propensity to amplify, out of all proportion, certain ideas that are typical of the particular denomination from which they hail. In this way Rozanov explained the asceticism and self-mortification of the *khlysty* (the flagellants) and *skoptsy* (the self-castrators): These Russian sects magnified *ab absurdum* the life-denying tendency that, in Rozanov's view, was latently present in Orthodoxy itself (Rozanov 1911, esp. 99–127).[1]

Seen from a theological-dogmatic point of view, Tolstoi was undoubtedly a heretic. That term, however, has little relevance for an inquiry into the history of ideas. I have sought to move beyond such labels to search for possible ideational connections behind all hostility and mutual recriminations between Russian Orthodoxy and Tolstoi's heterodoxy.

If Tolstoi's relation to the Orthodox faith were to be summed up in one word, "ambivalence" seems a far better expression than "rejection." Not "lie," but "truth interwoven with lies with the finest threads" was how Tolstoi characterized Orthodoxy in *A Confession* (Tolstoi PSS 23, 53), and this idea reappeared in several places in his later writings. To a surprising

[1] Laura Engelstein (Engelstein 2003, 31) makes the same point, describing the Skoptsy's relation to Orthodoxy as "an extreme variation on a common theme."

degree, the same contradictory attitude characterized also Orthodox reactions to Tolstoi. Time and again, Orthodox writers acknowledged that Tolstoi's views on the essence of faith resembled their own. Claims that Tolstoi had "rediscovered a long-discovered America" (Ledovskii 1911, 13); hid behind "a mask of goodness" (Il'menskii 1911, 1); "served his poison in microscopic doses"; appeared as "an angel of light" (Griniakin 1905, 551); peddled "contraband" and had "stolen the pearl of the gospel" (Nikolskii 1912, 4, 316) necessarily implied that there was significant coincidence between Tolstoi's teaching and Orthodox doctrine and religiosity.

The signature "Amicus." maintained that in Tolstoi's writings, the right (*pravda*) and the crooked (*krivda*) were always expressed side by side, truth mixed with lies; among correct ideas and assessments, one could also encounter extreme, one-sided, and erroneous opinions. For this Orthodox author, therefore, the task was to "separate the wheat from the chaff, and the grain of truth from the glitter of tinsel" (Amicus 1899, 1, 73). This expressed a program that was very similar to Tolstoi's task of "separating truth from falsehood" in Orthodoxy.

In 1939, the Russian-Orthodox Archbishop Ioann (Shakhovskoi) in his book *Tolstoi and the Church* expressed the view that Tolstoi was a very dangerous heretic, but he also admitted that "sometimes Tolstoi seems to speak like a Christian" (Ioann [Shakhovskoi] 1939, 106).[2] With reference to Tolstoi's philosophical-social and ethical ideas, Ioann claimed that Tolstoi almost always expressed truth (*pravda*) and falsehood (*nepravda*) simultaneously.

> In his truth, there is some falsehood and in his falsehood, there is some truth. His religious falsehood is braided with his religious truth like a liana around a tree trunk that sucks the tree dry. Like ivy, the Christian truth twines itself around the dead tree of Tolstoian ideas and gives this tree the appearance of blossom. (Ioann [Shakhovskoi] 1939, 101)

Archbishop Ioann's botanical metaphor is strikingly reminiscent of Tolstoi's tapestry image, "truths interwoven with lies." Their understandings of the relationship between Orthodoxy and Tolstoianism coincide, albeit with opposite signs: Tolstoi perceived those elements in Orthodoxy that distinguish it from his own doctrine as a lie, while Shakhovskoi replied

[2] Ioann was bishop in the West-European Exarchate which in 1930 split away from the Russian Orthodox Church outside Russia (ROCOR) and placed itself under the jurisdiction of the Ecumenical Patriarch of Constantinople.

in kind. However, inbetween, there was a significant common ground that both men agreed to consider as truth.

Without intending to, Ioann, even more than Tolstoi, revealed how interlaced in each other these two systems of belief were. So tightly united were the heretical and the Orthodox elements in Tolstoianism that this twentieth-century archbishop was unable to determine which was the parasite and which constituted the tree trunk: In the middle of his metaphor, the two elements change places.

Bibliography

Agapit, arkhimandrit, *Zhizneopisanie v Bozhe pochivshego optinskogo startsa, Ieromonakha Amvrosiia*, I–II vols, Moscow, 1900.

Aggeev, Konstantin, *Po povodu tolkov v sovremennom obrazovannom obshchestve, vozbuzhdennykh poslaniem Sv. Sinoda o grafe L. Tolstom*, Kiev, 1901.

Ahlberg, Alf, *Friedrich Nietzsche – hans liv och verk*, Stockholm, 1923.

Aivazov, Ivan, "Kto takoi L. N. Tolstoi? (Po povodu postanovleniia Moskovskoi gorodskoi dumy chestvovat' 80-letie Tolstogo)," *Tserkovnye vedomosti*, 1908, issue 34, pribavlenie, 1622–28.

Aksakov, Konstantin, "O vnutrennem polozhenii Rossii," in Brodskii, N. L., ed., *Rannie slavianofily: A. S. Khomiakov, I. V. Kireevskii, K. S. i I. S. Aksakovy*, Moscow, 1910, 69–102.

Akselrod-Ortodox, Liubov', *Tolstojs Weltanschauuung und ihre Entwicklung*, Stuttgart, 1902.

Aleksii (Kuznetsov), *Iurodstvo i stolpnichestvo: Religiozno-psikhologicheskoe izsledovanie*, St. Petersburg, 1913.

Alfeev, P., "*Kratkoe izlozhenie Evangeliia* Grafa L.N. Tolstogo," in *Missionerskii sbornik*, 1907, 4, 298–302; 6, 507–9; 1908, issue 2, 140–45, issue 5, 366–75; 1909, issue 1–2, 25–34, issue 3, 148–60, issue 5, 299–307; 1910, issue 1, 8–21, issue 3, 191–201, issue 8, 643–59; 1911, issue 2, 113–20, issue 4, 247–63.

Alston, Charlotte, *Tolstoy and His Disciples: The History of a Radical International Movement*, London, 2014.

Amicus, "Otkrytiia pis'ma k drugu intelligentu uvlekaiushchemusia ucheniem L.N. Tolstogo," in *Missionerskoe obozrenie*, 1899, issue 1, 72–81; 1899, issue 2, 209–13, issue 7–8, 32–39, issue 9, 212–15.

Amvrosii (Grenkov), *Sobranie pisem . . . : Optinskago startsa . . . : K mirskim osobam*, Sergiev Posad, 1908.

Amvrosii (Kliucharev), "O deiateliakh na zhatve Bozhiei," in *Tserkovnye vedomosti*, 1901, issue 15, 67–119.

Andreev, Leonid N., "Za polgoda do smerti," in *Solntse Rossii*, 1911, issue 53, 2.

Anninskii, A., "Tsenzura i L. N. Tolstoi," in *Krasnyi Arkhiv*, 1922, 1, 412–16.

Anninskii, L., *Graf Lev Nikolaevich Tolstoi kak moralist*, Riazan', 1914.

Antonii (Khrapovitskii), *Besedy o prevoskhodstve pravoslavnago ponimaniia Evangeliia sravnitel'no s ucheniem L. Tolstago*, St. Petersburg, 1891.

Nravstvennoe uchenie v sochinenii Tolstago "Tsarstvo Bozhie vnutri vas" pred sudom ucheniia khristianskago, Moscow, 1897.

Antonii (Khrapovitskii), "Besedy o pravoslavnom ponimanii zhizni i ego prevoskhodstvo nad ucheniem L. N. Tolstogo," St. Petersburg, 1889. In *Zhizneopisanie i tvoreniia blazhenneishago Antoniia, Mitropolita Kievskago i Galitskago v 17 tomakh*, New York, 1967a, XIV, 62–113.

"O narodnykh razskazakh gr. L. N. Tolstogo," in *Russkoe delo*, 1886, issue 18. In *Zhizneopisanie ...*, op. cit., 1967b, XIV, 167–73.

"Vozmozhna li nravstvennaia zhizn' bez khristianskoi religii? (Po povodu 'Kritiki dogmaticheskogo bogosloviia' L. N. Tolstogo)," in *Pravoslavnyi sobesednik*, 1897, issue April. In *Zhizneopisanie ...*, op. cit., 1967c, XIV, 174–201.

"Dve krainosti: papisty i tolstovtsy," in *Bogoslovskii Vestnik*, 1895, issue Febr. In *Zhizneopisanie* ... op. cit, 1967d, XIV, 219–46.

"V chem prodolzhalo otrazhat'sia vliianie pravoslaviia na posledniia proizvedeniia gr. L. N. Tolstogo," 1910. In *Zhizneopisanie ...*, op. cit., 1967e, XIV, 247–68.

Antonii, (Vadkovskii), "Otvet na pis'mo grafini S. A. Tolstoi," in *Po povodu otpadeniia ... Tolstogo*, op. cit., 1905a, 69–71.

"Mysli po povodu otveta Sv. Sinoda grafa L. N. Tolstogo," in *Po povodu otpadeniia ... Tolstogo*, op. cit., 1905b, 92–95.

Apokrif, N., "K. Leont'ev i graf L. Tolstoi," in *Rus'*, 1903, 96–141.

Apostolov, N., "L. N. Tolstoi pod udarami tsenzury," in *Krasnyi arkhiv*, 1929, 35, 215–35.

Arbuzov, Sergei, *Gr. L. N. Tolstoi: Vospominaniia byvshago slugi grafa L. N. Tolstogo*, Moscow, 1904.

Arseniev, Nicholas, *Russian Piety*, New York, [1964] 1975.

Arsenii (Zadinovskii), arkhimandrit, *Graf Tolstoi i nashe neverie*, Moscow, 1911.

Asketizm i monashestvo, Valaamo, n.d..

Augustine, *The City of God*, Harmondsworth, 1981.

B., "Po povodu otpevaniia, sovershennago na mogile L. N. Tolstogo," in *Tserkovno-obshchestvennyi vestnik*, 1913, issue 8, 11–13.

Bakunin, Mikhail, *God and the State*, New York, [1882] 1970.

Balasubramanian, Radha, *The Influence of India on Leo Tolstoy and Tolstoy's Influence on India*, Lewinston, 2013.

Balmuth, Daniel, *Censorship in Russia 1865–1905*, Washington, 1979.

Bartlett, Rosamund, *Tolstoy: A Russian Life*, London, 2010.

Basinskii, Pavel, *Lev Tolstoi: Begstvo iz raia*, Moscow, 2019.

Baskakov, Alexej, *"Ströme von Kraft": Thomas Mann und Tolstoi*, Cologne, 2014.

Belkin, Vasilii, "Bludnyi syn. (Grafu L. N. Tolstomu)," in *Missionerskii sbornik* 1909, issue 3, 146–47.

Berdiaev, Nikolai, "Tri iubileia. (L. Tolstoi, Gen. Ibsen, N.F. Fedorov)," in *Put'* 1928, issue 11, 76–94.

Samopoznanie. Opyt filosofskoi avtobiografii, Paris, 1949.

Istoki i smysl russkogo kommunizma, Paris, [1937] 1955.

Russkaia ideia, Paris, [1946] 1971.
"Vetkhii i Novyi Zavet v religioznom soznanii L. Tolstogo," in *O religii Tolstogo*, op. cit., [1912] 1978, 172–95.
Berger, Peter L. and Thomas Luckmann, *The Social Construction of Reality*, Harmondsworth, [1966] 1976.
Bessonov, Petr, *Kaleki perekhozhie*, I–II vols, Moscow, 1861–64.
"Bibliografiia," in *Vera i tserkov'*, 1903a, issue 1, 165–67.
Biblioteka L'va Tolstogo v Iasnoi Poliane, Moscow, 1975.
Billington, James H., *The Icon and the Axe: An Interpretive History of Russian Culture*, New York, 1970.
Biriukov, Pavel I., *Lev Nikolaevich Tolstoi. Biografiia*, I–IV vols, Moscow, 1905–23.
Biriukov, Pavel I., *Tolstoj und der Orient*, Zürich, 1925.
Bitovt, Iurii, *Tolstoi v literature i iskusstve, Podrobnyi bibliograficheskii ukazatel' russkoi i inostrannoi literatury*, Moscow, 1903.
Blane, Andrew, "Protestant sects in Late Imperial Russia," in Blane, Andrew, ed., *The Religious World of Russian Culture*, The Hague, 1975, II, 267–304.
Bodde, Derk, *Tolstoy and China*, Princeton, 1950.
Bodin, Per-Arne. "Lev Tolstoy and Folly in Christ," in Lunde, Ingunn, ed., *The Holy Fool in Byzantium and Russia: Papers Presented at a Symposium Arranged by the Norwegian Committee of Byzantine Studies*, August 28, 1993, at the University of Bergen, 35–46.
Bogdanovich, Savva, "Dve besedy missionera s predstavitelem shtundizma (tolstovstva)," in *Dushepoleznoe chtenie*, 1903, issue 1, 88–93, issue 3, 461–66.
Bogoslovskii, G., "K voprosu o tserkovnom brake po povodu dramy L. N. Tolstogo 'zhivoi trup'," in *Missionerskii sbornik*, 1912, issue 11, 923–39; issue 12, 1032–40; 1913 issue 1, 23–37.
Bogoslovskii, Sergei, "Neskol'ko slov po povodu lzheucheniia gr. Tolstogo," in *Moskovskie tserkovnye vedomosti*, 1887, issue 3, 48–49.
Bolshakoff, Serge, *Russian Nonconformity: The Story of Unofficial Religion in Russia*, Philadelphia, 1950.
Bolshakoff, Sergius, *Russian Mystics*, London, 1977.
Bonch-Bruevich, Vladimir, "Voina i sektanty," in *Sovremennyi mir*, December 1914, 102–15.
"Zhivaia tserkov'" i proletariat, Moscow, 1929.
Børtnes, Jostein, "Kristendommen i russisk litteratur indtil 1917," in *Svantevit* 1988, 2, 104–17.
Breitburg, S. M., "K tsenzurnoi istorii 'Skazki ob Ivane-durake' L. N. Tolstogo (po neizdannym materialam)," in Gusev, N. N., ed., *Tolstoi i o Tolstom*, Moscow, 1924, 87–95.
Bronnitskii, S., "Razgovory sredi druzei po povodu romana 'Voskresenie' L. N. Tolstogo," in *Missionerskoe obozrenie*, 1901, issue 3, 371–81; issue 4, 519–32; issue 9, 267–73; issue 10, 398–411.
Bronzov, Aleksandr, "Drug ili vrag Khristov – Tolstoi?," in *Khristianskoe chtenie*, 1912, issue 4, 463–82.

Bulgakov, N. "Pouchaiushchii koshchunnika nazhivet sebe bezslavie," in *Po povodu otpadeniia . . . Tolstogo*, op.cit. 1905, 177–86.

Bulgakov, Sergei, 1910, "Tolstoi i tserkov," in *Russkaia mysl'*, issue 12, 218–22.

"Samozashchita V.I. Ekzempliarskogo," in *Russkaia mysl'*, 1912a, issue 8, 39–40.

"L.N. Tolstoi," in *O religii Tolstogo op. cit.*, [1912] 1978a, 1–26.

"Die christliche Anthropologie," in Berdiaev, N., ed., *Kirche, Staat und Mensch. Russisch-orthodoxe Studien*, Genf, 1937, 209–55.

Bulgakov, Valentin, *Khristianskaia etika. Sistematicheskie ocherki mirovozzreniia Tolstogo*, Moscow, 1917.

Lev Tolstoi v poslednii god ego zhizni, Moscow, 1957.

Bunin, Ivan, "Osvobozhdenie Tolstogo," in *Sobranie* sochinenii vol IX, 7–38 Moscow, 1967.

Buss, Andreas E., *The Russian-Orthodox Tradition and Modernity*, Leiden, 2003.

Butkevich, Timofei, "Slovo v den' vosshestviia na prestol blagochestveishago Gosudaria Imperatora Aleksandra Aleksandrovicha. O lzheuchenii grafa L. N. Tolstogo," in *Vera i razum*, 1891, issue 1, part 1, 269–83.

"*Nagornaia propoved*," *Protiv Tolstogo*, Khar'kov, 1893.

Poslednee sochinenie grafa L. N. Tolstogo 'Tsarstvo Bozhie vnutri vas' (Kriticheskii razbor), Khar'kov, 1894.

"Tolstovstvo kak sekta," in Skvortsov, V., ed., *Deianiia 3-ogo Vserossiiskogo Missionerskogo s"ezda v Kazani po voprosam vnutrennem missii i raskolnichestva*, Kiev, 1897, 158–82.

Obzor russkikh sekt i ikh tolkov, Khar'kov, 1910, chapter 12: 'Tolstovstvo', 574–97.

Byford, Chas. T., *Peasants and Prophets (Baptist Pioneers in Russia, and South Eastern Europe)*, London, [1912] 2012.

Chadwick, Henry, *The Early Church*, Harmondsworth, 1978.

Charques, Richard, *The Twilight of Imperial Russia*, Oxford, 1958.

Chepurin, Nikolai, "Iz zhizni i ucheniia gr. L. N. Tolstogo," in *Vera i razum*, 1909, issue 19–20, 111–34.

Chertkov, Vladimir, *Ukhod Tolstogo*, Moscow, 1922.

Chetverikov, Sergii, *Opisanie zhizni . . . ieroskhimonakha Amvrosiia*, Kaluga, 1912.

Chisnikov, Vladimir, "Tainoe otpevanie na mogile L. N. Tolstogo 12 dekabria 1912 goda," in *Neva*, 2008, 9, 219–28.

Climacus, John, *Lestvitsa, Prepodobnago ottsa nashego Ioanna igumena Sinaiskoi gory*, [Sergiev Posad 1908] Jordanville, 1963.

Christian, Reginald, *Tolstoy: A Critical Introduction*, Cambridge, 1969.

Chrysostomus, Johannes, *Kommentar zum Evangelium des Hl. Mattaeus*, Munich, 1915.

Christoyannopoulos, Alexandre, "Leo Tolstoy's anticlericalism in its context and beyond: The case against churches and clerics, religious and secular," *Religions*, 2016, 7, 59, 1–20.

"The subversive potential of Leo Tolstoy's 'defamiliarisation': A case study in drawing on the imagination to denounce violence," *Critical Review of International Social and Political Philosophy*, 2019, 22, 5, 562–80.

Tolstoy's Political Thought: Christian Anarcho-Pacifist Iconoclasm Then and Now, Routledge, 2020.
Coates, Ruth, "The Light of the Truth': Russia's two enlightenments, with reference to Pavel Florenskii," in Michelson, Patrick Lally and Kornblatt, Judith Deutsch, eds., *Thinking Orthodox in Modern Russian: Culture, History, Context, Madison*, WI, 2014, 151–74.
Coleman, Heather J., "Theology on the ground: Dimitrii Bogoluibov, the Orthodox anti-Sectarian Mission, and the Russian Soul," in Michelson, Patrick Lally and Kornblatt, Judith Deutsch, eds., *Thinking Orthodox in Modern Russian: Culture, History, Context, Madison*, WI, 2014, 64–84.
Colliander, Tito, *Way of the Ascetics*, New York, 1985.
Corcoran, Donald (Sr.), "Spiritual guidance," in *Christian Spirituality. Origins to the Twelfth Century*, vol. 1, New York, 1985, 444–52.
Curtiss, John, *Church and State in Russia – the Last Years of the Empire – 1900-1917*, New York NY, 1940.
De Simone, Peter T., *The Old Believers in Imperial Russia: Oppression, Opportunism and Religious Identity in Tsarist Moscow*, London: Bloomsbury, 2019.
Dionysios, pseudo-, *O nebesnoi ierarkhii*, [Moscow 1898] Montréal 1974.
Dmitrievskii, I., "Lichnost' grafa Tolstogo i prichiny ego vliianiia na obshchestvo," *Vera i razum*, 1912, issue 10, 514–27; issue 11, 627–39, issue 12, 759–72.
Dobrotoliubie (Philokalia), I–IV vols, 5th ed., Moscow, 1851.
Dobrotoliubie (Philokalia), I–IV vols, Moscow, 1902.
Donahoo, Robert, "Towards a Definition of Resurrection: Tolstoy's Novel as Theology and Art," *Literature and Belief*, 1991, 1–12.
Donskov, Andrew, *Leo Tolstoy and the Canadian Doukhobors*, Ottawa, 2019.
Döpmann, Hans-Dieter, *Die Russische Orthodoxe Kirche in Geschichte und Gegenwart*, Berlin, 1981.
Dostoevskii, Fedor, *Polnoe sobranie sochinenii*, St. Petersburg, 1888.
Pis'ma, I–IV vols, Moscow, 1959.
Drozdov, N., "Tolstoi i tserkov'," in *Strannik*, 1911, issue 12, 781–84.
"Tseniteli Tolstogo," in *Strannik*, 1913, issue 4, 657–62.
Dunlop, John B., *Staretz Ambrosy: Model for Dostoevsky's Staretz Zossima*, Belmont, MA, 1972.
Eikhenbaum, Boris, *Lev Tolstoi: Semidesiatye gody*, Leningrad, 1960.
O literature: Raboty raznykh let, Moscow, 1987.
Ekzempliarskii, Vasilii, *Za chto menia osudili?*, Kiev, 1912.
"Gr. L. N. Tolstoi i sv. Ioann Zlatoust v ikh vzgliade na zhiznennoe znachenie zapovedei Khristovykh," in *O religii Tolstogo op. cit*[1912] 1978, 76–113.
Eleonskii, Nikolai, *O 'novom evangelii' gr. Tolstago*, 2nd ed., Moscow, 1889.
Engelstein, Laura, "Old and new, high and low: Straw Horsemen of Russian Orthodoxy," in Kivelson, Valerie A. and Greene, Robert H., eds., *Orthodox Russia: Belief and Practices under the Tsars*, University Park, 2003, 23–32.
"Ep. Parfenii o poezdke k L.N. Tolstomu," *Novoe Vremia*, November 10, 2010.

Ern, Vladimir, "Tolstoi protiv Tolstogo," in *O religii Tolstogo op. cit.*, 1978, 214–48.
"Eshche po povodu doklada v filosofskom obshchestve o gr. *L. N. Tolstom*," in *Missionerskoe obozrenie*, 1901, issue 4, 507–32.
Fischer, Claus M., *Lev N Tolstoj in Japan*, Wiesbaden, 1969.
Fedotov, George, *The Russian Religious Mind*, I–II vols, Belmont, MA, [1966] 1975.
ed., *A Treasury of Russian Spirituality*, London, [1950] 1981.
Feofan (Govorov), *Pis'ma o khristianskoi zhizni*, Moscow, [1860] 1880.
(Govorov), *Sobranie pisem*, I–VII vols, Moscow, 1898–1901.
Filaret (Drozdov), *Prostrannyi khristianskii katekhizis pravoslavnyia kafolicheskiia vostochnyia tserkvi*, [Moscow 1880] Jordanville, 1976.
Florovskii, Georgii, *Puti russkogo bogosloviia*, Paris, [1937] 1982.
Foster, John Burt Jr., *Transnational Tolstoy: Between the West and the World*, New York and London, 2013.
Fryszman, Alex, "Den russiske intelligentsia og glasnost," in Steffensen, Eigil, ed., *Magt og mening: Ruslands vej til ytringsfriheden*, Copenhagen, 1990, 39–72.
Fueloep-Miller, Rene, "Tolstoy the apostolic crusader," in *Russian Review*, 1960, 19, 2, 99–121.
Gasparov, Boris, "Introduction," in Nakhimovsky, Alexander D. and Nakhimovsky, Alice Stone, eds., *The Semiotics of Russian Culture*, Ithaca, 1985, 13–29.
George, Martin, "Gott," in George, Martin, Herlth, Jens, Münch, Christian and Schmid, Ulrich, eds, *Tolstoj als theologischer Denker und Kirchenkritiker*, Göttingen, 2014, 355–72.
"Lev Tolstoj – nichtchristlich oder christlich, konfessionslos oder orthodox?" in Flogaus, Reinhard and Wasmuth, Jennifer, eds., *Orthodoxie im Dialog: Historische und aktuelle Perspektiven*, Berlin, 2015, 197–250.
Givens, John, *The Image of Christ in Russian Literature: Dostoevsky, Tolstoy, Bulgakov, Pasternak*, DeKalb, 2018.
Gladkov, B. I., *Graf L. Tolstoi kak bogoiskatel'*, St Petersburg, 1914.
Glagolev, Feodor, "Gr. L. Tolstoi pri konchine rodnogo brata," in *Tul'skie eparkhial'nye vedomosti*, 1905, issue 19, 515–20.
Glagolev, Sergei, "Otsutstvie religioznago obrazovanie v sovremennom obshchestve," in *Bogoslovskii vestnik*, 1912, issue 10, 273–96.
Golubtsev, A. and Alekseev, Il'ia, *Polnoe razoblachenie iasnopolianskogo eretika*, St Petersburg, 1909.
Gorain, I., "O lzheuchenii L. Tolstogo. (K iubileiu L. Tolstogo)," in *Vera i razum*, 1908, issue 16, 535–39.
Gor'kii, Maksim, *Vospominaniia o L've Nikolaeviche Tolstom*, Peterburg, 1919.
Gorski, Philip, *Godseekers: Selected Literary and Theological Eessays: East and West*, Nottingham, 2019.
Goviadovskii, Ioann, "Uchenie sv. Ioanna Zlatousta o sobstvennosti," in *Dushepoleznoe chtenie*, 1906, issue 11, 412–28, issue 12, 523–42; 1907, issue 1, 101–13; issue 2, 196–208; issue 3, 372–88; issue 4, 605–13.

Greenwood, E. B., *Tolstoy: The Comprehensive Vision*, London, 1975.
Grigor'ev, Dmitrii, "O. Vasilii Zen'kovskii," in Poltoratskii, N. P., ed., *Russkaia religiozno-filosofskaia mysl' XX veka*, Pittsburg, 1975, 231–39.
Grigor'ev, I., "Khodish' i voskhishchaesh'sia," in *Ekaterinoslavskie eparkhial'nye vedomosti*, 1912, issue 4, 164–67.
Griniakin, N., "*Utverdi, Gospodi, tserkov*", St Petersburg, 1904.
Gruppa stolichnykh, sviashchennikov, "O neobkhodimosti peremen v russkom tserkovnom upravlenii," in *Tserkovnyi vestnik*, 1905, issue 11, 321–25.
Gusev, Aleksandr, "Lev Nikolaevich Tolstoi, ego ispoved' i mnimo-novaia vera," in *Pravoslavnoe obozrenie*, 1886, issue 1, 131–63; issue 2, 297–336; issue 3, 507–51; issue 4, 739–76; issue 5–6, 306–51; issue 9, 148–82; issue 10, 242–69; 1889, issue 10, 312–46; issue 11, 604–42; 1890, issue 1, 27–71; issue 2, 229–75; issue 4, 587–611.
O sushchnosti religiozno-nravstvennogo ucheniia L. N. Tolstogo, Kazan', 1902.
Gusev, Nikolai, *Letopis' zhizni i tvorchestva L'va Nikolaevicha Tolstogo 1891–1910*, Moscow, 1960.
L. N. Tolstoi. Materialy k biografii, s 1870 po 1881 god, Moscow, 1963.
L. N. Tolstoi. Materialy k biografii, s 1881 po 1885 god, Moscow, 1970.
Dva goda s L. N. Tolstym. Vospominaniia i dnevnik byvshego sekretaria L. N. Tolstogo 1907–1908, Moscow, 1973.
Gustafson, Richard F., *Leo Tolstoy: Resident and Stranger*, Princeton, 1986.
Haase, Felix, "Quellen der Weltanschauung L. N. Tolstojs," in *Jahrbücher für Kultur und Geschichte der Slaven*, 1928, 4, issue 2, 173–99.
Hägglund, Bengt, *Theologins historia. En dogmhistorisk översikt*, Lund, [1956] 1975.
Hamburg, G. M., "Tolstoy's Spirituality," in Orwin, Donna Tussing, ed., *Anniversary Essays on Tolstoy*, Cambridge, 2010, 138–58.
Harnack, Adolf von, *Das Mönchtum, seine Ideale und seine Geschichte*, Giessen, 1903.
Haupmann, Peter, *Die Katechismen der Russischen Orthodoxen Kirche*, Göttingen, 1971.
Hedda, Jennifer, *His Kingdom Come: Orthodox Pastorship and Social Activism in Revolutionary Russia*, DeKalb, IL, 2008.
Heier, Edmund, *Religious Schism in the Russian Aristocracy 1860-1900: Radstockism and Pashkovism*, The Hague 1970.
Ia., E., "Spravka po povodu tret'iago pechatnogo zaiavleniia iz sem'i Tolstykh," in *Po povodu otpadeniia .... Tolstogo, op. cit.*, 1905, 682–85.
Iastremskii, I., "Asketizm i khristianskaia liubov' i ikh vzaimootnoshenie," in *Vera i Razum*, 1913, issue 19, 37–54; issue 24, 819–36.
Ignatii (Malyshev), *Neskol'ko slov o tolkakh grafa L. N. Tolstogo*, St. Petersburg, 1888.
Il'menskii, Sergei, *Graf L. Tolstoi kak odin iz samykh iarkikh vyrazitelei dukha griadushchiago antikhrista*, Saratov, 1911.
Ioann (Shakhovskoi), *Tolstoi i tserkov'*, Berlin, 1939.

Ivanov, A. N., *O knizhkakh dlia naroda izdavaemykh firmoi 'Posrednik'*, Voronezh, 1886.

"Pis'mo k grafu L.Tolstomu," in *Tul'skie eparkhial'nye vedomosti*, 1901a, 257–72.

"Slovo v den' koronovaniia . . . Imperatora Nikolaia," in *Tul'skie eparkhial'nye vedomosti*, 1901b, 319–22.

"O grafe L've Tolstom," in *Tul'skie eparkhial'nye vedomosti*, 1901c, 507–11.

Ivanov, Sergei, *Blazhennye pokhaby: Kul'turnaia istoriia iurodstva*, Moscow, 2005.

Ivanovskii, N., "Graf Lev Nikolaevich Tolstoi i ego uchenie (Obshchii ocherk)," in *Po povodu otpadeniia . . . Tolstogo*, op. cit., 1905, 1–38.

"Iz materialov o L. N. Tolstom," *Krasnyi arkhiv*, 1923, 338–64.

Jahn, Gary R., "Tolstoj and Kant," in Gutsche, George J. and Leighton, Lauren G., eds, *New Perspectives on the Nineteenth-Century Russian Prose*, Columbus, OH, 1982, 60–70.

Jaspers, Karl, *Nietzsche og Kristendommen*, Oslo, [1938] 1977. Translated by Trond Berg Eriksen.

John (Damascenus), *Writings (Fathers of the church, volume 37)*, Washington, 1970.

Kadloubovsky, E. and Palmer, G. E. H. editors and translators, *Early Fathers from the Philokalia*, London, 1976 (6th impression).

Kadloubovsky, E. and Palmer, G. E. H. editors and translators, *Writing from the Philokalia on Prayer of the Heart*, London, 1977 (9th impression).

Kartashev, Anton, "Molitva o Tolstom," in *Russkoe slovo*, January 3, 1913.

Ocherki po istorii russkoi tserkvi, I–II vols, Paris, 1959.

Kazanskii, Dmitrii, "Dumy sel'skago sviashchennika po povodu smerti grafa L'va Nikolaevicha Tolstogo," in *Samarskie eparkhial'nye vedomosti*, 1910, issue 24, 1611–17.

Khilkov, Dmitrii, "Pis'ma k N. V. Kovalevu," in *Bogoslovskii vestnik*, June, 1916, 219–36.

Khitrov, Mikhail, *Khristianskii trud. Protiv stat'i gr. Tolstogo 'Nedelanie'*, Moscow, 1894.

Khomiakov, Aleksei, *Polnoe Sobranie Sochinenii*, I–VIII vols, Moscow, 1900–1914.

(Khrapovitskii), Antonii, se Antonii (Khrapovitskii).

Kizenko, Nadieszda, *The Prodigal Saint: father John of Kronstad and the Russian People*, University Park, PA, 2000.

Kline, George L., *Religious and Anti-Religious Thought in Russia*, Chicago, 1968.

(Kliucharev), Amvrosii, see Amvrosii (Kliucharev).

Koblov, Ia., "Graf L. N. Tolstoi i musul'mane," in *Pravoslavnyi sobesednik*, 1904, issue 4, 622–33; issue 6, 888–916.

Kohn, Hans, *Pan-Slavism: Its History and Ideology*, 2nd rev.ed., New York, 1960.

Kolstø, Pål, "Leo Tolstoy, A Church Critic influenced by Orthodox thought," in *Church, Nation and State in Russia and Ukraine (Studies in Russia and East Europe)*, London, 1991, 148–66.

Sannhet i løgn: Lev Tolstoj og den ortodokse tro, Acta Humaniora 14, Oslo: Scandinavian University press, 1997.

"A mass for a heretic? The controversy over Leo Tolstoi's Burial," in *Slavic Review*, 2000, 60, 1, 75-95.

"Orthodoxie,“ in George, Martin, Herlth, Jens, Münch, Christian and Schmid, Ulrich, eds., *Tolstoj als theologischer Denker und Kirchenkritiker*, Vandenhoeck & Ruprecht, 2014, 528–40.

"Konkurs na Makarievskuiu premiiu v Kievskoi Dukhovnoi Akademii,“ in *Trudy Kievskoi dukhovnoi akademii*, 1887, issue 11, 1–6, prilozhenie.

Konstantin (Zaitsev), arkhimandrit, "Tolstoi. K piatidesiatiletiiu ego konchiny," in *K piatidesiatiletiiu* . . ., op. cit., 1960, 3–26.

Kontsevich, Ivan, *Istoki dushevnoi katastrofy L. N. Tolstogo*, München, 1960.

Kornblatt, Judith Deutsch, "Soloviev on Salvation: The story of the 'Short Story of the Anti-Christ'," in Deutsch Kornblatt, Judith and Gustafson, Richard F., eds., *Russian Religious Thought*, Madison, 1996, 68–87.

Kovalev, I. F., "Bor'ba tsarizma i Tserkvi s L. N. Tolstym," *Voprosy istorii religii i ateizma. Sbornik stat'ei VIII*, Moscow, 1960.

Kovalevskii, Ioann, *Iurodstsvo vo Khriste i Khrista radi iurodivye vostochnoi i russkoi tserkvi*, Moscow, 1895.

Kozlov, Aleksander, *Religiia grafa L. N. Tolstogo, ego uchenie o zhizni i liubvi*, 2nd ed., St. Petersburg, 1895.

Kozubovskii, Stefan, *'Religiia i nauka': Sbornik statei protiv neveriia i tolstovstva*, Moscow, 1910.

K piatidesiatiletiiu konchiny L'va Tolstogo: Sbornik statei, Jordanville NY, 1960.

Kraniev, P., *'Otpevanie' grafa L. N. Tolstogo s evangel'skoi i tserkovnoi tochki zreniia. (Po povodu sovremennoi gazetnoi shumikhi)*, Riazan', 1913.

Kudriavtsev, N. P., "Uchenie Zlatousta o bogatstve i ego sotsial'nyi ideal," *Bogoslovskii vestnik*, 1907, issue 12, 85–97.

Kuliukin, S., "Otklik na nekotorie mysli grafa L. N. Tolstago v ego proizvedenii 'Chto takoe iskusstvo'," *Khristianskoe chtenie*, 1902, issue 6, 818–40.

Kurov, M. N., "Novye materialy ob otluchenii L. N. Tolstogo (k 150-letiiu so dnia rozhdeniia)," *Voprosy nauchnogo ateizma*, 1979, 24, 264–77.

Kuznetsov, Nikolai, "Vopros o molitve za gr. L. N. Tolstogo," in *Otdykh khristianina*, 1913, issue 5, 881–923.

Lebedev, A., "Vzgliad grafa L. N. Tolstogo na istoricheskuiu zhizn' Tserkvi Bozhiei," in *Bogoslovskii vestnik*, 1903, issue November, 394–417; 1904, issue January, 42–74.

Ledovskii, Sergei, *'Istinnyi oblik' L'va Tolstogo, nravstvennyi, religioznyi i politicheskii (po sochineniiam i po lichnoi zhizni)*, Saratov, 1911.

Lenin, Vladimir, *Lev Tolstoi kak zerkalo russkoi revoliutsii*, Moscow, 1973.

Levitskii, Sergei, "O. Sergii Bulgakov," in Poltoratskii, N. P., ed., *Russkaia religiozno-filosofskaia mysl' XX veka*, Pittsburg, 1975, 205–13.

Lialina, G. S., "Tsenzurnaia politika tserkvi v XIX – nachale XX v," in Klibanov, A. L., ed., *Russkaia pravoslavnaia tserkov', Vekhi istorii* Moscow, 1989, 463–500.

"L. N. Tolstoi (iz nashego korrespondenta)," *Novoe vremia*, November 10, 1910.

Lock, Charles, "Review of Richard Gustafson Leo Tolstoy: Resident and stranger," *St. Vladimir's Theological Quarterly*, 1987, 175–81.

Lomunov, K. N., 'Tolstoi i tserkovniki', preface to Pozoiskii, Semen, *K istorii otlucheniia L'va Tolstogo ot tserkvi*, Moscow, 1979, 1–8.

Losskii, Nikolai, "Tolstoi kak khudozhnik i myslitel'," *Sovremennye zapiski*, 1928, 37, 234–41.

Lossky, Vladimir, *The Mystical Theology of the Eastern Church*, London, [1957] 1973.

The Vision of God, New York, [1963] 1983.

Lotman, Jurij, 1985, "The Decembrists in daily life (everyday behavior as a historical-psychological category," in Nakhimovsky, Alexander D. and Stone Nakhimovsky, Alice, eds., *The Semiotics of Russian Culture*, Ithaca NY, 1985, 95–149.

"Problems in the typology of cultures," in Lucid, Daniel P., ed., *Soviet Semiotics: An Anthology*, Baltimore MD, 1988, 213–22.

Lotman, Jurij and Uspenskij, Boris, "Binary models in the dynamics of Russian culture (to the end of the eighteenth century," in Nakhimovsky, Alexander D. and Nakhimovsky, Alice Stone, eds., *The Semiotics of Russian Culture*, Ithaca NY, 1985, 30–66.

Lowrie, Donald, A., *A Rebellious Prophet: A Life of Nikolai Berdyaev*, New York NY, 1960.

M., "L. N. Tolstoi. Uchenie dvenadtsati Apostolov," in *Trudy Kievskoi dukhovnoi akademii*, 1906, issue 1, 694–700.

M. B., Antonii, *Mitropolit S-Peterburgskii i ladozhskii*, no place given, 1915.

M., I., "Pod vliianiem idei velikogo russkogo pisatelia," in *Missionerskii sbornik*, 1904, issue 2, 89–102; issue 4, 273–87.

M, Mirianin, *Mysli i razsuzhdeniia po povodu broshiury L'va Tolstago pod zaglaviem 'Ma religion'*, Sedlets, 1888.

Maevskii, Vladislav, *Tragediia bogoiskatel'stva L'va Tolstogo*, Buenos Aires, 1952.

Vnutrenniaia missiia i ee osnovopolozhnik, Buenos Aires, 1954.

Makarii (Bulgakov), *Pravoslavno-dogmaticheskoe bogoslovie*, I–II, 5th ed., St. Petersburg, 1895.

Makkaveiskii, Nikolai, *Pedagogicheskie vozzreniia grafa L. N. Tolstogo*, Kiev, 1902.

Lev Tolstoi v roli religioznago nastavnika detei, Kiev, 1909.

Makovitskii, Dushan, *U Tolstogo 1904–1910: 'Iasnopolianskie zapiski'*, Moscow, 1979.

Maksimov, Sergei, *Brodiachaia Rus' Khrista radi*, St. Petersburg, 1877.

Sibir' i katorga, St. Petersburg, 1891.

Maloney, George S. J., *A History of Orthodox Theology Since 1453*, Belmont MA, 1976.

Markovitch, Milan, *J.-J. Rousseau et Tolstoi*, Paris, 1928.

Matveev, Dmitrii, *Pravoslavnaia tserkov' v otnoshenii k otluchennym voobshche i gr. L. N. Tolstomu v chastnosti*, Tobol'sk, 1901.

Matveev, Pavel, "L. N. Tolstoi i N. N. Strakhov v Optinoi Pustyni," in *Istoricheskii vestnik*, 1907, issue 4, 151–57.
Maude, Aylmer, *Tolstoy and His Problems*, London, 1905.
The Life of Tolstoy, 2 vols, Oxford, [1908–10] 1987.
McLean, Hugh, *In quest of Tolstoy*, Boston MA, 2010.
Meilakh, Boris, *Ukhod i smert' L'va Tolstogo*, Moscow, [1960] 1979.
Men'shikov, Mikhail, "Urok molodezhi,"*Novoe vremia*, November 9, 1910.
Medzhibovskaya, Inessa, *Tolstoy and the Religious Culture of His Time: A Biography of a Long Conversion, 1845–1887*, Lanham, 2009.
Merezhkovskii, Dmitrii, "Revoliutsiia i religiia," in *Russkaia mysl*, 1907, issue 2, 64–85; issue 3, 17–34.
Meyendorff, John, *Byzantine Theology. Historical Trends and Doctrinal Themes*, New York NY, 1974.
Michelson, Patrick Lally and Kornblatt, Judith Deutsch, "Introduction," in Michelson, Patrick Lally and Kornblatt, Judith Deutsch, eds., *Thinking Orthodox in Modern Russian: Culture, History, Context*, Madison WI, 2014, 3–39.
Michelson, Patrick Lally, *Beyond the Monastery Walls: The Ascetic Revolution in Russian Orthodox Thought, 1814–1914*, Madison WI, 2017.
Mikhail (Semenov), "Mysli o boge. L. N. Tolstoi," in *Missionerskoe obozrenie*, 1902, issue September, 353–59.
Mikhailovskii, Nikolai, "Eshche o gr. L. N. Tolstom," in *Severnyi vestnik*, 1886, issue 6, 197–216.
Miliukov, Pavel, *Ocherki po istorii russkoi kul'tury*, I–III, Petrograd, 1909–16.
Miller, Orest, *Russkie pisateli posle Gogolia*, St. Petersburg, 1886.
Mironenko, Aleksandr, "Dostoino i pravedno (Po povodu otlucheniia grafa L. N. Tolstogo ot Tserkvi . . .)," in *Po povodu otpadenie . . . Tolstogo*, op. cit. 1905, 219–43.
Mochul'skii, Konstantin, *Vladimir Solov'ev. Zhizn' i uchenie*, Paris, 1951.
Møller, Peter Ulf, *Efterspil til Kreutzersonaten. Tolstoj og kønsmoraldebatten i russisk litteratur i 1890erne*, København, 1983.
M-ov, V., "Smert' L. N. Tolstogo," in *Staroobracheskaia mysl*, 1910, 704–07.
Muretov, Mitr., "Khristianin bez Khrista," in *Dushepoleznoe chtenie*, 1893, issue 3, 370–85.
N., F.: "Po prochtenii pis'ma grafini S. A. Tolstoi," in *Po povodu otpadeniia . . . Tolstogo*, op. cit., 1905, 80–81.
"Nepostizhimoe vmeshatel'stvo," in *Novoe vremia*, August 23, 1908.
Nichols, Robert L., "The Orthodox elders (Startsy) of Imperial Russia," *Modern Greek Studies Yearbook*, 1985, 1, 1–30.
Nickell, William, "Transfiguration's of Tolstoy's final journey: The church and the media in 1910," *Tolstoy Studies Journal*, 2006, 18, 32–51.
The Death of Tolstoy: Russia on the Eve, Astapovo Station 1910, Ithaca NY, 2010.
Nietzsche, Friedrich, *Werke*, I–V vols, Munich, 1979.
Nikanorov, I., "Pedagogicheskiia vozzreniia gr. Tolstogo pred sudom razuma, prosveshchennago istinoiu Khristovoiu," in *Vera i tserkov'*, 1900, issue 8, 365–97.

Nikiforov, Lev, *Poucheniia sv. Ioanna Zlatousta. Izvlecheniia iz ego besed*, Moscow, 1888.

Nikol'skii, Aleksandr, "L. N. Tolstoi pred sudom pokoinago filosofa Vl. S. Solov'eva," in *Missionskii sbornik*, 1910, 2, 109–18.

"Lev Tolstoi i russkaia intelligentsiia v eia pogone za kumirami," in *Missionerskii sbornik*, 1911, issue 5, 371–86; issue 6, 407–18; issue 7–8, 487–96; issue 10, s.731–53; issue 12, 901–18; 1912, issue 1, 29–39; issue 3, 198–218; issue 4, 302–17; issue 5, 380–93; issue 7–8, 603–16; issue 12, 1020–31.

Nikol'skii, Nikolai, *Istoriia Russkoi Tserkvi*, Moscow, 1983.

Nikon (Rozhdestvenskii), "Iz dnevnika . . . ," in *Moskovskie tserkovnye vedomosti*, 1910, issue 50, 895–901; issue 51–52, 924–34.

[Novikov, Valentin], *Il'ia Glazunov: Vechnaia Rossiia*, Moscow, 1994.

Novoselov, Mikhail, "Otkrytoe pis'mo grafu L. N. Tolstomu ot byvshago ego edinomyshlennika, po povodu otveta na postanovlenie Sviateishago Sinoda," in *Po povodu otpadeniia . . . Tolstogo*, op. cit., 1905, 113–25.

Nygren, Anders, *Filosofi och motivforskning*, Stockholm, 1940.

Nyström, Teodor, *Chrysostomi etik. Det sedligas accentuering i homiliarne*, Lund, 1911.

Oberländer, Erwin, *Tolstoj und die revolutionäre Bewegung*, Munich, 1965.

"Obozrenie zhurnal'nykh statei i otdel'nykh izdanii po povodu poslaniia Sv. Sinoda o gr. L. Tolstom," in *Vera i tserkov'*, 1901, issue 8, 519–30.

Olesnitskii, Akim, "Slovo ob istinnom i lozhnom zlu neprotivlenii (Po povodu prevratnago tolkovaniia na Matv 5,39, v uchenii grafa L. Tolstogo)," in *Trudy kievskoi dukhovnoi akademii*, 1892, issue 4, 521–36.

"Po povodu novago proizvedeniia grafa L. Tolstogo," in *Tserkovnye vedomosti*, 1895, issue 16, pribavlenie, 545–51.

Ol'shevskii, Iust, "Slovo v nedel'iu krestopoklonnuiu, po povodu lzheucheniia grafa L'va Tolstogo," *Poltavskie eparkhial'nye vedomosti*, 1901, issue 9, 389–92.

"Opredelenie Sv. Sinoda ot 20–22 fevralia 1901 goda, s poslaniem vernym chadam Pravoslavnyia Grekorossiiskiia Tserkvi o grafa L've Nikolaeviche Tolstom," in *Tserkovnye vedomosti*, 1901, issue 8, 46–48.

"Opredeleniie Sviateishago Sinoda. I. Ot 20-ogo avgusta sego goda za Nr.5492, po voprosu o gotoviashchemsia chestvovanii dnia rozhdeniia grafa L'va Nikolaevicha Tolstogo," in *Tserkovnye vedomosti*, 1908, issue 34, 270–72.

Opul'skaia, Lidiia, "Predislovie," in Petrov, G. I., *Otluchenie L'va Tolstogo ot tserkvi*, Moscow, 1978.

Orekhanov, Georgii, "Novye materialy po povodu otlucheniia L. N. Tolstogo," *Istoricheskii Arkhiv*, 2005, issue 3, 164–77.

Russkaia Pravoslavnaia tserkov' i Lev Tolstoi, Moscow, 2010.

Lev Tolstoi. 'Prorok bez chesti': Khronika katastrofy, Moscow, 2016.

O religii Tolstogo, Sbornik statei, [Moscow 1912] Paris, 1978.

Orfano, Aleksandr, *V chem dolzhna zakliuchat'sia istinnaia vera kazhdago cheloveka? (Kriticheskii razbor knigi gr. L. N. Tolstogo 'V chem moia vera')*, Moscow, 1890.

Orwin, Donna Tussing, *Tolstoi's Art and Thought: 1847–1880*, Princeton, 1993.

Ostroumov, N., "K voprosu o postanovke pamiatnika gr. L. N. Tolstomu. (Po povodu gazetnykh slukhov," in *Missionerskii Sbornik*, 1914, issue 3, 173–76.

Ostroumov, Stefan, "Religioznoe i nravstvennoe uchenie L. N. Tolstogo v ikh polozhitel'nom znachenii," in *Otdykh khristianina*, 1916, issue 1, 116–30; issue 2, 118–22; issue 3, 178–93; issue 5–6, 131–55; issue 7–8, 211–18; issue 10, 152–65.

"O vneshnykh obriadakh Pravoslaviia (Po povodu lzheucheniia grafa Tolstogo)," *Kormchii*, 1902, issue 4, 55–57.

P., I., "Carfhago elenda est! (sic)," in *Voronezhskie eparkhial'nye vedomosti*, 1912, issue 46, 1344–46.

Palimpsestov, Ivan, "Novyi razskaz grafa L. N. Tolstogo," in *Moskovskie tserkovnye vedomosti*, 1886a, issue 20, 302–03.

"Neskol'ko slov po povodu 'Ispovedi' grafa L. N. Tolstago," in *Strannik*, 1886b, issue 4, 800–14.

"Vlast' t'my: Drama L'va Tolstogo," in *Moskovskie tserkovnye vedomosti*, 1887, issue 10, 159–61.

Pamiati L. N. Tolstogo: Otkliki stolichnoi pechati poslednikh dnei, St. Petersburg, 1911.

Pankratov, Aleksandr, "Na mogile Tolstogo," *Russkoe slovo*, December 21, 1912.

Paperni, Vladimir M., "The transformation of the mystical tradition in Tolstoy's art and religious thought¨," in Medzhibovskaya, Inessa, ed., *Tolstoy and His Problems: Views from the Twenty-First-Century*, Evanston IL, 2019, 59–88.

Paperno, Irina, "Leo Tolstoy's correspondence with Nikolai Strakhov: The dialogue on faith," Orwin, Donna Tussing, ed., *Anniversary Essays on Tolstoy*, Cambridge, 2010, 96–119.

"Who, what am I?": Tolstoy Struggles to Narrate the Self, Ithaca and London, 2014.

Parfenii, *Skazanie o stranstvii i puteshestvii po Rossii, Moldavii, Turtsii i Sviatoi Zemle*, Moscow, 1855.

Pärt, Irina, *Spiritual Elders: Charisma and Tradition in Russian Orthodoxy*, DeKalb IL, 2010.

Rancour, David, "The human image divine: Tolstoy's Anthropic theology," in *Christianity & Literature*, 1990, Autumn, 23–36.

Pentkovsky, Aleksei, "Introduction," in *The Pilgrim's Tale*, New York NY, 1989, 1–36.

Petr (Mogila), *Pravoslavnoe ispovedanie katolicheskoi i apostolskoi tserkvi vostochnoi*, 12th ed., Moscow, 1841.

Petrov, G. I., *Otluchenie L'va Tolstogo ot tserkvi*, Moscow, 1978.

Petrov, Grigorii Spiridonovich, *Zakonchennyi krug: Pamiati L'va Nikolaevicha Tolstogo*, St. Petersburg, 1911.

Philipp, Franz-Heinrich, *Tolstoj und der Protestantismus*, Giessen, 1959.

Pickford, Henry W., *Thinking with Tolstoy and Wittgenstein: Expression, Emotion, and Art*, Evanston, 2016.

"Pis'ma K. P. Pobedonostseva k redaktoru 'Tserkovnykh vedomostei' P. Smirnovu ob otluchenii Tolstogo ot tserkvi," in *L. N. Tolstoi, Letopisi gosudarstvenngo muzeia*, Moscow, '1938, 208–09'.

Platon (Levshin), *The Orthodox Doctrine of the Apostolic Eastern Church, or a Compendium of Christian Theology*, New York, [1775] 1969.

Plekhanov, Gennadii, "Smeshenie predstavlenii (Uchenie L. N. Tolstogo)," in *Ob ateizme i religii v istorii obshchestva i ku'ltury*, Moscow, 1977, 311–33.

Ponomarev, Aleksandr, "Tserkovno-narodnyia legendy 'O sudakh Bozhiikh ne ispytaemykh' i razskaz gr. L. N. Tolstogo 'Chem liudi zhivy'," in *Strannik*, 1894, issue 1, 36–49.

Po povodu otpadeniia ot pravoslavnoi tserkvi grafa L'va Nikolaevicha Tolstogo. Sbornik statei "Missionerskago obozreniia," St. Petersburg, 1905.

"Po povodu poslaniia Sviateishago Sinoda o grafe L've Tolstom," in *Tserkovnye vedomosti*, 1901, issue 16, pribavlenie, 562–76.

Popovskii, Mark, *Russkie muzhiki rasskazyvaiut ... Posledovateli L. N. Tolstogo v Sovetskom Soiuze*, London, 1983.

Poslanie patriarkhov vostochno-kafolicheskiia tserkvi o pravoslavnoi very, n.d., no publisher.

Poslednie dni L'va Nikolaevicha Tolstogo, St. Petersburg, 1910.

"Poslednie izvestiia," *Simbirskie eparkhial'nye vedomosti*, 1910, issue 22, 733–36.

Pospelov, Ioann, *Razbor ucheniia L'va Nikolaevicha Tolstogo o vere i pravilakh zhizni cheloveka*, Kostroma, 1898.

Pospielovsky, Dimitry, *The Russian church under the Soviet regime 1917–1982*, I–II vols, Crestwood NY, 1984.

Pozoiskii, Semen, *Lev Tolstoi i tserkov'*, Tula, 1963.

K istorii otlucheniia L'va Tolstogo ot tserkvi, Moscow, 1979.

Pravoslavnyi, "Iazvy nashego vremeni," in *Dushepoleznoe chtenie*, 1901, issue 6, 327–33.

Pravoslavnyi, "Otkrytoe pis'mo k grafini S. A. Tolstoi," in *Po povodu otpadeniia ... Tolstogo*, op. cit., 1905, 72–79.

Pravoslavnyi mirianin, *Mysli po povodu vyskazannykh religioznykh vozzrenii grafa L'va Nikolaevicha Tolstogo*, St.Pb. 1901a.

"Komu zhe verit' i gde pravda? (Po povodu dvukh pisem grafa i grafini Tolstykh)," in *Tul'skie eparkhial'nye vedomosti*, 1901b, 649–66.

Prebsting, Liubov', "O neobkhodimosti obshchestvennykh tserkovnykh molitv za grafa Tolstogo i drugikh otstupnikov," in *Po povodu otpadeniia ... Tolstogo*, op. cit., 1905, 198–204.

Preobrazhenskii, Fedor, *Uchenie L. N. Tolstogo o smysle zhizni po sudu khristianstva*, Moscow, 1898.

"Preosviashchennyi Parfenii ob 'ukhode' L. N. Tolstogo," in *Russkoe Slovo*, November 3, 1910, issue 253.

Prugavin, Aleksandr, *Monastyrskie tiur'my v bor'be s sektanstvom*, Moscow, 1906.

"Publikatsii: Borba tsarizma i tserkvi s L. N. Tolstym," *Voprosy istorii religii i ateizma*, 1960, 348–76.

Pushkin, Aleksandr, "Strannik," in *Sobranie sochinenii*, I–IX vols, Moscow, 1974, II, 365–67.

Pustynnozhitel', "Starchestvo," in *Dushepoleznoe chtenie*, 1906, issue 2, 210–21.

Quiskamp, Robert, *Die Beziehungen L. N. Tolstojs zu den Philosophen des deutschen Idealismus*, Emsdetten, 1930.

Der Gottesbegriff bei Tolstoj, Emsdetten, 1937.

Rancour-Laferriere, Daniel, *Tolstoy's Quest for God*, New Brunswick NJ and London, 2007.

Rklitskii, Nikon, *Kratkoe zhizneopisanie blazhennogo Antoniia, Mitropolita Kievskago i Galitskago*, Belgrade, 1935.

Robinson, Douglas, "Tolstoy's infection theory and the aesthetics of de- and repersonalization," *Tolstoy Studies Journal*, 2007, 19, 33–53.

Romashkov, D. I., *O dukhovnoi smerti i dukhovnom voskresenii grafa L. N. Tolstogo*, Moscow, 1902.

Roslof, Edward E., *Red Priests: Renovationism, Russian Orthodoxy and the Revolution, 1905–1946*, Bloomington and Indianapolis, 2002.

Rovner, Arkadii, "V. F. Ern," in Poltoratskii, N. P., ed., *Russkaia religiozno-filosofskaia mysl' XX veka*, Pittsburg, 1975, 385–91.

Rozanov, Vasilii, "Seriia nedorazumeniia," *Novoe vremia*, 1901, February 16.

Temnyi lik: Metafizika khristianstva, [St. Petersburg, 1911] Wirzburg, 1975.

Rozenberg, S., "Iurodstvo i fariseistvo. K polemike s L'vom Tolstym," *Russkoe bogatstvo*, 1886, issue 10, 63–82.

(Rozhdestvenskii) Nikon, see Nikon (Rozhdestvenskii).

Rozhdestvin, Aleksandr, *Spravedlivy-li obvineniia vozvodimyia grafom L'vom Tolstym na pravoslavnuiu tserkov' v ego sochinenii "Tserkov' i gosudarstvo"*, Khar'kov, 1889.

"'Khristianstvo' grafa L'va Tolstogo," in *Chteniia v obshchestve liubitelei dukhovnogo prosveshcheniia*, 1892, issue February, otdel II, 81–144.

Ryan, W. F. "Magic and divination: Old Russian sources," in Rosenthal, Bernice Glatzer, ed., *The Occult in Russian and Soviet Culture*, Ithaca, 1997, 35–58.

Ryshkovskii, N., *Bratskoe slovo L. N. Tolstomu*, Kiev, 1888.

Scherrer, Jutta, *Die Peterburger religiös-philosophischen Vereinigungen*, Berlin, 1973.

Schmid, Ulrich, *Lew Tolstoi*, Munich, 2010.

"Islam," in George, Martin, Herlth, Jens, Münch, Christian and Schmid, Ulrich, eds., *Tolstoj als theologischer Denker und Kirchenkritiker*, Göttingen, 2014, 571–74.

Seludiakov, I., "Russkii narod i graf L. N. Tolstoi. (Golos iz naroda)," in *Missionerskii sbornik*, 1913, issue 7–8, 718–22.

Sergii (Stragorodskii), "Otzyv ... o novoi ispovedi grafa L. Tolstogo," in *Po povodu otpadeniia ... Tolstogo*, op. cit., 1905, 96–103.

"Kak pravoslavnyi khristianin dolzhen otnestis' k predstoiashchemu chestvovaniiu grafa Tolstogo?," in *Tserkovnye vedomosti*, 1908, issue 304 pribavlenie, 1619–22.

Sergiev, Ioann (Kronshtadtskii), *O. Ioann Kronshtadtskii o dushepogubnom ereticheste grafa L. N. Tolstogo*, St. Petersburg, 1907.
Otvet o. Ioanna Kronshtadtskago na obrashchenie gr. L. N. Tolstogo k dukhovenstvu: Prisnopamiatnyi Otets Ioann Kronshtadtskii i Lev Tolstoi, Jordanville (USA), 1960.
Shestov, Lev, *Umozrenie i otkrovenie*, Paris, 1964.
Shevzov, Vera, *Russian Orthodoxy on the Eve of the Revolution*, Oxford, 2004.
Shifman, A. I., *Lev Tolstoi i vostok*, Moscow, 1971.
Shishkin, Mikhail, "But to continue the life – for what purpose?," in Cicovacki, Predrag and Grek, Heidi Nada, eds., *Tolstoy and Spirituality*, Boston MA, 2018, 1–15.
Shklovskii, Viktor, *Lev Tolstoi*, Moscow, [1963] 1971.
Shubin, Daniel H., *Monastery Prisons: The History of Monasteries as Prisons, the Inmates Incarcerated There*, 2001.
Silin, Dmitrii, "Tragizm Tolstovstva i mir Evangeliia," in *Po povodu otpadeniia . . . Tolstogo*, op. cit., 1905, 422–41.
Simmons, Ernest J., *Leo Tolstoy*, London, 1947.
Dostoevsky: The Making of a Novelist, New York NY, 1962.
Introduction to Tolstoy's Writings, Chicago IL, 1969.
Sinod mstit Tolstogo anafemoi. Po povodu otlucheniia, Garouge-Genève, 1900.
Skvortsov, Dmitrii, "Tragediia dushi L. N. Tolstogo (Po povodu 'ukhoda' i smerti ego)," in *Tul'skie eparkhial'nye vedomosti*, 1911, issue 1–2, 8–18.
Skvortsov, Vasilii, *Dukhobory v Amerike i graf L. N. Tolstoi*, St. Petersburg, 1900.
Graf Lev Tolstoi i Sviateishii Sinod, Berlin, 1901a.
"Novaia ispoved' grafa L. N. Tolstogo. Neskol'ko predvaritel'nykh zamechanii," in *Missionerskoe obozrenie*, 1901b, issue June, 797–805.
"So skrizhalei serdtsa," in *Missionerskoe obozrenie*, 1902a, issue March, 612–20.
"So skrizhalei serdtsa: Graf Tolstoi o svobode sovesti i veroterpimosti," in *Missionerskoe obozrenie*, 1902b, issue April, 798–.812.
'So skrizhalei serdtsa' in *Missionerskoe obozrenie*, 1903 issue 17, 960-974.
"Predislovie izdatelia," in *Po povodu otpadeniia . . . Tolstogo*, op cit., 1905a, IX–XIV.
"Kak i kogda sovershilos' otpadenie gr. L'va Nik. Tolstogo ot pravoslavnoi tserkvi," in *Po povodu otpadeniia . . . Tolstogo*, op. cit., 1905b, 39–52.
"Kak otnosilas' pravoslavnaia Tserkov' k religioznomu bluzhdeniiu gr. Tolstogo," in *Po povodu otpadeniia . . . Tolstogo*, op. cit., 1905c, 53–62.
Smert' Tolstogo po novym materialam, Moscow, 1929.
Smirnov, S., "Ispoved' mirian pred startsam," in *Bogoslovskii vestnik*, 1905, issue September, 1–38.
Smirnov-Platonov, Grigorii, "Novoe proizvedenie grafa L. N. Tolstogo," in *Bogoslovskii vestnik*, 1896, issue 4, 129–32.
Smolenskii, N., "Tragediia very," in *Otdykh khristianina*, 1910, issue 12, 875–891.
Smolitsch, Igor, *Leben und Lehre der Starzen*, Wien, 1936.
Sofronii, priest-monk, *Ob osnovakh pravoslavnogo podvizhnichestva*, Paris, 1953.

Sokolov, A., "V zashchitu tserkovnykh molitvoslov," in *Vera i tserkov'*, 1904, issue 1, 64–90; issue 2, 227–60.

Sollertinskii, Sergei, Ob'iasnenie *Mf. V, 22; V, 38–42; VII, 1. Luk. VI, 37 u grafa Tolstogo*, St. Petersburg, 1887.

Solonikio, A., "Religiozno-filosofskiia vozzreniia gr. L. N. Tolstogo i ikh psikhologicheskii genezis," in *Vera i tserkov'*, 1901, issue 7, 316–44; issue 8, 491–504; issue 9, 659–84; issue 10, 851–74; 1902, issue 3, 473–96; issue 4, 609–29; issue 6, 83–116; issue 9, 591–619; issue 10, 758–92.

Solov'ev, Ioann, "Poslanie sviateishago sinoda o grafe L've Tolstom. (Opyt raskrytiia ego smysla i znacheniia)," in *Vera i tserkov'*, 1901, issue 4, 525–557.

Solov'ev, Vladimir, "Zametka po povodu novykh khristian," in *Rus'*, 1883, issue May, 39–43.

"Tri razgovora," in *Sobranie Sochinenii*, I–VIII vols, St. Petersburg, 1903, 453–586.

"Rossiia i Vselenskaia Tserkov'," in his *O khristianskom edinstve*, [Paris, 1889] Brussels, 1967, 249–383.

Sopots'ko, Mikhail, "Po povodu Iubileia 'grafa L. N. Tolstogo'," *Student-khristianin*, 1908, issue 11–12, 29–30.

Sorokin, Boris, *Tolstoy in Prerevolutionary Russian Criticism*, Columbus OH, 1979.

Spasskii, M. I. (pseudonym), "Lev Tolstoi i khristianskii brak," in Sharapov, Sergei, ed., *Sushchnost' braka*, Moscow, 1901, 14–33.

Spence, G. W., *Tolstoy, the Ascetic*, London, 1967.

Spiritual Regulation of Peter the Great, Seattle WA and London, 1972. Translated by Alexander V. Muller.

Spiro, Sergei, "L. N. Tolstoi i episkop Parfenii," *Russkoe slovo*, February 5, 1909.

"Sredi gazet i zhurnalov," *Novoe vremia*, November 11, 1910.

Sreznevskii, V. I., "L. N. Tolstoi v Peterburge v fevrale 1897 (po dannym Peterburgskogo Okhrannogo Otdeleniia," in Sreznevskii, V. I., ed., *Tolstoi. Pamiatniki tvorchestva i zhizni*, IV vols, Moscow, 1923.

Steinberg, Mark D. "'A path of thorns': The spiritual wounds and wandering of worker-poets," in Steinberg, Mark D. and Coleman, Heather J., eds., *Sacred Stories: Religion and Spirituality in Modern Russia*, Bloomington and Indianapolis, Indiana University press, 304–29.

Stepanov, I., *O "Zhivoi tserkvi"*, Moscow, 1922.

(Stragorodskii) Sergii, see Sergii (Stragorodskii).

Strakhov, Nikolai, *Perepiska L. N. Tolstogo s N. N. Strakhovym 1870–1894*, St. Petersburg, 1914.

Strakhov, Sergii, "Rokovoi punkt v religioznom lzheuchenii grafa L. N. Tolstogo (Otritsanie tserkvi so vsemi eia ustanovleniiami)," in *Vera i tserkov'*, 1903, issue 1, 30–47; issue 2, 173–88.

Strannika, otkrovennye rasskazy dukhovnomu svoemu ottsu, [Kazan' 1880–84] Paris, 1973.

Sukhotina-Tolstaia, Tat'iana, *Vospominaniia*, Moscow, [1932] 1981.

Suvorin, Aleksei, *Dnevnik*, Moscow, [1923] 1992.
Svod zakonov Rossiiskoi Imperii, St. Petersburg, 1857.
Szamuely, Tibor, *The Russian Tradition*, New York, 1975.
Szeftel, Marc, "Church and state in Imperial Russia," in Nichols, Robert L. and Stavrou, Theofanis George, eds., *Russian Orthodoxy under the Old Regime*, Minneapolis MN, 1978, 127–41.
T., P.P., "Otkrytoe pis'mo gr. L. N. Tolstomu," in *Po povodu otpadeniia . . . Tolstogo*, op. cit., 172–73.
Tal'berg, Nikolai, "Smert' gr. L. N. Tolstogo po ofitsial'nym doneseniiam," in *Pravoslavnaia Rus'*, 1956, issue 10, 5–7.
Teresa of Avila, "The life . . . ," in *The Complete Works*, 1 vol, London, [before 1567] 1963.
Terletskii, B., *Po povodu poslaniia sv. sinoda o gr. L've Tolstom*, Poltava, 1901. Printed also in *Poltavskie eparkhial'nye vedomosti*, 1901, issue 9, 402–10, issue 11, 525–43.
Thunberg, Lars, "The human being as image of God: I. Eastern Christianity," in McGinn, Bernard and Meyendorff, John, eds., *Christian Spirituality: Origins to the Twelfth century*, New York, 1985, 291–311.
Tikhomirov, Lev, "Novye plody ucheniia grafa L. Tolstogo," in *Missionerskoe obozrenie*, 1897, issue 1, 46–63.
"Iz dnevnika L. Tikhomirova," *Krasnyi arkhiv*, 1936, issue 74, 162–91.
Tkachenko, Aleksandr, "Prokliat'e, kotorogo ne bylo.Tserkov' i Tolstoi: Istoriia otnoshenii," *Pravoslavie i mir*, www.pravmir.ru/proklyate-kotorogo-ne-bylo cerkov-i-tolstoj-istoriya-otnoshenij/ January 13, 2006.
Tolstaia, Aleksandra Andreevna, *Perepiska L. N. Tolstogo s. gr. A. A. Tolstoi*, St. Petersburg, 1911.
Tolstaia, Aleksandra L'vovna, "Ob ukhode i smerti L. N. Tolstogo," in Sreznevskii, V. I., ed., *Tolstoi: Pamiatniki tvorchestva i zhizni*, vol IV Moscow, 1923, 131–84.
Tolstoy: A Life of My Father, Belmont MA, 1975.
Tolstaia, Sof'ia Andreevna, "Pis'mo k mitropolitu Antoniiu," reprinted in *Po povodu otpodeniia*, 1905, 67–69.
Pis'ma k L. N. Tolstomu 1862–1910, Moscow, 1936.
Dnevniki, I–II vols, Moscow, 1978.
Tolstoi, Il'ia, *Moi vospominaniia*, Moscow, [1913] 1969.
Tolstoi, Lev, *Mysli o boge*, Berlin, 1901.
Pis'ma k dukhobortsam, Berlin, 1902.
Polnoe sobranie sochinenii, Moscow, 1912–13.
Tolstoi, Lev, PSS, *Polnoe sobranie sochinenii: Iubileinoe izdanie*, Moscow, 1930–72. (The standard reference version of Tolstoi's collected works).
"Tolstovstvo kak sekta," in *Missionerskoe obozrenie*, 1897, issue 9–10, 807–31.
Troitskii, Dmitrii, *Pravoslavno-pastyrskoe uveshchanie grafa L. N. Tolstogo*, Sergiev Posad, 1913.
Troitskii, Vladimir, "Uchenie grafa L. N. Tolstogo o 'smysle zhizni', in *Pravoslavnoe obozrenie*, 1891, issue 2, 337–68.

Troyat, Henri, *Tolstoy*, Harmondsworth, 1980.

Trubetskoi, Evgenii, "Spor Tolstogo i Solov'eva o gosudarstve," in *O religii Tolstogo*, [Paris 1978] Moscow, 1912, 59–75.

Trubetskoi, Grigorii, *Krasnaia Rossiia i sviataia Rus'*, Paris, 1931.

Trubetskoi, Sergei, "Vladimir Solov'ev: Tri razgovora . . . ," in *Voprosy psikhologii i filosofii*, 1900, issue May-June, 358–63.

"Tsarskoe dostoinstvo Iisusa Khrista. Otvet E. Renanu i L. Tolstomu," *Pravoslavnoe obozrenie*, 1889, issue 4, 778–808.

"Tserkovnoe obozrenie," in *Otdykh khristianina*, 1910, issue 11, 733–42.

Tsvetkov, Zosima, "'Mysli o zhizni' grafa L. N. Tolstogo. Kriticheskii razbor," in *Blagovest'*, 1892, issue May, 1183–228.

Ulam, Adam, *In the Name of the People: Prophets and Conspirators in Prerevolutionary Russia*, New York NY, 1977.

Uspenskij, Boris, "Historia sub specie semiotica," in Lucid, Daniel P., ed., *Soviet Semiotics, An Anthology*, Baltimore MD, 1988, 107–16.

V., D., "Ushel . . . ," in *Moskovskie Tserkovnye Vedomosti*, 1910, issue 45, 809–14.

V., E., "L. N. Tolstoi i Optina Pustyn'," in *Dushepoleznoe chtenie*, 1911, issue 1, 19–27.

(Vadkovskii), Antonii, see Antonii (Vadkovskii).

Valliere, Paul, *Modern Russian Theology: Bukharev, Soloviev, Bulgakov: Orthodox Theology in a New Key*, Grand Rapids MI, 2000.

Varzhanskii, N., "Po povodu 'otpevaniia' L. N.Tolstogo," in *Missionerskoe obozrenie*, 1913, issue 4, 672–78.

V chem vera L. N. Tolstogo, [St. Petersburg, 1911] Jordanville NY, 1960.

Velikanova, Natalia and Whittaker, Robert, eds, *Tolstoi i SShA: Perepiska*, Moscow, 2004.

Volzhskii, A. S., "Okolo chuda," in *Russkie mysliteli o L've Tolstom*, Iasnaia Poliana, 2002, 415–31.

Vostorgov, Ioann, *Znameniia vremen*, Moscow, 1909.

Vyscheslavzev, B., "Das Ebenbild Gottes im Wesen des Menschen," in *Kirche, Staat und Mensch*, Geneva, 1937, 316–48.

Ware, Timothy (Kallistos), *The Orthodox Church*, Harmondsworth, 1978.

The Orthodox Way, London, [1979] 1981.

"Philocalie," in *Dictionnaire de Spiritualite*, Paris, 1984, XII, l 377–1352.

Weiant, E. T., *Sources of Modern Mass Atheism in Russia*, Mount Vernon, 1953.

Weisbein, Nicolas, *L'evolution religieuse de Tolstoi*, Paris, 1960.

Werth, Paul W., *The Tsar's Foreign Faiths: Toleration and the Fate of Religious Freedom in Imperial Russia*, Oxford, [2014] 2016.

Wilson, A. N., *Tolstoy*, Harmondsworth, 1988.

(Zhadanovskii) Arsenii, see Arsenii (Zhadanovskii).

Zaidenshnur, E. E. "O tolstovskoi bibliografii," *Iasnopolianskii sbornik*, Tula, 1981, 128–36.

Zaitsev, K. I., *Tolstoi, kak iavlenie religioznoe*, Harbin, 1937.

Zapiski Peterburgskikh Religiozno-Filosofskikh sobranii (1902–1903). St. Petersburg, 1906.

Zaraiskii, V., "O prave tserkovnogo otlucheniia ili anafemstvovaniia," in *Missionerskii sbornik*, 1911, issue 2, 120–27.

"Zasedanie sinoda po povodu bolezni L. N. Tolstogo," *Russkoe slovo*, November 5, 1910.

Zen'kovskii, Vasilii, "Problema bezsmertiia u L. N. Tolstogo," in *O religii Tolstogo*, [1912] 1978 op. cit., 27–58.

Das Bild vom Menschen in der Ostkirche, Stuttgart, 1951.

Zernov, Nicolas, *The Russian Religious Renaissance of the Twentieth Century*, London, 1963.

Ziolkowski, Margaret, "Hagiographical motifs in Tolstoy's 'Father Sergius'," in *South Atlantic Review*, 1982, 2, 63–80.

"Zmeia na mogile Tolstogo," in *Tul'skie eparkhial'nye vedomosti*, 1911, issue 47–48, 767–69; and in *Tomskie eparkhial'nye vedomosti*, 1911, issue 22, 1196–97.

Zorin, Andrei, *Critical Lives: Leo Tolstoy*, London, 2020.

Index

Milton Keynes UK
Ingram Content Group UK Ltd.
UKHW021007140524
442615UK00019B/149

9 781009 260411